Lenin Selected Writings: The Revolutions of 1917

The Revolutions of 1917

VI Lenin

Selected Writings: 2

Wellred Books
London

The Revolutions of 1917
Lenin Selected Writings: 2
VI Lenin

First edition
Wellred Books, August 2024

UK distribution: Wellred Books Britain, wellredbooks.co.uk
124 City Road
London
EC1V 2NX
contact@wellredbooks.co.uk

USA distribution: Marxist Books, marxistbooks.com
WR Books
250 44th Street #208
Brooklyn, New York
NY 11232
sales@marxistbooks.com

DK distribution: Forlaget Marx, forlagetmarx.dk
Degnestavnen 19, st. tv.
2400 København NV
forlag@forlagetmarx.dk

Cover image: *The Bolshevik* by Boris Kustodiev, 1920
Cover design by Jesse Murray-Dean and Sylvia Léo

Layout by Wellred Books

ISBN: 978 1 916936 12 6

Contents

October

Note on Dates

Until 14 February 1918, Russia used the Old Style (Julian) calendar, which was thirteen days behind the New Style (Gregorian) used in the West and which is standard today.

All dates referring to events that happened in Russia are given in the Old Style, with the New Style date also provided in brackets.

Introduction

In this epoch of deepening crisis for world capitalism, there has never been a more appropriate time for the republication of Lenin's writings. This new selection of Lenin's letters and articles written in 1917, the year which culminated in the victory of the Russian working class, is especially important. The October Revolution was, after all, the greatest event in world history and showed that society could be run without bankers and capitalists.

These writings provide a remarkable insight into the thinking of Lenin, the leader of the Bolshevik Party, without whom the revolution would not have succeeded. Above all, they trace how the October victory was achieved. They explain the abrupt changes throughout the year and how the Bolsheviks were able to prepare the working class for the eventual conquest of power.

These writings, which follow the torrents of revolution and counter-revolution in 1917, reveal the flexible approach of Lenin in addressing the problems thrown up at every stage. They are a classic application of the method of Marxism, applying a dialectical understanding to the ever-changing concrete situation. For the class-conscious worker, they constitute a veritable treasure trove of ideas.

The purpose of this introduction is not to provide a history of 1917, but simply to give a brief outline of Lenin's approach to events. There are a number of classic works, which comprehensively cover this period and provide an in-depth understanding of the revolution. First and foremost among these is Leon Trotsky's monumental study, *The History of the Russian Revolution*, which brilliantly dissects the revolution at every turn and explains the objective and subjective forces at play. Above all, he traces the passionate changes in consciousness in the masses, the motive force of the revolution. Trotsky writes in his opening lines:

> During the first two months of 1917 Russia was still a Romanov monarchy. Eight months later the Bolsheviks stood at the helm. They were little known to anybody when the year began, and their leaders were still under indictment for state treason when they came to power. You will not find another such sharp turn in history – especially if you remember that it involves a nation of 150 million people.[1]

The first news of the February Revolution – the forcible entry of the masses onto the stage of history – and the overthrow of Russian tsarism reached Lenin in Zurich on 2 March, according to the Old Style calendar (15 March in the New Style), a whole week after the revolution erupted.[2]

He had been in exile for most of his adult life, and was the leader of what proved to be the most revolutionary party in history. Looking back, it can be said that Lenin's whole life experience had prepared him for what was about to happen.

Foreign newspaper reports had confirmed that the revolution in Russia had established a bourgeois Provisional Government, and had thrown up a new power, the Petrograd Soviet of Workers' and Soldiers' Deputies, the predecessor of which in 1905 Lenin had described as "an embryo of a provisional revolutionary government".[3]

---

1 Trotsky, Leon, *History of the Russian Revolution*, Vol. 1, Wellred Books, 2022, p. 17.

2 See 'Note on Dates', p. ix.

3 Lenin, 'Our Tasks and the Soviet of Workers' Deputies', 2-4 (15-17) November 1905, *Collected Works* (henceforth referred to as *LCW*), Vol. 10, Progress

The emergence of these two entities reflected a regime of 'dual power' that had suddenly come into being.

The superiority of Lenin was in his ability to immediately grasp the significance of what was taking place, and he promptly set about drafting an article for the Bolshevik paper *Pravda* that put forward the steps that needed to be taken by the Party.

Lenin was always fond of quoting a phrase from Goethe's *Faust*: "Theory, my friend, is grey, but green is the eternal tree of life." Life is always more varied and richer than the most brilliant theory. The revolution had thrown up a situation not fully envisaged previously. The task of the revolutionary party was to adapt to changing circumstances. And these required a sharp change in the Bolshevik Party's orientation and tactics.

For Lenin, the fall of tsarism and the coming to power of a bourgeois Provisional Government was simply the first stage. The inability of this government to solve the problems confronting it placed the perspective of a new revolution on the agenda. In other words, the conquest of power by the working class was the only way the most elementary aspirations of the masses – peace, bread and freedom – could be achieved. Such a radical turn of events meant the abandonment of the old Bolshevik slogan of the democratic dictatorship of proletariat and peasantry, which had been an algebraic formula based on the continuation of capitalism, but which had now been superseded. "The formula is obsolete", he wrote later in a reply to Kamenev. "It is no good at all. It is dead. And it is no use trying to revive it."[4]

However, such a change was not straightforward or easily achieved. Whenever such a sharp turn is required, there is always resistance from those still tied to the past. And this was the case among the Bolshevik leaders. In fact, the only other person who independently came to the same conclusions as Lenin was Leon Trotsky, who was in exile in New York.

In his letter of farewell to Swiss workers, Lenin explained that the great honour of beginning the world revolution had fallen to

---

Publishers, 1960, p. 21.

4 Lenin, 'Letters on Tactics', 8-13 (21-26) April 1917, in this volume, p. 68.

the Russian proletariat. "Russia is a peasant country, one of the most backward of European countries. Socialism *cannot* triumph there *directly* and *immediately*", he explained.[5] Lenin demonstrated his internationalism by stating that the Russian revolution would be "the *prologue* to the world socialist revolution, a *step* towards it."[6] He went on to praise the German proletariat, which was "the most trustworthy, the most reliable ally of the Russian and the world proletarian revolution."[7]

For Lenin, internationalism was central, to which the fate of the Russian Revolution was inseparably linked. After all, Lenin knew full well, following in the footsteps of Marx and Engels, that the material basis for socialism, let alone a classless communist society, did not exist in backward Russia, but only on a world scale.

This selection of writings contains the first three of Lenin's famous *Letters From Afar*, a series of five letters that outlined his perspectives and tasks, the last of which was unfinished and written on the eve of his departure from Switzerland for revolutionary Russia. However, only the first letter was ever published in *Pravda*, not least due to the resistance of Kamenev and Stalin, who were the first Bolshevik leaders to return to Petrograd and who adopted a conciliatory attitude towards the Provisional Government.

Lenin had already sent an urgent telegram to the Bolshevik leaders in Russia stressing what needed to be done:

> Our tactics: no trust in and no support of the new government; Kerensky is especially suspect; arming of the proletariat is the only guarantee; immediate elections to the Petrograd City Council; no rapprochement with other parties. Telegraph this to Petrograd.[8]

First and foremost, Lenin demanded no confidence in the Provisional Government, which was a bourgeois, pro-imperialist government. The

---

5 Lenin, 'Farewell Letter to the Swiss Workers', 26 March (8 April) 1917, in this volume, p. 45.

6 Ibid., p. 46.

7 Ibid., p. 47.

8 Lenin, 'Telegram to the Bolsheviks Leaving for Russia', 6 (19) March 1917, *LCW*, Vol. 23, p. 292.

working class needed to defend their own independent class point of view. Consequently, anyone who championed support for the Provisional Government was in Lenin's view, "a traitor to the workers, traitor to the cause of the proletariat, to the cause of peace and freedom."[9]

This telegram was a shot over the bow of those leaders, especially Kamenev and Stalin, who succumbed to the euphoria of the first wave of the revolution and were responsible for pursuing a conciliatory line in *Pravda*. They used the columns in the Bolshevik paper to rally support for the Provisional Government and the war effort "insofar as" it assisted the revolution.

Lenin came out with guns blazing in his first *Letter* in his usual straightforward style:

> Ours is a bourgeois revolution, *therefore*, the workers must support the bourgeoisie, say the Potresovs, Gvozdevs and Chkheidzes, as Plekhanov said yesterday.[10]

No! Lenin replied emphatically:

> Ours is a bourgeois revolution, we Marxists say, *therefore* the workers must open the eyes of the people to the deception practised by the bourgeois politicians, teach them to put no faith in words, to depend entirely on their *own* strength, their *own* organisation, their *own* unity and their own *weapons*.[11]

While Lenin was enthusiastic about the intervention of the masses, he was not the type of man who was intoxicated with revolutionary phrases. He took a very sober view of things. For him, the first revolution was simply a prelude to a second. He stressed:

> You must perform miracles of organisation, organisation of the proletariat and of the whole people, to prepare the way for your victory in the second stage of the revolution...[12]

9 Lenin, 'First *Letter From Afar*', 7 (20) March 1917, in this volume, p. 11.
10 Ibid., p. 11, emphasis in original.
11 Ibid., emphasis in original.
12 Ibid. p. 12.

He again defined the Soviet of Workers' and Soldiers' Deputies, as in 1905, as:

> … the embryo of a workers' government, the representative of the interests of the entire mass of the *poor* section of the population, i.e. of nine-tenths of the population, which is striving for *peace, bread* and *freedom*.[13]

Through these writings, Lenin repeatedly explains that Marxist theory is not a dogma, but only a guide to action, and that the Bolsheviks needed to adapt their tactics to the swift and abrupt changes taking place.

The basic ideas contained in the *Letters*, especially the fifth letter, were developed in his other writings, such as 'Letters on Tactics' and 'The Tasks of the Proletariat in Our Revolution', all of which hammered home the change in the situation, which had to be met with a corresponding change in the political slogans raised by the Bolsheviks.

Prior to his return to Petrograd, Lenin was alone in this perspective. The 'old Bolsheviks' were stuck in the past and failed to see the significance of the changes taking place under their very nose. When Lenin's *April Theses* were published in *Pravda*, Kamenev as an editor wrote a note:

> As for the general scheme of Comrade Lenin, it seems to us unacceptable in that it starts from the assumption that the bourgeois-democratic revolution is ended, and counts upon an immediate transformation of this revolution into a socialist revolution.[14]

On his arrival in Russia, Lenin's immediate task was therefore to convince the Bolshevik Party of the new perspective. He needed to 'rearm' the party. Lenin arrived on the night of 3 (16) April and attended the Party conference the following day, where he presented his theses in his own name, such was his isolation. These are outlined in 'The Tasks of the Proletariat in the Present Revolution'. He deals here with his attitude to the imperialist war.

13 Ibid., p. 10, emphasis in original.
14 *Pravda*, 8 April 1917, quoted in Trotsky, *History of the Russian Revolution*, pp. 326-7.

> The slightest concession to revolutionary defencism is a *betrayal of socialism*, a complete renunciation of *internationalism*, no matter by what fine phrases and 'practical' considerations it may be justified.[15]

This was clearly aimed not only at the 'moderate' socialists, but at Kamenev and Stalin and the views they held.

Nevertheless, he explained the Party needed to approach "the broad mass of the people *in a different way*."[16] He said:

> The mass believers in revolutionary defencism are *honest*, not in a personal, but in a class sense, i.e. they belong to *classes* (workers and the peasant poor) which *in actual fact* have nothing to gain from annexations and the subjugation of other peoples.[17]

It was necessary to explain the real nature of the war and that only the overthrow of the capitalist governments could deliver a real democratic peace.

At the time of the outbreak of the war in 1914, given the isolation of the Party and the confusion that existed, Lenin aimed his ideas at the cadres. He had advocated revolutionary defeatism, namely opposition to the imperialist nature and aims of the war, to firm-up the cadres against the prevailing mood of defencism. Even then, Lenin had made a distinction between the honest defencist workers, and the imperialist standpoint of the social patriots and the bourgeois government.

Now, he was aiming his ideas at a mass audience, which meant a change in his presentation. While the content was the same as before, his approach was different.

He had to tailor his view to take into consideration the views of the honest defencists, 'patiently explaining' the nature of the imperialist war. This change is taken up fully in *Lenin Selected Writings: On Imperialist War*, recently published by Wellred Books, which contains his writings on this question.

15 Lenin, 'The Tasks of the Proletariat in Our Revolution', 10 (23) April 1917, in this volume, p. 86, emphasis in original.

16 Ibid., p. 87, emphasis in original.

17 Ibid., emphasis in original.

For Lenin, it was now time to break decisively with the traitors of the old International, as well as the 'bog' of Zimmerwald, the first gathering of internationalists in 1915, which was quite politically amorphous. Zimmerwald was linked to the centrists around Kautsky – 'Marxists' in words and phrases, but reformist in deeds. There was no time for prevarication.

> It is we who must found, and right now, without delay, a new, revolutionary, proletarian International.[18]
>
> ... it is time to cast off the soiled shirt and put on clean linen.[19]

Very few of the 'old Bolsheviks' were convinced of Lenin's stance about a new revolution. The old guard were wedded to the traditional position and simply repeated the old arguments against Lenin's position. The Mensheviks and others thought he had gone mad. Stalin had even come out in favour of unity with the Mensheviks, despite all that Lenin had said on the question.

Following the April Conference (24-29 April, Old Style), Lenin had managed to use his authority to win a majority, starting with the rank and file, for his new position that rearmed the Party with the perspective of workers' power. This rearming was absolutely decisive.

Despite the overthrow of tsarism, the masses were still faced with widespread misery and hunger, as the bread ration was steadily reduced. Rising prices provoked strikes and lockouts. Demonstrations became a daily occurrence. Land-hungry peasants seized the land. Buffeted by events, cracks began to emerge in the Provisional Government, which was under pressure from all sides.

With the growing disenchantment with the conduct of the war, the government was pressurised into renouncing all imperialist aims and was obliged to inform the Allies. The Foreign Minister and leader of the Constitutional Democrats (Cadets), Pavel Milyukov, went back on this promise, which, when made public, provoked uproar. Spontaneous demonstrations broke out. Banners appeared

18 Ibid., p. 104.
19 Ibid., p. 111.

bearing 'Down With the Provisional Government!' and 'Down With Milyukov!' The extent of the mass protests were such that Milyukov was forced to resign. He was later joined by another minister, Guchkov. This provoked the first government crisis.

Given the frustrations and fury, there were sections of workers who wanted to immediately overthrow the Provisional Government. This was clearly premature, as the rest of the country was lagging behind, where the government still had reserves of support. As a result, Lenin attempted to steer the Party as well as educate its ranks against adventurism. Lenin was therefore forced to intervene to restrain such moods. He explained:

> The slogan 'Down with the Provisional Government!' is an incorrect one at the present moment because, in the absence of a solid (i.e. a class-conscious and organised) majority of the people on the side of the revolutionary proletariat, such a slogan is either an empty phrase, or, objectively, amounts to attempts of an adventurist character.[20]

The task, as he saw it, was to 'patiently explain' the Bolshevik policies to the masses and not engage in ultra-left actions. While they were in a small minority, the Party needed to carry on its propaganda work and to systematically organise its forces. As part of this, Lenin was in favour of peaceful demonstrations that avoided violence, as a show of strength, while urging the workers to put pressure on the Soviets.

The Provisional Government was joined at the hip to the imperialists, given their reliance on foreign loans to continue the war. With Kerensky (a member of the Socialist-Revolutionary Party (SRs)) becoming Minister of War, they soon agreed to undertake a new military offensive in June, which was doomed to fail. This only made matters worse, further undermining their support. The growing influence of Bolshevism was reflected in the many banners with the inscription 'All Power to the Soviets', that were now carried on the streets of Petrograd and elsewhere.

---

20 'Resolution of the Central Committee of the RSDLP(B)', 22 April (5 May) 1917, in this volume, p. 130.

A renewed government crisis resulted in a reshuffle where Mensheviks and Socialist-Revolutionaries joined the capitalist parties in the new coalition government. Lenin skilfully opposed this move and called for the 'moderate socialists' to break with the bourgeoisie. This was summed up in the Bolshevik slogan: 'Down With the Ten Capitalist Ministers!'

The Menshevik and Socialist-Revolutionary leaders could feel the ground shifting under their feet. Through their control of the Soviet Executive Committee, they were able to ban a demonstration called by the Bolsheviks. When the Executive called its own demonstration for 18 June (1 July), it backfired and the influence of the Bolsheviks was for all to see. "In one way or another, 18 June will go down as a turning-point in the history of the Russian Revolution" wrote Lenin.[21]

A class shift was now taking place in the revolution. The ranks of the Bolshevik Party swelled with new recruits. The Menshevik and Socialist-Revolutionary leaders panicked, but behind them stood the bourgeoisie and the imperialist powers. In early July, a mass spontaneous demonstration led to violent outbreaks, stirred up by provocateurs. A huge campaign of slander was then launched against the Bolsheviks, accusing them of orchestrating an armed uprising. In fact, the Bolsheviks attempted to channel the demonstration along peaceful lines to avoid premature clashes. Lenin, feeling unwell, had left Petrograd before these events, but rushed back on 4 (17) July, where he delivered a speech from the balcony of Kshesinskaya's Palace that ended with an appeal for "firmness, steadfastness and vigilance."

Nevertheless, a hue and cry went up against Lenin and the Bolshevik Party. The counter-revolution went on the offensive to crush the movement. Lenin was accused of being a German agent and was forced into hiding. The Bolsheviks, hundreds of whom were arrested, were in effect driven underground. In face of the outrageous slanders against the Bolsheviks, Lenin concluded:

---

21 Lenin, 'The Eighteenth of June', 20 June (3 July) 1917, in this volume, p. 196.

> All hopes for a peaceful development of the Russian revolution have vanished for good. This is the objective situation: either complete victory for the military dictatorship, or victory for the workers' armed uprising...[22]

Given the fact that the Soviets were in the hands of the witch-hunters, Lenin now believed the slogan of 'All Power to the Soviets', while possible in April, June and early July, was now no longer appropriate. The July Days had transformed everything and signified the temporary victory of the counter-revolution, including the out-and-out betrayal of the Socialist-Revolutionaries and the Mensheviks.

Kerensky soon became the new Prime Minister and a government reshuffle drew in a majority of 'moderate socialists' into the coalition, although the capitalist Cadets still called the shots.

It was a period of sudden changes and abrupt turns. By the end of August, the Russian bourgeoisie was looking towards a real dictatorship – a real strongman – that would sweep away the 'democrats'. This came in the form of Kornilov, a general who led a revolt pledging to put an end to all this anarchy. This turn of events was described by Lenin as "downright unbelievably sharp".[23]

He wrote to the Central Committee (CC) at the end of August, in the midst of the crisis:

> It is possible that these lines will come too late, for events are developing with a rapidity that sometimes makes one's head spin.[24]

Faced with the Kornilov revolt, Lenin argued for the Party to take up the fight against the attempted coup, but at the same time that they must not offer the Kerensky government any political support. While they would fight alongside Kerensky's troops, they would also expose Kerensky's weaknesses and vacillations.

> It would be wrong to think that we have moved farther away from the task of the proletariat winning power. No, we have come very close to

22 Lenin, 'The Political Situation', 10 (23) July 1917, in this volume, p. 223.

23 Lenin, 'To the Central Committee of the RSDLP', 30 August (12 September) 1917, in this volume, p. 282.

24 Ibid.

> it, ***not directly***, but from the side. ***At the moment*** we must campaign not so much directly against Kerensky, as *indirectly* against him, namely, by demanding a more and more active, truly revolutionary war against Kornilov. [...] We must relentlessly fight against phrases about the defence of the country, about a united front of revolutionary democrats, about supporting the Provisional Government, etc., etc., since they are just empty *phrases*. We must say: now is the time for *action*; you SR and Menshevik gentlemen have long since worn those phrases threadbare. Now is the time for *action*; the war against Kornilov must be conducted in a revolutionary way, by drawing the masses in, by arousing them, by inflaming them (Kerensky is *afraid* of the masses, *afraid* of the people).[25]

We can see the way in which Lenin skilfully turns the situation to the advantage of the Bolsheviks in leading the fight against Kornilov, using revolutionary means. In this way he educates the party in the art of flexible tactics. We should remember that Lenin was still in hiding in Finland. Nevertheless, the Kerensky government was forced to lean for support on the Bolsheviks, given their growing influence. The Bolsheviks, in turn, seized the opportunity to arm the workers and revive the Red Guards, the factory based militias set up by workers to defend the revolution.

In the end, following the fraternisation of the Bolsheviks and workers of Petrograd with Kornilov's troops, his forces melted away. Following his defeat, a new situation opened up, as Kerensky's authority rapidly declined. Furthermore, during the struggle, the Soviets once more came to life. Lenin therefore renewed the call of 'All Power to the Soviets', in which again he raised the idea of a peaceful development of the revolution.

In the middle of September, Lenin offered a 'compromise' to the Mensheviks and SRs for them to agree to establish a government wholly and exclusively responsible to the Soviets, which would also take over power locally. This would guarantee, he said, the peaceful development of the revolution.

---

25 Ibid., p. 283, emphasis in original.

> Now, and only now, perhaps *during only a few days* or a week or two, such a government could be set up and consolidated in a perfectly peaceful way. In all probability it could secure the peaceful *advance* of the whole Russian revolution, and provide exceptionally good chances for great strides in the world movement towards peace and the victory of socialism.
>
> [...]
>
> I think the Bolsheviks would advance no other conditions, trusting that the revolution would proceed peacefully and party strife in the Soviets would be *peacefully overcome* thanks to really complete freedom of propaganda and to the immediate establishment of a new democracy in the composition of the Soviets (new elections) and in their functioning.
>
> Perhaps this is *already* impossible? Perhaps. But if there is even one chance in a hundred, the attempt at realising this opportunity is still worthwhile.[26]

These lines completely refute the false idea put out by bourgeois historians that Lenin was in favour of violence and bloodshed. For much of 1917, Lenin argued as a minority for 'peaceful propaganda', based upon the slogans of bread, land and peace. He nevertheless placed the responsibility for ensuring a peaceful development of the revolution on the shoulders of the Mensheviks and SRs, who should take the power.

The failure of the Provisional Government to deliver any of its promises led to a crumbling of its support. The experience of the Kornilov coup sealed its fate.

New elections to the Soviets, especially in Petrograd and Moscow, now led to a victory for the Bolsheviks. This opened up a new critical chapter in the revolution. "The majority of the people are *on our side*", wrote Lenin. "The majority gained in the Soviets of the metropolitan cities *resulted* from the people coming over *to our side*."[27] The Soviets now had to assume power. This was not Blanquism and

26 Lenin, 'On Compromises', 1-3 (14-16) September 1917, in this volume, p. 287, emphasis in original.

27 Lenin, 'The Bolsheviks Must Assume Power', 12-14 (25-27) September 1917, in this volume, p. 295, emphasis in original.

the seizure of power by a minority. It would represent the victory of the revolutionary masses, who were now looking to the Bolsheviks to translate words into deeds.

Kerensky attempted to regroup with the announcement of a so-called Democratic Conference, where all parties should participate. Lenin opposed participation, having now directed the Party's attention towards insurrection, but he was overruled. This, he felt, simply wasted time. The revolution was maturing and there was no time to lose. The trust of the masses could not be taken for granted.

Trotsky, who had worked closely with the Bolsheviks after his return to Russia in May, joined the Party in August and was elected to its Central Committee. His collaboration with Lenin was very close and he was elected the chairman of the Petrograd Soviet. He fully supported Lenin's opposition to participation in the Democratic Conference. This led Lenin to write:

> Trotsky was for the boycott. Bravo, Comrade Trotsky!
>
> Boycottism was defeated in the Bolshevik group at the Democratic Conference.
>
> Long live the boycott![28]

They soon carried the day and Trotsky led the Bolshevik walkout.

The situation was becoming critical, politically and economically. The situation of dual power in the country could not last: either the Soviets would take power and sweep away the Provisional Government, or the Soviets would be crushed by the counter-revolution. Everything was now in the balance, and Lenin fully realised it.

Using the Revolutionary Military Committee established by the Petrograd Soviet, Trotsky began to make links with the Petrograd garrison and preparations for the October insurrection. The seizure of power would mean that the slogan of 'All Power to the Soviets' would become a reality after almost nine months.

---

28 Lenin, 'From a Publicist's Diary', 22-24 September (5-7 October) 1917, in this volume, p. 339.

During August and September, as well as directing the attention of the Bolsheviks to the task of power, Lenin wrote his famous theoretical work while in hiding in Finland, *The State and Revolution*. This work, together with *The Impending Catastrophe and How to Combat It*, another important work, have been left out of this selection solely due to their length. They are, however, readily available. *The State and Revolution* is published by Wellred Books, and *The Impending Catastrophe* has been reproduced online by *In Defence of Marxism* (marxist.com), both of which are an essential read!

Towards the end of September, Lenin wrote that "we are on the threshold of a world proletarian revolution", to which he tied the fate of the second Russian Revolution.[29]

> The crisis has matured. The whole future of the Russian revolution is at stake. The honour of the Bolshevik Party is in question. The whole future of the international workers' revolution for socialism is at stake.[30]

However, Lenin, who was still in hiding in Finland, was fearful that the opportunity to take power would be missed. He saw a tendency in the Bolshevik leadership which was vacillating. He did not want the insurrection to be delayed until the opening of the Soviet Congress. He therefore wrote a stern letter to the CC and the Petrograd and Moscow leaderships urging immediate action. The foot-dragging of the CC and the deletion of his criticisms from his articles led him to tender his resignation from the CC to allow him the freedom to campaign openly within the ranks of the Party. But given the pace of events it was a threat that was not actually carried through.

However, on the eve of the October Revolution there was a crisis within the Bolshevik leadership. On 10 (23) October, Lenin, still in disguise, emerged from hiding to attend the CC meeting. He had been kicking his heels in Finland since July. Now he had the opportunity to address the Bolshevik leaders directly. Lenin delivered a report on the current situation and urged the immediate

---

29 Lenin, 'The Crisis Has Matured', 29 September (13 October) 1917, in this volume, p. 352.

30 Ibid., p. 357.

organisation of an uprising. With ten votes against two, they agreed to Lenin's proposal of an insurrection. But the date was left hanging in the air.

The next day, the two who voted against an insurrection, Zinoviev and Kamenev, issued a statement in opposition to the CC decision, which was distributed to the regional and executive leaderships.

Another extended CC meeting was called almost a week later on 16 (29) October, where Lenin reiterated his plea for an immediate insurrection, but there still existed some hesitation and reservations. Again, Zinoviev and Kamenev raised their opposition. After much heated discussion, Lenin put his resolution to the vote, with twenty in favour, three abstentions and two against.

However, breaking party discipline, on 18 (31) October, Zinoviev and Kamenev went public, writing in the non-party paper *Novaya Zhizn* about their opposition to the proposed insurrection. They instead urged the Party to form a large opposition in a future Constituent Assembly, and not undertake an adventure, as they saw it. Lenin replied angrily in a letter to the CC on 19 October (1 November) denouncing them as "strikebreakers" in shamefully warning the enemy of their plans.[31] He called for their expulsion from the Party.

The CC held on the following day, where Lenin was absent and hiding in Petrograd, heard Lenin's letter but refused to expel the strikebreakers, who received simply a reprimand.

By this time, Trotsky had been busy with the organisation of the insurrection. He was in favour of the insurrection on the date of the All-Russian Congress of Soviets, to give greater legitimacy to the revolution. Even the day before the insurrection, Lenin was still urging the Bolsheviks to take power, clearly unaware of Trotsky's advanced preparations: "The government is tottering. It must be *given the death-blow* at all costs. To delay action is fatal."[32] In the

31 Lenin, 'Letter to the Central Committee of the RSDLP(B)', 19 October (1 November) 1917, in this volume, p. 430.

32 Lenin, 'Letter to Central Committee Members', 24 October (6 November) 1917, in this volume, p. 435, emphasis in original.

end, Trotsky's tactics proved correct. The insurrection was carried through smoothly on 25 October (7 November) under his leadership of the Revolutionary Military Committee and in the name of the Petrograd Soviet.

It was none other than Stalin who acknowledged Trotsky's key role in the revolution. He wrote:

> All the work of practical organisation of the insurrection was conducted under the immediate leadership of the chairman of the Petrograd Soviet, Trotsky. It is possible to declare with certainty that the swift passing of the garrison to the side of the Soviet and the bold execution of the work of the Revolutionary Military Committee, the Party owes principally and above all to comrade Trotsky.[33]

Following the successful insurrection, Lenin was to emerge from hiding to appear at the All-Russian Congress of Soviets where the victory was announced.

According to John Reed, who was present:

> Now Lenin, gripping the edge of the reading stand, letting his little winking eyes travel over the crowd as he stood there waiting, apparently oblivious of the long-rolling ovation which lasted for several minutes.[34]

When the applause died down, Lenin, who was full of emotion, simply said:

> We shall now proceed to construct the socialist order.[35]

As head of the new government, Lenin announced a series of decrees on peace without annexations, the complete publication of all the secret treaties, then on land, which abolished private ownership and gave land to the peasants, the right of nations to self-determination and many more. Within the space of barely twenty-

---

33 Stalin, Joseph, 'The Role of the Most Eminent Party Leaders', *Pravda*, 6 November 1918, quoted in Trotsky, *History of the Russian Revolution*, Vol. 3, p. 1214, and also in Stalin, *The October Revolution*, Lawrence and Wishart, 1936, p. 30.

34 Reed, John, *Ten Days That Shook the World*, Penguin, 1970, p. 128.

35 Quoted in Trotsky, Leon, *History of the Russian Revolution*, Vol. 3, p. 1168.

four hours after the seizure of power, the new Soviet Government, the Council of People's Commissars, showed its determination to carry out its programme.

The All-Russian Congress of Soviets had become the highest power in the land. It represented the first blow against world capitalism and marked the beginning of the world socialist revolution.

This was no coup behind the backs of the masses, as the bourgeois historians claim. The left Menshevik Sukhanov wrote:

> To call it [the October Revolution] a military conspiracy rather than a national uprising is utterly absurd since the [Bolshevik] Party was already the *de facto* power in the land, and since it enjoyed the support of the enormous majority of the people.[36]

Lenin's writing in this period shows the thoughts of a man bound up with the revolutionary process, who saw much further than many of those around him. His role was crucial, as can be seen from these writings, which we now make available to a wider audience.

The socialist revolution will once again be placed on the agenda in the period ahead. These writings of Lenin from 1917 will help illuminate the path to a successful worldwide proletarian revolution.

Rob Sewell,
London,
August 2024

---

36 Quoted in Liebman, Marcel, *The Russian Revolution*, Vintage Books, 1972, p. 286.

The First Stage of the First Revolution (First 'Letter from Afar')

Written 7 (20) March 1917

The first revolution engendered by the imperialist world war has broken out. The first revolution but certainly not the last.

Judging by the scanty information available in Switzerland, the first stage of this first revolution, namely, of the *Russian* revolution of 1 (14) March 1917, has ended.[1] This first stage of our revolution will certainly not be the last.

How could such a 'miracle' have happened, that in only eight days – the period indicated by Mr. Milyukov[2] in his boastful telegram to all Russia's representatives abroad – a monarchy collapsed that had maintained itself for centuries, and that in spite of everything had managed to maintain itself throughout the three years of the tremendous, nation-wide class battles of 1905-07?

1 The February Revolution began on 23 February (8 March). The Tsar abdicated a week later, on 2 (15) March.

2 Milyukov was Foreign Minister in the first Provisional Government, and co-founder and leader of the Cadets, the party of the Russian liberal-monarchist bourgeoisie and the dominant force in the Provisional Government.

There are no miracles in nature or history, but every abrupt turn in history, and this applies to every revolution, presents such a wealth of content, unfolds such unexpected and specific combinations of forms of struggle and alignment of forces of the contestants, that to the lay mind there is much that must appear miraculous.

The combination of a number of factors of world-historic importance was required for the tsarist monarchy to have collapsed in a few days. We shall mention the chief of them.

Without the tremendous class battles and the revolutionary energy displayed by the Russian proletariat during the three years 1905-07, the second revolution could not possibly have been so rapid in the sense that its *initial stage* was completed in a few days. The first revolution (1905) deeply ploughed the soil, uprooted age-old prejudices, awakened millions of workers and tens of millions of peasants to political life and political struggle and revealed to each other – and to the world – *all* classes (and all the principal parties) of Russian society in their true character and in the true alignment of their interests, their forces, their modes of action and their immediate and ultimate aims. This first revolution, and the succeeding period of counter-revolution (1907-14), laid bare the very essence of the tsarist monarchy, brought it to the 'utmost limit', exposed all the rottenness and infamy, the cynicism and corruption of the tsar's clique, dominated by that monster, Rasputin.[3] It exposed all the bestiality of the Romanov family – those pogrom-mongers who drenched Russia in the blood of Jews, workers and revolutionaries, those *landlords*, 'first among peers', *who own millions* of dessiatins[4] of land and are prepared to stoop to any brutality, to any crime, to ruin and strangle any number of citizens in order to preserve the 'sacred right of property' for themselves *and their class*.

Without the Revolution of 1905-07 and the counter-revolution of 1907-14, there could not have been that clear 'self determination'

3 Russian Orthodox mystic in the tsarist court who was close with the family of Nicholas II

4 A dessiatin, used in tsarist Russia, was equivalent to 11,000 square meters.

of all classes of the Russian people and of the nations inhabiting Russia, that determination of the relation of these classes to each other and to the tsarist monarchy, which manifested itself during the eight days of the February-March Revolution of 1917. This eight-day revolution was 'performed', if we may use a metaphorical expression, as though after a dozen major and minor rehearsals; the 'actors' knew each other, their parts, their places and their setting in every detail, through and through, down to every more or less important shade of political trend and mode of action.

For the first great Revolution of 1905, which the Guchkovs[5] and Milyukovs and their hangers-on denounced as a "great rebellion", led after the lapse of twelve years, to the "brilliant", the "glorious" Revolution of 1917 – the Guchkovs and Milyukovs have proclaimed it "glorious" because it has put them in power (*for the time being*). But this required a great, mighty and all-powerful 'stage manager', capable, on the one hand, of vastly accelerating the course of world history, and, on the other, of engendering world-wide crises of unparalleled intensity – economic, political, national and international. Apart from an extraordinary acceleration of world history, it was also necessary that history make particularly abrupt turns, in order that at one such turn the filthy and blood-stained cart of the Romanov monarchy should be overturned at *one stroke*.

This all-powerful 'stage manager', this mighty accelerator was the imperialist world war.

That it is a world war is now indisputable, for the United States and China are already half-involved today, and will be fully involved tomorrow.

That it is an imperialist war on *both* sides is now likewise indisputable. Only the capitalists and their hangers-on, the social-patriots and social-chauvinists, or – if instead of general critical

---

5 Guchkov was a Moscow landowner and industrialist. He was the founder and leader of the Octobrists as well as Minister of War and Navy from March-May 1917. The Octobrists were the party of the big merchants, industrialists and big landowners who ran their estates on capitalist lines.

definitions we use political names familiar in Russia – only the Guchkovs and Lvovs, Milyukovs and Shingarevs[6] on the one hand, and only the Gvozdevs, Potresovs, Chkhenkelis, Kerenskys and Chkheidzes on the other,[7] can deny or gloss over this fact. *Both* the German and the Anglo-French bourgeoisie are waging the war for the plunder of foreign countries and the strangling of small nations, for financial world supremacy and the division and redivision of colonies and in order to save the tottering capitalist regime by misleading and dividing the workers of the various countries.

The imperialist war was bound, with objective inevitability, immensely to accelerate and intensify to an unprecedented degree the class struggle of the proletariat against the bourgeoisie; it was bound to turn into a civil war between the hostile classes.

This *transformation has been started* by the February-March Revolution of 1917, the first stage of which has been marked, firstly, by a joint blow at tsarism struck by two forces: one, the whole of bourgeois and landlord Russia, with all her unconscious hangers-on and all her conscious leaders, the British and French ambassadors and capitalists, and the other, *the Soviet of Workers' Deputies*, which has begun to win over the soldiers' and peasants' deputies.

These three political camps, these three fundamental political forces:

1. The tsarist monarchy, the head of the feudal landlords, of the old bureaucracy and the military caste;

---

6 Prince Lvov was a Cadet and Aristocrat, appointed Prime Minister of the first Provisional Government and Minister of the Interior until July. Shingarev was a leading Cadet who was Minister of Agriculture in the first Provisional Government and Minister of Finance in the second.

7 All these individuals were ministers in the Provisional Government.
Gvozdev, Potresov, Chkhenkeli and Chkheidze were Mensheviks, the party which originated as the opposition faction in the Russian Social-Democratic Labour Party (RSDLP), who pursued a policy of class collaboration with the bourgeoisie. Their leading body was the Organising Committee (OC).
Kerensky was a lawyer and nominally a member of the Socialist-Revolutionary Party (SRs), a petty-bourgeois party of agrarian socialists, who based themselves on the peasantry.

2. Bourgeois and landlord-Octobrist-Cadet Russia, behind which trailed the petty bourgeoisie (of which Kerensky and Chkheidze are the principal representatives);
3. The Soviet of Workers' Deputies, which is seeking to make the entire proletariat and the entire mass of the poorest part of the population its allies.

These three *fundamental* political forces fully and clearly revealed themselves even in the eight days of the 'first stage' and even to an observer so remote from the scene of events as the present writer, who is obliged to content himself with the meagre foreign press dispatches.

But before dealing with this in greater detail, I must return to the part of my letter devoted to a factor of prime importance, namely, the imperialist world war.

The war shackled the belligerent powers, the belligerent groups of capitalists, the 'bosses' of the capitalist system, the slave-owners of the capitalist slave system, to each other with *chains of iron. One bloody clot* – such is the social and political life of the present moment in history.

The socialists who deserted to the bourgeoisie on the outbreak of the war – all these Davids and Scheidemanns in Germany and the Plekhanovs, Potresovs, Gvozdevs and co. in Russia – clamoured loud and long against the 'illusions' of the revolutionaries, against the 'illusions' of the Basel Manifesto, against the 'farcical dream' of turning the imperialist war into a civil war.[8] They sang praises in every key to the strength, tenacity and adaptability allegedly revealed by capitalism – *they*, who had aided the capitalists to 'adapt', tame, mislead and divide the working classes of the various countries!

---

8 The Basel Manifesto was adopted at the Second International Congress in Basel in 1912. In it, the parties of the Second International all agreed on their firm stance against the war, and that they would turn the war between the nations into a war against capitalism itself. When the war broke out in 1914, the Second International betrayed its own anti-war resolutions and gave wholehearted support to the imperialist slaughter.
The Basel Manifesto is reproduced in *Lenin Selected Writings: On Imperialist War*, Wellred Books, 2024, p. 371.

But "he who laughs last laughs best". The bourgeoisie has been unable to delay for long the revolutionary crisis engendered by the war. That crisis is growing with irresistible force in all countries, beginning with Germany, which, according to an observer who recently visited that country, is suffering "brilliantly organised famine", and ending with England and France, where *famine is also* looming, but where organisation is far less 'brilliant'.

It was natural that the revolutionary crisis should have broken out *first of all* in tsarist Russia, where the disorganisation was most appalling and the proletariat most revolutionary (not by virtue of any special qualities, but because of the living traditions of 1905). This crisis was precipitated by the series of extremely severe defeats sustained by Russia and her allies. They shook up the old machinery of government and the old order and roused the anger of *all* classes of the population against them; they embittered the army, wiped out a very large part of the old commanding personnel, composed of die-hard aristocrats and exceptionally corrupt bureaucratic elements, and replaced it by a young, fresh, mainly bourgeois, commoner, petty-bourgeois personnel. Those who, grovelling to the bourgeoisie or simply lacking backbone, howled and wailed about 'defeatism', are now faced by the fact of the historical connection between the defeat of the most backward and barbarous tsarist monarchy and the *beginning* of the revolutionary conflagration.

But while the defeats early in the war were a negative factor that precipitated the upheaval, the *connection* between Anglo-French finance capital, Anglo-French imperialism and Russian Octobrist-Cadet capital was a factor that hastened this crisis by the direct *organisation of a plot* against Nicholas Romanov.[9]

This highly important aspect of the situation is, for obvious reasons, hushed up by the Anglo-French press and maliciously emphasised by the German. We Marxists must soberly face the truth and not allow ourselves to be confused either by the lies, the official sugary diplomatic and ministerial lies, of the first group of imperialist

9 Nicholas II was the last tsar of Russia, reigning from 1894 until his abdication on 2 (15) March 1917.

belligerents, or by the sniggering and smirking of their financial and military rivals of the other belligerent group. The whole course of events in the February-March Revolution clearly shows that the British and French embassies, with their agents and 'connections', who had long been making the most desperate efforts to prevent 'separate' agreements and a separate peace between Nicholas II (and last, we hope, and we will endeavour to make him that) and Wilhelm II,[10] directly organised a plot in conjunction with the Octobrists and Cadets, in conjunction with a section of the generals and army and St. Petersburg garrison officers, with the express object of *deposing* Nicholas Romanov.

Let us not harbour any illusions. Let us not make the mistake of those who – like certain OC supporters or Mensheviks who are oscillating between Gvozdev-Potresov policy and internationalism and only too often slip into petty-bourgeois pacifism – are now ready to extol 'agreement' between the workers' party and the Cadets, 'support' of the latter by the former, etc. In conformity with the old (and by no means Marxist) doctrine that they have learned by rote, they are trying to veil the plot of the Anglo-French imperialists and the Guchkovs and Milyukovs aimed at deposing the 'chief warrior', Nicholas Romanov, and putting more energetic, fresh and more capable *warriors* in his place.

That the revolution succeeded so quickly and – seemingly, at the first superficial glance – so radically, is only due to the fact that, as a result of an extremely unique historical situation, *absolutely dissimilar currents*, *absolutely heterogeneous* class interests, *absolutely contrary* political and social strivings have *merged*, and in a strikingly 'harmonious' manner. Namely, the conspiracy of the Anglo-French imperialists, who impelled Milyukov, Guchkov and co. to seize power *for the purpose of continuing the imperialist war*, for the purpose of conducting the war still more ferociously and obstinately, for the purpose of *slaughtering fresh millions* of Russian workers and peasants in order that the Guchkovs might obtain Constantinople,

10 Wilhelm II was Emperor of Germany from 1888 until the 1918 Revolution.

the French capitalists Syria, the British capitalists Mesopotamia and so on. This on the one hand. On the other, there was a profound proletarian and mass popular movement of a revolutionary character (a movement of the entire poorest section of the population of town and country) for *bread*, for *peace*, for *real freedom*.

It would simply be foolish to speak of the revolutionary proletariat of Russia 'supporting' the Cadet-Octobrist imperialism, which has been 'patched up' with English money and is as abominable as tsarist imperialism. The revolutionary workers were destroying, have already destroyed to a considerable degree and will destroy to its foundations the infamous tsarist *monarchy*. They are neither elated nor dismayed by the fact that at certain brief and exceptional historical conjunctures *they were aided* by the struggle of Buchanan,[11] Guchkov, Milyukov and co. to *replace* one monarch by *another monarch*, also preferably a Romanov!

Such, and only such, is the way the situation developed. Such, and only such, is the view that can be taken by a politician who does not fear the truth, who soberly weighs the balance of social forces in the revolution, who appraises every 'current situation' not only from the standpoint of all its present, current peculiarities, but also from the standpoint of the more fundamental motivations, the deeper interest-relationship of the proletariat and the bourgeoisie, both in Russia and throughout the world.

The workers of Petrograd, like the workers of the whole of Russia, self-sacrificingly fought the tsarist monarchy – fought for freedom, land for the peasants, and *for peace*, against the imperialist slaughter. To continue and intensify that slaughter, Anglo-French imperialist capital hatched Court intrigues, conspired with the officers of the Guards, incited and encouraged the Guchkovs and Milyukovs, and fixed up a *complete new government*, which in fact *did seize power* immediately after the proletarian struggle had struck the first blows at tsarism.

This new government, in which Lvov and Guchkov of the Octobrists and Peaceful Renovation Party,[12] yesterday's abettors of

---

11 British diplomat and ambassador to Russia from 1910-18.

12 The party of Peaceful Renovation was a constitutional-monarchist organisation of the big bourgeoisie and landlords.

Stolypin the Hangman,[13] control *really important* posts, vital posts, decisive posts, the army and the bureaucracy – this government, in which Milyukov and the other Cadets are more than anything decorations, a signboard – they are there to deliver sentimental professorial speeches – and in which the Trudovik Kerensky is a balalaika on which they play to deceive the workers and peasants – this government is not a fortuitous assemblage of persons.

They are representatives of the new class that has risen to political power in Russia, the class of capitalist landlords and bourgeoisie which has long been *ruling* our country economically, and which during the Revolution of 1905-07, the counter-revolutionary period of 1907-14 and finally – and with special rapidity – the war period of 1914-17, was quick to organise itself politically, taking over control of the local government bodies, public education, congresses of various types, the Duma,[14] the war industries committees, etc. This new class was already 'almost completely' *in* power by 1917, and therefore it needed only the first blows to bring tsarism to the ground and clear the way for the bourgeoisie. The imperialist war, which required an incredible exertion of effort, so accelerated the course of backward Russia's development that we have 'at one blow' (*seemingly* at one blow) *caught up* with Italy, England and almost with France. We have obtained a 'coalition', a 'national' (i.e. adapted for carrying on the imperialist slaughter and for fooling the people) 'parliamentary' government.

Side by side with this government – which as regards the *present* war is but the agent of the billion-dollar 'firm' 'England and France' – there has arisen the chief, unofficial, as yet undeveloped and comparatively weak *workers' government*, which expresses the interests of the proletariat and of the entire poor section of the urban and rural population. This is the *Soviet of Workers' Deputies* in Petrograd,

13 Landowner, appointed Prime Minister and Minister of the Interior from 1906 until his assassination in 1911. Stolypin oversaw the counter-revolutionary terror after the 1905 Revolution.

14 During the reign of Nicholas II the State Duma was the name given to the national parliament, which only had an advisory role. There were also local dumas, the equivalent of local councils.

which is seeking connections with the soldiers and peasants and also with the agricultural workers, with the latter particularly and primarily, of course, more than with the peasants.

Such is the *actual* political situation, which we must first endeavour to define with the greatest possible objective precision, in order that Marxist tactics may be based upon the only possible solid foundation – the foundation of *facts*.

The tsarist monarchy has been smashed, but not finally destroyed. The Octobrist-Cadet bourgeois government, which wants to fight the imperialist war 'to a finish', and which in reality is the agent of the financial firm 'England and France', is *obliged to promise* the people the maximum of liberties and sops compatible with the maintenance of its power over the people and the possibility of continuing the imperialist slaughter.

The Soviet of Workers' Deputies is an organisation of the workers, the embryo of a workers' government, the representative of the interests of the entire mass of the *poor* section of the population, i.e. of nine-tenths of the population, which is striving for *peace, bread* and *freedom*.

The conflict of these three forces determines the situation that has now arisen, a situation that is *transitional* from the first stage of the revolution to the second.

The antagonism between the first and second force is *not* profound, it is temporary, the result *solely* of the present conjuncture of circumstances, of the abrupt turn of events in the imperialist war. The *whole* of the new government is monarchist, for Kerensky's *verbal* republicanism simply cannot be taken seriously, is not worthy of a statesman and, *objectively*, is political chicanery. The new government, which has not dealt the tsarist monarchy the final blow, has already *begun to strike a bargain* with the landlord Romanov Dynasty. The bourgeoisie of the Octobrist-Cadet type *needs* a monarchy to serve as the head of the bureaucracy and the army in order to protect the privileges of capital against the working people.

He who says that the workers must *support* the new government in the interests of the struggle against tsarist reaction (and apparently this is being said by the Potresovs, Gvozdevs, Chkhenkelis and also, all *evasiveness* notwithstanding, by *Chkheidze*) is a traitor to the workers, a traitor to the cause of the proletariat, to the cause of peace and freedom. For actually, *precisely* this new government is *already* bound hand and foot by imperialist capital, by the imperialist policy of *war* and plunder, has *already* begun to strike bargain (without consulting the people!) with the dynasty, *is already working to restore the tsarist monarchy*, is already soliciting the candidature of Mikhail Romanov[15] as the new kinglet, is already taking measures to prop up the throne, to substitute for the legitimate (lawful, ruling by virtue of the old law) monarchy a Bonapartist, plebiscite monarchy (ruling by virtue of a fraudulent plebiscite).

No, if there is to lie a real struggle against the tsarist monarchy, if freedom is to be guaranteed in fact and not merely in words, in the glib promises of Milyukov and Kerensky, the workers must *not* support the new government; the government must 'support' the workers! For the only *guarantee* of freedom and of the complete destruction of tsarism lies in *arming the proletariat*, in strengthening, extending and developing the role, significance and power of the Soviet of Workers' Deputies.

All the rest is mere phrase-mongering and lies, self-deception on the part of the politicians of the liberal and radical camp, fraudulent trickery.

Help, or at least do not hinder, the arming of the workers, and freedom in Russia will be invincible, the monarchy irrestorable, the republic secure.

Otherwise the Guchkovs and Milyukovs will restore the monarchy and grant *none*, absolutely none of the 'liberties' they promised. All bourgeois politicians in *all* bourgeois revolutions 'fed' the people and fooled the workers with promises.

Ours is a bourgeois revolution, *therefore*, the workers must support the bourgeoisie, say the Potresovs, Gvozdevs and Chkheidzes, as Plekhanov said yesterday.

---

15 The younger brother of Nicholas II.

Ours is a bourgeois revolution, we Marxists say, *therefore* the workers must open the eyes of the people to the deception practised by the bourgeois politicians, teach them to put no faith in words, to depend entirely on their *own* strength, their *own* organisation, their *own* unity and their own *weapons.*

The government of the Octobrists and Cadets, of the Guchkovs and Milyukovs, *cannot,* even if it sincerely wanted to (only infants can think that Guchkov and Lvov are sincere), *cannot* give the people *either peace, bread, or freedom.*

It cannot give peace because it is a war government, a government for the continuation of the imperialist slaughter, a government of *plunder,* out to plunder Armenia, Galicia and Turkey, annex Constantinople, reconquer Poland, Courland, Lithuania, etc. It is a government bound hand and foot by Anglo-French imperialist capital. Russian capital is merely a branch of the world-wide 'firm' which manipulates *hundreds of billions* of roubles and is called 'England and France'.

It cannot give bread because it is a bourgeois government. *At best,* it can give the people 'brilliantly organised famine', as Germany has done. But the people will not accept famine. They will learn, and probably very soon, that there is bread and that it can be obtained, but only by methods that *do not respect the sanctity of capital and landownership.*

It cannot give freedom because it is a landlord and capitalist government which *fears* the people and has already begun to strike a bargain with the Romanov dynasty.

The tactical problems of our immediate attitude towards this government will be dealt with in another article. In it, we shall explain the peculiarity of the present situation, which is a *transition* from the first stage of the revolution to the second, and why the slogan, the 'task of the day', at *this* moment must be:

> 'Workers, you have performed miracles of proletarian heroism, the heroism of the people, in the civil war against tsarism. You must perform miracles of organisation, organisation of the proletariat and

of the whole people, to prepare the way for your victory in the second stage of the revolution.'

Confining ourselves for the *present* to an analysis of the class struggle and the alignment of class forces at this stage of the revolution, we have still to put the question: who are the proletariat's *allies* in *this* revolution?

It has *two* allies: first, the broad mass of the semi-proletarian and partly also of the small-peasant population, who number scores of millions and constitute the overwhelming majority of the population of Russia. For this mass peace, bread, freedom and land are *essential.* It is inevitable that to a certain extent this mass will be under the influence of the bourgeoisie, particularly of the petty bourgeoisie, to which it is most akin in its conditions of life, vacillating between the bourgeoisie and the proletariat. The cruel lessons of war, and they will be *the more* cruel the more vigorously the war is prosecuted by Guchkov, Lvov, Milyukov and co., will *inevitably* push this mass towards the proletariat, compel it to follow the proletariat. We must now take advantage of the relative freedom of the new order and of the Soviets of Workers' Deputies to *enlighten* and *organise* this mass first of all and above all. Soviets of Peasants' Deputies and Soviets of Agricultural Workers – that is one of our most urgent tasks. In this connection we shall strive not only for the agricultural workers to establish their own separate Soviets, but also for the propertyless and poorest peasants to organise *separately* from the well-to-do peasants. The special tasks and special forms of organisation urgently needed at the present time will be dealt with in the next letter.

Second, the ally of the Russian proletariat is the proletariat of all the belligerent countries and of all countries in general. At present this ally is to a large degree repressed by the war, and all too often the European social-chauvinists speak in its name – men who, like Plekhanov, Gvozdev and Potresov in Russia, have deserted to the bourgeoisie. But the liberation of the proletariat from their influence has progressed with every month of the imperialist war, and the Russian revolution will *inevitably* immensely hasten this process.

With these two allies, the proletariat, *utilising the peculiarities* of the present transition situation, can and will proceed, first, to the achievement of a democratic republic and complete victory of the peasantry over the landlords, instead of the Guchkov-Milyukov semi-monarchy, and then to *socialism*, which alone can give the war-weary people *peace, bread* and *freedom*.

N Lenin,[16]
Zurich,
7 (20) March 1917

16 Pseudonym used by Lenin.

The New Government and the Proletariat (Second 'Letter from Afar')

Written 9 (22) March 1917

The principal document I have at my disposal at today's date (8 (21) March) is a copy of that most conservative and bourgeois English newspaper *The Times* of 16 March, containing a batch of reports about the revolution in Russia. Clearly, a source more favourably inclined – to put it mildly – towards the Guchkov and Milyukov government it would not be easy to find.

This newspaper's correspondent reports from St. Petersburg on Wednesday, 1 (14) March, when the *first* Provisional Government still existed, i.e. the thirteen-member Duma Executive Committee, headed by Rodzianko[1] and including two 'socialists', as the newspaper puts it, Kerensky and Chkheidze:

> A group of twenty two elected members of the Upper House [State Council] including M. Guchkov, M. Stakhovich, Prince Trubetskoi, and Professor Vassiliev, Grimm and Vernadsky, yesterday addressed a telegram to the Tsar…

1 Landowner and a leading Octobrist.

... imploring him in order to save the 'dynasty', etc., etc., to convoke the Duma and to name as the head of the government someone who enjoys the 'confidence of the nation'.

> What the Emperor may decide to do on his arrival today is unknown at the hour of telegraphing, [writes the correspondent] but one thing is quite certain. Unless His Majesty immediately complies with the wishes of the most moderate elements among his loyal subjects, the influence at present exercised by the Provisional Committee of the Imperial Duma will pass wholesale into the hands of the socialists, who want to see a republic established, but who are unable to institute any kind of orderly government and would inevitably precipitate the country into anarchy within and disaster without...

What political sagacity and clarity this reveals. How well this Englishman, who thinks like (if he does not guide) the Guchkovs and Milyukovs, understands the alignment of class forces and interests! "The most moderate elements among his loyal subjects", i.e. the monarchist landlords and capitalists, want to take power into their hands, fully realising that otherwise "influence" will pass "into the hands of the socialists". Why the "socialists" and not somebody else? Because the English Guchkovite is fully aware that there is *no* other social force in the political arena, *nor can there be*. The revolution was made by the proletariat. It displayed heroism; it shed its blood; it swept along with it the broadest masses of the toilers and the poor; it is demanding bread, peace and freedom; it is demanding a republic; it sympathises with socialism. But the handful of landlords and capitalists headed by the Guchkovs and Milyukovs want to betray the will, or strivings, of the vast majority and conclude a *deal with the tottering monarchy*, bolster it up, save it: appoint Lvov and Guchkov, Your Majesty, and we will be with the monarchy against the people. Such is the entire meaning, the sum and substance of the new government's policy!

But how to justify the deception, the fooling of the people, the violation of the will of the overwhelming majority of the population?

By slandering the people – the old but eternally new method of the bourgeoisie. And the English Guchkovite slanders, scolds, spits and splutters: "anarchy within and disaster without", no "orderly government"!

That is not true, Mr. Guchkovite! The workers want a republic; and a republic represents far more 'orderly' government than monarchy does. What guarantee have the people that the second Romanov will not get himself a second Rasputin? Disaster will be brought on precisely by continuation of the war, i.e. precisely by the new government. Only a proletarian republic, backed by the rural workers and the poorest section of the peasants and town dwellers, can secure peace, provide bread, order and freedom.

All the shouts about anarchy are merely a screen to conceal the selfish interests of the capitalists, who want to make profit out of the war, out of war loans, who want to restore the monarchy *against* the people.

> ... Yesterday, [continues the correspondent] the Social-Democratic Party issued a proclamation of a most seditious character, which was spread broadcast throughout the city. They [i.e. the Social-Democratic Party] are mere doctrinaires, but their power for mischief is enormous at a time like the present. M. Kerensky and M. Chkheidze, who realise that without the support of the officers and the more moderate elements of the people they cannot hope to avoid anarchy, have to reckon with their less prudent associates, and are insensibly driven to take up an attitude which complicates the task of the Provisional Committee...

O great English, Guchkovite diplomat! How 'imprudently' you have blurted out the truth!

"The Social-Democratic Party" and their "less prudent associates" with whom "Kerensky and Chkheidze have to reckon", evidently mean the Central or the St. Petersburg Committee of our Party, which was restored at the January 1912 Conference, those very same 'Bolsheviks' at whom the bourgeoisie always hurl the abusive term "doctrinaires", because of their faithfulness to the 'doctrine', i.e. the fundamentals, the principles, teachings, aims of *socialism*. Obviously, the English Guchkovite hurls the abusive terms seditious and doctrinaire at the manifesto and at the conduct of our Party in urging a fight for a republic, peace, complete destruction of the tsarist monarchy, bread for the people.

Bread for the people and peace – that's sedition, but ministerial posts for Guchkov and Milyukov – that's 'order'. Old and familiar talk!

What, then, are the tactics of Kerensky and Chkheidze as characterised by the English Guchkovite?

Vacillation: on the one hand, the Guchkovite praises them: they "realise" (Good boys! Clever boys!) that without the "support" of the army officers and the more moderate elements, anarchy cannot be avoided. (We, however, have always thought, in keeping with our doctrine, with our socialist teachings, that it is the capitalists who introduce anarchy and war into human society, that only the transfer of *all* political power to the proletariat and the poorest people can rid us of war, of anarchy and starvation!) On the other hand, they "have to reckon with their less prudent associates", i.e. the Bolsheviks, the Russian Social-Democratic Labour Party, restored and united by the Central Committee.

What is the force that compels Kerensky and Chkheidze to "reckon" with the Bolshevik Party to which they have *never* belonged, which they, or their literary representatives (Socialist-Revolutionaries, Popular Socialists,[2] the Menshevik OC supporters and so forth), have always abused, condemned, denounced as an insignificant underground circle, a sect of doctrinaires and so forth? Where and when has it ever happened that in time of revolution, at a time of predominantly *mass* action, sane-minded politicians should "reckon" with "doctrinaires"?

He is all mixed up, our poor English Guchkovite; he has failed to produce a logical argument, has failed to tell either a whole lie or the whole truth, he has merely given himself away.

Kerensky and Chkheidze are compelled to reckon with the Social-Democratic Party of the Central Committee by the influence it exerts on the proletariat, on the masses. Our Party was found to be with the masses, with the revolutionary proletariat, *in spite* of the arrest and deportation of our Duma deputies to Siberia, as far back

---

2 Party formed in 1906 in a right-wing split from the SRs.

as 1914, in spite of the fierce persecution and arrests to which the St. Petersburg Committee was subjected for its underground activities during the war, *against* the war and against tsarism.

"Facts are stubborn things", as the English proverb has it. Let me remind you of it, most esteemed English Guchkovite! That our Party guided, or at least rendered devoted assistance to, the St. Petersburg workers in the great days of revolution is a fact the English Guchkovite '*himself*' was *obliged* to admit. And he was equally obliged to admit the fact that Kerensky and Chkheidze are oscillating *between* the bourgeoisie and the proletariat. The Gvozdevites, the 'defencists', i.e. the social-chauvinists, i.e. the defenders of the imperialist, predatory war, are now completely following the bourgeoisie; Kerensky, by entering the ministry, i.e. the second Provisional Government, has also completely deserted to the bourgeoisie; Chkheidze has not; he continues to *oscillate* between the Provisional Government of the bourgeoisie, the Guchkovs and Milyukovs and the 'provisional government' of the proletariat and the poorest masses of the people, the Soviet of Workers' Deputies and the Russian Social-Democratic Labour Party united by the Central Committee.

Consequently, the revolution has confirmed what we especially insisted on when we urged the workers clearly to realise the class difference between the principal parties and principal trends in the working-class movement and among the petty bourgeoisie – what we wrote, for example, in the Geneva *Sotsial-Demokrat*, No. 47, nearly eighteen months ago, on 13 October 1915:

> As hitherto, we consider it admissible for Social-Democrats to join a provisional revolutionary government together with the democratic petty bourgeoisie, but *not* with the revolutionary chauvinists. By revolutionary chauvinists we mean those who want a victory over tsarism so as to achieve victory over Germany – plunder other countries – consolidate Great-Russian rule over the other peoples of Russia, etc. Revolutionary chauvinism is based on the class position of the petty bourgeoisie. The latter always vacillates between the bourgeoisie and the proletariat. At present it is vacillating between chauvinism (which

> prevents it from being consistently revolutionary, even in the meaning of a democratic revolution) and proletarian internationalism. At the moment the Trudoviks, the Socialist-Revolutionaries, *Nasha Zarya* (now *Dyelo*),[3] Chkheidze's Duma group, the Organising Committee, Mr. Plekhanov and the like are political spokesmen for this petty bourgeoisie in Russia. If the revolutionary chauvinists won in Russia, we would be opposed to a defence of *their* 'fatherland' in the present war. Our slogan is: against the chauvinists, even if they are revolutionary and republican – *against* them and *for* an alliance of the international proletariat for the socialist revolution.

But let us return to the English Guchkovite. He continues:

> … The Provisional Committee of the Imperial Duma, appreciating the dangers ahead, have purposely refrained from carrying out the original intention of arresting Ministers, although they could have done so yesterday without the slightest difficulty. The door is thus left open for negotiations, thanks to which we ["we" = British finance capital and imperialism] may obtain all the benefits of the new regime without passing through the dread ordeal of the Commune and the anarchy of civil war…

The Guchkovites were *for* a civil war from which *they* would benefit, but they are *against* a civil war from which the people, i.e. the actual majority of the working people, would benefit.

> The relations between the Provisional Committee of the Duma, which represents the whole nation [imagine saying this about the committee of the landlord and capitalist Fourth Duma!], and the Council of Labour Deputies, representing purely class interests [this is the language of a diplomat who has heard learned words with one ear and wants to conceal the fact that the Soviet of Workers' Deputies represents the proletariat and the poor, i.e. nine-tenths of the population], but in a crisis like the present wielding enormous power, have aroused no small misgivings among reasonable men regarding the possibility of a conflict between them – the results of which might be too terrible to describe.

---

3 A Menshevik paper.

> Happily this danger has been averted, at least for the present [note the "at least"!], thanks to the influence of M. Kerensky, a young lawyer of much oratorical ability, who clearly realises [unlike Chkheidze, who also 'realised', but evidently less clearly in the opinion of the Guchkovite?] the necessity of working with the Committee in the interests of his Labour constituents [i.e. to catch the workers' votes, to flirt with them]. A satisfactory agreement was concluded today [Wednesday 1 (14) March], whereby all unnecessary friction will be avoided.[4]

What this agreement was, whether it was concluded with the *whole* of the Soviet of Workers' Deputies and on what terms, we do not know. On this *chief* point, the English Guchkovite says nothing at all this time. And no wonder! It is not to the advantage of the bourgeoisie to have these terms made clear, precise and known to all, for it would then be more difficult for it to violate them!

* * *

The preceding lines were already written when I read two very important communications. First, in that most conservative and bourgeois Paris newspaper *Le Temps* of 20 March, the text of the Soviet of Workers' Deputies manifesto appealing for 'support' of the new government; second, excerpts from Skobelev's[5] speech in the State Duma on 1 (14) March, reproduced in a Zurich newspaper (*Neue Zürcher Zeitung*, 1 Mit.-bl., 8 (21) March) from a Berlin newspaper (*National-Zeitung*).

The manifesto of the Soviet of Workers' Deputies, if the text has not been distorted by the French imperialists, is a most remarkable document. It shows that the St. Petersburg proletariat, at least at the time the manifesto was issued, was under the predominating influence of petty-bourgeois politicians. You will recall that in this category of politicians I include, as has been already mentioned above, people of the type of Kerensky and Chkheidze.

4 Reference is to the agreement between the Duma Provisional Committee and the Socialist-Revolutionary and Menshevik leaders of the Petrograd Soviet Executive Committee. The latter voluntarily surrendered power to the bourgeoisie and authorised the Duma Provisional Committee to form a Provisional Government of its own choice.

5 Menshevik and a leader of the Petrograd Soviet after the February Revolution.

In the manifesto we find two political ideas, and two slogans corresponding to them:

Firstly. The manifesto says that the government (the new one) consists of 'moderate elements'. A strange description, by no means complete, of a purely liberal, not of a Marxist character. I too am prepared to agree that in a certain sense – in my next letter I will show in precisely what sense – now, with the first stage of the revolution completed, every government must be 'moderate'. But it is absolutely impermissible to conceal from ourselves and from the people that this government wants to continue the imperialist, war, that it is an agent of British capital, that it wants to restore the monarchy and strengthen the rule of the landlords and capitalists.

The manifesto declares that all democrats must 'support' the new government and that the Soviet of Workers' Deputies requests and authorises Kerensky to enter the Provisional Government. The conditions – implementation of the promised reforms already during the war, guarantees for the 'free cultural' (only?) development of the nationalities (a purely Cadet, wretchedly liberal programme) and the establishment of a special committee consisting of members of the Soviet of Workers' Deputies and of 'military men' to supervise the activities of the Provisional Government.

This Supervising Committee, which comes within the second category of ideas and slogans, we will discuss separately further on.

The appointment of the Russian Louis Blanc,[6] Kerensky, and the appeal to support the new government is, one may say, a classical example of betrayal of the cause of the revolution and the cause of the proletariat, a betrayal which doomed a number of nineteenth-century revolutions, irrespective of how sincere and devoted to socialism the leaders and supporters of such a policy may have been.

The proletariat cannot and must not support a war government, a restoration government. To fight reaction, to rebuff all possible

6 French petty-bourgeois socialist in the nineteenth century opposed to the proletarian revolution, wanting a compromise with the bourgeoisie. Lenin often used his name as an epithet denoting opportunist and conciliatory tactics.

and probable attempts by the Romanovs and their friends to restore the monarchy and muster a counter-revolutionary army, it is necessary not to support Guchkov and co., but to *organise*, expand and strengthen a *proletarian* militia, to arm the people under the leadership of the workers. Without this principal, fundamental, radical measure, there can be no question either of offering serious resistance to the restoration of the monarchy and attempts to rescind or curtail the promised freedoms, or of firmly taking the road that will give the people bread, *peace* and freedom.

If it is true that Chkheidze, who, with Kerensky, was a member of the first Provisional Government (the Duma committee of thirteen), refrained from entering the second Provisional Government out of principled considerations of the above-mentioned or similar character, then that does him credit. That must be said frankly. Unfortunately, such an interpretation is contradicted by the facts, and primarily by the speech delivered by Skobelev, who has always gone hand in hand with Chkheidze.

Skobelev said, if the above-mentioned source is to be trusted, that "the social [? evidently the Social-Democratic] group and the workers are only slightly in touch (have little contact) with the aims of the Provisional Government", that the workers are demanding peace, and that if the war is continued there will be disaster in the spring anyhow, that "the workers have concluded with society [liberal society] a temporary agreement, although their political aims are as far removed from the aims of society as heaven is from earth", that "the liberals must abandon the senseless aims of the war", etc.

This speech is a sample of what we called above, in the excerpt from *Sotsial-Demokrat*, 'oscillation' between the bourgeoisie and the proletariat. The liberals, while remaining liberals, *cannot* 'abandon' the 'senseless' aims of the war, which, incidentally, are not determined by them alone, but by Anglo-French finance capital, a world-mighty force measured by hundreds of billions. The task is not to 'coax' the liberals, but to *explain* to the workers why the liberals find themselves in a blind alley, why *they* are bound hand and foot, why they *conceal* both the treaties tsarism concluded with England and other countries and the deals between Russian and Anglo-French capital and so forth.

If Skobelev says that the workers have concluded an agreement with liberal society, no matter of what character, and since he does not protest against it, does not explain from the Duma rostrum how harmful it is for the workers, he thereby *approves* of the agreement. And that is exactly what he should not do.

Skobelev's direct or indirect, clearly expressed or tacit, approval of the agreement between the Soviet of Workers' Deputies and the Provisional Government is Skobelev's swing towards the bourgeoisie. Skobelev's statement that the workers are demanding peace, that their aims are as far removed from the liberals' aims as heaven is from earth, is Skobelev's swing towards the proletariat.

Purely proletarian, truly revolutionary and profoundly correct in design is the second political idea in the manifesto of the Soviet of Workers' Deputies that we are studying, namely, the idea of establishing a 'Supervising Committee' (I do not know whether this is what it is called in Russian; I am translating freely from the French), of proletarian-soldier supervision over the Provisional Government.

Now, that's something real! It is worthy of the workers who have shed their blood for freedom, peace, bread for the people! It is a *real step* towards *real guarantees* against tsarism, against a monarchy and against the monarchists Guchkov, Lvov and co.! It is a sign that the Russian proletariat, in spite of everything, has made progress compared with the French proletariat in 1848, when it 'authorised' Louis Blanc! It is proof that the instinct and mind of the proletarian masses are not satisfied with declamations, exclamations, promises of reforms and freedoms, with the title of 'minister authorised by the workers', and similar tinsel, but are seeking support *only* where it is to be found, in the *armed* masses of the people organised and led by the proletariat, the class-conscious workers.

It is a step along the right road, but *only* the first step.

If this 'Supervising Committee' remains a purely political-type parliamentary institution, a committee that will 'put questions' to the Provisional Government and receive answers from it, then it will remain a plaything, will amount to nothing.

If, on the other hand, it leads, immediately and despite all obstacles, to the formation of a *workers' militia*, or *workers' home guard*, extending to the whole people, to all men and women, which would not only replace the exterminated and dissolved police force, not only make the latter's restoration *impossible* by *any* government, constitutional-monarchist or democratic-republican, *either* in St. Petersburg *or* anywhere else in Russia – then the advanced workers of Russia will really take the road towards new and great victories, the road to victory over war, to the realisation of the slogan which, as the newspapers report, adorned the colours of the cavalry troops that demonstrated in St. Petersburg, in the square outside the State Duma: "Long Live Socialist Republics in All Countries!"

I will set out my ideas about this workers' militia in my next letter.

In it I will try to show, on the one hand, that the formation of a militia embracing the entire people and led by the workers is the correct slogan of the day, one that corresponds to the tactical tasks of the peculiar transitional moment through which the Russian revolution (and the world revolution) is passing; and, on the other hand, that to be successful, this workers' militia must, firstly, embrace the entire people, must be a mass organisation to the degree of being *universal*, must really embrace the *entire* able-bodied population of both sexes; secondly, it must proceed to combine not only purely police, but general state functions with military functions and with the control of social production and distribution.

N Lenin,
Zurich,
9 (22) March 1917

PS: I forgot to date my previous letter 7 (20) March.

Concerning a Proletarian Militia (Third 'Letter from Afar')

Written 11 (24) March 1917

The conclusion I drew yesterday about Chkheidze's vacillating tactics has been fully confirmed today, 10 (23) March, by two documents. First – a telegraphic report from Stockholm in the *Frankfurter Zeitung* containing excerpts from the manifesto of the Central Committee of our Party, the Russian Social-Democratic Labour Party, in St. Petersburg. In this document there is not a word about either supporting the Guchkov government or overthrowing it; the workers and soldiers are called upon to organise around the Soviet of Workers' Deputies, to elect representatives to it for the fight against tsarism and for a republic, for an eight-hour day, for the confiscation of the landed estates and grain stocks, and chiefly, for an end to the predatory war. Particularly important and particularly urgent in this connection is our Central Committee's absolutely correct idea that to obtain peace relations must be established with *the proletarians of all the belligerent countries.*

To expect peace from negotiations and relations between the bourgeois governments would be self-deception and deception of the people.

The second document is a Stockholm report, also by telegraph, to another German newspaper (*Vossische Zeitung*) about a conference between the Chkheidze group in the Duma, the workers' group (? *Arbeiterfraction*) and representatives of fifteen workers' unions on 2 (15) March and a manifesto published next day. Of the eleven points of this manifesto, the telegram reports only three; the first, the demand for a republic; the seventh, the demand for peace and immediate peace negotiations; and the third, the demand for "adequate participation in the government of representatives of the Russian working class".

If this point is correctly reported, I can understand why the bourgeoisie is praising Chkheidze. I can understand why the praise of the English Guchkovites in *The Times* which I quoted elsewhere has been supplemented by the praise of the French Guchkovites in *Le Temps*. This newspaper of the French millionaires and imperialists writes on 22 March:

> The leaders of the workers' parties, particularly M. Chkheidze, are exercising all their influence to moderate the wishes of the working classes.

Indeed, to demand workers' 'participation' in the Guchkov-Milyukov government is a theoretical and political absurdity: to participate as a minority would mean serving as a pawn; to participate on an 'equal footing' is impossible, because the demand to continue the war cannot be reconciled with the demand to conclude an armistice and start peace negotiations; to 'participate' as a majority requires the strength to *overthrow* the Guchkov-Milyukov government. In practice, the demand for 'participation' is the worst sort of Louis Blanc-ism, i.e. oblivion to the class struggle and the actual conditions under which it is being waged, infatuation with a most hollow-sounding phrase, spreading illusions among the workers, loss, in negotiations with Milyukov or Kerensky, of *precious* time which must be used to create a *real* class and revolutionary force, a proletarian militia that will *enjoy the confidence of all* the poor strata of the population, and they constitute the vast majority, and will *help them to organise*, help *them* to fight for bread, peace, freedom.

This mistake in the manifesto issued by Chkheidze and his group (I am not speaking of the OC, Organising Committee *party*, because in the sources available to me there is not a word about the OC) – this mistake is all the more strange considering that at the 2 (15) March conference, Chkheidze's closest collaborator, Skobelev, said, according to the newspapers: "Russia is on the eve of a second, real [*wirklich*] revolution".

Now that is the truth, from which Skobelev and Chkheidze have forgotten to draw the practical conclusions. I cannot judge from here, from my accursed afar, how near this second revolution is. Being on the spot, Skobelev can see things better. Therefore, I am not raising for myself problems, for the solution of which I have not and cannot have the necessary concrete data. I am merely emphasising the confirmation by Skobelev, an 'outside witness', i.e. one who does not belong to our Party, of the *factual* conclusion I drew in my first letter, namely: that the February-March Revolution was merely the *first* stage of the revolution. Russia is passing through a peculiar historical moment of *transition* to the next stage of the revolution, or, to use Skobelev's expression, to a 'second revolution'.

If we want to be Marxists and learn from the experience of revolution in the whole world, we must strive to understand in what, precisely, lies the *peculiarity* of this *transitional* moment, and what tactics follow from its objective specific features.

The peculiarity of the situation lies in that the Guchkov-Milyukov government gained the first victory with extraordinary ease due to the following three major circumstances:

1. Assistance from Anglo-French finance capital and its agents;
2. Assistance from part of the top ranks of the army;
3. The already existing organisation of the entire Russian bourgeoisie in the shape of the rural and urban local government institutions, the State Duma, the war industries committees and so forth.

The Guchkov government is held in a vice: bound by the interests of capital, it is compelled to strive to continue the predatory, robber war, to protect the monstrous profits of capital and the landlords, to restore the monarchy. Bound by its revolutionary origin and by the need for an abrupt change from tsarism to democracy, pressed by the bread-hungry and peace-hungry masses, the government is compelled to lie, to wriggle, to play for time, to 'proclaim' and promise (promises are the only things that are very cheap even at a time of madly rocketing prices) as much as possible and do as little as possible, to make concessions with one hand and to withdraw them with the other.

Under certain circumstances, the new government can at best postpone its collapse somewhat by leaning on all the organising ability of the entire Russian bourgeoisie and bourgeois intelligentsia. But even in that case it is *unable* to avoid collapse, because it is *impossible* to escape from the claws of the terrible monster of imperialist war and famine nurtured by world capitalism unless one renounces bourgeois relationships, passes to revolutionary measures, appeals to the supreme historic heroism of both the Russian and world proletariat.

Hence the conclusion: we cannot overthrow the new government at one stroke, or, if we can (in revolutionary times the limits of what is possible expand a thousandfold), we will not be able to maintain power *unless we counter* the magnificent organisation of the entire Russian bourgeoisie and the entire bourgeois intelligentsia with an equally magnificent *organisation of the proletariat*, which must lead the entire vast mass of urban and rural poor, the semi-proletariat and small proprietors.

Irrespective of whether the 'second revolution' has already broken out in St. Petersburg (I have said that it would be absolutely absurd to think that it is possible from abroad to assess the actual tempo at which it is maturing), whether it has been postponed for some time, or whether it has already begun in individual areas (of which some signs are evident) – in *any* case, the slogan of the moment on the eve of the new revolution, during it, and on the morrow of it, must be *proletarian organisation.*

Comrade workers! You performed miracles of proletarian heroism yesterday in overthrowing the tsarist monarchy. In the more or less near future (perhaps even now, as these lines are being written) you will again have to perform the same miracles of heroism to overthrow the rule of the landlords and capitalists, who are waging the imperialist war. You will not achieve *durable victory* in this next 'real' revolution if you do not perform *miracles of proletarian organisation!*

Organisation is the slogan of the moment. But to confine oneself to that is to say nothing, for, on the one hand, organisation is *always* needed; hence, mere reference to the necessity of 'organising the masses' explains absolutely nothing. On the other hand, he who confines himself solely to this becomes an abettor of the liberals, for the *very thing* the *liberals* want in order to strengthen their rule is that the workers *should not go beyond their ordinary* 'legal' (from the standpoint of 'normal' bourgeois society) organisations, i.e. that they should *only* join their party, their trade union, their cooperative society, etc., etc.

Guided by their class instinct, the workers have realised that in revolutionary times they need *not only* ordinary, but an entirely different organisation. They have rightly taken the path indicated by the experience of our 1905 Revolution and of the 1871 Paris Commune; they have set up a *Soviet of Workers' Deputies*; they have begun to develop, expand and strengthen it by drawing in *soldiers'* deputies, and, undoubtedly, deputies from rural *wage*-workers, and then (in one form or another) from the entire peasant poor.

The prime and most important task, and one that brooks no delay, is to set up organisations of this kind in all parts of Russia without exception, for all trades and strata of the proletarian and semi-proletarian population without exception, i.e. for all the working and exploited people, to use a less economically exact but more popular term. Running ahead somewhat, I shall mention that for the entire mass of the peasantry our Party (its *special* role in the new type of proletarian organisations I hope to discuss in one of my next letters) should especially recommend Soviets of wage-workers and Soviets of small tillers who do not sell grain, to be formed *separately* from the well-to-do peasants. Without this, it will be impossible either to conduct a truly proletarian policy in general, or correctly to approach the extremely important practical question which is a matter of life and death for millions of people: the proper distribution of *grain*, increasing its production, etc.[1]

It might be asked: What should be the function of the Soviets of Workers' Deputies? They "must be regarded as organs of insurrection, of revolutionary rule", we wrote in No. 47 of the Geneva *Sotsial-Demokrat*, of 13 October 1915.

This theoretical proposition, deduced from the experience of the Commune of 1871 and of the Russian Revolution of 1905, must be explained and concretely developed on the basis of the practical experience of precisely the present stage of the present revolution in Russia.

We need revolutionary *government*, we need (for a certain transitional period) a *state*. This is what distinguishes us from the anarchists. The difference between the revolutionary Marxists and the anarchists is not only that the former stand for centralised, large-scale communist production, while the latter stand for disconnected small production. The difference between us precisely on the question of government, of the state, is that we are *for*, and the anarchists *against*, utilising revolutionary forms of the state in a revolutionary way for the struggle for socialism.

We need a state. But *not the kind* of state the bourgeoisie has created everywhere, from constitutional monarchies to the most democratic republics. And in this we differ from the opportunists and Kautskyites[2] of the old, and decaying, socialist parties, who have

1 In the rural districts a struggle will now develop for the small and, partly, middle peasants. The landlords, leaning on the well-to-do peasants, will try to lead them into subordination to the bourgeoisie. Leaning on the rural wage-workers and rural poor, we must lead them into the closest alliance with the urban proletariat. – *Lenin*

2 Kautsky was one of the leading theoreticians of the German Social-Democratic Party (SPD) and the Second International. After the outbreak of the First World War, he abandoned revolutionary Marxism and took up an indecisive position between revolutionary opposition to the war and patriotic support for the

distorted, or have forgotten, the lessons of the Paris Commune and the analysis of these lessons made by Marx and Engels.[3]

We need a state, but *not* the kind the bourgeoisie needs, with organs of government in the shape of a police force, an army and a bureaucracy (officialdom) separate from and opposed to the people. All bourgeois revolutions merely perfected *this* state machine, merely transferred *it* from the hands of one party to those of another.

The proletariat, on the other hand, if it wants to uphold the gains of the present revolution and proceed further, to win peace, bread and freedom, must '*smash*', to use Marx's expression, this 'ready-made' state machine and substitute a new one for it by *merging* the police force, the army and the bureaucracy with *the entire armed people*. Following the path indicated by the experience of the Paris Commune of 1871 and the Russian Revolution of 1905, the proletariat must organise and arm *all* the poor, exploited sections of the population in order that they *themselves* should take the organs of state power directly into their own hands, in order that *they themselves should constitute* these organs of state power.

And the workers of Russia have already *taken* this path in the first stage of the first revolution, in February-March 1917. The whole task now is clearly to understand what this new path is, to proceed along it further, boldly, firmly and perseveringly.

The Anglo-French and Russian capitalists wanted 'only' to remove, or only to 'frighten', Nicholas II and to leave intact the old state machine, the police force, the army and the bureaucracy.

The workers went further and smashed it. And now, not only the Anglo-French, but also the German capitalists are *howling* with

---

German bourgeoisie. As such, he became the theoretician of this 'centrism' in the socialist movement, and a bitter opponent of the Russian Revolution.

3 In one of my next letters, or in a special article, I will deal in detail with this analysis, given in particular in Marx's *The Civil War in France*, in Engels' preface to the third edition of that work, in the letters: Marx's of 12 April 1871, and Engels' of 18-28 March 1875, and also with the utter distortion of Marxism by Kautsky in his controversy with Pannekoek in 1912 on the question of the so-called 'destruction of the state'. – *Lenin*
This was to become Lenin's pamphlet, *The State and Revolution*.

rage and horror as they see, for example, Russian soldiers shooting their officers, as in the case of Admiral Nepenin, that supporter of Guchkov and Milyukov.

I said that the workers have smashed the old state machine. It will be more correct to say: *have begun* to smash it.

Let us take a concrete example.

In St. Petersburg and in many other places the police force has been partly wiped out and partly dissolved. The Guchkov-Milyukov government *cannot* either restore the monarchy or, in general, maintain power *without restoring* the police force as a special organisation of armed men under the command of the bourgeoisie, separate from and opposed to the people. That is as clear as daylight.

On the other hand, the new government must reckon with the revolutionary people, must feed them with half-concessions and promises, must play for time. That is why it resorts to half-measures: it establishes a 'people's militia' with elected officials (this sounds awfully respectable, awfully democratic, revolutionary and beautiful!) – *but... but*, firstly, it places this militia under the control of the rural and urban local government bodies, i.e. under the command of landlords and capitalists who have been elected in conformity with laws passed by Nicholas the Bloody and Stolypin the Hangman! Secondly, although calling it a 'people's militia' in order to throw dust in the eyes of the 'people', it does *not* call upon the *entire* people to join this militia, *and does not compel* the employers and capitalists to *pay* workers and office employees their ordinary wages *for the hours and days* they spend in the *public service*, i.e. in the militia.

That's their trick. That is how the landlord and capitalist government of the Guchkovs and Milyukovs manages to have a 'people's militia' on paper, while in reality, it is restoring, gradually and on the quiet, the *bourgeois*, anti-people's militia. At first it is to consist of '8,000 students and professors' (as foreign newspapers describe the present St. Petersburg militia) – an obvious plaything! – and will gradually be built up of the old and new *police force*.

Prevent restoration of the police force! Do not let the local government bodies slip out of your hands! Set up a militia that will really embrace the entire people, be really universal, and be led by the proletariat! – such is the task of the day, such is the slogan of the moment which equally conforms with the properly understood interests of furthering the class struggle, furthering the revolutionary movement, and the democratic instinct of every worker, of every peasant, of every exploited toiler who cannot help hating the policemen, the rural police patrols, the village constables, the command of landlords and capitalists over armed men with power over the people.

What kind of police force do *they* need, the Guchkovs and Milyukovs, the landlords and capitalists? The same kind as existed under the tsarist monarchy. After the briefest revolutionary periods *all* the bourgeois and bourgeois-democratic republics in the world set up or restored *precisely such* a police force, a special organisation of armed men subordinate to the bourgeoisie in one way or another, separate from and opposed to the people.

What kind of militia do we need, the proletariat, all the toiling people? A genuine *people's* militia, i.e. one that, first, consists of the *entire* population, of all adult citizens of *both* sexes; and, second, one that combines the functions of a people's army with police functions, with the functions of the chief and fundamental organ of public order and public administration.

To make these propositions more comprehensible I will take a purely schematic example. Needless to say, it would be absurd to think of drawing up any kind of a 'plan' for a proletarian militia: when the workers and the entire people set about it practically, on a truly mass scale, they will work it out and organise it a hundred times better than any theoretician. I am not offering a 'plan', I only want to illustrate my idea.

St. Petersburg has a population of about 2 million. Of these, more than half are between the ages of fifteen and sixty-five. Take half – 1 million. Let us even subtract an entire fourth as physically unfit etc., taking no part in public service at the present moment for justifiable reasons. There remain 750,000 who, serving in the militia, say one day in fifteen (and receiving their pay for this time from their employers), would form an army of 50,000.

That's the type of 'state' we need!

That's the kind of militia that would be a 'people's militia' in deed and not only in words.

That is how we must proceed in order to *prevent* the restoration either of a special police force, or of a special army separate from the people.

Such a militia, ninety-five-hundredths of which would consist of workers and peasants, would express the *real* mind and will, the strength and power of the vast majority of the people. Such a militia would really arm, and provide military training for, the entire people, would be a safeguard, but *not* of the Guchkov or Milyukov type, against all attempts to restore reaction, against all the designs of tsarist agents. Such a militia would be the executive organ of the Soviets of Workers' and Soldiers' Deputies, it would enjoy the *boundless* respect and confidence of the people, for it itself would be an organisation of the entire people. Such a militia would transform democracy from a beautiful signboard, which covers up the enslavement and torment of the people by the capitalists, into a means of actually *training the masses* for participation in *all* affairs of state. Such a militia would draw the young people into political life and teach them not only by words, but also by action, by *work*. Such a militia would develop those functions which, speaking in scientific language, come within the purview of the 'welfare police', sanitary inspection and so forth, and would enlist for such work all adult women. If women are not drawn into public service, into the militia, into political life, if women are not torn out of their stupefying house and kitchen environment, it will be *impossible* to guarantee real freedom, it will be *impossible* to build even democracy let alone socialism.

Such a militia would be a proletarian militia, for the industrial and urban workers would exert a guiding influence on the masses of the poor as naturally and inevitably as they came to hold the leading place in the people's revolutionary struggle both in 1905-07 and in 1917.

Such a militia would ensure absolute order and devotedly observed comradely discipline. At the same time, in the severe crisis that all the belligerent countries are experiencing, it would make it possible to combat this crisis in a really democratic way, properly and rapidly to distribute grain and other supplies, introduce 'universal labour service', which the French now call 'civilian mobilisation' and the Germans 'civilian service' and without which *it is impossible – it has proved to be impossible* – to heal the wounds that have been and are being inflicted by the predatory and horrible war.

Has the proletariat of Russia shed its blood only in order to receive fine promises of political democratic reforms and nothing more? Can it be that it will not demand, and secure, that *every* toiler should *forthwith* see and feel some improvement in his life? That every family should have bread? That every child should have a bottle of good milk and that not a single adult in a rich family should dare take extra milk until children are provided for? That the palaces and rich apartments abandoned by the tsar and the aristocracy should not remain vacant, but provide shelter for the homeless and the destitute? Who can carry out these measures except a people's militia, to which women must belong equally with men?

These measures do *not yet* constitute socialism. They concern the distribution of consumption, not the reorganisation of production. They would not yet constitute the 'dictatorship of the proletariat', only the 'revolutionary-democratic dictatorship of the proletariat and the poor peasantry'. It is not a matter of finding a theoretical classification. We would be committing a great mistake if we attempted to force the complex, urgent, rapidly developing practical tasks of the revolution into the Procrustean bed of narrowly conceived 'theory' instead of regarding theory primarily and predominantly as a *guide to action.*

Do the masses of the Russian workers possess sufficient class-consciousness, fortitude and heroism to perform 'miracles of proletarian organisation' after they have performed miracles of daring, initiative and self-sacrifice in the direct revolutionary struggle? That we do not know, and it would be idle to indulge in guessing, for practice *alone* furnishes the answers to such questions.

What we do know definitely, and what we, as a party, must explain to the masses is, on the one hand, the immense power of the locomotive of history that is engendering an unprecedented crisis, starvation and incalculable hardship. That locomotive is the war, waged for predatory aims by the capitalists of *both* belligerent camps. This 'locomotive' has brought a number of the richest, freest and most enlightened nations to the brink of doom. It is *forcing* the peoples to strain to the utmost all their energies, placing them in unbearable conditions, putting on the order of the day not the application of certain 'theories' (an illusion against which Marx always warned socialists), but implementation of the most extreme practical measures; for *without* extreme measures, death – immediate and certain death from starvation – awaits millions of people.

That the revolutionary enthusiasm of the advanced class can do a *great deal* when the objective situation *demands* extreme measures from the entire people, needs no proof. *This* aspect is clearly seen and *felt* by everybody in Russia.

It is important to realise that in revolutionary times the objective situation changes with the same swiftness and abruptness as the current of life in general. And we must *be able to adapt* our tactics and immediate tasks to the *specific features* of every given situation. Before February 1917, the immediate task was to conduct bold revolutionary-internationalist propaganda, summon the masses to fight, rouse them. The February-March days required the heroism of devoted struggle to crush the immediate enemy – tsarism. Now we are in *transition* from that first stage of the revolution to the second, from 'coming to grips' with tsarism to 'coming to grips' with Guchkov-Milyukov landlord and capitalist imperialism. The immediate task is *organisation*, not only in the stereotyped sense of working to form stereotyped organisations, but in the sense of drawing unprecedentedly broad masses of the oppressed classes into an organisation that would take over the military, political and economic functions of the state.

The proletariat has approached, and will approach, this singular task in different ways. In some parts of Russia the February-March Revolution puts nearly complete power in its hands. In others the proletariat may, perhaps, in a 'usurpatory' manner, begin to form and develop a proletarian militia. In still others, it will probably strive for immediate elections of urban and rural local government bodies on the basis of universal, etc. suffrage, in order to turn them into revolutionary centres, etc. until the growth of proletarian organisation, the coming together of the soldiers with the workers, the movement among the peasantry and the disillusionment of very many in the war-imperialist government of Guchkov and Milyukov bring near the hour when this government will be replaced by the 'government' of the Soviet of Workers' Deputies.

Nor ought we to forget that close to St. Petersburg we have one of the most advanced, factually republican, countries, namely, Finland, which, from 1905 to 1917, shielded by the revolutionary battles of Russia, has in a relatively peaceful way developed democracy and has won the *majority* of the people for socialism. The Russian proletariat will guarantee the Finnish Republic complete freedom, including freedom to secede (it is doubtful now whether a single Social-Democrat will waver on this point when the Cadet Rodichev is so meanly haggling in Helsingfors for bits of privileges for the Great Russians) – and precisely in this way will win the *complete* confidence and comradely assistance of the Finnish workers for the all-Russian proletarian cause. In a difficult and big undertaking mistakes are inevitable, nor will we avoid them. The Finnish workers are better organisers, they will help us in this sphere, they will, *in their own way*, push forward the establishment of the socialist republic.

Revolutionary victories in Russia proper – peaceful organisational successes in Finland shielded by these victories – the Russian workers' transition to revolutionary organisational tasks on a new scale – capture of power by the proletariat and poorest strata of the population – encouragement and development of the socialist revolution in the West – this is the road that will lead us to *peace* and *socialism*.

N Lenin,
Zurich,
11 (24) March 1917

Farewell Letter to the Swiss Workers

Written on 26 March (8 April) 1917

Comrades, Swiss workers,

Leaving Switzerland for Russia, to continue revolutionary-internationalist activity in our country, we, members of the Russian Social-Democratic Labour Party united under the Central Committee (as distinct from *another* party bearing the *same* name, but united under the Organising Committee), wish to convey to you our fraternal greetings and expression of our profound comradely gratitude for your comradely treatment of the political émigrés.

If the *avowed* social-patriots and opportunists, the Swiss Grütlians who, like the social-patriots of all countries, have deserted the camp of the proletariat for the camp of the bourgeoisie; if these people have *openly* called upon you to fight the harmful influence of foreigners upon the Swiss labour movement; if the disguised social-patriots and opportunists who constitute a majority among the leaders of the Swiss Socialist Party have been pursuing similar tactics *under cover*, we consider it our duty to state that on the part of the revolutionary, internationalist socialist workers of Switzerland we have met with warm sympathy, and have greatly benefited from comradely relations with them.

We have always been particularly careful in dealing with questions, acquaintance with which requires prolonged participation in the Swiss movement. But those of us – and there were hardly more than ten or fifteen – who have been members of the Swiss Socialist Party have considered it our duty steadfastly to maintain our point of view, the point of view of the Zimmerwald Left,[1] on general and fundamental questions of the international socialist movement. We considered it our duty determinedly to fight not only social-patriotism, but also the so-called 'Centrist' trend to which belong R Grimm, F Schneider, Jacques Schmid and others in Switzerland; Kautsky, Haase and the *Arbeitsgemeinschaft* in Germany; Longuet, Pressemane and others in France; Snowden, Ramsay MacDonald and others in England; Turati, Treves and their friends in Italy; and the above-mentioned party headed by the Organising Committee (Axelrod, Martov, Chkheidze, Skobelev and others) in Russia.

We have worked hand in hand with the revolutionary Social-Democrats of Switzerland grouped, in particular, around the magazine *Freie Jugend*. They formulated and circulated (in the German and French languages) the proposals for a referendum in favour of a party congress in April 1917 to discuss the party's attitude on the war. At the Zurich cantonal congress in Töss they tabled a resolution on behalf of the youth and the 'Lefts' on the war issue, and in March 1917 issued and circulated in certain localities of French Switzerland a leaflet, in the German and French languages, entitled 'Our Peace Terms', etc.

To these comrades, whose views we share, and with whom we worked hand in hand, we convey our fraternal greetings.

1 The Zimmerwald Left group was founded on Lenin's initiative at the International Socialist Conference held in Zimmerwald in September 1915. Headed by Lenin, it waged a struggle against the centrist majority of the Conference and moved resolutions condemning the imperialist war, exposing the betrayal by the social-chauvinists, and urging the necessity of active revolutionary struggle against the war.
For Lenin's articles on the Zimmerwald Left, including its draft resolution and statements, see *Lenin Selected Writings: On Imperialist War.*

We have never had the slightest doubt that the imperialist government of England will under no circumstances permit the Russian internationalists, who are implacable opponents of the imperialist government of Guchkov-Milyukov and co. and of Russia continuing the *imperialist* war, to return to Russia.

In this connection, we must briefly explain our understanding of the tasks of the Russian revolution. We believe this all the more necessary because through the Swiss workers we can and must address ourselves to the German, French and Italian workers, who speak the same languages as the population of Switzerland, a country that still enjoys the benefits of peace and, relatively, the largest measure of political freedom.

We abide unconditionally by our declaration, which appeared in the Central Organ of our Party, *Sotsial-Demokrat* (No. 47, 13 October 1915), published in Geneva. In it we stated that, should the revolution prove victorious in Russia, and should a *republican* government come to power, a government intent on continuing the imperialist war, a war in alliance with the imperialist bourgeoisie of England and France, a war for the seizure of Constantinople, Armenia, Galicia, etc. – we would most resolutely oppose such a government and would be *against* the 'defence of the fatherland' in *such* a war.

A contingency approaching the above has now arisen. The new government of Russia, which has negotiated with the brother of Nicholas II for restoration of the monarchy, and in which the most important and influential posts are held by the *monarchists* Lvov and Guchkov, this government is trying to deceive the Russian workers with the slogan, 'the Germans must overthrow Wilhelm' (correct! but why not add: the English, the Italians, etc. must overthrow their kings, and the Russians their monarchists, Lvov and Guchkov?). By issuing this slogan, but *refusing* to publish the imperialist, predatory treaties concluded by the tsar with France, England, etc. and *confirmed by the government of Guchkov-Milyukov-Kerensky*, this government is trying to represent its *imperialist* war with Germany as a war of 'defence' (i.e. as a just war, legitimate even from the standpoint of the proletariat). It is trying to represent a war for the defence of the rapacious, imperialist, predatory aims of capital – Russian, English, etc. – as 'defence' of the Russian republic (which does *not* yet exist, and which the Lvovs and the Guchkovs have *not* even *promised!*).

If there is any truth in the latest press reports about a rapprochement between the avowed Russian social-patriots (such as Plekhanov, Zasulich, Potresov, etc.) and the 'Centre party', the party of the 'Organising Committee', the party of Chkheidze, Skobelev, etc. based on the common slogan: 'Until the Germans overthrow Wilhelm, our war remains a defensive war' – if this is true, then we shall redouble our energy in combating the party of Chkheidze, Skobelev, etc. which we have *always* fought for its opportunist, vacillating, unstable political behaviour.

Our slogan is: 'No support for the Guchkov-Milyukov government!' He who says that such support is necessary to prevent restoration of the monarchy is deceiving the people. On the contrary, the Guchkov government has *already* conducted negotiations for restoration of the monarchy in Russia. *Only* the arming and organisation of the proletariat can *prevent* Guchkov and co. from *restoring* the monarchy in Russia. Only the revolutionary proletariat of Russia and the *whole of Europe*, remaining loyal to internationalism, is capable of ridding humanity of the horrors of the imperialist war.

We do not close our eyes to the tremendous difficulties facing the revolutionary-internationalist vanguard of the Russian proletariat. The most abrupt and swift changes are possible in times such as the present. In No. 47 of *Sotsial-Demokrat* we gave a clear and direct answer to the question that naturally arises: What would our Party do, if the revolution *immediately* placed it in power? Our answer was:

1. We would forthwith offer peace to *all* the warring nations;
2. We would announce our peace terms – immediate liberation of *all* the colonies and *all* the oppressed and non-sovereign peoples;

3. We would immediately begin and carry out the liberation of all the peoples oppressed by the Great Russians;
4. We do not deceive ourselves for one moment, we know that these terms would be *unacceptable* not only to the monarchist, but also to the republican bourgeoisie of Germany, and *not only* to Germany, but also to the capitalist governments of England and France.

We would be forced to wage a revolutionary war against the German – and not only the German – bourgeoisie. *And we would wage this war*. We are not pacifists. We are opposed to imperialist wars over the division of spoils among the capitalists, but we have always considered it absurd for the revolutionary proletariat to disavow revolutionary wars that *may* prove necessary *in the interests of socialism*.

The task we outlined in No. 47 of *Sotsial-Demokrat* is a gigantic one. It can be accomplished only by a long series of great class battles between the proletariat and the bourgeoisie. However, it was not our impatience, nor our wishes, but the *objective conditions* created by the imperialist war that brought the *whole* of humanity to an impasse, that placed it in a dilemma: either allow the destruction of more millions of lives and utterly ruin European civilisation, or hand over power in all the civilised countries to the revolutionary proletariat, carry through the socialist revolution.

To the Russian proletariat has fallen the great honour of *beginning* the series of revolutions which the imperialist war has made an objective inevitability. But the idea that the Russian proletariat is the chosen revolutionary proletariat among the workers of the world is absolutely alien to us. We know perfectly well that the proletariat of Russia is less organised, less prepared and less class-conscious than the proletariat of other countries. It is not its special qualities, but rather the special conjuncture of historical circumstances that *for a certain, perhaps very short, time* has made the proletariat of Russia the vanguard of the revolutionary proletariat of the whole world.

Russia is a peasant country, one of the most backward of European countries. Socialism *cannot* triumph there *directly* and *immediately*.

But the peasant character of the country, the vast reserve of land in the hands of the nobility, *may*, to judge from the experience of 1905, give tremendous sweep to the bourgeois-democratic revolution in Russia and *may* make our revolution the *prologue* to the world socialist revolution, a *step* toward it.

Our Party was formed and developed in the struggle for these ideas, which have been fully confirmed by the experience of 1905 and the spring of 1917, in the uncompromising struggle against all the other parties; and we shall continue to fight for these ideas.

In Russia, socialism cannot triumph directly and immediately. But the peasant mass *can* bring the inevitable and matured agrarian upheaval to the point of *confiscating* all the immense holdings of the nobility. This has always been our slogan and it has now again been advanced in St. Petersburg by the Central Committee of our Party and by *Pravda*, our Party's newspaper. The proletariat will fight for *this* slogan, without closing its eyes to the inevitability of cruel class conflicts between the agricultural labourers and the poorest peasants closely allied with them, on the one hand, and the *rich peasants*, whose position has been strengthened by Stolypin's agrarian 'reform' (1907-14), on the other. The fact should not be overlooked that the 104 peasant deputies in the First (1906) and Second (1907) Dumas introduced a revolutionary agrarian bill demanding the nationalisation of all lands and their distribution by local committees elected on the basis of complete democracy.

Such a revolution would not, in itself, be socialism. But it would give a great impetus to the world labour movement. It would immensely strengthen the position of the socialist proletariat in Russia and its influence on the agricultural labourers and the poorest peasants. It would enable the city proletariat to develop, on the strength of this influence, such revolutionary organisations as the Soviets of Workers' Deputies to replace the old instruments of oppression employed by bourgeois states, the army, the police, the bureaucracy; to carry out – under pressure of the unbearably burdensome imperialist war and its consequences – a series of revolutionary measures to *control* the production and distribution of goods.

Single-handed, the Russian proletariat cannot bring the socialist revolution to a *victorious conclusion*. But it can give the Russian revolution a mighty sweep that would create the most favourable conditions for a socialist revolution, and would, in a sense, *start* it. It can facilitate the rise of a situation in which its *chief*, its most trustworthy and most reliable collaborator, the *European* and American *socialist* proletariat, could join the decisive battles.

Let the sceptics despair because of the temporary triumph within the European socialist movement of such disgusting lackeys of the imperialist bourgeoisie as the Scheidemanns, Legiens, Davids and co. in Germany; Sembat, Guesde, Renaudel and co. in France; the Fabians and the Labourites in England. We are firmly convinced that this filthy froth on the surface of the world labour movement will be soon swept away by the waves of revolution.

In Germany there is already a *seething* unrest of the proletarian masses, who contributed so much to humanity and socialism by their persistent, unyielding, sustained organisational work during the long decades of European 'calm', from 1871 to 1914. The future of German socialism is represented not by the traitors, the Scheidemanns, Legiens, Davids and co., nor by the vacillating and spineless politicians, Haase, Kautsky and their ilk, who have been enfeebled by the routine of the period of 'peace'.

The future belongs to the trend that has given us Karl Liebknecht, created the Spartacus group, has carried on its propaganda in the Bremen *Arbeiterpolitik*.

The objective circumstances of the imperialist war make it certain that the revolution will not be limited to the first stage of the Russian revolution, that the revolution will not be limited to Russia.

The German proletariat is the most trustworthy, the most reliable ally of the Russian and the world proletarian revolution.

When, in November 1914, our Party put forward the slogan: 'Turn the imperialist war into a civil war' of the oppressed against the oppressors for the attainment of socialism, the social-patriots met this slogan with hatred and malicious ridicule, and the Social-Democratic 'Centre', with incredulous, sceptical, meek and expectant silence. David, the German social-chauvinist and social-imperialist, called it 'insane', while Mr. Plekhanov, the representative of Russian (and Anglo-French) social-chauvinism, of socialism in words, imperialism in deeds, called it a 'farcical dream' (*Mittelding zwischen Traum und Komödie* [Something between a dream and a comedy]) The representatives of the Centre confined themselves to silence or to cheap little jokes about this 'straight line drawn in empty space'.

Now, after March 1917, only the blind can fail to see that it is a correct slogan. Transformation of the imperialist war into civil war is *becoming* a fact.

Long live the proletarian revolution that is *beginning* in Europe!

On behalf of the departing comrades,
members of the RSDLP (united under the
Central Committee), who approved this letter
at a meeting held 26 March (8 April) 1917

N Lenin

Lenin's Speech in the Finland Station Square to Workers, Soldiers and Sailors

3 (16) April 1917

Editor's note:
No complete record survives of Lenin's speech on his arrival in Russia at the Finland Station. We produce here a report from *Pravda* of the event, and a part of Lenin's speech as recorded by Nikolai Sukhanov in his *Russian Revolution 1917*, Oxford University Press, 1955 p. 273.

* * *

Newspaper Report

Pravda, No. 24

In the street, standing on top of an armoured car, Comrade Lenin greeted the revolutionary Russian proletariat and the revolutionary Russian army, who had succeeded not only in liberating Russia from tsarist despotism, but in starting a social revolution on an international scale, and added that the proletariat of the whole world looked with hope to the Russian proletariat's bold steps.

The whole crowd walked in a body behind the car to the Kshesinskaya mansion, where the meeting continued.

* * *

Part of Lenin's Speech

Quoted by Nikolai Sukhanov

Dear comrades, soldiers, sailors and workers! I am happy to greet in your persons the victorious Russian Revolution, and greet you as the vanguard of the worldwide proletarian army… The piratical imperialist war is the beginning of civil war throughout Europe… The hour is not far distant when at the call of our comrade, Karl Liebknecht, the peoples will turn their arms against their own capitalist exploiters… The worldwide Socialist revolution has already dawned… Germany is seething… Any day now the whole of European capitalism may crash. The Russian Revolution accomplished by you has prepared the way and opened a new epoch. Long live the worldwide Socialist revolution!

The Tasks of the Proletariat in the Present Revolution (April Theses)

4 (17) April 1917

Editor's note:

This article contains Lenin's famous *April Theses* read by him at two meetings held at the Tauride Palace on 4 (17) April 1917, at a meeting of Bolsheviks and at a joint meeting of Bolshevik and Menshevik delegates to the All-Russia Conference of Soviets of Workers' and Soldiers' Deputies.

* * *

I did not arrive in Petrograd until the night of 3 (16) April, and therefore at the meeting on 4 (17) April I could, of course, deliver the report on the tasks of the revolutionary proletariat only on my own behalf, and with reservations as to insufficient preparation.

The only thing I could do to make things easier for myself – and for *honest* opponents – was to prepare the theses *in writing*. I read them out, and gave the text to Comrade Tsereteli.[1] I read them *twice*

1 Tsereteli was a Menshevik who had a leading position in the Petrograd Soviet from February 1917.

very slowly: first at a meeting of Bolsheviks and then at a meeting of both Bolsheviks and Mensheviks.

I publish these personal theses of mine with only the briefest explanatory notes, which were developed in far greater detail in the report.

Theses

1. In our attitude towards the war, which under the new government of Lvov and co. unquestionably remains on Russia's part a predatory imperialist war owing to the capitalist nature of that government, not the slightest concession to 'revolutionary defencism' is permissible.

   The class-conscious proletariat can give its consent to a revolutionary war, which would really justify revolutionary defencism, only on condition: (a) that the power pass to the proletariat and the poorest sections of the peasants aligned with the proletariat; (b) that all annexations be renounced in deed and not in word; (c) that a complete break be effected in actual fact with all capitalist interests.

   In view of the undoubted honesty of those broad sections of the mass believers in revolutionary defencism who accept the war only as a necessity, and not as a means of conquest, in view of the fact that they are being deceived by the bourgeoisie, it is necessary with particular thoroughness, persistence and patience to explain their error to them, to explain the inseparable connection existing between capital and the imperialist war, and to prove that without overthrowing capital *it is impossible* to end the war by a truly democratic peace, a peace not imposed by violence.

   The most widespread campaign for this view must be organised in the army at the front.

   Fraternisation.

2. The specific feature of the present situation in Russia is that the country is *passing* from the first stage of the revolution – which,

owing to the insufficient class-consciousness and organisation of the proletariat, placed power in the hands of the bourgeoisie – to its *second* stage, which must place power in the hands of the proletariat and the poorest sections of the peasants.

This transition is characterised, on the one hand, by a maximum of legally recognised rights (Russia is *now* the freest of all the belligerent countries in the world); on the other, by the absence of violence towards the masses, and, finally, by their unreasoning trust in the government of capitalists, those worst enemies of peace and socialism.

This peculiar situation demands of us an ability to adapt ourselves to the *special* conditions of Party work among unprecedentedly large masses of proletarians who have just awakened to political life.

3. No support for the Provisional Government; the utter falsity of all its promises should be made clear, particularly of those relating to the renunciation of annexations. Exposure in place of the impermissible, illusion-breeding 'demand' that *this* government, a government of capitalists, should *cease* to be an imperialist government.

4. Recognition of the fact that in most of the Soviets of Workers' Deputies our Party is in a minority, so far a small minority, as against *a bloc of all* the petty-bourgeois opportunist elements, from the Popular Socialists and the Socialist-Revolutionaries down to the Organising Committee (Chkheidze, Tsereteli, etc.), Steklov, etc., etc., who have yielded to the influence of the bourgeoisie and spread that influence among the proletariat.

   The masses must be made to see that the Soviets of Workers' Deputies are the *only possible* form of revolutionary government, and that therefore our task is, as long as *this* government yields to the influence of the bourgeoisie, to present a patient, systematic and persistent explanation of the errors of their tactics, an *explanation* especially adapted to the practical needs of the masses.

As long as we are in the minority we carry on the work of criticising and exposing errors and at the same time we preach the necessity of transferring the entire state power to the Soviets of Workers' Deputies, so that the people may overcome their mistakes by experience.

5. Not a parliamentary republic – to return to a parliamentary republic from the Soviets of Workers' Deputies would be a retrograde step – but a republic of Soviets of Workers', Agricultural Labourers' and Peasants' Deputies throughout the country, from top to bottom.

   Abolition of the police, the army and the bureaucracy.[2]

   The salaries of all officials, all of whom are elective and displaceable at any time, not to exceed the average wage of a competent worker.

6. The weight of emphasis in the agrarian programme to be shifted to the Soviets of Agricultural Labourers' Deputies.

   Confiscation of all landed estates.

   Nationalisation of *all* lands in the country, the land to be disposed of by the local Soviets of Agricultural Labourers' and Peasants' Deputies. The organisation of separate Soviets of Deputies of Poor Peasants. The setting up of a model farm on each of the large estates (ranging in size from 100 to 300 dessiatins, according to local and other conditions, and to the decisions of the local bodies) under the control of the Soviets of Agricultural Labourers' Deputies and for the public account.

7. The immediate amalgamation of all banks in the country into a single national bank, and the institution of control over it by the Soviet of Workers' Deputies.

8. It is not our *immediate* task to 'introduce' socialism, but only to bring social production and the distribution of products at once under the *control* of the Soviets of Workers' Deputies.

---

2 I.e. the standing army to be replaced by the arming of the whole people. – *Lenin*

9. Party tasks:
   a. Immediate convocation of a Party congress;
   b. Alteration of the Party Programme, mainly:
      i. On the question of imperialism and the imperialist war;
      ii. On our attitude towards the state and *our* demand for a 'commune state';[3]
      iii. Amendment of our out-of-date minimum programme;
   c. Change of the Party's name.[4]

10. A new International.

    We must take the initiative in creating a revolutionary International, an International against the *social-chauvinists* and against the 'Centre'.[5]

In order that the reader may understand why I had especially to emphasise as a rare exception the 'case' of honest opponents, I invite him to compare the above theses with the following objection by Mr. Goldenberg: Lenin, he said, "has planted the banner of civil war in the midst of revolutionary democracy" (quoted in No. 5 of Mr. Plekhanov's *Yedinstvo*).

Isn't it a gem?

I write, announce and elaborately explain:

> In view of the undoubted honesty of those *broad* sections of the *mass* believers in revolutionary defencism… in view of the fact that they are being deceived by the bourgeoisie, it is necessary with *particular* thoroughness, persistence and *patience* to explain their error to them…

Yet the bourgeois gentlemen who call themselves Social-Democrats, who *do not* belong either to the *broad* sections or to the *mass* believers

---

3 I.e. a state of which the Paris Commune was the prototype. – *Lenin*

4 Instead of 'Social-Democracy', whose official leaders *throughout* the world have betrayed socialism and deserted to the bourgeoisie (the 'defencists' and the vacillating 'Kautskyites'), we must call ourselves the *Communist Party*. – *Lenin*

5 The 'Centre' in the international Social-Democratic movement is the trend which vacillates between the chauvinists (= 'defencists') and internationalists, i.e. Kautsky and co. in Germany; Longuet and co. in France; Chkheidze and co. in Russia; Turati and co. in Italy; MacDonald and co. in Britain; etc. – *Lenin*

in defencism, with serene brow present my views thus: "The banner [!] of civil war" (of which there is not a word in the theses and not a word in my speech!) has been planted (!) "in the midst [!!] of revolutionary democracy…"

What does this mean? In what way does this differ from riot-inciting agitation, from *Russkaya Volya*?

I write, announce and elaborately explain:

> The Soviets of Workers' Deputies are the *only possible* form of revolutionary government, and therefore our task is to present a patient, systematic, and persistent *explanation* of the errors of their tactics, an explanation especially adapted to the practical needs of the masses.

Yet opponents of a certain brand present my views as a call to "civil war in the midst of revolutionary democracy"!

I attacked the Provisional Government for *not* having appointed an early date or any date at all, for the convocation of the Constituent Assembly, and for confining itself to promises. I argued that *without* the Soviets of Workers' and Soldiers' Deputies the convocation of the Constituent Assembly is not guaranteed and its success is impossible.

And the view is attributed to me that I am opposed to the speedy convocation of the Constituent Assembly!

I would call this 'raving', had not decades of political struggle taught me to regard honesty in opponents as a rare exception.

Mr. Plekhanov in his paper called my speech "raving". Very good, Mr. Plekhanov! But look how awkward, uncouth and slow-witted you are in your polemics. If I delivered a raving speech for two hours, how is it that an audience of hundreds tolerated this "raving"? Further, why does your paper devote a whole column to an account of the "raving"? Inconsistent, highly inconsistent!

It is, of course, much easier to shout, abuse and howl than to attempt to relate, to explain, to recall *what* Marx and Engels said in 1871, 1872 and 1875 about the experience of the Paris Commune and about the *kind* of state the proletariat needs.[6]

6 See Marx's *The Civil War in France*, and Marx and Engels' *Critique of the Gotha Programme.*

Ex-Marxist Mr. Plekhanov evidently does not care to recall Marxism.

I quoted the words of Rosa Luxemburg, who on 4 August 1914 called *German* Social-Democracy a "stinking corpse". And the Plekhanovs, Goldenbergs and co. feel 'offended'. On whose behalf? On behalf of the *German* chauvinists, because they were called chauvinists!

They have got themselves in a mess, these poor Russian social-chauvinists – socialists in word and chauvinists in deed.

Letters on Tactics

Written 8-13 (21-26) April 1917

Foreword

On 4 (17) April 1917, I had occasion to make a report on the subject indicated in the title, first, at a meeting of Bolsheviks in Petrograd. These were delegates to the All-Russia Conference of Soviets of Workers' and Soldiers' Deputies, who had to leave for their homes and therefore could not allow me to postpone it. After the meeting, the chairman, Comrade G Zinoviev, asked me on behalf of the whole assembly to repeat my report immediately at a joint meeting of Bolshevik and Menshevik delegates, who wished to discuss the question of unifying the Russian Social-Democratic Labour Party.

Difficult though it was for me immediately to repeat my report, I felt that I had no right to refuse once this was demanded of me by *my comrades-in-ideas* as well as by the Mensheviks, who, because of their impending departure, really could not grant me a delay.

In making my report, I read the theses which were published in No. 26 of *Pravda*, on 7 (20) April 1917.[1]

---

1 I reprint these theses together with the brief comment from the same issue of *Pravda* as an appendix to this letter. – *Lenin*

Both the theses and my report gave rise to differences of opinion among the Bolsheviks themselves and the editors of *Pravda*. After a number of consultations, we unanimously concluded that it would be advisable *openly* to discuss our differences, and thus provide material for the All-Russia Conference of our Party (the Russian Social-Democratic Labour Party, united under the Central Committee) which is to meet in Petrograd on 20 April (3 May) 1917.

Complying with this decision concerning a discussion, I am publishing the following *letters* in which I do not claim to have made an *exhaustive* study of the question, but wish merely to outline the principal arguments, which are especially essential for the *practical* tasks of the working-class movement.

First Letter: Assessment of the Present Situation

Marxism requires of us a strictly exact and objectively verifiable analysis of the relations of classes and of the concrete features peculiar to each historical situation. We Bolsheviks have always tried to meet this requirement, which is absolutely essential for giving a scientific foundation to policy.

"Our theory is not a dogma, but a guide to action", Marx and Engels always said, rightly ridiculing the mere memorising and repetition of 'formulas', that at best are capable only of marking out *general* tasks, which are necessarily modifiable by the *concrete* economic and political conditions of each particular *period* of the historical process.[2]

What, then, are the clearly established objective *facts* which the party of the revolutionary proletariat must now be guided by in defining the tasks and forms of its activity?

Both in my first *Letter From Afar* ('The First Stage of the First Revolution') published in *Pravda* Nos. 14 and 15, 21 and 22 March 1917, and in my theses, I define 'the specific feature of the present situation in Russia' as a period of *transition* from the first stage of the

---

2 See Engels, Friedrich, 'Letter to FA Sorge', 29 November 1886, *Marx and Engels Collected Works* (henceforth referred to as *MECW*), Vol. 47, Lawrence and Wishart, 1975, pp. 531-2.

revolution to the second. I therefore considered the basic slogan, the 'task of the day' at *this* moment to be:

> Workers, you have performed miracles of proletarian heroism, the heroism of the people, in the civil war against tsarism. You must perform miracles of organisation, organisation of the proletariat and of the whole people, to prepare the way for your victory in the second stage of the revolution.[3]

What, then, is the first stage?

It is the passing of state power to the bourgeoisie.

Before the February-March Revolution of 1917, state power in Russia was in the hands of one old class, namely, the feudal landed nobility, headed by Nicholas Romanov.

After the revolution, the power is in the hands of a *different* class, a new class, namely, the *bourgeoisie*.

The passing of state power from one *class* to another is the first, the principal, the basic sign of a *revolution*, both in the strictly scientific and in the practical political meaning of that term.

To this extent, the bourgeois, or the bourgeois-democratic, revolution in Russia is *completed*.

But at this point we hear a clamour of protest from people who readily call themselves 'old Bolsheviks'. Didn't we always maintain, they say, that the bourgeois-democratic revolution is completed only by the 'revolutionary-democratic dictatorship of the proletariat and the peasantry'? Is the agrarian revolution, which is also a bourgeois-democratic revolution, completed? Is it not a fact, on the contrary, that it has *not even* started?

My answer is: The Bolshevik slogans and ideas *on the whole* have been confirmed by history; but *concretely* things have worked out *differently*; they are more original, more peculiar, more variegated than anyone could have expected.

To ignore or overlook this fact would mean taking after those 'old Bolsheviks' who more than once already have played so regrettable a role in the history of our Party by reiterating formulas senselessly

3 Lenin, 'The First Stage of the First Revolution – First *Letter from Afar*', in this volume, p. 12.

learned by rote instead of *studying* the specific features of the new and living reality.

'The revolutionary-democratic dictatorship of the proletariat and the peasantry' has *already* become a reality[4] in the Russian revolution, for this 'formula' envisages only a *relation of classes*, and not a *concrete political institution implementing* this relation, this cooperation. 'The Soviet of Workers' and Soldiers' Deputies' – there you have the 'revolutionary-democratic dictatorship of the proletariat and the peasantry' already accomplished in reality.

This formula is already antiquated. Events have moved it from the realm of formulas into the realm of reality, clothed it with flesh and bone, concretised it and *thereby* modified it.

A new and different task now faces us: to effect a split *within* this dictatorship between the proletarian elements (the anti-defencist, internationalist, 'Communist' elements, who stand for a transition to the commune) and the *small-proprietor* or *petty-bourgeois* elements (Chkheidze, Tsereteli, Steklov, the Socialist-Revolutionaries and the other revolutionary defencists, who are opposed to moving towards the commune and are in favour of 'supporting' the bourgeoisie and the bourgeois government).

The person who *now* speaks only of a 'revolutionary democratic dictatorship of the proletariat and the peasantry' is behind the times, consequently, he has in effect *gone over* to the petty bourgeoisie against the proletarian class struggle; that person should be consigned to the archive of 'Bolshevik' pre-revolutionary antiques (it may be called the archive of 'old Bolsheviks').

The revolutionary-democratic dictatorship of the proletariat and the peasantry has already been realised, but in a highly original manner, and with a number of extremely important modifications. I shall deal with them separately in one of my next letters. For the present, it is essential to grasp the incontestable truth that a Marxist must take cognisance of real life, of the true facts of *reality*, and not cling to a theory of yesterday, which, like all theories, at best only

4 In a certain form and to a certain extent. – *Lenin*

outlines the main and the general, only *comes near* to embracing life in all its complexity.

"Theory, my friend, is grey, but green is the eternal tree of life."[5] To deal with the question of 'completion' of the bourgeois revolution *in the old way* is to sacrifice living Marxism to the dead letter.

According to the old way of thinking, the rule of the bourgeoisie could and should be *followed* by the rule of the proletariat and the peasantry, by their dictatorship.

In real life, however, things have *already* turned out *differently*; there has been an extremely original, novel and unprecedented *interlacing of the one with the other*. We have side by side, existing together, simultaneously, *both* the rule of the bourgeoisie (the government of Lvov and Guchkov) and a revolutionary-democratic dictatorship of the proletariat and the peasantry, which is *voluntarily* ceding power to the bourgeoisie, voluntarily making itself an appendage of the bourgeoisie.

For it must not be forgotten that actually, in Petrograd, the power is in the hands of the workers and soldiers; the new government is *not* using and cannot use violence against them, because *there is no* police, *no* army standing apart from the people, *no* officialdom standing all-powerful *above* the people. This is a fact, the kind of fact that is characteristic of a state of the Paris Commune type. This fact does not fit into the old schemes. One must know how to adapt schemes to facts, instead of reiterating the now meaningless words about a 'dictatorship of the proletariat and the peasantry' *in general*.

To throw more light on this question let us approach it from another angle.

A Marxist must not abandon the ground of careful analysis of class relations. The bourgeoisie is in power. But is not the mass of the peasants *also* a bourgeoisie, only of a different social stratum, of a different kind, of a different character? Whence does it follow that *this* stratum *cannot* come to power, thus 'completing' the bourgeois-democratic revolution? Why should this be impossible?

---

5 Lenin here quotes the words of Mephistopheles from Goethe's tragedy, *Faust*.

This is how the 'old Bolsheviks' often argue.

My reply is that it is quite possible. But, in assessing a given situation, a Marxist must proceed *not* from what is possible, but from what is real.

And the reality reveals the *fact* that freely elected soldiers' and peasants' deputies are freely joining the second, parallel government, and are freely supplementing, developing and completing it. And, just as freely, they are *surrendering* power to the bourgeoisie – a fact which does not in the least contravene the theory of Marxism, for we have always known and repeatedly pointed out that the bourgeoisie maintains itself in power *not* only by force but, also by virtue of the lack of class-consciousness and organisation, the routinism and downtrodden state of the masses.

In view of this present-day reality, it is simply ridiculous to turn one's back on the fact and talk about 'possibilities'.

Possibly the peasantry may seize all the land and all the power. Far from forgetting this possibility, far from confining myself to the present, I definitely and clearly formulate the agrarian programme, taking into account the *new* phenomenon, i.e. the deeper cleavage between the agricultural labourers and the poor peasants on the one hand, and the peasant proprietors on the other.

But there is also another possibility; it is possible that the peasants will take the advice of the petty-bourgeois party of the Socialist-Revolutionaries, which has yielded to the influence of the bourgeoisie, has adopted a defencist stand, and which advises waiting for the Constituent Assembly, although not even the date of its convocation has yet been fixed.[6]

It is possible that the peasants will *maintain* and prolong their deal with the bourgeoisie, a deal which they have now concluded

6 Lest my words be misinterpreted, I shall say at once that I am positively in favour of the Soviets of Agricultural Labourers and Peasants immediately taking over all the land; but they should themselves observe the strictest order and discipline, not permit the slightest damage to machines, structures, or livestock, and in no case disorganise agriculture and grain production, but rather develop them, for the soldiers need twice as much bread, and the people must not be allowed to starve. – *Lenin*

through the Soviets of Workers' and Soldiers' Deputies not only in form, but in fact.

Many things are possible. It would be a great mistake to forget the agrarian movement and the agrarian programme. But it would be no less a mistake to forget the *reality*, which reveals the *fact* that an *agreement*, or – to use a more exact, less legal, but more class-economic term – *class collaboration* exists between the bourgeoisie and the peasantry.

When this fact ceases to be a fact, when the peasantry separates from the bourgeoisie, seizes the land and power despite the bourgeoisie, that will be a new stage in the bourgeois-democratic revolution; and that matter will be dealt with separately.

A Marxist who, in view of the possibility of such a future stage, were to forget his duties in *the present*, when the peasantry is *in agreement* with the bourgeoisie, would turn petty bourgeois. For he would in practice be preaching to the proletariat *confidence* in the petty bourgeoisie ('this petty bourgeoisie, this peasantry, must separate from the bourgeoisie while the bourgeois-democratic revolution is still on'). Because of the 'possibility' of so pleasing and sweet a future, in which the peasantry would *not* be the tail of the bourgeoisie, in which the Socialist-Revolutionaries, the Chkheidzes, Tseretelis and Steklovs would *not* be an appendage of the bourgeois government – because of the 'possibility' of so pleasing a future, he would be forgetting *the unpleasant present*, in which the peasantry still forms the tail of the bourgeoisie, and in which the Socialist-Revolutionaries and Social-Democrats have not yet given up their role as an appendage of the bourgeois government, as 'His Majesty' Lvov's Opposition.

This hypothetical person would resemble a sweetish Louis Blanc, or a sugary Kautskyite, but certainly not a revolutionary Marxist.

But are we not in danger of falling into subjectivism, of wanting to arrive at the socialist revolution by 'skipping' the bourgeois-democratic revolution – which is not yet completed and has not yet exhausted the peasant movement?

I might be incurring this danger if I said: "No Tsar, but a *workers'* government." But I did *not* say that, I said something else. I said that there *can be no* government (barring a bourgeois government) in Russia *other than* that of the Soviets of Workers', Agricultural Labourers', Soldiers' and Peasants' Deputies. I said that power in Russia now can pass from Guchkov and Lvov *only* to these Soviets. And in these Soviets, as it happens, it is the peasants, the soldiers, i.e. petty bourgeoisie, who preponderate, to use a scientific, Marxist term, a class characterisation, and not a common, man-in-the-street, professional characterisation.

In my theses, I absolutely ensured myself against skipping over the peasant movement, which has not outlived itself, or the petty-bourgeois movement in general, against any *playing* at 'seizure of power' by a workers' government, against any kind of Blanquist[7] adventurism; for I pointedly referred to the experience of the Paris Commune. And this experience, as we know, and as Marx proved at length in 1871 and Engels in 1891,[8] absolutely excludes Blanquism, absolutely ensures the direct, immediate and unquestionable rule of the *majority* and the activity of the masses only to the extent that the majority itself acts *consciously*.

In the theses, I very definitely reduced the question to one of *a struggle for influence within* the Soviets of Workers', Agricultural Labourers', Peasants' and Soldiers' Deputies. To leave no shadow of doubt on this score, I *twice* emphasised in the theses the need for patient and persistent "explanatory" work "adapted to the *practical* needs of the *masses*".

Ignorant persons or renegades from Marxism, like Mr. Plekhanov, may shout about anarchism, Blanquism and so forth. But those who want to think and learn cannot fail to understand that Blanquism means the seizure of power by a minority, whereas the Soviets are *admittedly* the direct and immediate organisation of the *majority* of the people. Work confined to a struggle for influence *within* these

7 Louis-Auguste Blanqui was a French nineteenth century socialist who put forward that the revolution must be carried out, not by the masses, but as a *coup de main* of a small revolutionary minority.

8 Lenin is referring to Marx's *The Civil War in France*, written in 1871, and Engels' introduction to the 1891 edition of the book.

Soviets cannot, simply *cannot*, stray into the swamp of Blanquism. Nor can it stray into the swamp of anarchism, for anarchism denies *the need for a state and state power* in the period of *transition* from the rule of the bourgeoisie to the rule of the proletariat, whereas I, with a precision that precludes any possibility of misinterpretation, *advocate* the need for a state in this period, although, in accordance with Marx and the lessons of the Paris Commune, I advocate not the usual parliamentary bourgeois state, but a state *without* a standing army, *without* a police opposed to the people, *without* an officialdom placed above the people.

When Mr. Plekhanov, in his newspaper *Yedinstvo*, shouts with all his might that this is anarchism, he is merely giving further proof of his break with Marxism. Challenged by me in *Pravda*, No. 26, to tell us what Marx and Engels taught on the subject in 1871, 1872 and 1875,[9] Mr. Plekhanov can only preserve silence on the question at issue and shout out abuse after the manner of the enraged bourgeoisie.

Mr. Plekhanov, the ex-Marxist, has *absolutely* failed to understand the Marxist doctrine of the state. Incidentally, the germs of this lack of understanding are also to be found in his German pamphlet on anarchism.[10]

* * *

Now let us see how Comrade L Kamenev, in *Pravda*, No. 27, formulates his 'disagreements' with my theses and with the views expressed above. This will help us to grasp them more clearly.

> As for Comrade Lenin's general scheme, [writes Comrade Kamenev,] it appears to us unacceptable, inasmuch as it proceeds from the assumption that the bourgeois-democratic revolution is *completed*, and builds on the immediate transformation of this revolution into a socialist revolution.

There are two big mistakes here.

---

9 See Lenin, 'The Tasks of the Proletariat in the Present Revolution (April Theses)', 4 (17) April 1917, in this volume, p. 51.

10 Plekhanov's *Anarchism and Socialism*, first published in German in 1894.

First. The question of 'completion' of the bourgeois-democratic revolution is *stated* wrongly. The question is put in an abstract, simple, so to speak one-colour, way, which does *not* correspond to the objective reality. To put the question *this way*, to ask *now* 'whether the bourgeois-democratic revolution is completed' and say *no more*, is to prevent oneself from seeing the exceedingly complex reality, which, is at least two-coloured. This is in theory. In practice, it means surrendering helplessly to *petty-bourgeois revolutionism.*

Indeed, reality shows us *both* the passing of power into the hands of the bourgeoisie (a 'completed' bourgeois-democratic revolution of the usual type) and, side by side with the real government, the existence of a parallel government which represents the 'revolutionary-democratic dictatorship of the proletariat and the peasantry'. This 'second government' has *itself* ceded the power to the bourgeoisie, has chained *itself* to the bourgeois government.

Is this reality covered by Comrade Kamenev's old-Bolshevik formula, which says that 'the bourgeois-democratic revolution is not completed'?

It is not. The formula is obsolete. It is no good at all. It is dead. And it is no use trying to revive it.

Second. A practical question. Who knows whether it is still possible at present for a *special* 'revolutionary-democratic dictatorship of the proletariat and the peasantry', *detached* from the bourgeois government, to emerge in Russia? Marxist tactics cannot be based on the unknown.

But *if* this is still possible, then there is one, and only one, way towards it, namely, an immediate, resolute, and irrevocable separation of the proletarian Communist elements from the petty-bourgeois elements.

Why?

Because the entire petty bourgeoisie has, not by chance but of necessity, turned towards chauvinism (= defencism), towards 'support' of the bourgeoisie, towards dependence on it, towards the *fear* of having to do without it, etc., etc.

How can the petty bourgeoisie be 'pushed' into power, if even now it can take the power, but *does not want to*?

This can be done only by separating the proletarian, the Communist, party, by waging a proletarian class struggle *free from* the timidity of those petty bourgeois. Only the consolidation of the proletarians who are free from the influence of the petty bourgeoisie in deed and not only in word can make the ground so hot under the feet of the petty bourgeoisie that it will be *obliged* under certain circumstances to take the power; it is even within the bounds of possibility that Guchkov and Milyukov – again under certain circumstances – will be for giving full and sole power to Chkheidze, Tsereteli, the SRs and Steklov, since, after all, these are '*defencists*'.

To separate the proletarian elements of the Soviets (i.e. the proletarian, Communist, party) from the petty-bourgeois elements right now, immediately and irrevocably, is to give correct expression to the interests of the movement in *either* of two possible events: in the event that Russia will yet experience a special 'dictatorship of the proletariat and the peasantry' independent of the bourgeoisie, and in the event that the petty bourgeoisie will not be able to tear itself away from the bourgeoisie and will oscillate eternally (that is, until socialism is established) between us and it.

To be guided in one's activities merely by the simple formula, 'the bourgeois-democratic revolution is not completed', is like taking it upon oneself to guarantee that the petty bourgeoisie is definitely capable of being independent of the bourgeoisie. To do so is to throw oneself at the given moment on the mercy of the petty bourgeoisie.

Incidentally, in connection with the 'formula' of the dictatorship of the proletariat and the peasantry, it is worth mentioning that, in *Two Tactics* (July 1905), I made a point of emphasising this:

> Like everything else in the world, the revolutionary-democratic dictatorship of the proletariat and the peasantry has a past and a future. Its past is autocracy, serfdom, monarchy and privilege. [...]
>
> Its future is the struggle against private property, the struggle of the wage-worker against the employer, the struggle for socialism.[11]

11 Lenin, *Two Tactics of Social-Democracy in the Democratic Revolution*, July 1905, *Collected Works* (henceforth referred to as *LCW*), Vol. 9, Progress Publishers,

Comrade Kamenev's mistake is that even in 1917 he sees only *the past* of the revolutionary-democratic dictatorship of the proletariat and the peasantry. As a matter of fact its *future* has already begun, for the interests and policies of the wage-worker and the petty proprietor have *actually* diverged already, even in such an important question as that of 'defencism', that of the attitude towards the imperialist war.

This brings me to the second mistake in Comrade Kamenev's argument quoted above. He criticises me, saying that my scheme "builds" on "the immediate transformation of this [bourgeois-democratic] revolution into a socialist revolution".

This is incorrect. I not only do not "build" on the "immediate transformation" of our revolution into a *socialist* one, but I actually warn against it, when in Thesis No. 8, I state: "It is *not* our *immediate* task to 'introduce' socialism..."[12]

Is it not clear that no person who builds on the immediate transformation of our revolution into a socialist revolution could be opposed to the immediate task of introducing socialism?

Moreover, even a 'commune state' (i.e. a state organised along the lines of the Paris Commune) *cannot* be introduced in Russia 'immediately', because to do that it would be necessary for the *majority* of the deputies in all (or in most) Soviets to clearly recognise all the erroneousness and harm of the tactics and policy pursued by the SRs, Chkheidze, Tsereteli, Steklov, etc. As for me, I declared unmistakably that in this respect I 'build' only on 'patient' explaining (does one have to be patient to bring about a change which can be effected 'immediately'?).

Comrade Kamenev has somewhat overreached himself in his eagerness, and has repeated the bourgeois prejudice about the Paris Commune having wanted to introduce socialism 'immediately'. This is not so. The Commune, unfortunately, was too slow in introducing socialism. The real essence of the Commune is not

---

1960, pp. 84-85.

12 See Lenin, 'The Tasks of the Proletariat in the Present Revolution (April Theses)', 4 (17) April 1917, in this volume, p. 54

where the bourgeois usually looks for it, but in the creation of a *state* of a special type. Such a state has *already* arisen in Russia, it is the Soviets of Workers' and Soldiers' Deputies!

Comrade Kamenev has not pondered on the *fact*, the significance, of the *existing* Soviets, their identity, in point of type and socio-political character, with the commune state, and instead of studying the *fact*, he began to talk about something I was supposed to be 'building' on for the 'immediate' future. The result is, unfortunately, a repetition of the method used by many bourgeois: from the question as to *what are* the Soviets, whether they are of a *higher* type than a parliamentary republic, whether they are *more useful* for the people, *more democratic, more convenient* for the struggle, for combating, for instance, the grain shortage, etc. – from this real, urgent, vital issue, attention is diverted to the empty, would-be scientific, but actually hollow, professorially dead question of 'building on an immediate transformation'.

An idle question falsely presented. I 'build' *only* on this, *exclusively* on this – that the workers, soldiers and peasants will deal better than the officials, better than the police, with the difficult *practical* problems of producing more grain, distributing it better and keeping the soldiers better supplied, etc., etc.

I am deeply convinced that the Soviets will make the independent activity of the *masses* a reality more quickly and effectively than will a parliamentary republic (I shall compare the two types of states in greater detail in another letter). They will more effectively, more practically and more correctly decide what *steps* can be taken towards socialism and how these steps should be taken. Control over a bank, the merging of all banks into one, is *not yet* socialism, but it is *a step towards* socialism. Today such steps are being taken in Germany by the Junkers and the bourgeoisie against the people. Tomorrow the Soviet will be able to take these steps more effectively for the benefit of the people if the whole state power is in its hands.

What *compels* such steps?

Famine. Economic disorganisation. Imminent collapse. The horrors of war. The horrors of the wounds inflicted on mankind by the war.

Comrade Kamenev concludes his article with the remark that:

> … in a broad discussion he hopes to carry his point of view, which is the only possible one for revolutionary Social-Democracy if it wishes to and should remain to the very end the party of the revolutionary masses of the proletariat and not turn into a group of Communist propagandists.

It seems to me that these words betray a completely erroneous estimate of the situation. Comrade Kamenev contraposes to a "party of the masses" a "group of propagandists". But the "masses" have now succumbed to the craze of 'revolutionary' defencism. Is it not more becoming for internationalists at this moment to show that they can resist 'mass' intoxication rather than to 'wish to remain' with the masses, i.e. to succumb to the general epidemic? Have we not seen how in all the belligerent countries of Europe the chauvinists tried to justify themselves on the grounds that they wished to 'remain with the masses'? Must we not be able to remain for a time in the minority against the 'mass' intoxication? Is it not the work of the propagandists at the present moment that forms the key point for *disentangling* the proletarian line from the defencist and petty-bourgeois 'mass' intoxication? It was this fusion of the masses, proletarian and non-proletarian, regardless of class differences within the masses, that formed one of the conditions for the defencist epidemic. To speak contemptuously of a 'group of propagandists' advocating a *proletarian* line does not seem to be very becoming.

The Dual Power

Published 9 (22) April 1917

The basic question of every revolution is that of state power. Unless this question is understood, there can be no intelligent participation in the revolution, not to speak of guidance of the revolution.

The highly remarkable feature of our revolution is that it has brought about a *dual power*. This fact must be grasped first and foremost: unless it is understood, we cannot advance. We must know how to supplement and amend old 'formulas', for example, those of Bolshevism, for while they have been found to be correct on the whole, their concrete realisation *has turned out to be* different. *Nobody* previously thought, or could have thought, of a dual power.

What is this dual power? Alongside the Provisional Government, the government of the *bourgeoisie*, *another government* has arisen, so far weak and incipient, but undoubtedly a government that actually exists and is growing – the Soviets of Workers' and Soldiers' Deputies.

What is the class composition of this other government? It consists of the proletariat and the peasants (in soldiers' uniforms). What is the political nature of this government? It is a revolutionary dictatorship, i.e. a power directly based on revolutionary seizure, on the direct initiative of the people from below, and *not on a law* enacted by a centralised state power. It is an entirely different kind of power from the one that generally exists in the parliamentary bourgeois-democratic republics of the usual type still prevailing in the advanced countries of Europe and America. This circumstance often overlooked, often not given enough thought, yet it is the crux of the matter. *This* power is of *the same type* as the Paris Commune of 1871. The fundamental characteristics of this type are:

1. The source of power is not a law previously discussed and enacted by parliament, but the direct initiative of the people from below, in their local areas – direct 'seizure', to use a current expression;
2. The replacement of the police and the army, which are institutions divorced from the people and set against the people, by the direct arming of the whole people; order in the state under such a power is maintained by the armed workers and peasants *themselves*, by the armed people *themselves*;
3. Officialdom, the bureaucracy, are either similarly replaced by the direct rule of the people themselves or at least placed under special control; they not only become elected officials, but are also *subject to recall* at the people's first demand; they are reduced to the position of simple agents; from a privileged group holding '*jobs*' remunerated on a high, bourgeois scale, they become workers of a special 'arm of the service', whose remuneration *does not exceed* the ordinary pay of a competent worker.

This, and this *alone*, constitutes the *essence* of the Paris Commune as a special type of state. This essence has been forgotten or perverted by the Plekhanovs (downright chauvinists who have betrayed Marxism), the Kautskys (the men of the 'Centre', i.e. those who vacillate between chauvinism and Marxism), and generally by all those Social-Democrats, Socialist-Revolutionaries, etc., etc., who now rule the roost.

They are trying to get away with empty phrases, evasions, subterfuges; they congratulate each other a thousand times upon the revolution, but refuse to *consider what* the Soviets of Workers' and Soldiers' Deputies *are*. They refuse to recognise the obvious truth that in as much as these Soviets exist, *in as much as* they are a power, we have in Russia a state of the *type* of the Paris Commune.

I have emphasised the words 'in as much as', for it is only an incipient power. By direct agreement with the bourgeois Provisional Government and by a series of actual concessions, it has itself *surrendered and is surrendering* its positions to the bourgeoisie.

Why? Is it because Chkheidze, Tsereteli, Steklov and co. are making a 'mistake'? Nonsense. Only a philistine can think so – not a Marxist. The reason is *insufficient class-consciousness* and organisation of the proletarians and peasants. The 'mistake' of the leaders I have named lies in their petty-bourgeois position, in the fact that instead of clarifying the minds of the workers, they are *befogging* them; instead of dispelling petty-bourgeois illusions, they are *instilling* them; instead of freeing the people from bourgeois influence, they are *strengthening* that influence.

It should be clear from this why our comrades, too, make so many mistakes when putting the question 'simply': Should the Provisional Government be overthrown immediately?

My answer is:

1. It should be overthrown, for it is an oligarchic, bourgeois, and not a people's government, and *is unable* to provide peace, bread, or full freedom;

2. It cannot be overthrown just now, for it is being kept in power by a direct and indirect, a formal and actual *agreement* with the Soviets of Workers' Deputies, and primarily with the chief Soviet, the Petrograd Soviet;

3. Generally, it can not be 'overthrown' in the ordinary way, for it rests on the '*support*' given to the bourgeoisie by the *second* government – the Soviet of Workers' Deputies, and that government is the only possible revolutionary government, which directly expresses the mind and will of the majority of the workers and peasants. Humanity has not yet evolved and we do not as yet know a type of government superior to and better

than the Soviets of Workers', Agricultural Labourers', Peasants' and Soldiers' Deputies.

To become a power the class-conscious workers must win the majority to their side. *As long as no* violence is used against the people there is no other road to power. We are not Blanquists, we do not stand for the seizure of power by a minority. We are Marxists, we stand for proletarian class struggle against petty-bourgeois intoxication, against chauvinism-defencism, phrase-mongering and dependence on the bourgeoisie.

Let us create a proletarian Communist Party; its elements have already been created by the best adherents of Bolshevism; let us rally our ranks for proletarian class work; and larger and larger numbers from among the proletarians, from among the *poorest* peasants will range themselves on our side. For *actual experience* will from day to day shatter the petty-bourgeois illusions of those 'Social-Democrats', the Chkheidzes, Tseretelis, Steklovs and others, the 'Socialist-Revolutionaries', the petty bourgeoisie of an even purer water, and so on and so forth.

The bourgeoisie stands for the undivided power of the bourgeoisie.

The class-conscious workers stand for the undivided power of the Soviets of Workers', Agricultural Labourers', Peasants' and Soldiers' Deputies – for undivided power made possible not by adventurist acts, but by *clarifying* proletarian minds, by *emancipating* them from the influence of the bourgeoisie.

The petty bourgeoisie – 'Social-Democrats', Socialist-Revolutionaries, etc. – vacillate and, thereby, *hinder* this clarification and emancipation.

This is the actual, the *class* alignment of forces that determines our tasks.

N Lenin

The Tasks of the Proletariat in Our Revolution

Draft Platform for the Proletarian Party

Written 10 (23) April 1917

The moment of history through which Russia is now passing is marked by the following main characteristics:

The class character of the revolution that has taken place

1. The old tsarist power, which represented only a handful of feudal landowners who commanded the entire state machinery (the army, the police and the bureaucracy), has been overthrown and removed, but not completely destroyed. The monarchy has not been formally abolished; the Romanov gang continues to hatch monarchist intrigues. The vast landed possessions of the feudal squirearchy have not been abolished.

2. State power in Russia has passed into the hands of a new *class*, namely, the bourgeoisie and landowners who had become bourgeois. *To this extent* the bourgeois-democratic revolution in Russia is completed.

Having come to power, the bourgeoisie has formed a bloc (an alliance) with the overt monarchists, who are notorious for their exceptionally ardent support of Nicholas the Bloody and Stolypin the Hangman in 1906-14 (Guchkov and other politicians to the right of the Cadets). The new bourgeois government of Lvov and co. has attempted and has begun to negotiate with the Romanovs for the restoration of the monarchy in Russia. Behind a screen of revolutionary phrases, this government is appointing partisans of the old regime to key positions. It is striving to reform the whole machinery of state (the army, the police and the bureaucracy) as little as possible, and has turned it over to the bourgeoisie. The new government has already begun to hinder in every way the revolutionary initiative of mass action and the seizure of power by the people *from below*, which is the *sole* guarantee of the real success of the revolution.

Up to now this government has not even fixed a date for the convocation of the Constituent Assembly. It is not laying a finger on the landed estates, which form the material foundation of feudal tsarism. This government does not even contemplate starting an investigation into, and making public, the activities of the monopolist financial organisations, the big banks, the syndicates and cartels of the capitalists, etc. or instituting control over them.

The key positions, the decisive ministerial posts in the new government (the Ministry of the Interior and the War Ministry, i.e. the command over the army, the police, the bureaucracy – the entire apparatus for oppressing the people) are held by outright monarchists and supporters of the system of big landed estates. The Cadets, those day-old republicans, republicans against their own will, have been assigned minor posts, having no direct relation to the *command* over the people or to the apparatus of state power. A Kerensky, a Trudovik and 'would-be socialist', has no function whatsoever, except to lull the vigilance and attention of the people with sonorous phrases.

For all these reasons, the new bourgeois government does not deserve the confidence of the proletariat even in the sphere of internal policy, and no support of this government by the proletariat is admissible.

The foreign policy of the new government

3. In the field of foreign policy, which has now been brought to the forefront by objective circumstances, the new government is a government for the continuation of the imperialist war, a war that is being waged in alliance with the imperialist powers – Britain, France and others – for division of the capitalist spoils and for subjugating small and weak nations.

Subordinated to the interests of Russian capitalism and its powerful protector and master – Anglo-French imperialist capitalism, the wealthiest in the world – the new government, notwithstanding the wishes expressed in no uncertain fashion on behalf of the obvious majority of the peoples of Russia through the Soviet of Soldiers' and Workers' Deputies, has taken no real steps to put an end to the slaughter of peoples for the interests of the capitalists. It has not even published the secret treaties of an obviously predatory character (for the partition of Persia, the plunder of China, the plunder of Turkey, the partition of Austria, the annexation of Eastern Prussia, the annexation of the German colonies, etc.), which, as everybody knows, bind Russia to Anglo-French predatory imperialist capital. It has *confirmed* these treaties concluded by tsarism, which for centuries robbed and oppressed more nations than other tyrants and despots, and which not only oppressed, but also disgraced and demoralised the Great-Russian nation by making it an executioner of other nations.

The new government has confirmed these shameful depredatory treaties and has not proposed an immediate armistice to all the belligerent nations, in spite of the clearly expressed demand of the majority of the peoples of Russia, voiced through the Soviets of Workers' and Soldiers' Deputies. It has evaded the issue with the help of solemn, sonorous, bombastic, but absolutely empty declarations and phrases, which, in the mouths of bourgeois diplomats, have always served, and still serve, to deceive the trustful and naive masses of the oppressed people.

4. Not only, therefore, is the new government unworthy of the slightest confidence in the field of foreign policy, but to go on demanding that it should proclaim the will of the peoples of Russia for peace, that it should renounce annexations, and so on and so forth, is in practice merely to deceive the people, to inspire them with false hopes and to retard the clarification of their minds. It is indirectly to reconcile them to the continuation of a war the true social character of which is determined not by pious wishes, but by the class character of the government that wages the war, by the connection between the class represented by this government and the imperialist finance capital of Russia, Britain, France, etc. by *the real and actual policy* which that class is pursuing.

The peculiar nature of the dual power and its class significance

5. The main feature of our revolution, a feature that most imperatively demands thoughtful consideration, is the *dual power* which arose in the very first days after the triumph of the revolution.

   This dual power is evident in the existence of *two* governments: one is the main, the real, the actual government of the bourgeoisie, the 'Provisional Government' of Lvov and co., which holds in its hands all the organs of power; the other is a supplementary and parallel government, a 'controlling' government in the shape of the Petrograd Soviet of Workers' and Soldiers' Deputies, which holds no organs of state power, but directly rests on the support of an obvious and indisputable majority of the people, on the armed workers and soldiers.

   The class origin and the class significance of this dual power is the following: the Russian Revolution of March 1917 not only swept away the whole tsarist monarchy, not only transferred the entire power to the bourgeoisie, but also *moved close towards* a revolutionary-democratic dictatorship of the proletariat and the peasantry. The Petrograd and the other, the local, Soviets constitute precisely such a dictatorship (that is, a power resting not on the law but directly on the force of armed masses of the population), a dictatorship precisely of the above-mentioned classes.

6. The second highly important feature of the Russian Revolution is the fact that the Petrograd Soviet of Soldiers' and Workers' Deputies, which, as everything goes to show, enjoys the confidence of most of the local Soviets, is *voluntarily* transferring state power to the bourgeoisie and *its* Provisional Government, is voluntarily *ceding* supremacy to the latter, having entered into an agreement to support it, and is limiting its own role to that of an observer, a supervisor of the convocation of the Constituent Assembly (the date for which has not even been announced as yet by the Provisional Government).

   This remarkable feature, unparalleled in history in such a form, has led to the *interlocking of two* dictatorships: the dictatorship of the bourgeoisie (for the government of Lvov and co. is a dictatorship, i.e. a power based not on the law, not on the previously expressed will of the people, but on seizure by force, accomplished by a definite class, namely, the bourgeoisie) and the dictatorship of the proletariat and the peasantry (the Soviet of Workers' and Soldiers' Deputies).

   There is not the slightest doubt that such an 'interlocking' *cannot* last long. Two powers *cannot exist* in a state. One of them is bound to pass away; and the entire Russian bourgeoisie is already trying its hardest everywhere and in every way to keep out and weaken the Soviets, to reduce them to nought, and to establish the undivided power of the bourgeoisie.

   The dual power merely expresses a *transitional* phase in the revolution's development, when it has gone farther than the ordinary bourgeois-democratic revolution, *but has not yet reached* a 'pure' dictatorship of the proletariat and the peasantry.

The class significance (and the class explanation) of this transitional and unstable situation is this: like all revolutions, our revolution required the greatest heroism and self-sacrifice on the part of the people for the struggle against tsarism; it also immediately *drew* unprecedentedly vast numbers of ordinary citizens *into the movement.*

From the point of view of science and practical politics, one of the chief symptoms of *every* real revolution is the unusually rapid, sudden and abrupt increase in the number of 'ordinary citizens' who begin to participate actively, independently and effectively in political life and in the *organisation of the state.*

Such is the case in Russia. Russia at present is seething. Millions and tens of millions of people, who had been politically dormant for ten years and politically crushed by the terrible oppression of tsarism and by inhuman toil for the landowners and capitalists, *have awakened and taken eagerly* to politics. And who are these millions and tens of millions? For the most part small proprietors, petty bourgeois, people standing midway between the capitalists and the wage-workers. Russia is the most petty-bourgeois of all European countries.

A gigantic petty-bourgeois wave has swept over everything and overwhelmed the class-conscious proletariat, not only by force of numbers but also ideologically; that is, it has infected and imbued very wide circles of workers with the petty-bourgeois political outlook.

The petty bourgeoisie are in real life dependent upon the bourgeoisie, for they live like masters and not like proletarians (from the point of view of their *place* in social *production*) and follow the bourgeoisie in their outlook.

An attitude of unreasoning trust in the capitalists – the worst foes of peace and socialism – characterises the politics of the *popular masses* in Russia at the present moment; this is the fruit that has *grown* with revolutionary rapidity on the social and economic soil of the most petty-bourgeois of all European countries. This is the *class* basis for the '*agreement*' between the Provisional Government and the Soviet of Workers' and Soldiers' Deputies (I emphasise that I am referring not so much to the formal agreement as to *actual support*, a tacit agreement, the surrender of power inspired by unreasoning trust), an agreement which has given the Guchkovs a fat piece – real power – and the Soviet merely promises and honours (for the time being), flattery, phrases, assurances and the bowings and scrapings of the Kerenskys.

On the other side we have the inadequate numerical strength of the proletariat in Russia and its insufficient class-consciousness and organisation.

All the Narodnik parties, including the Socialist-Revolutionaries, have always been petty-bourgeois.[1] This is also true of the party of the Organising Committee (Chkheidze, Tsereteli, etc.). The non-party revolutionaries (Steklov and others) have similarly yielded to the tide, or have not been able to stand up to it, have not had the time to do it.

The peculiar nature of the tactics which flow from the above

7. For the Marxist, who must reckon with objective facts, with the masses and classes, and not with individuals and so on, the peculiar nature of the actual situation as described above must determine the peculiar nature of the tactics for the *present* moment.

   This peculiarity of the situation calls, in the first place, for the 'pouring of vinegar and bile into the sweet water of revolutionary-democratic phraseology' (as my fellow member on the Central Committee of our Party, Teodorovich, so aptly put it at yesterday's session of the All-Russia Congress of Railwaymen

1 Lenin uses the term 'Narodnik' to denote the three petty-bourgeois parties of the Narodnik trend, namely, the SRs and the two parties that had emerged from splits from the SRs: the Trudoviks and the Popular Socialists. For more, see the Narodnik glossary entry.

in Petrograd). Our work must be one of criticism, of *explaining* the mistakes of the petty-bourgeois Socialist-Revolutionary and Social-Democratic parties, of preparing and welding the elements of a *consciously* proletarian Communist Party and of *curing* the proletariat of the 'general' petty-bourgeois intoxication.

This *seems* to be 'nothing more' than propaganda work, but in reality it is most *practical revolutionary* work; for there is no advancing a revolution that has come to a standstill, that has choked itself with phrases and that keeps 'marking time', *not because* of external obstacles, *not because of the violence* of the bourgeoisie (Guchkov is still only threatening to employ violence against the soldier mass), but *because* of the unreasoning trust of the people.

Only by overcoming this unreasoning trust (and we can and should overcome it only ideologically, by comradely persuasion, by pointing to the *lessons of experience*) can we set ourselves free from the prevailing *orgy of revolutionary phrase-mongering* and really stimulate the consciousness both of the proletariat and of the mass in general, as well as their bold and determined initiative *in the localities* – the independent realisation, development and consolidation of liberties, democracy and the principle of people's ownership of all the land.

8. The world-wide experience of bourgeois and landowner governments has evolved *two* methods of keeping the people in subjection. The first is violence. Nicholas Romanov I, nicknamed Nicholas of the Big Stick, and Nicholas II, the Bloody, demonstrated to the Russian people the maximum of what can and cannot be done in the way of these hangmen's practices. But there is another method, best developed by the British and French bourgeoisie, who 'learned their lesson' in a series of great revolutions and revolutionary movements of the masses. It is the method of deception, flattery, fine phrases, promises by the million, petty sops and concessions of the unessential while retaining the essential.

The peculiar feature of the present situation in Russia is the transition at a dizzy speed from the first method to the second, from violent oppression of the people to *flattering* and deceiving the people by promises. Vaska the Cat listens, but goes on eating.[2] Milyukov and Guchkov are holding power, they are protecting the profits of the capitalists, conducting an imperialist war in the interests of Russian and Anglo-French capital, and trying to get away with promises, declamation and bombastic statements in reply to the speeches of 'cooks' like Chkheidze, Tsereteli and Steklov, who threaten, exhort, conjure, beseech, demand and proclaim… Vaska the Cat listens, but goes on eating.

But from day to day trustful lack of reasoning and unreasoning trust will be falling away, especially among the proletarians and *poor* peasants, who are being taught by experience (by their social and economic position) to distrust the capitalists.

The leaders of the petty bourgeoisie 'must' teach the people to trust the bourgeoisie. The proletarians must teach the people to distrust the bourgeoisie.

Revolutionary defencism and its class significance

9. *Revolutionary defencism* must be regarded as the most important, the most striking manifestation of the petty-bourgeois wave that has swept over 'nearly everything'. It is the worst enemy of the further progress and success of the Russian Revolution.

   Those who have yielded on this point and have been unable to extricate themselves are lost to the revolution. But the masses yield in a different way from the leaders, and they extricate themselves *differently*, by a different course of development, by different means.

   Revolutionary defencism is, on the one hand, a result of the deception of the masses by the bourgeoisie, a result of the trustful lack of reasoning on the part of the peasants and a section of the workers; it is, on the other, an expression of the interests and point

2 A quotation from Ivan Krylov's fable 'The Cat and the Cook'.

of view of the small proprietor, who is to some extent interested in annexations and bank profits, and who 'sacredly' guards the traditions of tsarism, which demoralised the Great Russians by making them do a hangman's work against the other peoples.

The bourgeoisie deceives the people by working on their noble pride in the revolution and by pretending that the *social and political* character of the war, as far as Russia is concerned, underwent a change because of this stage of the revolution, because of the substitution of the near republic of Guchkov and Milyukov for the tsarist monarchy. And the people believed it – for a time – largely owing to age-old prejudices, which made them look upon the other peoples of Russia, i.e. the non-Great Russians, as something in the nature of a property and private estate of the Great Russians. This vile demoralisation of the Great Russian people by tsarism which taught them to regard the other peoples as something inferior, something belonging 'by right' to Great Russia, could not disappear *instantly*.

What is required of us is the *ability* to explain to the masses that the social and political character of the war is determined not by the 'good will' of individuals or groups, or even of nations, but by the position of the *class* which conducts the war, by the class *policy* of which the war is a continuation, by the *ties* of capital, which is the dominant economic force in modern society, by the *imperialist character* of international capital, by Russia's dependence in finance, banking and diplomacy upon Britain, France and so on. To explain this skilfully in a way the people would understand *is not easy*; none of us would be able to do it at once without committing errors.

But this, and only this, must be the aim or, rather, the message of our propaganda. The slightest concession to revolutionary defencism is *a betrayal of socialism*, a complete renunciation of *internationalism*, no matter by what fine phrases and 'practical' considerations it may be justified.

The slogan 'Down with the War!' is, of course, correct. But it fails to take into account the specific nature of the tasks of the present moment and the necessity of *approaching* the broad mass of the people *in a different way*. It reminds me of the slogan 'Down with the Tsar!' with which the inexperienced agitator of the 'good old days' went simply and directly to the countryside – and got a beating for his pains. The mass believers in revolutionary defencism are *honest*, not in the personal, but in the class sense, i.e. they belong to *classes* (workers and the peasant poor) which *in actual fact* have nothing to gain from annexations and the subjugation of other peoples. This is nothing like the bourgeois and the 'intellectual' fraternity, who know very well that you *cannot* renounce annexations without renouncing the rule of capital, and who unscrupulously deceive the people with fine phrases, with unlimited promises and endless assurances.

The rank-and-file believer in defencism regards the matter in the simple way of the man in the street: "I don't want annexations, but the Germans are 'going for' *me*, therefore I'm defending a just cause and not any kind of imperialist interests at all". To a man like this it must be explained again and again that it is not a question of his personal wishes, but of mass, *class*, political relations and conditions, of the connection between the war and the interests of capital and the international network of banks, and so forth. Only such a struggle against defencism will be serious and will promise success – perhaps not a very rapid success, but one that will be real and enduring.

How can the war be ended?

10. The war cannot be ended 'at will'. It cannot be ended by the decision of one of the belligerents. It cannot be ended by 'sticking your bayonet into the ground', as one soldier, a defencist, expressed it.

The war cannot be ended by an 'agreement' among the socialists of the various countries, by the 'action' of the proletarians of all countries, by the 'will' of the peoples, and so forth. All the phrases of this kind, which fill the articles of the defencist, semi-defencist and semi-internationalist papers as well as innumerable resolutions, appeals, manifestos and the resolutions of the Soviet of Soldiers' and Workers' Deputies – all such phrases are nothing but idle, innocent and pious wishes of the petty bourgeois. There is nothing more harmful than phrases like 'ascertaining the will of the peoples for peace', like the *sequence* of revolutionary actions of the proletariat (after the Russian proletariat comes the turn of the German), etc. All this is Blancism, fond dreams, a playing at 'political campaigning', and in reality just a repetition of the fable of Vaska the Cat.

The war is not a product of the evil will of rapacious capitalists, although it is undoubtedly being fought *only* in their interests and they alone are being enriched by it. The war is a product of half a century of development of world capitalism and of its billions of threads and connections. It is *impossible* to slip out of the imperialist war and achieve a democratic, non-coercive peace without overthrowing the power of capital and transferring state power to *another* class, the proletariat.

The Russian Revolution of February-March 1917 was the beginning of the transformation of the imperialist war into a civil war. This revolution took the *first* step towards ending the war; but it requires a *second* step, namely, the transfer of state power to the proletariat, to make the end of the war a *certainty*. This will be the beginning of a 'breakthrough' on a world-wide scale, a breakthrough in the front of capitalist interests; and only by breaking through *this* front *can* the proletariat save mankind from the horrors of war and endow it with the blessings of peace.

It is directly to such a 'breakthrough' in the front of capitalism that the Russian Revolution has *already* brought the Russian proletariat by creating the Soviets of Workers' Deputies.

A new type of state emerging from our revolution

11. The Soviets of Workers', Soldiers', Peasants' and other Deputies are not understood, not only in the sense that their class significance, their role in the *Russian* revolution, is not clear to

the majority. They are not understood also in the sense that they constitute a new form or rather a new *type of state*.

The most perfect, the most advanced type of bourgeois state is the *parliamentary democratic republic*: power is vested in parliament; the state machine, the apparatus and organ of administration, is of the customary kind: the standing army, the police and the bureaucracy – which in practice is undisplaceable, is privileged and stands *above* the people.

Since the end of the nineteenth century, however, revolutionary epochs have advanced a *higher* type of democratic state, a state which in certain respects, as Engels put it, ceases to be a state, is "no longer a state in the proper sense of the word".[3] This is a state of the Paris Commune type, one in which a standing army and police divorced from the people are *replaced* by the direct arming of the people themselves. It is *this feature* that constitutes the very essence of the Commune, which has been so misrepresented and slandered by the bourgeois writers, and to which has been erroneously ascribed, among other things, the intention of immediately 'introducing' socialism.

This is the type of state which the Russian Revolution *began* to create in 1905 and in 1917. A Republic of Soviets of Workers', Soldiers', Peasants' and other Deputies, united in an All-Russia Constituent Assembly of people's representatives or in a Council of Soviets, etc. is what is *already being realised* in our country now, at this juncture. It is being realised by the initiative of the nation's millions, who are creating a democracy on their own, *in their own way* without waiting until the Cadet professors draft their legislative bills for a parliamentary bourgeois republic, or until the pedants and routine-worshippers of petty-bourgeois 'Social-Democracy', like Mr. Plekhanov or Kautsky, stop distorting the Marxist teaching on the state.

Marxism differs from anarchism in that it recognises the *need* for a state and for state power in the period of revolution

3 See Engels, Friedrich, 'Letter to A Bebel', 18-28 March 1875, *MECW*, Vol. 45, p. 64.

in general, and in the period of transition from capitalism to socialism in particular.

Marxism differs from the petty-bourgeois, opportunist 'Social-Democratism' of Plekhanov, Kautsky and co. in that it recognises that what is required during these two periods is *not* a state of the usual parliamentary bourgeois republican type, but a state of the Paris Commune type.

The main distinctions between a state of the latter type and the old state are as follows.

It is quite easy (as history proves) to revert from a parliamentary bourgeois republic to a monarchy, for all the machinery of oppression – the army, the police and the bureaucracy – is left intact. The Commune and the Soviet *smash* that machinery and do away with it.

The parliamentary bourgeois republic hampers and stifles the independent political life of the *masses* – their direct participation in the *democratic* organisation of the life of the state from the bottom up. The opposite is the case with the Soviets.

The latter reproduce the type of state which was being evolved by the Paris Commune and which Marx described as "the political form at last discovered under which to work out the economic emancipation of labour".[4]

We are usually told that the Russian people are not yet prepared for the 'introduction' of the Commune. This was the argument of the serf-owners when they claimed that the peasants were not prepared for emancipation. The Commune, i.e. the Soviets, does not 'introduce', does not intend to 'introduce', and must not introduce *any* reforms which have not absolutely matured both in economic reality and in the minds of the overwhelming majority of the people. The deeper the economic collapse and the crisis produced by the war, the more urgent becomes the need for the most perfect political form, which will *facilitate* the healing of the terrible wounds inflicted on mankind by

4 Marx, Karl, *The Civil War in France*, Wellred Books, 2021, p. 48.

the war. The less the organisational experience of the Russian people, the more resolutely must we *proceed* to organisational development by the *people themselves* and not merely by the bourgeois politicians and 'well-placed' bureaucrats.

The sooner we shed the old prejudices of pseudo-Marxism, a Marxism falsified by Plekhanov, Kautsky and co., the more actively we set about helping the people to organise Soviets of Workers' and Peasants' Deputies everywhere and immediately, and helping the latter to take life *in its entirety* under their control, and the longer Lvov and co. delay the convocation of the Constituent Assembly, the easier will it be for the people (through the medium of the Constituent Assembly, or independently of it, if Lvov delays its convocation too long) to cast their decision in favour of a republic of Soviets of Workers' and Peasants' Deputies. Errors in the new work of organisational development by the people themselves are at first inevitable; but it is better to make mistakes and go forward than to *wait* until the professors of law summoned by Mr. Lvov draft their laws for the convocation of the Constituent Assembly, for the perpetuation of the parliamentary bourgeois republic and for the strangling of the Soviets of Workers' and Peasants' Deputies.

If we organise ourselves and conduct our propaganda skilfully, not only the proletarians, but nine-tenths of the peasants will be opposed to the restoration of the police, will be opposed to an undisplaceable and privileged bureaucracy and to an army divorced from the people. And that is all the new type of state stands for.

12. The substitution of a people's militia for the police is a reform that follows from the entire course of the revolution and that is now being introduced in most parts of Russia. We must explain to the people that in most of the bourgeois revolutions of the usual type, this reform was always extremely short-lived, and that the bourgeoisie – even the most democratic and republican – restored the police of the old, tsarist type, a police divorced

from the people, commanded by the bourgeoisie and capable of oppressing the people in every way.

There is only one way to *prevent* the restoration of the police, and that is to create a people's militia and to fuse it with the army (the standing army to be replaced by the arming of the entire people). Service in this militia should extend to all citizens of both sexes between the ages of fifteen and sixty-five without exception, if these tentatively suggested age limits may be taken as indicating the participation of adolescents and old people. Capitalists must pay their workers, servants, etc. for days devoted to public service in the militia. Unless women are brought to take an independent part not only in political life generally, but also in daily and universal public service, it is no use talking about full and stable democracy, let alone socialism. And such 'police' functions as care of the sick and of homeless children, food inspection, etc. will never be satisfactorily discharged until women are on an equal footing with men, not merely nominally but in reality.

The tasks which the proletariat must put before the people in order to safeguard, consolidate and develop the revolution are prevention of the restoration of the police and enlistment of the organisational forces of the entire people in forming a people's militia.

The agrarian and national programmes

13. At the present moment we cannot say for certain whether a mighty agrarian revolution will develop in the Russian countryside in the near future. We cannot say exactly how profound the class cleavage is among the peasants, which has undoubtedly grown more profound of late as a division into agricultural labourers, wage-workers and poor peasants ('semi-proletarians'), on the one hand, and wealthy and middle peasants (capitalists and petty capitalists), on the other. Such questions will be, and can be, decided only by experience.

Being the party of the proletariat, however, we are unquestionably in duty bound not only immediately to advance an agrarian (land) programme but also to advocate practical measures which can be immediately realised in the *interests* of the peasant agrarian revolution in Russia.

We must demand the nationalisation of *all* the land, i.e. that all the land in the state should become the property of the central state power. This power must fix the size, etc. of the resettlement land fund, pass legislation for the conservation of forests, for land improvement, etc. and absolutely prohibit any middlemen to interpose themselves between the owner of the land, i.e. the state, and the tenant, i.e. the tiller (prohibit all subletting of land). However, the *disposal* of the land, the determination of the *local regulations* governing ownership and tenure of land, must in no case be placed in the hands of bureaucrats and officials, but wholly and exclusively in the hands of the regional and local *Soviets of Peasants' Deputies.*

In order to improve grain production techniques and increase output, and in order to develop rational cultivation on a large scale under public control, we must strive within the peasants' committees to secure the transformation of every confiscated landed estate into a large model farm controlled by the *Soviet of Agricultural Labourers' Deputies.*

In order to counteract the petty-bourgeois phrase-mongering and the policy prevailing among the Socialist-Revolutionaries, particularly the idle talk about 'subsistence' standards or 'labour' standards, 'socialisation of the land', etc., the party of the proletariat must make it clear that small-scale farming under commodity production cannot save mankind from poverty and oppression.

Without necessarily splitting the Soviets of Peasants' Deputies at once, the party of the proletariat must explain the need for organising separate Soviets of Agricultural Labourers' Deputies and separate Soviets of deputies from the poor (semi-proletarian) peasants, or, at least, for holding regular separate conferences of deputies of *this class status* in the shape of separate groups or parties within the general Soviets of Peasants' Deputies. Otherwise all the honeyed petty-bourgeois talk of the Narodniks regarding the peasants in general will serve as a shield for the deception of the propertyless mass by the wealthy peasants, who are merely a variety of *capitalists.*

To counteract the bourgeois-liberal or purely bureaucratic sermons preached by many Socialist-Revolutionaries and Soviets of Workers' and Soldiers' Deputies, who advise the peasants not to seize the landed estates and not to start the agrarian reform pending the convocation of the Constituent Assembly, the party of the proletariat must urge the peasants to carry out the agrarian reform at once on their own, and to confiscate the landed estates immediately, upon the decisions of the peasants' deputies in the localities.

At the same time, it is most important to insist on the necessity of *increasing* food production for the soldiers at the front and for the towns, and on the absolute inadmissibility of causing any damage or injury to livestock, implements, machinery, buildings, etc.

14. As regards the national question, the proletarian party first of all must advocate the proclamation and immediate realisation of complete freedom of secession from Russia for all the nations and peoples who were oppressed by tsarism, or who were forcibly joined to, or forcibly kept within the boundaries of, the state, i.e. annexed.

All statements, declarations and manifestos concerning renunciation of annexations that are not accompanied by the realisation of the right of secession in practice, are nothing but bourgeois deception of the people, or else pious petty-bourgeois wishes.

The proletarian party strives to create as large a state as possible, for this is to the advantage of the working people; it strives to *draw* nations *closer together*, and bring about their *further fusion*; but it desires to achieve this aim not by violence, but exclusively through a free fraternal union of the workers and the working people of all nations.

The more democratic the Russian republic, and the more successfully it organises itself into a Republic of Soviets of Workers' and Peasants' Deputies, the more powerful will be the force of *voluntary* attraction to such a republic on the part of the working people of *all* nations.

Complete freedom of secession, the broadest local (and national) autonomy, and elaborate guarantees of the rights of national minorities – this is the programme of the revolutionary proletariat.

Nationalisation of the banks and capitalist syndicates

15. Under no circumstances can the party of the proletariat set itself the aim of 'introducing' socialism in a country of small peasants so long as the overwhelming majority of the population has not come to realise the need for a socialist revolution.

But only bourgeois sophists, hiding behind 'near-Marxist' catchwords, can deduce from this truth a justification of the policy of postponing immediate revolutionary measures, the time for which is fully ripe; measures which *have been* frequently *resorted to during the war by a number of bourgeois states*, and which are absolutely indispensable in order to combat impending total economic disorganisation and famine.

Such measures as the nationalisation of the land, of all the banks and capitalist syndicates, or, at least, the *immediate* establishment of the *control* of the Soviets of Workers' Deputies, etc. over them – measures which do not in any way constitute the 'introduction' of socialism – must be absolutely insisted on, and, whenever possible, carried out in a revolutionary way. Without such measures, which are only steps towards socialism, and which are perfectly feasible economically, it will be impossible to heal the wounds caused by the war and to avert the impending collapse; and the party of the revolutionary proletariat will never hesitate to lay hands on the fabulous profits of the capitalists and bankers, who are enriching themselves on the war in a particularly scandalous manner.

The situation within the Socialist International

16. The international obligations of the working class of Russia are precisely now coming to the forefront with particular force.

Only lazy people do not swear by internationalism these days. Even the chauvinist defencists, even Plekhanov and Potresov, even Kerensky, call themselves internationalists. It becomes the duty of the proletarian party all the more urgently, therefore, to clearly, precisely and definitely counterpoise internationalism in deed to internationalism in word.

Mere appeals to the workers of all countries, empty assurances of devotion to internationalism, direct or indirect attempts to fix a 'sequence' of action by the revolutionary proletariat in the various belligerent countries, laborious efforts to conclude 'agreements' between the socialists of the belligerent countries *on the question* of the revolutionary struggle, all the fuss over the summoning of socialist congresses *for the purpose* of a peace campaign, etc., etc. – no matter how sincere the authors of such ideas, attempts and plans may be – amount, as far as their *objective* significance is concerned, to mere phrase-mongering, and *at best* are innocent and pious wishes, fit only to conceal the *deception* of the people by the chauvinists. The *French* social-chauvinists, who are the most adroit and accomplished in methods of parliamentary hocus-pocus, have long since broken the record for ranting and resonant pacifist and internationalist phrases *coupled with* the incredibly brazen betrayal of socialism and the International, the acceptance of posts in governments which conduct the imperialist war, the voting of credits *or loans* (as Chkheidze, Skobelev, Tsereteli and Steklov have been doing recently in Russia), opposition to the revolutionary struggle in *their own country*, etc., etc.

Good people often forget the brutal and savage setting of the imperialist world war. This setting does not tolerate phrases, and mocks at innocent and pious wishes.

There is one, and only one, kind of real internationalism, and that is – working whole-heartedly for the development of the revolutionary movement and the revolutionary struggle in *one's own* country and supporting (by propaganda, sympathy, and material aid) *this struggle*, this, and *only this*, line, in *every* country without exception.

Everything else is deception and Manilovism.[5]

During the two odd years of the war the international socialist and working-class movement in *every* country has evolved three trends. Whoever ignores *reality* and refuses to recognise the existence of these three trends, to analyse them, to fight consistently for the trend that is really internationalist, is doomed to impotence, helplessness and errors.

The three trends are:

1) The social-chauvinists, i.e. socialists in word and chauvinists in deed. People who support 'defence of the fatherland' in an imperialist war (and above all in the present imperialist war).

These people are our *class* enemies. They have gone over to the bourgeoisie.

They are the majority of the official leaders of the official Social-Democratic parties in *all* countries – Plekhanov and co. in Russia; the Scheidemanns in Germany; Renaudel, Guesde and Sembat in France; Bissolati and co. in Italy; Hyndman, the Fabians and the Labourites (the leaders of the 'Labour Party') in Britain; Branting and co. in Sweden; Troelstra and his party in Holland; Stauning and his party in Denmark; Victor Berger and the other 'defenders of the fatherland' in America and so forth.

2) The second trend, known as the 'Centre', consists of people who vacillate between the social-chauvinists and the true internationalists.

The 'Centre' all vow and declare that they are Marxists and internationalists, that they are for peace, for bringing every kind of 'pressure' to bear upon the governments, for 'demanding' in every way that their own government should 'ascertain the

---

5 From Manilov, a character in Gogol's *Dead Souls*, represented as a type of easy-going sentimental landowner, whose name has become a synonym for an idle weak-willed dreamer.

will of the people for peace', that they are for all sorts of peace campaigns, for peace without annexations, etc., etc. – *and for peace with the social-chauvinists.* The 'Centre' is for 'unity', the Centre is opposed to a split.

The 'Centre' is a realm of honeyed petty-bourgeois phrases, of internationalism in word and cowardly opportunism and fawning on the social-chauvinists in deed.

The crux of the matter is that the 'Centre' is not convinced of the necessity for a revolution against one's own government; it does not preach revolution; it does not carry on a whole-hearted revolutionary struggle; and in order to evade such a struggle it resorts to the tritest ultra-'Marxist'-sounding *excuses.*

The social-chauvinists are our *class enemies*, they are *bourgeois* within the working-class movement. They represent a stratum, or groups, or sections of the working class which *objectively* have been bribed by the bourgeoisie (by better wages, positions of honour, etc.), and which help *their own* bourgeoisie to plunder and oppress small and weak peoples and to fight *for* the division of the capitalist spoils.

The 'Centre' consists of routine-worshippers, eroded by the canker of legality, corrupted by the parliamentary atmosphere, etc. – bureaucrats accustomed to snug positions and soft jobs. Historically and economically speaking, they are not a *separate* stratum but represent only a *transition* from a past phase of the working-class movement – the phase between 1871 and 1914, which gave much that is valuable to the proletariat, particularly in the indispensable art of slow, sustained and systematic organisational work on a large and very large scale – to a new *phase* that became *objectively* essential with the outbreak of the first imperialist world war, which inaugurated *the era of social revolution.*

The chief leader and spokesman of the 'Centre' is Karl Kautsky, the most outstanding authority in the Second International (1889 – 1914), since August 1914 a model of utter bankruptcy as a Marxist, the embodiment of unheard-of spinelessness, and the most wretched vacillations and betrayals. This 'Centrist' trend includes Kautsky, Haase, Ledebour and the so-called workers' or labour group in the Reichstag; in France it includes Longuet, Pressemane and the so-called minorities (Mensheviks) in general; in Britain, Philip Snowden, Ramsay MacDonald and many other leaders of the Independent Labour Party, and some leaders of the British Socialist Party; Morris Hillquit and many others in the United States; Turati, Tréves, Modigliani and others in Italy; Robert Grimm and others in Switzerland; Victor Adler and co. in Austria; the party of the Organising Committee, Axelrod, Martov, Chkheidze, Tsereteli and others in Russia, and so forth.

Naturally, at times individuals unconsciously drift from the social-chauvinist to the 'Centrist' position, and vice versa. Every Marxist knows that classes are distinct, even though individuals may move freely from one class to another; similarly, *trends* in political life are distinct in spite of the fact that individuals may change freely from one trend to another, and in spite of all attempts and efforts to *amalgamate* trends.

3) The third trend, that of the true internationalists, is best represented by the 'Zimmerwald Left'. (We reprint as a supplement its manifesto of September 1915, to enable the reader to learn of the inception of this trend at first hand.)[6]

Its distinctive feature is its complete break with both social-chauvinism and 'Centrism', and its gallant revolutionary struggle against *its own* imperialist government and *its own* imperialist bourgeoisie. Its principle is: 'Our chief enemy is at home'. It wages a ruthless struggle against honeyed social-pacifist phrases (a social-pacifist is a socialist in word and a bourgeois pacifist in deed; bourgeois pacifists dream of an everlasting peace *without* the overthrow of the yoke and domination of capital) and against all *subterfuges* employed to deny the possibility, or the appropriateness, or the timeliness of a proletarian revolutionary

6 Reproduced in *Lenin Selected Writings: On Imperialist War*, p. 387.

struggle and of a proletarian socialist revolution *in connection* with the present war.

The most outstanding representative of this trend in Germany is the Spartacus group or the *Internationale* group, to which Karl Liebknecht belongs. Karl Liebknecht is a most celebrated representative of this trend and of the *new*, and genuine, proletarian International.

Karl Liebknecht called upon the workers and soldiers of Germany to *turn their guns* against *their own* government. Karl Liebknecht did that openly from the rostrum of parliament (the Reichstag). He then went to a demonstration in Potsdamer Platz, one of the largest public squares in Berlin, with illegally printed leaflets proclaiming the slogan 'Down with the Government!' He was arrested and sentenced to *hard labour*. He is now serving his term in a German convict prison, like *hundreds*, if not thousands, of other *true* German socialists who have been imprisoned for their anti-war activities.

Karl Liebknecht in his speeches and letters mercilessly attacked not only *his own* Plekhanovs and Potresovs (Scheidemanns, Legiens, Davids and co.), *but also his own Centrists*, his own Chkheidzes and Tseretelis (Kautsky, Haase, Ledebour and co.).

Karl Liebknecht and his friend Otto Rühle, two out of 110 deputies, violated discipline, destroyed the 'unity' with the 'Centre' and the chauvinists and *went against all of them*. Liebknecht *alone* represents socialism, the proletarian cause, the proletarian revolution. All the rest of German Social-Democracy, to quote the apt words of Rosa Luxemburg (also a member and one of the leaders of the Spartacus group), is a '*stinking corpse*'.

Another group of true internationalists in Germany is that of the Bremen paper *Arbeiterpolitik*.

Closest to the internationalists in deed are: in France, Loriot and his friends (Bourderon and Merrheim have slid down to social-pacifism), as well as the Frenchman Henri Guilbeaux, who publishes in Geneva the journal *Demain*; in Britain, the newspaper

The Trade Unionist, and some of the members of the British Socialist Party and of the Independent Labour Party (for instance, Russell Williams, who openly called for a break with the leaders who have *betrayed* socialism), the Scottish socialist schoolteacher *Maclean*, who was sentenced to *hard labour* by the bourgeois government of Britain for his revolutionary fight against the war, and hundreds of British socialists who are in jail for the same offence. They, and they alone, are internationalists in deed. In the United States, the Socialist Labour Party and those within the opportunist Socialist Party who in January 1917 began publication of the paper, *The Internationalist*; in Holland, the Party of the 'Tribunists' which publishes the paper *De Tribune* (Pannekoek, Herman Gorter, Wijnkoop and Henriette Roland-Holst, who, although Centrist at Zimmerwald, has now joined our ranks); in Sweden, the Party of the Young, or the Left, led by Lindhagen, Ture Nerman, Carleson, Ström and Z Höglund, who at Zimmerwald was personally active in the organisation of the 'Zimmerwald Left' and who is now in prison for his revolutionary fight against the war; in Denmark, Trier and his friends who have left the now purely *bourgeois* 'Social-Democratic' Party of Denmark, headed by the *Minister* Stauning; in Bulgaria, the 'Tesnyaki'; in Italy, the nearest are Constantino Lazzari, secretary of the party, and Serrati, editor of the central organ *Avanti!*; in Poland, Radek, Hanecki and other leaders of the Social-Democrats united under the 'Regional Executive', and Rosa Luxemburg, Tyszka and other leaders of the Social-Democrats united under the 'Chief Executive'; in Switzerland, those of the Left who drew up the argument for the 'referendum' (January 1917) in order to fight the social-chauvinists and the 'Centre' in *their own* country and who at the Zurich Cantonal Socialist Convention, held at Töss on 11 February 1917, moved a consistently revolutionary resolution against the war; in Austria, the young Left-wing friends of Friedrich Adler, who acted partly through the Karl Marx Club in Vienna, now closed by the arch-reactionary Austrian Government, which is ruining Adler's life for his heroic though ill-considered shooting at a minister, and so on.

It is not a question of shades of opinion, which certainly exist even among the Lefts. It is a question of *trend*. The thing is that it is not easy to be an internationalist in deed during a terrible imperialist war. Such people are few; but it is on such people *alone* that the future of socialism depends; they *alone* are *the leaders of the people*, and not their corrupters.

The distinction between the reformists and the revolutionaries, among the Social-Democrats, and socialists generally, was objectively bound to undergo a change under the conditions of the imperialist war. Those who confine themselves to 'demanding' that the bourgeois governments should conclude peace or 'ascertain the will of the peoples for peace', etc., are *actually* slipping into reforms. For, objectively, *the problem of the war* can be solved only in a *revolutionary way*.

There is no possibility of this war ending in a democratic, non-coercive peace or of the people being relieved of the burden of *billions* paid in interest to the capitalists, who have made fortunes out of the war, except through a revolution of the proletariat.

The most varied reforms can and must be demanded of the bourgeois governments, but one cannot, without sinking to Manilovism and reformism, demand that people and classes entangled by the thousands of threads of imperialist capital should *tear* those threads. And unless they are torn, all talk of a war against war is idle and deceitful prattle.

The 'Kautskyites', the 'Centre', are revolutionaries in word and reformists in deed, they are internationalists in word and accomplices of the social-chauvinists in deed.

The collapse of the Zimmerwald International – The need for founding a Third International

17. From the very outset, the Zimmerwald International adopted a vacillating, 'Kautskyite', 'Centrist' position, which immediately compelled the *Zimmerwald Left* to dissociate itself, to separate itself from the rest and to issue *its own* manifesto (published in Switzerland in Russian, German and French).

The chief shortcoming of the Zimmerwald International and the cause of its *collapse* (for politically and ideologically it has already collapsed), was its vacillation and indecision on such a momentous issue of *crucial* practical significance as that of breaking completely with social-chauvinism and the old social-chauvinist International, headed by Vandervelde and Huysmans at The Hague (Holland), etc.

It is not as yet known in Russia that the Zimmerwald majority *are nothing but Kautskyites*. Yet this is the fundamental fact, one which cannot be ignored, and which is now generally known in Western Europe. Even that chauvinist, that extreme German chauvinist, Heilmann, editor of the ultra-chauvinistic *Chemnitzer Volksstimme* and contributor to Parvus' ultra-chauvinistic *Glocke* (a 'Social-Democrat', of course, and an ardent partisan of Social-Democratic 'unity'), was compelled to acknowledge in the press that the Centre, or 'Kautskyism', and the *Zimmerwald majority* were one and the same thing.

This fact was definitely established at the end of 1916 and the beginning of 1917. Although social-pacifism was condemned by the Kienthal Manifesto,[7] the *whole* Zimmerwald Right, the *entire* Zimmerwald majority, sank to social-pacifism: Kautsky and co. in a series of utterances in January and February 1917; Bourderon and Merrheim in France, who cast their votes *in unanimity* with the social-chauvinists for the pacifist resolutions of the Socialist Party (December 1916) and of the Confédération Générale du Travail (the national organisation of the French trade unions, also in December 1916); Turati and co. in Italy, where the entire party took up a social-pacifist position, while Turati himself, in a speech delivered on 17 December 1916, 'slipped' (not by accident, of course) into *nationalist* phrases whitewashing the imperialist war.

In January 1917, the chairman of the Zimmerwald and Kienthal conferences, Robert Grimm, joined the social-

7 Reproduced in *Lenin Selected Writings: On Imperialist War*, p. 397. The Kienthal Conference was the second Zimmerwald Conference, held in April 1916.

chauvinists in *his own* party (Greulich, Pflüger, Gustav Mümller and others) *against* the internationalists in deed.

At two conferences of *Zimmerwaldists* from various countries in January and February 1917, this equivocal, double-faced behaviour of the Zimmerwald majority was formally stigmatised by the Left internationalists of several countries: by Munzenberg, secretary of the international youth organisation and editor of the excellent internationalist publication *Die Jugendinternationale*; by Zinoviev, representative of the Central Committee of our Party; by K Radek of the Polish Social-Democratic Party (the 'Regional Executive') and by Hartstein,[8] a German Social-Democrat and member of the Spartacus group.

Much is given to the Russian proletariat; nowhere in the world has the working class yet succeeded in developing so much revolutionary energy as in Russia. But to whom much is given, of him much is required.

The Zimmerwald bog can no longer be tolerated. We must not, for the sake of the Zimmerwald 'Kautskyites', continue the semi-alliance with the chauvinist International of the Plekhanovs and Scheidemanns. We must break with this International immediately. We must remain in Zimmerwald only for purposes of information.

It is we who must found, and right now, without delay, a new, revolutionary, proletarian International, or rather, we must not fear to acknowledge publicly that this new International is *already established* and operating.

This is the International of those 'internationalists in deed' whom I precisely listed above. They and they alone are representatives of the revolutionary, internationalist mass, and not their corrupters.

And if socialists *of that type* are few, let every Russian worker ask himself whether there were many really class-conscious

8 Pseudonym of Paul Levi.

revolutionaries in Russia *on the eve* of the February-March revolution of 1917.

It is not a question of numbers, but of giving correct expression to the ideas and policies of the truly revolutionary proletariat. The thing is not to 'proclaim' internationalism, but to be able to be an internationalist in deed, even when times are most trying.

Let us not deceive ourselves with hopes of agreements and international congresses. As long as the imperialist war is on, international intercourse is held in the iron vice of the military dictatorship of the imperialist bourgeoisie. If even the 'republican' Milyukov, who is obliged to tolerate the parallel government of the Soviet of Workers' Deputies, *did not allow Fritz Platten*, the Swiss socialist, secretary of the party, an internationalist and participant in the Zimmerwald and Kienthal conferences, to enter Russia in April 1917, in spite of the fact that Platten has a Russian wife and was on his way to visit his wife's relatives, and in spite of the fact that he had taken part in the Revolution of 1905 in Riga, for which he had been confined in a Russian prison, had given bail to the tsarist government for his release and wished to recover that bail – if the 'republican' Milyukov could *do* such a thing in April 1917 in Russia, one can judge what value can be put on the promises and assurances, the phrases and declarations of the bourgeoisie on the subject of peace without annexations, and so on.

And the arrest of Trotsky by the British Government? And the refusal to allow Martov to leave Switzerland, and the attempt to lure him to Britain, where Trotsky's fate awaits him?

Let us harbour no illusions. We must not deceive ourselves.

To 'wait' for international congresses or conferences is simply to *betray* internationalism, since it has been shown that even from Stockholm neither socialists loyal to internationalism *nor even their letters* are allowed to come here, although this is quite possible and although a ferocious military censorship exists.

Our Party must not 'wait', but must immediately *found* a Third International. Hundreds of socialists imprisoned in Germany and Britain will then heave a sigh of relief, thousands and thousands of German workers who are now holding strikes and demonstrations that are frightening that scoundrel and brigand, Wilhelm, will learn from *illegal* leaflets of our decision, of our fraternal confidence in Karl Liebknecht, and in him alone, of *our* decision to fight 'revolutionary defencism' *even now*; they will read this and be strengthened in their revolutionary internationalism.

To whom much is given, of him much is required. No other country in the world is as free as Russia is *now*. Let us make use of this freedom, not to advocate support for the bourgeoisie, or bourgeois 'revolutionary defencism', but in a bold, honest, proletarian, Liebknecht way to *found the Third International*, an International uncompromisingly hostile both to the social-chauvinist traitors and to the vacillating 'Centrists'.

18. After what has been said, there is no need to waste many words explaining that the amalgamation of Social-Democrats in Russia is out of the question.

It is better to remain with one friend only, like Liebknecht, and *that means remaining with the revolutionary proletariat*, than to entertain even for a moment any thought of amalgamation with the party of the Organising Committee, with Chkheidze and Tsereteli, who can tolerate a bloc with Potresov in *Rabochaya Gazeta*, who voted for the loan in the Executive Committee of the Soviet of Workers' Deputies,[9] and who have sunk to 'defencism'.

Let the dead bury their dead.

Whoever wants to *help* the waverers must first stop wavering himself.

9 On 7 (20) April 1917, the Executive Committee of the Petrograd Soviet, by a majority of twenty-one votes against fourteen, adopted a resolution in favour of supporting the so-called 'Liberty Loan' issued by the Provisional Government to finance the continuing imperialist war.

What should be the name of our party – one that will be correct scientifically and help to clarify the mind of the proletariat politically?

19. I now come to the final point, the name of our Party. We must call ourselves the *Communist Party* – just as Marx and Engels called themselves.

We must repeat that we are Marxists and that we take as our basis *The Communist Manifesto*, which has been distorted and betrayed by the Social-Democrats on its two main points: (1) the working men have no country: 'defence of the fatherland' in an imperialist war is a betrayal of socialism; and (2) the Marxist doctrine of the state has been distorted by the Second International.

The name 'Social-Democracy' is *scientifically* incorrect, as Marx frequently pointed out, in particular, in the *Critique of the Gotha Programme* in 1875, and as Engels re-affirmed in a more popular form in 1894.[10] From capitalism mankind can pass directly only to socialism, i.e. to the social ownership of the means of production and the distribution of products according to the amount of work performed by each individual. Our Party looks farther ahead: socialism must inevitably evolve gradually into communism, upon the banner of which is inscribed the motto: "From each according to his ability, to each according to his needs".

That is my first argument.

Here is the second: the second part of the name of our Party (Social-*Democrats*) is also scientifically incorrect. Democracy is a form of *state*, whereas we Marxists are opposed to *every kind* of state.

The leaders of the Second International (1889-1914), Plekhanov, Kautsky and their like, have vulgarised and distorted Marxism.

Marxism differs from anarchism in that it recognises *the need for a state* for the purpose of the transition to socialism; but (and

---

10 See Engels, Friedrich, 'Preface to *Internationales aus dem "Volksstaat"*', *MECW*, Vol. 27, pp. 414-8.

here is where we differ from Kautsky and co.) *not a state of the type* of the usual parliamentary bourgeois-democratic republic, but a state like the Paris Commune of 1871 and the Soviets of Workers' Deputies of 1905 and 1917.

My third argument: *living reality*, the revolution, has *already actually* established in our country, albeit in a weak and embryonic form, precisely this new type of 'state', which is not a state in the proper sense of the word.

This is *already* a matter of the practical action of the people, and not merely a theory of the leaders.

The state in the proper sense of the term is domination over the people by contingents of armed men divorced from the people.

Our *emergent*, new state is also a state, for we too need contingents of armed men, we too need the *strictest* order, and must *ruthlessly* crush by force all attempts at either a tsarist or a Guchkov-bourgeois counter-revolution.

But our *emergent*, new state is *no longer* a state in the proper sense of the term, for in some parts of Russia these contingents of armed men are *the masses themselves*, the entire people, and not certain privileged persons placed over the people, and divorced from the people, and for all practical purposes undisplaceable.

We must look forward, and not backward to the usual bourgeois type of democracy, which consolidated the rule of the bourgeoisie with the aid of the old, *monarchist* organs of administration, the police, the army and the bureaucracy.

We must look forward to the emergent new democracy, which is already ceasing to be a democracy, for democracy means the domination of the people, and the armed people cannot dominate themselves.

The term democracy is not only scientifically incorrect when applied to a Communist Party; it has now, since March 1917, simply become *blinkers* put on the eyes of the revolutionary people and *preventing* them from boldly and freely, on their own initiative, building up the new: the Soviets of Workers',

Peasants' and all other Deputies, as *the sole power* in the 'state' and as the harbinger of the 'withering away' of the state *in every form.*

My fourth argument: we must reckon with the actual situation in which socialism finds itself internationally.

It is not what it was during the years 1871 to 1914, when Marx and Engels knowingly put up with the inaccurate, opportunist term 'Social-Democracy'. For *in those days*, after the defeat of the Paris Commune, history made slow organisational and educational work the task of the day. Nothing else was possible. The anarchists were then (as they are now) fundamentally wrong not only theoretically, but also economically and politically. The anarchists misjudged the character of the times, for they failed to understand the world situation: the worker of Britain corrupted by imperialist profits, the Commune defeated in Paris, the recent (1871) triumph of the bourgeois national movement in Germany, the age-long sleep of semi-feudal Russia.

Marx and Engels gauged the times accurately; they understood the international situation; they understood that the approach to the beginning of the social revolution must be *slow*.

We, in our turn, must also understand the specific features and tasks of the new era. Let us not imitate those sorry Marxists of whom Marx said: "I have sown dragon's teeth and harvested fleas".[11]

The objective inevitability of capitalism which grew into imperialism brought about the imperialist war. The war has brought mankind to the *brink of a precipice*, to the brink of the destruction of civilisation, of the brutalisation and destruction of more millions, countless millions, of human beings.

The *only* way out is through a proletarian revolution.

At the very moment when such a revolution is beginning, when it is taking its first hesitant, groping steps, steps betraying too great a confidence in the bourgeoisie, at such a moment the

11 Marx, *The German Ideology*, *MECW*, Vol. 5, p. 510, quoting Heinrich Heine.

majority (that is the truth, that is a fact) of the 'Social-Democratic' leaders, of the 'Social-Democratic' parliamentarians, of the 'Social-Democratic' newspapers – and these are precisely the *organs* that influence the people – have *deserted* socialism, have *betrayed* socialism and have gone over to the side of 'their own' national bourgeoisie.

The people have been confused, led astray and deceived by *these* leaders.

And we shall aid and abet that deception if we retain the old and out-of-date Party name, which is as decayed as the Second International!

Granted that 'many' workers *understand* Social-Democracy in an honest way; but it is time to learn how to distinguish the subjective from the objective.

Subjectively, such Social-Democratic workers are most loyal leaders of the proletarians.

Objectively, however, the world situation is such that the old name of our Party *makes it easier* to fool the people and *impedes* the onward march; for at every step, in every paper, in every parliamentary group, the masses see *leaders*, i.e. people whose voices carry farthest and whose actions are most conspicuous; yet they are all 'would-be Social-Democrats', they are all 'for unity' with the betrayers of socialism, with the social-chauvinists; and they are all presenting for payment the old bills issued by 'Social-Democracy'…

And what are the arguments against?… "We'll be confused with the Anarchist-Communists", they say…

Why are we not afraid of being confused with the Social-Nationalists, the Social-Liberals, or the Radical-Socialists, the foremost bourgeois party in the French Republic and the most adroit in the bourgeois deception of the people?… We are told: The people are used to it, the workers have come to 'love' *their* Social-Democratic Party.

That is the only argument. But it is an argument that dismisses the science of Marxism, the tasks of the morrow in the revolution, the objective position of world socialism, the shameful collapse of the Second International, and the harm done to the practical cause by the packs of 'would-be Social-Democrats' who surround the proletarians.

It is an argument of routinism, an argument of inertia, an argument of stagnation.

But we are out to rebuild the world. We are out to put an end to the imperialist world war into which hundreds of millions of people have been drawn and in which the interests of billions and billions of capital are involved, a war which cannot end in a truly democratic peace without the greatest proletarian revolution in the history of mankind.

Yet we are afraid of our own selves. We are loath to cast off the 'dear old' soiled shirt...

But it is time to cast off the soiled shirt and to put on clean linen.

N Lenin,
Petrograd,
10 (23) April 1917

A Shameless Lie of the Capitalists

Written 11 (24) April 1917

It is not enough that the capitalist newspapers lie and carry on a riot-mongering campaign against *Pravda*, that *Rech* vies in this respect with *Russkaya Volya* – a paper which it cannot but despise.[1]

Now the ministers of the capitalist government, too, have begun to speak in the language of *Russkaya Volya*. *Rech* quotes today Minister Nekrasov's statement made before a meeting of the Cadet Party in Moscow on 9 (22) April: "The preaching of violence that comes from the Kamennoostrovsky Prospekt is a terrible thing."

Re-echoing *Russkaya Volya*, the worthy Minister lies shamelessly, deceives the people, and aids the riot-mongers while hiding behind their backs. He dares not name directly a single person, a single newspaper, a single orator, or a single party.

The worthy Minister prefers dark hints – hoping that someone will fall for it!

But all politically minded people will understand that the worthy Minister is referring to the organ of the Central Committee of the RSDLP, *Pravda* and its followers.

1 *Rech* was the central organ of the Cadets, and *Russkaya Volya* was a daily founded and run by the big banks in Moscow.

You are lying, Mr. Minister, worthy member of the 'people's freedom' party. It is Mr. Guchkov who is preaching violence when be threatens to punish the soldiers for dismissing the authorities. It is *Russkaya Volya*, the riot-mongering newspaper of the riot-mongering 'republicans', a paper that is friendly to you, that preaches violence.

Pravda and its followers do not preach violence. On the contrary, they declare most clearly, precisely and definitely that our main efforts should now be concentrated on *explaining* to the proletarian masses their proletarian problems, as distinguished from the petty bourgeoisie which has succumbed to chauvinist intoxication.

So long as *you*, capitalist gentlemen, Guchkov and co., confine yourselves only to threats of violence, so long as you have not yet resorted to violence, so long as the Soviets of Workers' and Soldiers' Deputies exist, *so long as* you have not yet carried out your threats against the Soviets (such threats, for example, have actually been printed by Mr. Milyukov's associate, Mr. Wilson, *The Times* correspondent), so long as you have not yet perpetrated violence upon the masses, we Pravdists declare and reiterate that we regard the Soviets as the *only possible* form of government.

So long as *you*, capitalist gentlemen, who are in control of the army command, *have not yet begun to use violence*, it is our tactics, the tactics of all Pravdists and of all our Party, to fight for influence among the proletarian masses, to fight for influence among the Soviets of Workers' and Soldiers' Deputies, to *show up* the errors in their tactics, to show up all the falsity of the chauvinist (revolutionary-defencist) intoxication.

The worthy Minister Nekrasov knows this perfectly well, if only from the quotations which *Rech* itself was forced to print. The worthy Minister re-echoes *Russkaya Volya*; he is bent on *preventing* a calm demonstration of the truth by resorting to lies, slander, baiting and threats.

It won't work, Messrs. Nekrasovs!

The workers and soldiers want to know the truth, they want to clear up for themselves the questions of war and peace, and state systems, and they will certainly do so.

The Provisional Government's Note

Written 20 April (3 May) 1917

The cards are on the table. We have every reason to be grateful to Guchkov and Milyukov for their Note, printed today in all the newspapers.

The majority of the Executive Committee of the Soviet of Workers' and Soldiers' Deputies, the Narodniks, Mensheviks, all those who until now have appealed for confidence in the Provisional Government, have received fitting punishment. They hoped, expected and believed that the Provisional Government, under the beneficent influence of 'contact' with Chkheidze, Skobelev and Steklov, would forever repudiate annexations. Things have turned out somewhat differently…

In its Note of 18 April (1 May), the Provisional Government speaks of

> … the desire of the whole nation [!] to fight the world war out *to a decisive victory*. […] Needless to say, [the Note adds], the Provisional Government […] will fully stand by its obligations towards our Allies.

Short and clear. War to a decisive victory. The alliance with the British and French bankers is sacred…

Who concluded this alliance with 'our' Allies, i.e. with the British and French multi-millionaires? The tsar, Rasputin, the tsar's gang, of course. But to Milyukov and co. this treaty is sacred.

Why?

Some say: because Milyukov is insincere, he is a crafty person and so on.

But that is not the point. The point is that Guchkov, Milyukov, Tereshchenko and Konovalov are spokesmen of the *capitalists*. And the seizure of foreign lands is necessary to the capitalists. They will receive new markets, new places to export capital to, new opportunities to arrange profitable jobs for tens of thousands of their sons, etc. The point is that at the present moment the *interests* of the Russian capitalists are identical with those of the British and French capitalists. That, and that alone, is the reason why the tsar's treaties with the British and French capitalists are precious to the Provisional Government of the Russian capitalists.

The new Note of the Provisional Government will pour oil on the flames. It can only arouse a bellicose spirit in Germany. It will help Wilhelm the Brigand to go on deceiving 'his own' workers and soldiers and drag them into a war 'to a finish'.

The new Note of the Provisional Government puts the issue squarely: what next?

From the very first moment of our revolution, the British and French capitalists have been assuring us that the Russian revolution was made solely and exclusively in order to fight the war out 'to a finish'. The capitalists want to plunder Turkey, Persia and China. If this should entail the slaughter of another 10 million or so Russian *muzhiks*[1] – what of it? What we need is a 'decisive victory'… And now the Provisional Government, with utter frankness, has adopted the same course.

> 'Fight – because we want to plunder. Die in your tens of thousands every day – because "we" have not yet fought it out and have not yet got our share of the spoils!'

---

1 The Russian word for 'peasants'.

No class-conscious worker, no class-conscious soldier will support the policy of 'confidence' in the Provisional Government any longer. The policy of confidence is bankrupt.

Our Social-Democratic City Conference stated in its resolution that the correctness of *our* view would be corroborated now every day.[2] But not even we had expected events to move so fast.

The present Soviet of Workers' and Soldiers' Deputies is faced with the alternative: either to swallow the pill offered by Guchkov and Milyukov, which would mean renouncing an independent political role once and for all, for tomorrow Milyukov would put his 'feet on the table' and reduce the Soviet to a mere cipher; or to reject Milyukov's Note, which would mean breaking with the old policy of confidence and adopting the course proposed by *Pravda*.

Naturally, a middle-of-the-road course might be found. But would it be for long?

Workers and soldiers, you must now loudly declare that there must be only one power in the country – the Soviets of Workers' and Soldiers' Deputies. The Provisional Government, the government of a handful of capitalists, must make way for these Soviets.

---

2 See *LCW*, Vol. 24, pp. 154-55.

Icons versus Cannons, Phrases versus Capital

Published 21 April (4 May) 1917

The Note of the Provisional Government on war to a victorious finish has aroused indignation even among those who nourished illusory hopes for a possible renunciation of annexations on the part of the government of capitalists. The newspapers that have been acting as mouthpieces of this petty-bourgeois policy of illusory hopes are today either mumbling in dismay, like *Rabochaya Gazeta*,[1] or are trying to turn this indignation against individuals. *Novaya Zhizn*[2] writes:

> There is no place in the government of democratic Russia for a champion of the interests of international capital! We are sure the Soviet of Workers' and Soldiers' Deputies will act promptly in taking the most energetic measures towards rendering Mr. Milyukov harmless.

And *Dyelo Naroda*[3] expresses the same piece of philistine wisdom in the following words. Milyukov's Note, it says, "tries to reduce

1 Central organ of the Mensheviks.

2 Daily newspaper of a Menshevik trend, organ of a group of Social-Democrats known as Menshevik-Internationalists, adherents of Martov and non-aligned intellectuals.

3 Daily paper of the SRs.

to nought a statement of the greatest international importance approved by the entire cabinet."

Icons versus cannons. Phrases versus capital. The government's statement renouncing annexations was a piece of utterly worthless diplomatic verbiage, which might deceive an ignorant *muzhik*, but could not 'confuse' the leaders of the petty-bourgeois Social-Democratic and Socialist-Revolutionary parties, the writers of *Novaya Zhizn* and *Dyelo Naroda*, unless they were willing to be deceived. What empty phrases are these about there being "no place in the government of democratic Russia for a champion of the interests of international capital!" Educated people ought to be ashamed of themselves, writing such nonsense.

The whole Provisional Government is a government of the capitalist class. It is a matter of class, not of persons. To attack Milyukov personally, to demand, directly or indirectly, his dismissal, is a silly comedy, for *no* change of personalities can change anything so long as the *classes* in power are unchanged.

To draw a line between the 'democracy' of Russia, Britain, France, etc., and the championing of capital is to sink to the level, of the economic and political wisdom of a Gapon.[4]

It is pardonable for ignorant *muzhiks* to demand of the capitalist a 'promise' that he 'live righteously' and not capitalistically, that he should *not* 'champion the interests of capital'. But for the leaders of the Petrograd Soviet, for the writers of *Novaya Zhizn* and *Dyelo Naroda* to adopt such methods means to nourish the illusory hopes which the people place in the capitalists, hopes that are most harmful and ruinous to the cause of freedom, to the cause of the revolution.

---

4 Father Georgy Gapon was a Russian Orthodox priest and a popular working-class leader before the 1905 Revolution. On 9 (22) January 1905, he led a peaceful protest for democratic freedoms and better living conditions, to which the Imperial Army responded by firing upon the crowd. This event, later known as 'Bloody Sunday', served as the starting point of the 1905 Revolution.

Resolution of the CC of the RSDLP(B)

Adopted 21 April (4 May) 1917

Having considered the situation which has arisen in Petrograd after the imperialist, annexationist and predatory Note of the Provisional Government of 18 April (1 May) 1917, and after a number of meetings and demonstrations of the people held in the streets of Petrograd on 20 April (3 May), the Central Committee of the RSDLP resolves:

1. Party propagandists and speakers must refute the despicable lies of the capitalist papers and of the papers supporting the capitalists to the effect that we are holding out the threat of *civil war*. This is a despicable lie, for only at the present moment, as long as the capitalists and their government cannot and dare not use force against the masses, as long as the mass of soldiers and workers are freely expressing their will and freely electing and displacing *all* authorities – at *such a moment* any thought of civil war would be naive, senseless, preposterous; at such a moment *there must be compliance with the will of the majority of the population* and free criticism of this will by the discontented minority; should violence be resorted to, the responsibility will fall on the Provisional Government and its supporters.

2. By their outcries against civil war, the government of the capitalists and its newspapers are only trying to conceal the reluctance of the capitalists, who admittedly constitute an insignificant minority of the people, to submit to the will of the majority.
3. In order to learn the will of the majority of the population in Petrograd, where there is now an unusually large number of soldiers who are familiar with the sentiment of the peasants and correctly express it, a popular vote must at once be arranged in all the districts of Petrograd and its suburbs to ascertain what the attitude is towards the government's Note, what support the various parties enjoy, and what kind of Provisional Government is desired.
4. All Party propagandists must advocate these views and this proposal at factories, in regiments, in the streets, etc., by means of *peaceful* discussion and peaceful demonstrations, as well as meetings everywhere; we must endeavour to organise regular voting in factories and regiments, taking care that order and comradely discipline are strictly observed.
5. Party propagandists must again and again protest against the despicable slander spread by the capitalists alleging that our Party stands for a separate peace with Germany. We consider Wilhelm II as bad a crowned brigand meriting execution as Nicholas II, and the German Guchkovs, i.e. the German capitalists, just as much annexationists, robbers and imperialists as the Russian, British and all other capitalists. We *are against* negotiating with the capitalists, we are for negotiating and fraternising *with the revolutionary workers and soldiers of all countries.* We are convinced that the reason why the Guchkov-Milyukov government is trying to aggravate the situation is because it knows that the workers' revolution in Germany is beginning, and that this revolution will be a blow to the capitalists of all countries.

6. When the Provisional Government spreads rumours about utter and unavoidable economic chaos, it is not only trying to frighten the people into leaving the power in the hands of this Provisional Government, but is also vaguely, fumblingly expressing the profound and indubitable truth that *all* the nations of the world have been led into a blind alley, that the war waged in the interests of the capitalists has driven them to the brink of an abyss, and that there is really no way out except through the transfer of power to the revolutionary class, i.e. to the revolutionary proletariat, which is capable of adopting revolutionary measures.

   If there are any stocks of grain, etc., in the country, the new government of the workers and soldiers will know how to dispose of them too. But if the capitalist war has brought economic ruin to a stage where there is no bread at all, the capitalist government will only aggravate the condition of the people instead of improving it.

7. We consider the policy of the present majority of leaders of the Soviet of Workers' and Soldiers' Deputies, of the Narodnik and Menshevik parties, to be profoundly erroneous, since confidence in the Provisional Government, attempts to compromise with it, dickering over amendments, etc., would in fact mean only so many more useless scraps of paper and useless delays; and besides, this policy threatens to create a divergence between the will of the Soviet on the one hand, and that of the majority of revolutionary soldiers at the front and in Petrograd, and of the majority of workers, on the other.

8. We call upon those workers and soldiers who believe that the Soviet must change its policy and renounce the policy of confidence in and compromise with the capitalist government, to hold new elections of delegates to the Soviet of Workers' and Soldiers' Deputies and to send to that body only people who would steadfastly hold to a quite definite opinion consonant with the actual will of the majority.

Honest Defencism Reveals Itself

Published 22 April (5 May) 1917

Events in Petrograd during the last few days, especially yesterday, illustrate how right we were in speaking of the 'honest' defencism of the *mass* as distinguished from the defencism of the leaders and parties.

The mass of the population is made up of proletarians, semi-proletarians, and poor peasants. They are the vast majority of the nation. *These* classes are not at all interested in annexations. Imperialist policies, the profits of banking capital, incomes from railways in Persia, lucrative jobs in Galicia and Armenia, putting restraints on the freedom of Finland – all these are things in which these classes are *not* interested.

But all these things taken together just go to make up what is known in science and the press as imperialist, annexationist, predatory policy.

The crux of the matter is that the Guchkovs, Milyukovs and Lvovs – be they even all paragons of virtue, disinterestedness and love of their fellow-man – are the spokesmen, leaders and chosen representatives of the capitalist *class*, a class which has a vested interest in a predatory, annexationist policy. This class invested billions 'in the war', and is making hundreds of millions 'out of the war' and annexations (i.e. out of the subjugation or forced *incorporation* of alien nationalities).

To believe that the capitalist *class* will 'mend its ways', will cease to be a capitalist class, will give up its profits, is a fatuous hope, an idle dream, and in effect a deception of the people. Only petty-bourgeois politicians, fluctuating between capitalist and proletarian policies, can entertain or encourage such fatuous hopes. Herein lies the mistake of the present leaders of the Narodnik parties and the Mensheviks, Chkheidze, Tsereteli, Chernov and the others.

The mass representatives of defencism are not at all versed in politics. They have not been able to learn politics from books, from participation in the Duma, or from close observation of people engaged in politics.

The mass representatives of defencism still do not know that wars are waged by *governments*, that governments represent the interests of certain *classes*, that the present war, on the part of both belligerent groups, is waged by the capitalists in the predatory interests of and for the predatory aims of the capitalists.

Unaware as they are of this, the mass representatives of defencism argue quite simply: we do not want annexations, we demand a democratic peace, we do not want to fight for Constantinople, for putting down Persia, for plundering Turkey and so on; we 'demand' that the Provisional Government give up its policy of annexations.

The mass representatives of defencism are *sincere* in wishing this, not in a personal but in a class sense, because they speak for classes that are *not interested* in annexations. But what these representatives of the masses do not know is that the capitalists and their government may throw over the policy of annexations in words, may dangle promises and mouth fine phrases, but cannot *really* abandon the idea of annexations.

That is why the mass representatives of defencism were so strongly and legitimately shocked by the Provisional Government's Note of 18 April (1 May).

People familiar with politics could not have been surprised by this Note, for they knew only too well that when the capitalists 'renounce annexations' they do not really mean it. It is just the usual trick and phrase-mongering of diplomats.

But the 'honest' mass representatives of defencism were surprised, shocked, indignant. They *felt* – they did not understand it quite clearly, but they felt that they had been tricked.

This is the *essence* of the crisis and it should be clearly distinguished from the opinions, expectations and suppositions of single individuals and parties.

To patch up this crisis for a while with a new declaration, with a new Note (that is what Mr. Plekhanov's advice in *Yedinstvo* and the aspirations of Milyukov and co., on the one hand, and those of Chkheidze and Tsereteli, on the other, amount to) – to paper over the cracks with a new promise is of course possible, but this can do nothing but harm. A new promise would inevitably mean a new deception of the masses; therefore a new outburst of indignation, and such an outburst, if lacking intelligent orientation, might easily become very harmful.

The masses should be told the whole truth. The government of the capitalists *cannot* abandon annexations; it is caught in its own meshes and there is no escape. It feels, it realises, it sees that without revolutionary measures (of which only a revolutionary class is capable) *there is no way out*, and it is becoming panicky, losing its head; it promises one thing, but does another; at one minute it threatens the masses with violence (Guchkov and Shingarev), at the next it proposes that the power be taken out of its hands.

Economic ruin, crisis, the horrors of war, an impasse from which there is no way out – this is what the capitalists have brought *all* the nations to.

Indeed there is no way out – *except* through the transfer of power to the revolutionary class, to the revolutionary proletariat, which alone, supported by the majority of the population, is capable of aiding the revolution to victory in *all* the belligerent countries and leading humanity to lasting peace and liberation from the yoke of capitalism.

Resolution of the CC of the RSDLP(B)

Adopted in the Morning of 22 April (5 May) 1917

The political crisis that developed between 19 and 21 April (2-4 May) must be regarded, at least in its initial stage, as having passed.

The petty-bourgeois mass, angered by the capitalists, first swung *away from* them *towards* the workers; but two days later they again followed the Menshevik and Narodnik leaders, who stand for 'confidence' in and 'compromise' with the capitalists.

These leaders have compromised, completely surrendered all their positions, contenting themselves with the empty and purely verbal reservations of the capitalists.

The causes of the crisis have not been removed, and the recurrence of such crises is unavoidable.

The nature of the crisis is that the petty-bourgeois mass is vacillating between its age-old faith in the capitalists and its resentment against them, a tendency to place its faith in the revolutionary proletariat.

The capitalists are dragging out the war and covering up the fact by phrase-mongering. Only the revolutionary proletariat can put an end to, and is working towards putting an end to the war by means of a world revolution of the workers, a revolution which is obviously mounting in our country, ripening in Germany, and drawing closer in a number of other countries.

The slogan 'Down with the Provisional Government!' is an incorrect one at the present moment because, in the absence of a solid (i.e. a class-conscious and organised) majority of the people on the side of the revolutionary proletariat, such a slogan is either an empty phrase, or, objectively, amounts to attempts of an adventurist character.

We shall favour the transfer of power to the proletarians and semi-proletarians only when the Soviets of Workers' and Soldiers' Deputies adopt our policy and are willing to take the power into their own hands.

The organisation of our Party, the consolidation of the proletarian forces, clearly proved inadequate at the time of the crisis.

The slogans of the moment are:

1. To *explain* the proletarian line and the proletarian way of ending the war;
2. To *criticise* the petty-bourgeois policy of placing trust in the government of the capitalists and compromising with it;
3. To carry on propaganda and agitation from group to group *in every regiment*, in *every* factory and, particularly, among the most backward masses, such as domestic servants, unskilled labourers, etc. since it was their backing in the first place that the bourgeoisie tried to gain during the crisis;
4. To *organise*, *organise* and once more *organise* the proletariat, in every factory, in every district and in every city quarter.

The resolution of the Petrograd Soviet of 21 April (4 May) banning all street meetings and demonstrations for two days must be unconditionally obeyed by every member of our Party. The Central Committee already distributed yesterday morning, and is today publishing in *Pravda*, a resolution which states that "at such a moment any thought of civil war would be senseless and preposterous", that all demonstrations must be peaceful ones, and that the responsibility for violence will fall on the Provisional Government and its supporters.[1] Our Party therefore considers that the above mentioned resolution of the Soviet of Workers' and Soldiers' Deputies as a whole (and especially the part banning armed demonstrations and shooting in the air) is entirely correct and must be *unconditionally obeyed.*

We call upon all the workers and soldiers to consider carefully the results of the crisis of the last two days and to send as delegates to the Soviet of Workers' and Soldiers' Deputies and to the Executive Committee only such comrades as express the will of the majority, in all cases where a delegate does not express the opinion of the majority, new elections should be held in the factories and barracks.

1 See 'Resolution of the Central Committee of the RSDLP(B) – Adopted 21 April (4 May) 1917', in this volume, p. 121.

Lessons of the Crisis

Written 22 April (5 May) 1917

Petrograd and the whole of Russia have passed through a serious political crisis, the first political crisis since the revolution.

On 18 April (1 May) the Provisional Government issued its unhappily notorious Note, which confirmed the predatory aims of the war clearly enough to arouse the indignation of the masses, who had honestly believed in the desire (and ability) of the capitalists to 'renounce annexations'. On 20-21 April (3-4 May) Petrograd was in a turmoil. The streets were crowded; day and night knots and groups of people stood about, and meetings of various sizes sprang up everywhere; big street processions and demonstrations went on without a break. Yesterday evening, 21 April, the crisis, or, at any rate, the first stage of the crisis, apparently came to an end with the Executive Committee of the Soviet of Workers' and Soldiers' Deputies, and later the Soviet itself, declaring themselves satisfied with the 'explanations', the amendments to the Note and the 'elucidations' made by the government (which in fact boil down to empty phrases, saying absolutely nothing, changing nothing and committing the government to nothing). They considered the 'incident settled'.

Whether the masses consider the 'incident settled', the future will show. Our task now is to make a careful study of the *forces*, the classes, that revealed themselves in the crisis, and to draw the relevant lessons for our proletarian party. For it is the great significance of all crises that they make manifest what has been hidden; they cast aside all that is relative, superficial and trivial; they sweep away the political litter and reveal the real mainsprings of the *class struggle.*

Strictly speaking, the capitalist government on 18 April (1 May) merely reiterated its previous notes, in which the imperialist war was invested with diplomatic equivocations. The soldiers were angry because they had honestly believed in the sincerity and peaceful intentions of the capitalists. The demonstrations began as *soldiers'* demonstrations, under the contradictory, misguided and ineffectual slogan: 'Down with Milyukov' (as though a change of persons or groups could change the *substance* of policy!).

This means that the broad, unstable and vacillating mass, which is closest to the peasantry and which by its scientific class definition is petty-bourgeois, swung *away from* the capitalists *towards* the revolutionary workers. It was the swing or movement of this mass, strong enough to be a *decisive* factor, that caused the crisis.

It was at this point that other sections began to stir: *not* the middle but the extreme elements, *not* the intermediary petty bourgeoisie but the bourgeoisie and the proletariat, started to come out on to the streets and organise.

The bourgeoisie seized Nevsky Prospekt – or 'Milyukov' Prospekt as one paper called it – and the adjacent quarters of prosperous Petrograd, the Petrograd of the capitalists and the government officials. Officers, students and 'the middle classes' demonstrated *in favour* of the Provisional Government. Among the slogans, "Down with Lenin" frequently appeared on the banners.

The proletariat rallied in *its own* centres, the working-class suburbs, around the slogans and appeals of our Party's Central Committee. On 20-21 April the Central Committee adopted resolutions, which were immediately passed on to the proletariat through the Party organisations. The workers poured through the *poor,* less central districts, and then in groups got through to Nevsky. By their mass character and solidarity, these demonstrations were very different from those of the bourgeoisie. Many banners carried the inscription "All Power to the Soviet of Workers' and Soldiers' Deputies".

On Nevsky there were clashes. The 'hostile' demonstrations tore down each other's banners. The Executive Committee received news by telephone from various places that there was shooting on both sides, that there were killed and wounded; but the information was extremely contradictory and unconfirmed.

The bourgeoisie shouted about the 'spectre of civil war', thus expressing its fear that the real masses, the actual majority of the nation, might seize power. The petty-bourgeois leaders of the Soviet, the Mensheviks and Narodniks – who since the revolution in general, and during the crisis in particular, have had no definite party policy – allowed themselves to be intimidated. In the Executive Committee almost half the votes were cast against the Provisional Government on the eve of the crisis, but now thirty-four votes (with nineteen against) are cast *in favour* of returning to a policy of confidence in and agreement with the capitalists.

And the 'incident' was considered 'settled'.

What is the *essence* of the class struggle? The capitalists are *for* dragging out the war under cover of empty phrases and false promises. They are caught in the meshes of Russian, Anglo-French and *American* banking capital. The proletariat, as represented by its class-conscious vanguard, stands *for* the transfer of power to the revolutionary class, the working class and the semi-proletarians, *for* the development of a world workers' revolution, a revolution which is clearly developing also in Germany, and *for* terminating the war by means of *such* a revolution.

The vast mass of people, chiefly the petty bourgeoisie, who still believe the Menshevik and Narodnik leaders and who have been absolutely intimidated by the bourgeoisie and are carrying out *its* policy, although with reservations, are swinging now to the right, now to the left.

The war is terrible; it has hit the vast mass of the people hardest of all; it is these people who are becoming aware, albeit still very vaguely, that the war is criminal, that it is being carried on through the rivalry and scramble of the capitalists, for the division of *their* spoils. The world situation is growing more and more involved. *The only way out* is a world workers' revolution, a revolution which is *now* more advanced in Russia than in any other country, but which is clearly mounting (strikes, fraternisation) in Germany too. And the people are wavering: wavering between confidence in their old masters, the capitalists, and bitterness towards them; between confidence in the new class, the only consistently revolutionary class, which opens up the prospect of a bright future for all the working people – the proletariat – and a vague awareness of its role in world history.

This is not the first time the petty bourgeoisie and semi proletarians have wavered *and it will not be the last!*

The lesson is clear, comrade workers! There is no time to be lost. The first crisis will be followed by others. You must devote *all* your efforts to enlightening the backward, to making extensive, comradely and direct contact (not only by meetings) with every regiment and with every group of working people who have not had their eyes opened yet! *All* your efforts must be devoted to consolidating your own ranks, to organising the workers from the bottom upwards, including every district, every factory, every quarter of the capital and its suburbs! Do *not* be misled by those of the petty bourgeoisie who 'compromise' with the capitalists, by the defencists and by the 'supporters', nor by individuals who are inclined to be in a hurry and to shout 'Down with the Provisional Government!' before the majority of the people are solidly united. The crisis cannot be overcome by violence practised by individuals against individuals, by the local action of small groups of armed people, by Blanquist attempts to 'seize power', to 'arrest' the Provisional Government, etc.

Today's task is to explain more precisely, more clearly, more widely the proletariat's policy, *its* way of terminating the war. Rally more resolutely, more widely, wherever you can, to the ranks and columns of the proletariat! Rally round your Soviets; and within them endeavour to rally behind you a majority by comradely persuasion and by re-election of individual members!

The 'Crisis of Power'

Published 2 (15) May 1917

The whole of Russia remembers the days of 19-21 April (2-4 May), when civil war was about to break out in the streets of Petrograd.

On 21 April the Provisional Government penned a new 'reassuring missive' purporting to 'explain' its predatory Note of the 18th.[1]

After this the majority of the Executive Committee of the Soviet of Workers' and Soldiers' Deputies decided to consider the 'incident settled'.

Another couple of days passed, and the question of a coalition cabinet cropped up. The Executive Committee was almost equally divided: twenty-three against a coalition cabinet, twenty-two for it. The incident had been 'settled' only on paper.

Two more days passed, and we now have another 'incident'. War Minister Guchkov, one of the leaders of the Provisional Government, has resigned. There is talk of the whole Provisional Government having decided to resign. (At the time of writing, we still do not know for certain whether the government has resigned.) A new

1 The Provisional Government's statement published in the central newspapers on 22 April (5 May) 1917 'elucidating' Foreign Minister Milyukov's Note of 18 April (1 May) 1917. By this 'elucidation' the Provisional Government tried to cover up the imperialist character of the Note, which had announced the intention of continuing the war 'to decisive victory'.

'incident' has occurred, one that throws all previous 'incidents' into the shade.

Whence this spate of 'incidents'? Is there no root cause which inevitably engenders 'incident' upon 'incident'?

There *is* such a cause. It is what we know as the dual power, that state of unstable equilibrium resulting from the agreement between the Soviet and the Provisional Government.

The Provisional Government is a government of the capitalists. It cannot give up its dreams of conquests (annexations), it cannot end the predatory war by a democratic peace, it cannot but protect the profits of its own class (the capitalist class), it cannot but protect the estates of the landowners.

The Soviet represents other classes. Most of the workers and soldiers in the Soviet do not want this predatory war, they are not interested in the profits of the capitalists or in preserving the privileges of the landowners. At the same time, however, they still have faith in the Provisional Government of the capitalists, they are for having agreements with it, for keeping in contact with it.

The Soviets of Workers' and Soldiers' Deputies are themselves a government in embryo. On some questions they attempt to exercise power parallel with the Provisional Government. We thus have an overlapping of power, or, as it is now called, a 'crisis of power'.

This cannot go on for long. Such a state of affairs is bound every day to cause new 'incidents' and fresh complications. It is easy enough to inscribe on a bit of paper 'the incident is settled'. In real life, however, these incidents do not disappear. And this for the simple reason that they are not 'incidents' at all, they are not chance happenings, not trifles. They are the outward signs of a deep-rooted inner crisis. They are a result of the impasse in which humanity now finds itself. There can be no way out of this predatory war unless we accept the measures proposed by the internationalist socialists.

The Russian people are offered three ways of ending this 'crisis of power'. Some say: "Leave things as they are, put still greater trust in the Provisional Government. The threat to resign may be a trick calculated to make the Soviet say: We trust you still more. The

Provisional Government wants the Soviet to beg it: Come and rule over us; what shall we do without you…"

Others propose a coalition cabinet. "Let us share the ministerial portfolios with Milyukov and co.", they say, "let us get some of our own people into the cabinet; it will be quite another pair of shoes then."

We propose a third way: A complete change of the Soviets' policy, no confidence in the capitalists, and the *transfer of all power to the Soviets of Workers' and Soldiers' Deputies.* A change of *personalities* will give nothing; the whole *policy* must be changed. Another class must assume power. A government of workers and soldiers would be trusted by the whole world, for everyone knows that a worker and a poor peasant would want to rob no one. Only this can put a speedy end to the war, only this can help us through the economic debacle.

All power to the Soviets of Workers' and Soldiers' Deputies! No confidence in the government of the capitalists!

Every 'incident', every day, every hour will confirm the *soundness* of this watchword.

They Have Forgotten the Main Thing

The Municipal Platform of the Proletarian Party

Published 5 (18) May 1917

Elections to the district councils being close at hand, the two petty-bourgeois democratic parties, the Narodniks and the Mensheviks, have come out with high-sounding platforms. These platforms are exactly the same as those of the European bourgeois parties who are engaged in angling for the gullible uneducated mass of voters from among the petty proprietors, etc., such as, for instance, the platform of the Radical and Radical-Socialist Party of France. The same specious phrases, the same lavish promises, the same vague formulations, the same silence on or forgetfulness of the main thing, namely, the *actual conditions* on which the practicability of these promises depends.

At present these conditions are:

1. The imperialist war;

2. The existence of a capitalist government;

3. The impossibility of seriously improving the condition of the workers and the whole mass of working people without revolutionary encroachment on the 'sacred right, of capitalist private property';
4. The impossibility of carrying out the reforms promised by those parties while the old organs and machinery of government remain intact, while there exists a police force which is bound to back the capitalists and put a thousand and one obstacles in the way of such reforms.

For example: "House rents is in war time to be controlled", "such stocks to be requisitioned for the public needs" (that is stocks of foodstuffs kept in stores or by private individuals) "communal stores, bakeries, canteens and kitchens to be organised", write the Mensheviks. "Proper attention to be paid to sanitation and hygiene", echo the Narodniks (the Socialist-Revolutionaries).

Excellent wishes, to be sure. The trouble is that they cannot be carried out unless one *stops* supporting the imperialist war, stops supporting the loan (which is profitable to the capitalists), stops supporting the capitalist government, which safeguards capitalist profits, stops preserving the police, who are bound to obstruct, thwart and kill any such reform, even if the government and the capitalists themselves did not present an ultimatum to the reformers (and they certainly will, once capitalist profits are involved).

The trouble is that once we forget the harsh and rigid conditions of capitalist domination, then all such platforms, all such lists of sweeping reforms are empty words, which in practice turn out to be either harmless 'pious wishes', or simple hoodwinking of the masses by ordinary bourgeois politicians.

We must face the truth squarely. We must not gloss it over, we must tell it to people in a straightforward manner. We must not brush the class struggle under the carpet, but clarify what relation it bears to the high-sounding, specious, delightful 'radical' reforms.

Comrade workers, and all other citizens of Petrograd! In order to give the people all those pressing and essential reforms of which the Narodniks and the Mensheviks speak, one must throw over the policy of support for the imperialist war and war loans, support for the capitalist government and for the principle of the inviolability of capitalist profits. To carry out those reforms, one must *not allow the police to be reinstated*, as the Cadets are now doing, but have it replaced by a people's militia. This is what the party of the proletariat should tell the people at elections, this is what it must say *against* the petty-bourgeois parties of the Narodniks and the Mensheviks. This is the essence of the proletarian municipal platform that is being glossed over by the petty-bourgeois parties.

Foremost in this platform, topping the list of reforms, there must be, as a basic condition for their actual realisation, the following three fundamental points:

1. No support for the imperialist war (either in the form of support for the war loan, or in any other form).
2. No support to the capitalist government.
3. No reinstatement of the police, which must be replaced by a people's militia.

Unless attention is focused on these cardinal questions, unless it is shown that all municipal reforms are contingent upon them, the municipal programme inevitably becomes (at best) a pious wish.

Let us examine point 3.

In all bourgeois republics, even the most democratic, the police (like the standing army) is the chief instrument of oppression of the masses, an instrument making for a possible restoration of the monarchy. The police beats up the 'common people' in the police stations of New York, Geneva and Paris; it favours the capitalists either because it is bribed to do so (America and other countries), or because it enjoys wealthy 'patronage' and 'protection' (Switzerland), or because of a combination of both (France). Separated as it is from the people, forming a professional caste of men trained in the practice of violence upon the poor, men who receive somewhat higher pay and the privileges that go with authority (to say nothing of 'gratuities'), the police everywhere, in every republic, however democratic, where the bourgeoisie is in power, always remains the unfailing weapon, the chief support and protection of the bourgeoisie. No important radical reforms in favour of the working masses can be implemented through the police. That is objectively impossible.

A people's militia instead of the police force and the standing army is a *prerequisite* of effective municipal reforms in the interests of the working people. At a time of revolution this prerequisite is practicable. And it is on this that we must concentrate the whole municipal platform, for the other two cardinal conditions apply to the state as a whole, and not only to municipal governments.

Just how this people's militia can be brought into existence is something which experience will show. To enable the proletarians and semi-proletarians to serve in this militia, the employers must be made to pay them their full wages for the days and hours they spend in service. This is practicable. Whether we should *first* organise a workers' militia by drawing upon the workers employed at the large factories, i.e. the workers who are best organised and most capable of fulfilling the task of militiamen, or whether we should *immediately* organise general compulsory service for all adult men and women, who would devote to this service one or two weeks a year and so on, is not a question of fundamental importance. There is no harm in the different districts adopting different procedures – in fact, it would make for richer experience, and the process of organisation would develop more smoothly and come closer to life's practical requirements.

A people's militia would mean education of the *masses* in the practices of democracy.

A people's militia would mean government of the poor by the people themselves, chiefly by the poor, and *not* by the rich, not through *their* police.

A people's militia would mean that control (over factories, dwellings, the distribution of products, etc.) would be *real* and not merely on paper.

A people's militia would mean distribution without any bread queues, *without any* privileges for the rich.

A people's militia would mean that quite a number of the serious and radical reforms listed also by the Narodniks and the Mensheviks would *not* remain mere pious wishes.

Comrades, working men and women of Petrograd! Go to the district council elections. Protect the interests of the poor population. Come out against the imperialist war, against support of the capitalist government, against the restoration of the police and for the immediate unqualified replacement of the police by a people's militia.

Nothing Has Changed

Published 11 (24) May 1917

Now that 'socialists' have become members of the cabinet,[1] things will be different, the defencists have been assuring us. It did not take more than a few days to reveal the falsity of these assurances.

We all know what indignation was aroused among the soldiers and workers by ex-Minister Milyukov's statement that he had no intention of publishing the secret treaties which ex-Tsar Nicholas II had concluded with the British and French capitalists. And now, what does Mr. Tereshchenko, the *new* Minister of Foreign Affairs, the associate of Skobelev and Tsereteli, have to say on this question?

Tereshchenko admits that "this question [i.e. the secret treaties] arouses passions". But what does he do to cool these passions? He simply *repeats* what Milyukov, who has just been deposed, said before him.

"Immediate publication of the treaties would amount to a break with the Allies", Tereshchenko declared in a statement to the press.

And the 'socialist' ministers are silent and condone the system of secret diplomacy.

---

1 The representatives of the 'socialist' parties who joined the coalition Provisional Government formed on 5 (18) May 1917 were Tsereteli and Skobelev (Mensheviks), Kerensky and Chernov (SRs), Pereverzev (closely connected with the SRs) and Peshekhonov (Popular Socialist Party).

The coalition cabinet has brought no changes. The tsar's secret treaties remain sacred to it.

And you, gentlemen, want this not to 'arouse passions'? What do you take the class-conscious workers and soldiers for? Or do you really regard them as 'rebellious slaves'?

Impending Debacle

Published 14 (27) May 1917

News, speculation, apprehensions and rumours of an impending disaster are becoming more and more frequent. The capitalist newspapers are trying to frighten people; they are fulminating against the Bolsheviks and making play of Kutler's[1] cryptic allusions to "a certain" factory, to "certain" factories, to "a certain" enterprise and so forth. Peculiar methods, strange 'proofs'. Why not *name* a definite factory? Why not give the public *and the workers* a chance to verify these rumours, which are deliberately calculated to excite alarm?

It should not be difficult for the capitalists to understand that by withholding the exact facts about definite specified factories they are only making themselves ridiculous. Why, gentlemen – you capitalists are the government, you have ten out of the sixteen ministers, you bear the responsibility, you give the orders. Is it not ridiculous that people who run the government, people who have a majority in it, should confine themselves to Kutler's anonymous references, should be afraid to come out in the open and should try to shift responsibility to other parties that are not at the helm of the state?

The newspapers of the petty-bourgeois parties, the Narodniks and Mensheviks, are also complaining, though in a somewhat different

1 Cadet and prominent politician in Russia from 1904.

tone. They do not so much level accusations against the terrible Bolsheviks (that, of course, is all in the day's work) as heap one good wish upon another. Most typical in this respect is *Izvestia*, which is run by a bloc of the two above-named parties. In its issue No. 63 for 11 (24) May are two articles on the subject of combating economic chaos. The articles are identical in character. One of them, to put it mildly, is injudiciously headed (altogether as 'injudicious' as the very fact of the Narodniks and Mensheviks joining the imperialist cabinet): 'What Does the Provisional Government Want?' It would have been more correct to say: 'What the Provisional Government Does *Not* Want and What it Promises'.

The other article is a 'resolution of the Economic Department of the Executive Committee of the Soviet of Workers' and Soldiers' Deputies'. Here are some quotations from it, best illustrative of its contents:

> Many branches of industry are ripe for a state trade monopoly (grain, meat, salt, leather), others are ripe for the organisation of state – controlled trusts (coal, oil, metallurgy, sugar, paper); and, finally, present conditions demand in the case of nearly all branches of industry state control of the distribution of raw materials and manufactures, as well as price filing… Simultaneously, it is necessary to place all banking institutions under state and public control in order to combat speculation in goods subject to state control… At the same time, the most energetic measures should be taken against the workshy, even if labour conscription has to be introduced for that purpose… The country is already in a state of catastrophe, and the only thing that can save it is the creative effort of the whole nation *headed by a government* which has consciously shouldered [ahem! ahem!] the stupendous task of rescuing a country ruined by war and the tsarist regime.

With the exception of the last phrase beginning with the words we have italicised, a phrase which with purely philistine credulity places on the 'shoulders' of the capitalists tasks they are incapable of fulfilling, the programme is an excellent one. We have here control, state-controlled trusts, the combating of speculation, labour conscription – in what way does this differ from 'terrible' Bolshevism, what more could these 'terrible' Bolsheviks want?

That is just the point, that is the crux of the matter, that is just what petty bourgeoisie and philistines of all shades and colours stubbornly refuse to see. They are *forced* to accept the programme of 'terrible' Bolshevism, because no other programme offers a way out of the really calamitous debacle that is impending. *But* – there is this but – the capitalists 'accept' this programme (see the famous section 3 of the declaration of the 'new' Provisional Government)[2] *in order not to carry it out.* And the Narodniks and Mensheviks trust the capitalists, and encourage the people to share this fatal trust. That is the sum and substance of the political situation.

Control over the trusts, with publication of their full reports, with immediate conferences of their employees, with the unqualified participation in this control of the *workers themselves*, with independent control on the part of representatives of every important political party – all this can be introduced by decree which can be drafted in a *single day*.

What is the difficulty then, Citizens Shingarevs, Tereshchenkos, Konovalovs? What is stopping you, Citizens, near-socialist ministers Chernov and Tsereteli? What is stopping you, Citizens Narodnik and Menshevik leaders of the Executive Committee of the Soviet of Workers' and Soldiers' Deputies?

Neither we nor anybody else could have proposed anything but the *immediate* establishment of such control over the trusts, banks, trade, food supply and the *workshy* (a surprisingly good word to come from the pen of the *Izvestia* editors!). Nothing better could be devised than "the creative effort of the whole nation".

Only we must not trust the word of the capitalists; we must not believe the naive (at best, naive) hope of the Mensheviks and Narodniks that the capitalists can establish such control.

2 Issued on 6 (19) May 1917 by the first coalition Provisional Government. Paragraph 3 of this document read:

> The Provisional Government will redouble its determined efforts to combat economic disorganisation by developing planned state and public control of production, transport, commerce and distribution of products, and where necessary will resort also to the organisation of production.

A debacle is impending. Disaster is imminent. The capitalists are heading all countries to destruction. There is only one way out: revolutionary discipline, revolutionary measures by the *revolutionary class*, the proletarians and semi proletarians, the transfer of all power in the state to that class, a class that is really capable of instituting such control, that is able to cope effectively with the 'workshy'.

Has Dual Power Disappeared?

Published 20 May (2 June) 1917

It has not. Dual power still remains. The basic question of every revolution, that of state power, is still in an uncertain, unstable and obviously transitory state.

Compare the papers of the cabinet, *Rech*, for instance, with *Izvestia*, *Dyelo Naroda* and *Rabochaya Gazeta*. Scan the meagre – unfortunately all too meagre – official reports of what is going on at the meetings of the Provisional Government, of how the government 'postpones' discussion of the most vital issues, because of its inability to take any definite course. Study the resolution of the Soviet's Executive Committee passed on 16 (29) May, which deals with such a crucial and momentous question as that of how to cope with economic chaos and avert imminent debacle – and you will see that dual power is absolutely intact.

Everyone admits that the country is swiftly heading for disaster – yet all that is done about it is to brush the question under the carpet.

Is it not sidestepping the issue when a resolution on such a grave question as impending economic catastrophe, at such a grave moment, merely creates a spate of commissions, departments and sub-departments; when the same Executive Committee passes a resolution expressing nothing but pious wishes on such a scandalous affair as that of the Donets coal mine owners who were found guilty of deliberately disorganising production? Price fixing, profit regulation, the establishment of a minimum wage and the formation of state-controlled trusts – yes, but how, through whom?

> Through the central and local institutions in the Donets Krivoi Rog Basin. These institutions must be democratic in character and made up of representatives of the workers, employers, the government and democratic revolutionary organisations[!].

This would be comical if the matter involved were not a tragedy.

It is common knowledge that such 'democratic' institutions have existed and still exist locally and in Petrograd (the very same Executive Committee of the Soviet) but they are powerless to do anything. Meetings between the Donets workers and the employers have been going on since the end of March – *March!* Over six weeks have passed and the result is that the Donets workers have been forced to the conclusion that the coal mine owners are deliberately disorganising production!

And again the people are fed with promises, commissions, meetings between representatives of the workers and employers (in equal numbers?), and the old red tape starts all over again.

The root of the evil is in the dual power. The root of the Narodniks' and Mensheviks' error is that they do not understand the class struggle, and want to replace or cloak it, reconcile it by means of phrases, promises, resolutions, commissions 'with the participation' of representatives... of the same dual government!

The capitalists have made fantastic, outrageous fortunes out of the war. They have the majority of the government on their side. They want to rule supreme; in view of their class position they are bound to make a bid for supreme power and fight for it.

The working masses constitute the vast majority of the population, they control the Soviets, they are aware of their power as a majority, they see everywhere the promise of a 'democratised' life, they know that democracy is the rule of the majority over the minority (*and not the reverse* – which is what the capitalists want), they have been striving to better their lives only since the revolution (and then not everywhere), and not since the beginning of the war – therefore they cannot but aspire towards supreme rule by the people, i.e. the majority of the population, towards affairs being managed according to the will of the worker majority as opposed to the capitalist minority, and not according to an 'agreement' between the majority and the minority.

Dual power still remains. The government of the capitalists remains a government of the capitalists, despite the appended tag of Narodniks and Mensheviks in a minority capacity. The Soviets remain the organisation of the majority. The Narodnik and Menshevik leaders are floundering helplessly in an attempt to straddle two stools.

Meanwhile the crisis is growing. Things have reached a point where the capitalists – the coal mine owners – are brazenly committing outrageous *crimes* – *they* are *disorganising and stopping* production. Unemployment is spreading. There is talk of lockouts. Actually they have *started* in the form of disorganisation of production by the capitalists (for coal is the *bread of industry!*), in the form of growing unemployment.

Sole responsibility for this crisis, for the impending catastrophe, rests with the Narodnik and Menshevik leaders. For it is they who are at present the leaders of the Soviets, i.e. of the majority. That the minority (the capitalists) should be unwilling to submit to the majority is inevitable. No person who has not forgotten the lessons which science and the experience of all countries teach us, no person who has not forgotten the class struggle, will look trustfully towards 'an agreement' with the capitalists on such an essential, burning question.

The majority of the population, i.e. the Soviets, the workers and peasants, would be fully able to save the situation, prevent the capitalists from disorganising and stopping production, establish *their own* immediate and effective control over production if it were not for the 'conciliatory' policy of the Narodnik and Menshevik leaders. They bear full responsibility for the crisis and the catastrophe.

There is *no* way out, however, other than by the worker and peasant majority deciding to act against the capitalist minority. Playing for time will not help, it will only make matters worse.

Viewed from a Marxist angle, the 'conciliatory' attitude of the Narodnik and Menshevik leaders is a manifestation of petty-bourgeois indecision. The petty bourgeoisie is afraid to trust the workers, and is afraid to break with the capitalists. Such wavering is inevitable, as inevitable as our struggle, the struggle of the proletarian party, to overcome indecision, and to make the people see the necessity for rehabilitating, organising and increasing production in the teeth of capitalist opposition.

There is no other way out. Either we go back to supreme rule by the capitalists, or forward towards real democracy, towards majority decisions. This dual power cannot last long.

A Question of Principle

'Forgotten Words' of Democracy

Written before 25 May (7 June) 1917

Editor's note:

The sailors, soldiers and workers of the military workshops in Kronstadt played a very important part in preparing the victory of the October armed uprising in Petrograd. The Kronstadt Soviet of Workers' and Soldiers' Deputies followed the lead of the Bolsheviks from the very first day of its existence. This was due to the revolutionary traditions of Kronstadt (the mutinies of 1905 and 1906, the uprising on the battleship *Gangut* in 1915) and to the existence of a strong Bolshevik organisation there which carried on revolutionary work all through the war.

Owing to the conflict between the Kronstadt Soviet and the Commissar of the Provisional Government, Pepelyaev, a resolution moved by the non-party section of the Soviet and supported by the Bolsheviks was passed on 17 (30) May 1917 abolishing the office of Government Commissar and vesting all power in the Kronstadt Soviet. This resolution stated that the sole authority in the town of Kronstadt was the Soviet of Workers' and Soldiers' Deputies, which, on affairs of state concern, entered into direct contact with the Petrograd Soviet of Workers' and Soldiers' Deputies.

The bourgeois, SR and Menshevik press raised a hue and cry against the men of Kronstadt and the Bolsheviks, declaring that Russia was on the verge of collapse and anarchy, that Kronstadt was seceding and so on.

A delegation from the Petrograd Soviet (Chkheidze, Gotz and others) followed by one from the Provisional Government (Ministers Skobelev and Tsereteli) went out to settle the Kronstadt incident. The latter succeeded in getting a decision passed through the Kronstadt Soviet arranging a compromise settlement, under which the Commissar was to be elected by the Soviet and endorsed by the Provisional Government. In addition, a general political resolution was adopted in which the Kronstadt Soviet declared that it recognised the authority of the Provisional Government, but that this "recognition does not, of course, exclude criticism and the desire that revolutionary democracy should create a new organisation of central authority by vesting all power in the Soviets of Workers' and Soldiers' Deputies". The resolution also expressed the hope that the Bolsheviks would succeed in achieving this. It ended with a strong protest against attempts to ascribe to the Kronstadt Bolsheviks the intention of separating Kronstadt from the rest of Russia.

Lenin considered the revolutionary action in Kronstadt to have been premature. The negotiations by the Bolshevik group of the Kronstadt Soviet to settle the conflict and the further work of the Kronstadt Party organisation were directed by Lenin.

* * *

The filthy torrent of lies and slander which the capitalist papers have spewed out against the Kronstadt comrades has revealed once more how dishonest these papers are. They have seized on a quite ordinary and unimportant incident and magnified it to the dimensions of a 'state' affair, of 'secession' from Russia and so on and so forth.

Izvestia of the Petrograd Soviet, No. 74, reports that the Kronstadt incident has been settled. As was to have been expected, Ministers Tsereteli and Skobelev easily came to an understanding with the Kronstadt people on the basis of a compromise resolution. Needless to say, we express our hope and confidence that this compromise resolution, provided *both* sides faithfully live up to it, will, for a sufficiently lengthy period of time, eliminate conflicts in the work of the *revolution* both in Kronstadt and the rest of Russia.

The Kronstadt incident is a matter of principle to us in two respects.

First, it has revealed a fact long ago observed by us and officially recognised in our Party's resolution (on the Soviets), namely, that in the *local areas* the revolution has gone farther than it has in Petrograd. Succumbing to the current craze for the revolutionary phrase, the Narodniks and Mensheviks as well as the Cadets did not wish to or could not grasp the significance of this fact.

Secondly, the Kronstadt incident raised an important, fundamental issue of programmatic significance, which no honest democrat, to say nothing of a socialist, can afford to treat with indifference. It is the question of whether the central authority has the right to *endorse* officials elected by the local population or not.

The Mensheviks, to whose party ministers Tsereteli and Skobelev belong, still claim to be Marxists. Tsereteli and Skobelev got a resolution passed in favour of such endorsement. In doing so, did they stop to think of their duty as Marxists?

Should the reader find this question naive and pass a remark to the effect that the Mensheviks now have really become a petty-bourgeois, even defencist (i.e. chauvinist) party, and therefore it would be ludicrous even to talk about Marxism, we shall not argue the point. All we shall say is that Marxism always gives close attention to questions of democratism, and the name of democrats can hardly be denied to citizens Tsereteli and Skobelev.

Did they stop to think of their duty as democrats, of their 'title' as democrats, when they passed the resolution authorising the Provisional Government to 'endorse' officials elected by the Kronstadt population?

Obviously, they did not.

In support of this conclusion, we shall quote the opinion of a writer who, we hope, even in the eyes of Tsereteli and Skobelev, is considered something of a scientific and Marxian authority. That writer is Friedrich Engels.

In criticising the draft programme of the German Social-Democrats (now known as the Erfurt Programme) Engels wrote in 1891 that the German proletariat was in need of a single and united republic.

> But not such a republic as the present French Republic, which is really an empire founded in 1798 but without an emperor. From 1792 to 1798 every French department, every commune enjoyed complete self-government after the American pattern. That is what we [the German Social-Democrats] should have too. How self-government can be organised and how a bureaucracy can be dispensed with has been demonstrated to us by America and the First French Republic, as well as by Australia, Canada and other British colonies even today. Such provincial and communal self-government is much freer than, for instance, Swiss federalism, where each canton is really independent of the confederation [i.e. the central government] but at the same time is the supreme authority as far as the minor subdivisions of the canton are concerned – the Bezirk and the Commune. The cantonal governments appoint the Bezirksstatthalter[1] and Prefects. This right of appointing local officers is entirely unknown in English-speaking countries, and in future we must politely abolish this right [i.e. appointment from above], just as we should the Prussian Landräthe and Regierungsräthe.[2]

Such was Engels' opinion on questions of democracy as applied to the right of appointing officers from above. To express these views with greater precision and accuracy, he proposed that the German Social-Democrats should insert in their programme the following demand:

> Complete self-government in the communes, districts and regions through officers elected by universal suffrage; *abolition of all state-appointed local and regional authorities.*[3]

The italicised words leave nothing to be desired in the way of clarity and definiteness.

---

1 District governors.

2 See Engels, Friedrich, 'A Critique of the Draft Social-Democratic Programme of 1891', *MECW*, Vol. 27, pp. 228-9.

3 Ibid., p. 229.

Worthy citizens, Ministers Tsereteli and Skobelev! You are probably flattered to have your names mentioned in history books. But will it be flattering to have every Marxist – and every honest democrat – say that Ministers Tsereteli and Skobelev helped the Russian capitalists to build such a republic in Russia as would turn out to be not a republic at all, but *a monarchy without a monarch?*

* * *

PS: This article was written *before* the Kronstadt incident entered its last stage, as reported in today's papers. The Kronstadt people have *not* broken the compromise agreement. *Not a single fact* remotely suggesting a breach of this agreement has been cited. *Rech's* reference to newspaper articles is mere subterfuge, since you can only break an agreement by deeds and not by newspaper articles. The fact then remains, that Ministers Tsereteli, Skobelev and co. have allowed themselves to be scared for the hundredth and thousandth time by the screams of the frightened bourgeoisie and have resorted to *gross threats* against the people of Kronstadt. Crude, absurd threats, that merely serve the counter-revolution.

The Harm of Phrase-Mongering

Published 31 May (13 June) 1917

The answers of the French and the British governments clearly demonstrate the soundness of our repeated assertions that neither the Russian, nor the French, nor the British, nor the German capitalist governments can throw over the policy of annexations, and that all such promises are designed to deceive the peoples.[1]

We are fighting to seize Alsace-Lorraine, we are fighting for victory, the French replied. Be good enough to comply with the treaty and fight for Russian and German Poland, the British replied.

The bitter truth that capitalism cannot be reconciled to a non-annexationist policy has been exposed once more. The policy of the 'conciliators', of those who wish to reconcile the capitalists and the proletariat, the policy of the Narodnik and Menshevik ministerialists, is an obvious failure. All their hopes on a coalition government have been shattered, all their promises have been exposed as mere verbiage.

And most harmful of all, as far as the cause of the revolution and the interests of the toiling masses are concerned, is the attempt to cover up the whole thing with phrases. Two shadings stand out in this torrent of phrases, one as bad as the other.

---

1 This refers to the replies of the French and British governments to the declaration of the Provisional Government of 27 March (9 April) 1917, both expressing the hope of Russia's continued cooperation in fighting to win the war.

Rabochaya Gazeta, the organ of the Menshevik ministerialists, brings grist to the Cadet mill. On the one hand, it says:

> On this basis [on the basis of the answers of the two Allied powers] there can be no agreement between them and us…

When they say "us", do they mean the Russian *capitalists*? The theory of the class struggle is thrown overboard; it is much more profitable to spout phrases about 'democracy' in the abstract, while trampling underfoot the elementary truth of Marxism, namely, that it is precisely *within* a 'democracy' that the gulf between the capitalists and the proletarians is widest.

On the other hand, *Rabochaya Gazeta* wishes to make:

> … an attempt at revision [of the agreements and treaties] through a conference of representatives of the Allied governments to be specially convened.

The same old story: agreement with the capitalists, which, in fact, signifies *deception of the workers* by playing at negotiations with their class foes.

"The pressure of the rank and file of the French and British democracies, even pressure by the French and British proletariat alone upon their respective governments", writes *Rabochaya Gazeta*.

In Russia the Mensheviks are supporting *their own* imperialist government, but in other countries they want *pressure* to be brought to bear…

What is this, if not sheer phrase-mongering and humbug from beginning to end?

"We are working for it [for world peace] by convening an international socialist conference…" to be attended by ministers from among those ex-socialists who have sided with *their* governments! This is 'working' with a vengeance to deceive the people on a major scale by means of a series of minor deceptions.

We have *Dyelo Naroda* phrase-mongering 'à la Jacobin'. That stern tone, those spectacular revolutionary exclamations:

> … we know enough […] faith in the victory of our Revolution [with a capital letter, of course] upon this or that step […] of the Russian revolutionary democracy depend the destinies […] of the *entire* Uprising [with a capital letter, of course] which the working people have so happily and so victoriously begun.

Obviously, if you write the words Revolution and Uprising with capital letters it makes the thing look 'awfully' frightening, just like the Jacobins. Plenty of effect at small expense. For the people who write this are virtually helping to crush the revolution and impede the uprising of the working people by supporting the *Russian* government of the imperialists, by supporting *their* methods of concealing from the people the secret treaties, *their* tactics of putting off the immediate abolition of the landed estates, by supporting *their* war policy of 'offensive', *their* high-handed insulting behaviour towards the local representative bodies, *their* presumption to appoint or endorse the local officers elected by the local population, and so on *ad infinitum*.

Gentlemen, heroes of the phrase, knights of revolutionary bombast! Socialism demands that we distinguish between capitalist democracy and proletarian democracy, between bourgeois revolution and proletarian revolution, between a rising of the rich against the tsar and a rising of the working people *against the rich*. Socialism demands that we distinguish our bourgeois revolution, which has ended (the bourgeoisie now is counter-revolutionary), from the mounting revolution of the proletarians and poor peasants. The former revolution is *for* war, *for* preserving the landed estates, *for* 'subordinating' the local organs of self-government to the central government, *for* secret treaties. The latter revolution has *begun* to throttle the war by revolutionary fraternisation, by abolishing the power of the landowners in the local areas, by increasing the number and the power of the Soviets and by introducing everywhere the elective principle.

The Narodnik and Menshevik ministerialists are spouting phrases about 'democracy' in the abstract, about 'Revolution' in the abstract in order to *cover up* their agreement with the imperialist, now definitely counter-revolutionary, bourgeoisie of their own country – an agreement which, in effect, is turning into a struggle *against* the revolution of the proletarians and semi-proletarians.

The Petty-Bourgeois Stand on the Question of Economic Disorganisation

Written 31 May (13 June) 1917

Novaya Zhizn today publishes a resolution introduced by Comrade Avilov at a meeting of shop committees.[1] Unfortunately, this resolution must be regarded as an example of a petty-bourgeois attitude that is neither Marxist nor socialist. Because this resolution accentuates in sharp focus all the weaknesses peculiar to the Menshevik and Narodnik Soviet resolutions, it is typical and worthy of attention.

The resolution begins with an excellent general statement, with a splendid indictment of the capitalists:

> The present economic debacle [...] is a result of the war and the *predatory anarchic rule of the capitalists and the government.*

Correct! That capital is oppressive, that it is a predator, that it is the original source of anarchy – in this the petty bourgeoisie is

1 Avilov left the Bolsheviks in 1917 and joined Bazarov, Lindov and others to form the United Social-Democrat Internationalists, who aimed to bring together the Menshevik-Internationalists with the more moderate Bolsheviks into a new group. The group's organ was *Novaya Zhizn.*

ready to agree with the proletariat. But there the similarity ends. The proletarian regards capitalist economy as a robber economy, and therefore wages a class struggle against it, shapes his whole policy on unconditional distrust of the capitalist class, and in dealing with the question of the state his first concern is to distinguish which class the 'state' serves, whose class interests it stands for. The petty bourgeois, at times, gets 'furious' with capital, but as soon as the fit of anger is over he goes back to his old faith in the capitalists, to the hopes placed in the 'state'... of the capitalists!

The same thing has happened with Comrade Avilov.

After a splendid, strongly worded, formidable introduction accusing the capitalists and even the government of the capitalists of running a 'robber' economy, Comrade Avilov, throughout his resolution, in all its concrete substance and all its practical proposals, *forgets the class stand point*, and, like the Mensheviks and Narodniks, lapses into bombast about the 'state' in general, about 'revolutionary democracy' in the abstract.

Workers! Predatory capital is creating anarchy and economic chaos, and the government of the capitalists, too, is ruling by anarchy. Salvation lies in control on the part of "the state with the cooperation of revolutionary democracy". This is the substance of Avilov's resolution.

What are you talking about, Comrade Avilov! How can a Marxist forget that the state is an organ of class rule? Is it not ridiculous to appeal to a *capitalist state* to take action against 'predatory capitalists'?

How can a Marxist forget that in the history of all countries the capitalists, too, have often been 'revolutionary democrats', as in England in 1649, in France in 1789, in 1830, 1848 and 1870 and in Russia in February 1917?

Can you have forgotten that the revolutionary democracy of the capitalists, of the petty bourgeoisie and of the proletariat must be distinguished one from the other? Does not the *whole* history of *all* the revolutions I have just mentioned show a distinction of classes *within* 'revolutionary democracy'?

To continue in Russia to speak of 'revolutionary democracy' in general after the experience of February, March, April and May 1917 is to deceive the people knowingly or unknowingly, consciously or unconsciously. The 'moment' of general fusion of classes against tsarism has come and gone. The very first agreement between the first 'Provisional Committee' of the Duma and the Soviet marked the *end* of the class fusion and the beginning of the class struggle.

The April crisis (20 April), followed by that of 6 May, then 27-29 May (the elections), etc., etc., have brought about a definite cleavage of *classes* in the Russian revolution within the Russian 'revolutionary democracy'. To ignore this is to sink to the helpless level of the petty bourgeois.

To appeal now to the 'state' and to 'revolutionary democracy' on the matter of predatory capitalism of all questions, is to drag the working class backward. *In effect* it means preaching complete stoppage of the revolution. For our 'state' *today*, after April, after May, is a state of 'predator' capitalists, who, in the persons of Chernov, Tsereteli and co., have *tamed* a fairly considerable portion of 'revolutionary (petty-bourgeois) democracy'.

This state is hindering the revolution everywhere, in all fields of home and foreign policy.

To hand over to *this* state the job of fighting the capitalist 'predators' is like *throwing the pike into the river.*[2]

2 The offending fish, in Ivan Krylov's fable, was sentenced to be drowned by being thrown into the river.

A Mote in the Eye

Published 1 (14) June 1917

Algeria let them down... Our ministerial 'Socialist-Revolutionaries' had almost succeeded in stunning the public – and themselves – into believing all their talk about 'peace without annexations', but... Algeria let them down. *Dyelo Naroda*, a newspaper to which two Socialist-Revolutionary ministers, Kerensky and Chernov, contribute, was incautious enough to invite the views of three Allied cabinet ministers (belonging to the same near-socialist camp) on Algeria. How terribly careless this was on the part of the newspaper of the Kerenskys and Chernovs will be seen from the following.

The three Allied ministers – Henderson, Thomas and Vandervelde of Britain, France and Belgium, stated that they did not want "annexation", but only "liberation of territories". The paper of the Kerenskys and Chernovs described this – quite rightly – as a "sleight of hand" on the part of the 'tamed socialists', and poured out on them the following angry and sarcastic tirade:

> True, they [the three ministers] demand the liberation of territories only "in conformity with the will of the population". Very well! But in that case we ought to demand that they, and we, be consistent and recognise the 'liberation' of Ireland and Finland on the one hand and Algeria or

> Siam on the other. It would be very interesting to hear the opinion of, say, the socialist Albert Thomas on 'self-determination' for Algeria.

Indeed, "it would be very interesting to hear the opinion" also of Kerensky, Tsereteli, Chernov and Skobelev on "self-determination" for Armenia, Galicia, Ukraine and Turkestan.

Don't you see, you Narodnik and Menshevik members of the Russian Government, that by citing the example of Ireland and Algeria you have exposed the whole lie and falsity of your own position and behaviour. You have shown that 'annexation' *cannot* be interpreted merely as the seizure of territory *in this war*. In other words, you have refuted yourselves and *Izvestia* of the Petrograd Soviet, which only the other day declared with proud ignorance that the term annexation could be applied only to territories seized in the present war. But who does not know that Ireland and Algeria were annexed decades and centuries before the outbreak of this war?

Careless, very careless of *Dyelo Naroda*! It has exposed its utter confusion of ideas, and that of the Mensheviks and *Izvestia*, on such a key issue as annexations.

Nor is that all. You question Henderson about Ireland and Albert Thomas about Algeria; you contrast the views on annexation of the "French *bourgeoisie* now in power" with the views of the French *people*; you call Henderson and Albert Thomas "tamed socialists" – but what about yourselves?

What are you, Kerensky, Tsereteli, Chernov, Skobelev, if not "tamed socialists"? Did *you* raise the question of the *Russian* Ireland and the *Russian* Algeria, i.e. of Turkestan, Armenia, Ukraine, Finland, etc., before the government of the 'Russian *bourgeoisie* now in power'? When did you raise this question? Why don't you tell the Russian 'people' about it? Why don't you qualify as "sleight of hand" the *Russian* Narodniks' and Mensheviks' blether about "peace without annexations" in the Soviet, in the government and before the people, *without raising*, clearly and unambiguously, the question of *all Russian* annexations of the same type as Ireland and Algeria?

The Russian ministeriable Narodniks and Mensheviks are in a hopeless muddle; every passing day adds to their self-exposure.

Their 'final' stock argument is that we are having a revolution. But that argument is false from beginning to end. For our revolution *so far* has only brought the *bourgeoisie* to power, as in France and Britain, with a 'harmless minority' of 'tamed socialists', as in France and Britain. What our revolution will produce tomorrow – whether a return to the monarchy, the strengthening of the bourgeoisie, or the transfer of power to more advanced classes – neither we nor anyone else knows. Consequently, the plea of 'revolution' in general is a gross deception of the people and of oneself.

The annexation issue is a good touchstone for the Narodniks and Mensheviks, who are entangled in a web of lies. They are *just as* muddled as Plekhanov, Henderson, Scheidemann and co.; they are distinguishable from each other *only in words*, for as far as *deeds* are concerned they are all alike – dead to socialism.

The Enemies of the People

Published 7 (20) June 1917

Plekhanov's *Yedinstvo* (which even the Socialist-Revolutionary *Dyelo Naroda* justly calls a newspaper at one with the liberal bourgeoisie) has recently recalled the law of the French Republic of 1793 relating to enemies of the people. A very timely recollection.

The Jacobins of 1793 belonged to the most revolutionary class of the eighteenth century, the town and country poor. It was against this class, which had in fact (and not just in words) done away with its monarch, its landowners and its moderate bourgeoisie by the most revolutionary measures, including the guillotine – against this truly revolutionary class of the eighteenth century – that the monarchs of Europe combined to wage war.

The Jacobins proclaimed enemies of the people those "promoting the schemes of the allied tyrants directed against the Republic".

The Jacobins' example is instructive. It has not become obsolete to this day, except that it must be applied to the revolutionary class of the twentieth century, to the workers and semi-proletarians. To this class, the enemies of the people in the twentieth century are not the monarchs, but the landowners and capitalists as a class.

If the 'Jacobins' of the twentieth century, the workers and semi-proletarians, assumed power, they would proclaim enemies of the people the capitalists who are making thousands of millions in profits from the imperialist war, *that is*, a war for the division of capitalist spoils and profits.

The 'Jacobins' of the twentieth century would not guillotine the capitalists – to follow a good example does not mean copying it. It would be enough to arrest fifty to a hundred financial magnates and bigwigs, the chief knights of embezzlement and of robbery by the banks. It would be enough to arrest them for a few weeks *to expose their frauds* and show all exploited people 'who needs the war'. Upon exposing the frauds of the banking barons, we could release them, placing the banks, the capitalist syndicates and all the contractors 'working' for the government under workers' control.

The Jacobins of 1793 have gone down in history for their great example of a truly revolutionary struggle against *the class of the exploiters by the class of the working people and the oppressed* who had taken *all* state power into their own hands.

The miserable *Yedinstvo* (with which the Menshevik defencists were ashamed to form a bloc) wants to borrow Jacobinism in letter and not in spirit, its exterior trappings and not the content of its policy. This amounts in effect to a betrayal of the revolution of the twentieth century, a betrayal disguised by spurious reference to the revolutionaries of the eighteenth century.

'The Great Withdrawal'

Published 8 (21) June 1917

"The great withdrawal of the bourgeoisie from the government." This is what the main speaker of the Executive Committee, in a report he submitted last Sunday, called the formation of the coalition government and the entry of former socialists into the Ministry.

Only the first three words in this phrase are correct. "The great withdrawal" does indeed characterise and explain 6 (19) May (the formation of the coalition government). It was on that day that "the great withdrawal" really began, or, to be exact, manifested itself most clearly. Only, it was not a great withdrawal of the bourgeoisie from the government but a great withdrawal of the Menshevik and Narodnik leaders *from* the revolution.

The significance of the Congress of Soviets of Soldiers' and Workers' Deputies now in session lies in the fact that it has made this circumstance clearer than ever.

6 May was a triumph for the bourgeoisie. The bourgeois government was on the verge of defeat. The masses were definitely and absolutely, sharply and irreconcilably opposed to it. One word from the Narodnik and Menshevik leaders of the Soviet would have sufficed to induce the government to relinquish its power unquestioningly. Lvov had to admit that openly at the sitting in the Mariinsky Palace.

The bourgeoisie resorted to a skilful manoeuvre which was new to the Russian petty bourgeoisie and to Russia's masses in general, which intoxicated the intellectual Menshevik and Narodnik leaders, and which took proper account of their Louis Blanc nature. The reader may recall that Louis Blanc was a renowned petty-bourgeois socialist who entered the French Government in 1848 and became as sadly famed in 1871. Louis Blanc imagined himself to be *the leader* of the 'labour democrats' or 'socialist democrats' (the term 'democracy' was used in the France of 1848 as frequently as in *Socialist-Revolutionary* and Menshevik writing in 1917), but in reality he was the *tail-end* of the bourgeoisie, a play thing in their hands.

During the almost seventy years that have elapsed since then, that manoeuvre, which is a novelty in Russia, has been made many times by the bourgeoisie in the West. The purpose of this manoeuvre is to make the 'socialist democratic' leaders who 'withdraw' from socialism and from the revolution harmless *appendages* of a bourgeois government, to shield this government from the people by means of near-socialist Ministers, to cover up the counter-revolutionary nature of the bourgeoisie by a glittering, spectacular facade of 'socialist' ministerialism.

This method has been developed to a veritable art in France. It has also been tested on many occasions in Anglo-Saxon, Scandinavian and many of the Latin countries. It is this manoeuvre that was made in Russia on 6 May 1917.

'Our' near-socialist Ministers found themselves in a situation in which the bourgeoisie began to use *them* as their cat's paw, to do *through them* what the bourgeoisie could never have done without them.

Through Guchkov it would have been impossible to lure the people into continuing the *imperialist*, predatory war, a war *for redivision* of the colonies and annexed territories in general. Through Kerensky (and Tsereteli, who was busier defending Tereshchenko than defending the post and telegraph workers), the bourgeoisie were able, as correctly admitted by Milyukov and Maklakov, to begin 'organising' the continuation of this kind of war.

Through Shingarev it would have been impossible to ensure the preservation of the landed estates system at least until the convocation of the Constituent Assembly (if an offensive were to take place, it would "enable Russia to recover completely", said Maklakov. That means that the Constituent Assembly itself would be 'healthier'). Through Chernov, this can be brought about. The peasants have been told, although they have not been very glad to hear it, that to rent land from the landowners by agreement with each individual owner is 'order', while to abolish the landed estates at one stroke and rent *from the people*, pending the convocation of the Constituent Assembly, land formerly owned by the landowners is 'anarchy'. This counter-revolutionary idea of the landowners could only be put into effect through Chernov.

Through Konovalov it would have been impossible to ensure the safeguarding (*and the increase* – see what the ministerial newspaper, *Rabochaya Gazeta*, writes about the coal industrialists) of the scandalous profits from war contracts. Through Skobelev, or with his participation, this safeguarding can be ensured by allegedly preserving the old order, by near-'Marxist' rejection of the possibility of 'introducing' socialism.

Because socialism cannot be introduced, the scandalously high profits made by the capitalists – not from their purely capitalist business *but from supplies to the armed forces, to the* state – these profits *can* be both concealed from the people and retained! This is the wonderful Struvean argument which has brought together Tereshchenko and Lvov, on the one hand, and the 'Marxist' Skobelev, on the other.[1]

Popular meetings and the Soviets cannot be influenced through Lvov, Milyukov, Tereshchenko, Shingarev and the rest. But they can be influenced through Tsereteli, Chernov and co. in the same old

1 Referring to Peter Struve, who before the turn of the twentieth century was a member of the RSDLP. He moved progressively to the right, working first exclusively as a leading 'Legal Marxist', a trend of intellectuals in the RSDLP who spread their ideas in a watered-down form in legal journals. He continued this shift and in 1905 co-founded the Cadets.

bourgeois direction. And one can pursue *the same old* bourgeois-imperialist policy by means of particularly impressive, particularly 'nice'-sounding phrases, to the point of denying the people the elementary democratic right to *elect* local authorities and prevent both their appointment and confirmation from above.

By denying this right, Tsereteli, Chernov and co. have unwittingly turned from ex-socialists into ex-democrats.

A "great withdrawal", all right!

Confused and Frightened

Published 11 (24) June 1917

Editor's note:

Early in June, tensions in Petrograd grew. The prolongation of the war by the Provisional Government, preparations for an offensive at the front and food shortages caused resentment and indignation among the workers and soldiers. The government's order for troops to take over the Durnovo country-house and evict the workers' organisations of the Vyborgskaya Storona district from it gave rise to a strike. On 7 (20) June four factories went on strike and the next day, twenty-eight. The masses were eager to hold a street demonstration.

To ward off provocation and unnecessary loss of life, a joint meeting of the Central and Petrograd Committees, the Military Organisation, district delegates from the workers, and delegates from troop units, held on 8 (21) June, carried Lenin's motion to organise a peaceful organised demonstration. The action was set for Saturday 10 (23) June.

The Bolshevik's decision to hold a demonstration brought a ready response from the masses and alarmed the government, as well as the Mensheviks and SRs, who resolved to foil the demonstration. On the evening of 9 (22) June the First All-Russia Congress of Soviets, led by the Mensheviks and SRs, passed a resolution banning all street demonstrations for three days.

> On a motion by Lenin, the CC of the Bolshevik Party, not wishing to go against the Congress decision, resolved that night to call off the demonstration. Members of the Central and Petrograd Committees and other prominent members of the Party were sent to factories and barracks to dissuade the workers and soldiers from demonstrating. As a result of their explanatory work, the workers and soldiers agreed that it would be unwise to hold a demonstration at that time.

* * *

The atmosphere in Petrograd is one of fright and confusion reaching truly unparalleled dimensions.

This was illustrated by a small incident prior to the big incident of banning the demonstration fixed by our Party for Saturday.

This small incident was the seizure of Durnovo's country house. Minister Pereverzev first ordered the house cleared, but then declared at the Congress that he was letting the people use the garden and that the trade unions were not to be evicted from the house! All that was necessary, he said, was to arrest certain anarchists.[1]

If the seizure of Durnovo's country house was unlawful, then it was *wrong* either to leave the garden for the people's use or to allow the trade unions to remain in the house. If there were

1 After the victory of the February Revolution the workers' organisations of the Vyborgskaya Storona district (the bakers' union, the district branch of the people's militia, etc.), joined by the anarchists, took over the vacant country house of tsarist ex-Minister Durnovo and the adjoining garden (20 dessiatins in area), re-purposing the property as recreation grounds.
On 7 (20) June the Provisional Government, backed by the SR and Menshevik majority in the Petrograd Soviet and then by the First All-Russia Congress of Soviets, ordered the property to be vacated. The order brought protests from the Petrograd workers, particularly those of Vyborgskaya Storona. Several factories went on strike. The government yielded, but on the night of 18-19 June (1-2 July) it sent a contingent of Cossacks and soldiers which took the country house by assault, killing two anarchists and arresting fifty-nine people. As the overwhelming majority of the arrested had nothing to do with the anarchists, they had to be released shortly after. The raid deeply angered the workers.
For several weeks the bourgeois press was busy playing up the 'horrors' which it alleged to have taken place at the country house and used this particular incident to campaign against the revolutionary-minded masses and the Bolsheviks.

lawful grounds for arrest, the arrest had *no* bearing on the house, for it could have occurred *either* in the house *or* outside it. As it happened, the house was not 'vacated', nor were any arrests made. The government found itself confused and frightened. Had they not become nervous, there would have been no 'incident', for nothing has changed anyway.

The big incident was the demonstration. Our Party's Central Committee, together with a number of other organisations, including the Trade Union Bureau, resolved to call a peaceful demonstration, a march through the streets of the capital. In all constitutional countries, the holding of such a demonstration is an absolutely incontestable civil right. A peaceful street demonstration calling, incidentally, for an amendment of the Constitution or a change in the government is in no way regarded as unlawful by the legislation of any free country.

People who were confused and frightened, including, in particular, the majority at the Congress of Soviets, made an awful 'fuss' over the demonstration. The Congress majority adopted a devastating resolution against the demonstration, full of abuse against our Party, and *prohibited* all demonstrations, including peaceful ones, for three days.

When this formal decision had been adopted, the Central Committee of our Party, as early as 2 am on Saturday, resolved to cancel the demonstration. The cancellation was effected on Saturday morning at an emergency meeting with district representatives.

The question remains: *how* does our second 'government' the Congress of Soviets, *explain* its ban? Agreed that every party in a free country has the right to hold demonstrations, and every government can, after proclaiming a state of emergency, prohibit them. But the political question remains: why was the demonstration banned?

Here is the only political motive, clearly stated in the resolution of the Congress of Soviets:

> We know that concealed counter-revolutionaries want to take advantage of your demonstration [i.e. the one planned by our Party]…

That is the reason why the peaceful demonstration was banned. The Congress of Soviets 'knows' that there are 'concealed counter-revolutionaries' and that they wanted to 'take advantage' of the action which our Party had planned.

This statement by the Congress of Soviets is highly significant. And we must re-emphasise this *factual* statement, which by virtue of its factualness stands out from the spate of abuse levelled at us. What measures is our second government taking against the 'concealed counter-revolutionaries'? What exactly does this government 'know'? How exactly did the counter-revolutionaries want to take advantage of one pretext or another?

The people cannot and will not wait patiently and passively until those concealed counter-revolutionaries act.

If our second government does not want to remain like people who by bans and torrents of abuse try to cover up their confusion and the fact that they have allowed themselves to be frightened by the Right, it will have to *tell* the people a great deal about the "concealed counter-revolutionaries" and *do* a great deal to combat them seriously.

Speech on the Cancellation of the Demonstration

Delivered at a Meeting of the Petrograd Committee of the RSDLP(B)

11 (24) June 1917

The dissatisfaction voiced by most comrades over the cancellation of the demonstration is quite natural, but the Central Committee had no alternative for two reasons: first, we were formally banned from holding the demonstration by the semi-organ of power; secondly, the motive for the ban was stated as follows:

> We know that concealed forces of the counter-revolution want to take advantage of your demonstration.

In support of this motive, we were given names, such as that of a general, whom they promised to arrest within three days, and others. And they declared that a demonstration of the Black Hundreds had been arranged for 10 (23) June with the intention of breaking into our demonstration and turning it into a skirmish.

Even in ordinary warfare, it sometimes happens that a planned offensive has to be cancelled for strategic reasons. This is all the more likely to occur in class warfare, depending on the vacillation of the middle, petty-bourgeois groups. We must be able to take account of the situation and be bold in adopting decisions.

The cancellation was absolutely necessary, as subsequent developments proved. Today Tsereteli has delivered his historical and hysterical speech.[1] Today the revolution has entered a new phase of its development. They began by banning our peaceful demonstration for three days, and now they want to ban it for the entire duration of the Congress. They demand that we obey the decision of the Congress under threat of expulsion from the Congress. But we have declared that we prefer arrest rather than renounce freedom of propaganda.

Tsereteli, whose speech showed him up as a blatant counter-revolutionary, declared that the Bolsheviks must not be fought by words and resolutions, but must be deprived of all the technical means they have at their disposal. The result of all bourgeois revolutions is: first arm the proletariat and then disarm it to prevent it from going any further. The fact that a peaceful demonstration had to be banned shows that the situation must be very serious.

Tsereteli, who emerged from the depths of the Provisional Government to attend the Congress, clearly expressed a desire to disarm the workers. He was savagely furious in demanding that the Bolshevik Party be ousted from the ranks of the revolutionary democrats. The workers must clearly realise that there can now be no question of a peaceful demonstration. The situation is far more serious than we thought. We were going to hold a peaceful demonstration in order to exercise maximum pressure on the decisions of the Congress – that is our right – but we are accused of hatching a plot to arrest the government.

---

1 Reference is to the speech made by the Menshevik Irakli Tsereteli, member of the Provisional Government, on 11 (24) June 1917. In his speech, Tsereteli said the demonstration which the Bolsheviks had scheduled for 10 (23) June was "a Bolshevik conspiracy to overthrow the government and seize power". The speech was slanderous and counter-revolutionary throughout.

Tsereteli says that there are no counter-revolutionaries apart from the Bolsheviks. The meeting that passed judgment on us was organised with particular solemnity. It consisted of the Congress Steering Committee, the Executive Committee of the Soviet of Workers' and Soldiers' Deputies in full force and the bureaus of the groups of all the parties attending the Congress. At that meeting they blurted out the whole truth, namely, that they are calling an offensive against us.

The proletariat must reply by showing the maximum calmness, caution, restraint and organisation, and must remember that peaceful processions are a thing of the past.

We must give them no pretext for attack. Let them attack, and the workers will realise that it is an attack on the very existence of the proletariat. But reality is on our side, and it is a moot point whether their attack will succeed – at the front there are the troops, among whom discontent is very strong, and in the rear there is the high cost of living, economic dislocation and so on.

The Central Committee does not want to force your decision. Your right, the right to protest against the actions of the Central Committee, is a legitimate one, and your decision must be a free one.

The Turning-Point

Published 13 (26) June 1917

At the first stage of its development the Russian revolution transferred power to the imperialist bourgeoisie, and created, alongside of that power, the Soviets of Deputies, with the petty-bourgeois democrats in the majority. The second stage of the revolution (6 (19) May) formally removed from power the cynically frank spokesmen of imperialism, Milyukov and Guchkov, and virtually transformed the majority parties in the Soviets into governing parties. Our Party remained, before and after 6 May, a minority opposition. This was inevitable, for we are the party of the socialist proletariat, a party holding an internationalist position. A socialist proletariat whose outlook during an imperialist war is internationalist cannot but be in opposition to any power waging that war, regardless of whether that power is a monarchy or republic, or is held by defencist 'socialists'. And the party of the socialist proletariat is bound to attract an increasingly large mass of people who are being ruined by the protracted war and are growing distrustful of 'socialists' committed to the service of imperialism, in the same way as they previously grew distrustful of imperialists themselves.

The struggle against our Party, therefore, began in the very first days of the revolution. And however infamous and abominable the forms of struggle carried on by the Cadets and the Plekhanov people against the party of the proletariat, the meaning of the struggle is quite clear. It is the same struggle as the imperialists and the Scheidemann people waged against Liebknecht and Adler (both of whom were, in fact, declared 'mad' by the central organ of the German 'socialists', to say nothing of the bourgeois press, which described these comrades simply as 'traitors' working for Britain). This is a struggle of the *whole* of bourgeois society, *including the petty-bourgeois democrats,* however r-r-revolutionary they may be, against the socialist, internationalist proletariat.

In Russia, this struggle has reached a stage where the imperialists are trying, through the petty-bourgeois-democratic leaders, the Tseretelis, Chernovs, etc. to destroy the growing power of the workers' party at a single hard and decisive blow. As a pretext for this decisive blow, Minister Tsereteli has struck upon a method repeatedly used by counter-revolutionaries: *the charge of conspiracy.* This charge is a mere pretext. The point is that the petty-bourgeois democrats, who take their cue from the Russian and the Allied imperialists, need to do away with the internationalist socialists once and for all. They think that the moment is ripe for the blow. They are agitated and frightened, and under the whip of their masters they have made up their minds: now or never.

The socialist proletariat and our Party must be as cool and collected as possible, must show the greatest staunchness and vigilance. Let the future Cavaignacs begin first.[1] Our Party conference has already given warning of their arrival. The workers of Petrograd will give them no opportunity to disclaim responsibility. They will bide their time, gathering their forces and preparing for resistance *when* those gentlemen decide to turn from words to action.

---

1 Louis-Eugène Cavaignac was the notorious French general who, as Minister of War, led the suppression of the Paris workers' uprising in June 1848. Appointed Chief of the Executive Power in France from June-December 1848.

The Class Origins of Present-Day and 'Future' Cavaignacs

Published 16 (29) June 1917

"When a real Cavaignac comes, we shall fight in the same ranks with you", we were told in No. 80 of *Rabochaya Gazeta*, organ of the very same Menshevik party whose member, Minister Tsereteli, in his notorious speech, went to such lengths as to threaten to disarm the Petrograd workers.

The above-quoted statement clearly brings out the fundamental errors of Russia's two ruling parties, the Mensheviks and Socialist-Revolutionaries, and therefore deserves attention. The ministerial organ's arguments mean that you are looking for Cavaignacs at the wrong time and in the wrong place.

Remember the class role played by Cavaignac. In February 1848 the French monarchy was overthrown. The bourgeois republicans came to power. Like our Cadets, they wanted 'order', by which they meant the restoration and strengthening of monarchic instruments for oppressing the masses: the police, the standing army and the privileged bureaucracy. Like our Cadets, they wanted to put an end to the revolution, for they hated the revolutionary workers with their 'social' (i.e. socialist) aspirations, at that time very hazy. Like our Cadets, they were implacably hostile to the policy of extending the

French Revolution to the rest of Europe, the policy of transforming it into a world proletarian revolution. Like our Cadets, they skilfully used the petty-bourgeois 'socialism' of Louis Blanc by making him a Minister and so transforming him from leader of the socialist workers, which he had wanted to be, into an appendage, a hanger-on, of the bourgeoisie.

These were the class interests, the position and policy of the ruling class.

The petty bourgeoisie, vacillating, frightened by the red spectre, and falling for the outcries against the 'anarchists', were another basic social force. Dreamily and bombastically 'socialist' in their aspirations, and readily calling themselves 'socialist democrats' (even this term is now taken up by the Socialist-Revolutionaries and the Mensheviks!), the petty bourgeoisie were afraid to entrust themselves to the leadership of the revolutionary proletariat, and did not realise that fear condemned them to entrusting themselves to the bourgeoisie. For there can be *no* 'middle' course in a society rent by bitter class struggle between the bourgeoisie and the proletariat, particularly when this struggle is inevitably aggravated by a revolution. And the whole essence of the class position and aspirations of the petty bourgeoisie is that they want the impossible, that they aspire to the impossible, i.e. to a 'middle course'.

The third decisive class force was the proletariat, which aspired not to 'reconcile itself' with the bourgeoisie, but to defeat them, to fearlessly promote the revolution, doing so, moreover, on an international scale.

That was the objective historical soil which *brought forth* Cavaignac. The vacillation of the petty bourgeoisie 'debarred' them from an active role, and the French Cadet, General Cavaignac, taking advantage of the petty bourgeoisie's fear of entrusting themselves to the proletariat, decided to *disarm* the Paris workers and shoot them down *en masse*.

The revolution ended in that historic shooting. The petty bourgeoisie, while numerically superior, had been and remained the politically impotent tail of the bourgeoisie, and three years later France saw the restoration of a particularly vile form of Caesarist monarchy.

Tsereteli's historic speech on 11 (24) June, clearly inspired by the Cadet Cavaignacs (perhaps directly inspired by the bourgeois Ministers, or perhaps indirectly prompted by the bourgeois press and bourgeois public opinion – it does not matter which), was remarkable and historic in that Tsereteli *let out*, with inimitable naivety, the 'secret malady' of the entire petty bourgeoisie, both Socialist-Revolutionary and Menshevik. This 'secret malady' consists, first, in a complete inability to pursue an independent policy; secondly, in the fear to entrust themselves to the revolutionary proletariat and wholeheartedly support the independent policy *of the latter*; thirdly, in a drift – inevitably following from this – towards submitting to the Cadets or to the bourgeoisie in general (*i.e. submitting to the Cavaignacs*).

This is the heart of the matter. Tsereteli, Chernov and even Kerensky are not destined as individuals to play the role of Cavaignacs. There will be other people to do that, people who at the right moment will tell the Russian Louis Blancs: "Step aside". But the Tseretelis and Chernovs are leaders pursuing a petty-bourgeois policy that makes the appearance of Cavaignacs possible and necessary.

"When a real Cavaignac comes, we shall be with you" – an excellent promise, a splendid intention! Only, it is a pity that it reveals a misunderstanding of the class struggle, typical of the sentimental or timid petty bourgeoisie. For a Cavaignac is not an accident, his 'advent' is not an isolated development. A Cavaignac represents a class (the counter-revolutionary bourgeoisie) and carries out the policies of that class. And it is that class and those policies that you Socialist-Revolutionary and Menshevik gentlemen support *today*. It is to that class and its policies that *you*, who at the moment admittedly command a majority in the country, give *predominance* in the government, i.e. an excellent basis on which to work.

Indeed, the All-Russia Peasant Congress was almost entirely dominated by the Socialist-Revolutionaries. At the All-Russia Congress of Workers' and Soldiers' Deputies, the Socialist-Revolutionary and

Menshevik bloc had a vast majority. The same is true of the elections to the Petrograd district councils. The fact is there: the Socialist-Revolutionaries and Mensheviks are the ruling party now. And this ruling party is voluntarily ceding power (the majority in the government) to the *party of the Cavaignacs!!*

Wherever there's a swamp there's sure to be the devil. Once there is a shaky, vacillating petty bourgeoisie dreading the revolution's progress, the Cavaignacs are sure to appear.

In Russia there are many things now that make our revolution different from the French Revolution of 1848: the imperialist war, the proximity of more advanced countries (and not of more backward ones, as was the case of France at the time), an agrarian and a national movement. But all this may modify only the form in which the Cavaignacs come forward, the moment, the external causes, etc. It cannot change the essence of the matter, for the essence lies in the *class relationships*.

In words, Louis Blanc, too, was as far removed from Cavaignac as heaven is from earth. Louis Blanc, too, made countless promises "to fight in the same ranks" as the revolutionary workers against the bourgeois counter-revolutionaries. Nevertheless, no Marxist historian, no socialist, would venture to doubt that it was the weakness, the instability, the credulity of the Louis Blancs with regard to the bourgeoisie that brought forth Cavaignac and assured his success.

The Russian Cavaignacs are inevitable products of the counter-revolutionary character of the Russian bourgeoisie led by the Cadets and of the instability, timidity and vacillation of the petty-bourgeois parties of the Socialist-Revolutionaries and the Mensheviks. Whether the Russian Cavaignacs will win or lose the battle depends solely on the staunchness, vigilance and strength of Russia's revolutionary workers.

The Eighteenth of June

Published 20 June (3 July) 1917

Editor's note

On 12 (25) June, the SR and Menshevik leadership of the Congress of Soviets decided to hold a demonstration on 18 June (1 July) – the day when the Russian troops were to start an offensive – as proof of the people's 'confidence' in the Provisional Government.

Under Lenin's personal leadership, the Central and Petrograd Committees did a great deal to ensure that the demonstration reflected the true sentiment of the people and win that important peaceful battle against the Mensheviks and SRs for influence among the people.

Lenin took part in preparations for the demonstration by formulating slogans, checking the preparation of streamers and banners, giving directions to correspondents, writing telegrams to be sent to local Bolshevik organisations, taking steps to guarantee that there would be an adequate number of Bolshevik speakers, and putting his own name on the speakers list.

On 18 June (1 July) the demonstration brought some 500,000 Petrograd workers and soldiers out into the streets. By far most of the demonstrators carried Bolshevik revolutionary slogans. Only small groups carried the conciliating parties' slogans expressing confidence in the Provisional Government. The demonstration revealed the heightened revolutionary spirit of the people and the vastly increased influence and prestige of the Bolshevik Party. It also revealed the complete failure of the petty-bourgeois conciliating parties backing the Provisional Government. Lenin dealt with the June demonstration in this article, 'Three Crises' (see p. 215 of this volume) and in other articles.

* * *

In one way or another, 18 June (1 July) will go down as a turning-point in the history of the Russian revolution.

The mutual position of the classes, their correlation in the struggle against each other, their strength, particularly in comparison with the strength of the parties, were all revealed so distinctly, so strikingly, so impressively by last Sunday's demonstration that, whatever the course and pace of further development, the gain in political awareness and clarity has been tremendous.

The demonstration in a few hours scattered to the winds, like a handful of dust, the empty talk about Bolshevik conspirators and showed with the utmost clarity that the vanguard of the working people of Russia, the industrial proletariat of the capital and the overwhelming majority of the troops support slogans that our Party has always advocated.

The measured step of the battalions of workers and soldiers. Nearly half a million demonstrators. A concerted onslaught. Unity around the slogans, among which overwhelmingly predominated: 'All power to the Soviets', 'Down with the ten capitalist Ministers', 'Neither a separate peace treaty with the Germans nor secret treaties with the Anglo-French capitalists', etc. No one who saw the demonstration has any doubt left about the victory of these slogans among the organised vanguard of Russia's workers and soldiers.

The demonstration of 18 June was a demonstration of the strength and policy of the revolutionary proletariat, which is showing the direction for the revolution and indicating the way out of the impasse. This is the tremendous historical significance of last Sunday's demonstration, and its essential difference from the demonstrations during the funeral of the victims of the revolution and on May Day. Then it was a universal *tribute* to the revolution's first victory and to its heroes. The people looked back over the first stage of the road to freedom, which they had passed very rapidly and very successfully. May Day was a *holiday* of hopes and aspirations linked with the history of the world labour movement and with its ideal of peace and socialism.

Neither of the two demonstrations was intended to point the *direction* for the revolution's further development, nor could it do so. Neither demonstration put before the people, or raised in the name of the people, specific, definite and urgent questions as to how and in what direction the revolution should proceed.

In this sense, 18 June was the first political demonstration of *action*, an explanation of how the various classes act, how they want to and will act, in order to further the revolution – an explanation not given in a book or newspaper, but on the streets, not through leaders, but through the people.

The bourgeoisie kept out of the way. They refused to participate in that peaceful demonstration of a clear majority of the people, in which there was freedom of party slogans, and the chief aim of which was to protest against counter-revolution. That is natural. The bourgeoisie are the counter-revolution. They hide from the people. They organise real counter-revolutionary conspiracies against the people. The parties now ruling Russia, the Socialist-Revolutionaries and Mensheviks, clearly showed themselves on that historic day, 18 June, as waverers. Their slogans spoke of wavering, and it was obvious to all that the supporters of their slogans were in a minority. By their slogans and wavering *they* advised the people to remain where they were, to leave everything unchanged for the time being. And the people felt, and they themselves felt, that that was impossible.

Enough of wavering, said the vanguard of the proletariat, the vanguard of Russia's workers and soldiers. Enough of wavering. The policy of trust in the capitalists, in *their* government, in *their vain* attempts at reform, in *their war*, in *their* policy of an offensive, is a hopeless policy. Its collapse is imminent. Its collapse is inevitable. And that collapse will also be the collapse of the ruling parties, the Socialist-Revolutionaries and the Mensheviks. Economic disruption is coming nearer. There is *no* escaping it except by the revolutionary measures of the revolutionary class which has taken power.

Let the people break with the policy of trust in the capitalists. Let them put their trust in the revolutionary class – the proletariat. The source of power lies in it and only *in it*. It alone is the pledge that the interests of the *majority* will be served, the interests of the working and exploited people, who, though held down by war and capital, are capable of defeating war and capital!

A crisis of unprecedented scale has descended upon Russia and the whole of humanity. The only way out is to put trust in the most organised and advanced contingent of the working and exploited people, and support its policy.

We do not know whether the people will grasp this lesson soon or how they will put it into effect. But we do know for certain that apart from this lesson there is no way out of the impasse, that possible waverings or brutalities on the part of the counter-revolutionaries will lead nowhere.

There is no way out unless the masses put complete confidence in their leader, the proletariat.

The Revolution, the Offensive and Our Party

Published 21 June (4 July) 1917

Editor's note:

At the insistence of the Russian and Anglo-French imperialists, the Provisional Government launched an offensive, ordered by the War Minister Kerensky on 16 (29) June. On 18 June (1 July) the Russian troops went on the offensive on the South-Western Front. The operation was successful at first, but later, given inadequate technical preparation as well as the troops' fatigue and lack of understanding of the purpose of the offensive, the German troops forced the Russian troops into a disorderly retreat. The Russian Army sustained a crushing defeat, losing about 60,000 men and officers in ten days.

The news of the enormous casualties angered the working people and hastened a new political crisis in the country.

* * *

"The Russian revolution has reached a turning-point", said Tsereteli informing the Congress of Soviets that the offensive had begun. Yes, the whole course of the world war as well as the Russian revolution has reached a turning-point. After three months of vacillation the Russian Government has actually come to the decision demanded by the 'Allied' governments.

The offensive has been declared in the name of peace. And it is also 'in the name of peace' that the imperialists of the world send their troops into battle. Every time there is an offensive the generals in every belligerent country try to raise their troops' morale by holding out the real hope of that particular offensive leading to early peace.

The Russian 'socialist' Ministers have garnished this common imperialist method with very high-sounding phrases in which words about socialism, democracy and revolution sound like rattles in the hands of a clever juggler. But no high-sounding phrases can conceal the fact that the revolutionary armies of Russia have been sent into battle in the name of the imperialist designs of Britain, France, Italy, Japan and America. No arguments from Chernov, once a Zimmerwaldist and now Lloyd George's[1] partner, can conceal the fact that while the Russian Army and the Russian proletariat do not really pursue any annexationist aims, this does not in the least change the imperialist, predatory nature of the struggle between the two world trusts. Until the secret treaties binding Russia to the imperialists of other countries are revised, and as long as Ribot,[2] Lloyd George and Sonnino,[3] Russia's allies, continue to talk about the annexationist aims of their foreign policy, the offensive of the Russian troops will continue to serve the imperialists.

Tsereteli and Chernov object, however, that they have repeatedly declared their renunciation of all annexations. So much the worse, we reply. That means your actions do not accord with your words, for your actions serve both Russian and foreign imperialism. And when you begin to cooperate actively with the imperialist 'Allies' you render splendid service to the Russian counter-revolution. The joy of all the Black Hundreds and all counter-revolutionaries over the decisive turn in your policy is the best evidence of that. Yes, the Russian revolution has come to a turning-point. Through its

1 Welsh MP for the Liberal Party from 1890 to 1945. British Prime Minister from 1916-22.

2 Four-time French Prime Minister including during 1914 and from March to September 1917.

3 Prime Minister of Italy in 1909-10 and Minister of Foreign Affairs in 1914-19.

'socialist' Ministers, the Russian Government has done something which the imperialist Ministers, Guchkov and Milyukov, could not do. It has put the Russian Army at the disposal of the general staffs and the diplomats who act in the name and on the basis of unabrogated secret treaties, in the name of designs frankly proclaimed by Ribot and Lloyd George. The government could only fulfil its task, however, because the army trusted and followed it. The army marched to death because it believed it was making sacrifices for freedom, the revolution and early peace.

But the army did so because it is only a part of the people, who at this stage of the revolution are following the Socialist-Revolutionary and the Menshevik parties. This general and basic fact, the trust of the majority in the petty-bourgeois policy of the Mensheviks and the Socialist-Revolutionaries which is dependent on the capitalists, determines our Party's stand and conduct.

We shall keep up our efforts to expose government policy, resolutely warning the workers and soldiers, as in the past, against pinning their hopes on uncoordinated and disorganised actions.

It is a question of a phase in the people's revolution. The Tseretelis and Chernovs, having become dependent on imperialism, are putting into effect a phase of petty-bourgeois illusions and petty-bourgeois phrases, which serve to disguise the same old cynical imperialism.

This phase must be brought to an end. Let us help to end it as speedily and as painlessly as possible. This will rid the people of the *last* petty-bourgeois illusions and bring about the transfer of power to the revolutionary class.

To What State Have the SRs and the Mensheviks Brought the Revolution?

Published 22 June (5 July) 1917

They have brought it to a state of subjection to the imperialists.

The offensive is a renewal of the imperialist war. Nothing essential has changed in the relations between the two gigantic capitalist blocs waging war on one another. Even after the revolution of 27 February, Russia remains under the complete sway of the capitalists, who are bound to Anglo-French imperialist capital by alliance and by the old, tsarist, secret treaties. Both the economics and politics of the continuing war are the same as before: the same old imperialist banking capital dominating economic life, and the same old secret treaties, the same old foreign policy of alliances of one group of imperialists against another.

The empty phrases of the Mensheviks and Socialist-Revolutionaries are still empty phrases, in practice only serving to adorn the resumption of the imperialist war, which quite naturally meets with enthusiastic howls of approval from all the counter-revolutionaries, the whole bourgeoisie and Plekhanov, "who tails after the bourgeois press", as the Menshevik *Rabochaya Gazeta* put it, which itself tails after the whole horde of social-chauvinists.

But we must not overlook the distinguishing features of this particular resumption of the imperialist war. The resumption came after three months of hesitation, during which time the mass of workers and peasants thousands of times expressed their condemnation of a war of conquest (while continuing in practice to support the government of the predatory Russian bourgeoisie bent on conquest). The masses hesitated, as though they were about to carry out *at home* the advice which the 14 (27) March appeal to the peoples of the world gave to *other* peoples, namely: "Refuse to serve as tools of conquest and violence in the hands of the *bankers*!" But here at home, in 'revolutionary-democratic' Russia, the masses have remained in effect an instrument of conquest and violence in 'the hands of the bankers'.

A distinguishing feature of this situation is that it was created by the Socialist-Revolutionary and Menshevik parties at a time when the people enjoyed a comparatively large measure of freedom of organisation. It is these parties that have gained the majority at the moment: the All-Russia Congress of Soviets and the All-Russia Peasants' Congress have undoubtedly proved this.

It is these parties that are at present responsible for Russia's policy.

It is these parties that are responsible for the resumption of the imperialist war, for more hundreds of thousands of lives sacrificed virtually with the aim of enabling certain capitalists to 'overcome' other capitalists, and for the further aggravation of the economic dislocation inevitably resulting from the offensive.

Here we had, in the purest form, the self-deception of the petty-bourgeois masses and the deception of them by the bourgeoisie with the aid of the Socialist-Revolutionaries and Mensheviks. These parties both claim to be 'revolutionary democrats'. But in fact it was they who placed the people's fate in the hands of the counter-revolutionary bourgeoisie, the Cadets; it was they who deserted the revolution to continue the imperialist war, who deserted democracy to make 'concessions' to the Cadets on the issue of power (take, for instance, the 'confirmation' from above of the election of authorities by the local population), on the land issue (the Mensheviks' and Socialist-Revolutionaries' renunciation of *their own* programme, namely, to support the revolutionary actions of the peasants, *including confiscation* of the landed estates) and on the national question (defence of the undemocratic attitude of the Cadets towards the Ukraine and Finland).

The petty-bourgeois masses cannot help vacillating between the bourgeoisie and the proletariat. This has been the case in all countries, especially between 1789 and 1871. And it is also the case in Russia. The Mensheviks and Socialist-Revolutionaries have *induced the masses* to submit to the policy of the counter-revolutionary bourgeoisie.

That is the heart of the matter. That is the meaning of the offensive. That is the peculiarity of the situation: it was not violence, but trust in the Socialist-Revolutionaries and Mensheviks that led the people astray.

Will it be for long?

No, not long. The masses will learn from their own experience. The sad experience of the new stage of the war (a stage already begun), of further ruin accentuated by the offensive, will inevitably lead to the *political* downfall of the Socialist-Revolutionary and Menshevik parties.

The task of the workers' party is, first of all, to help the masses realise and take proper account of this experience, to prepare properly for this great downfall, which will show the masses their true leader – the organised urban proletariat.

A Class Shift

Published 27 June (10 July) 1917

Every revolution, if it is a real revolution, amounts to a class shift. Therefore, the best way of enlightening the people, and of fighting those who deceive the people by invoking the revolution, is to analyse the class shift that has taken or is taking place in the present revolution.

From 1904 to 1916, in the last years of tsarism, the relative positions of the classes in Russia became particularly clear. A handful of semi-feudal landowners, headed by Nicholas II, was in power and maintained the closest alliance with the financial magnates who were reaping profits unheard of in Europe and for whose benefit predatory treaties were concluded with foreign countries.

The liberal bourgeoisie, led by the Cadets, were in opposition. They were more afraid of the people than of reaction and were moving closer and closer to power by compromising with the monarchy.

The people, i.e. the workers and peasants, whose leaders had been driven underground, were revolutionary. They constituted the 'revolutionary democrats' – proletarian and petty-bourgeois.

The revolution of 27 February 1917 swept away the monarchy and put the liberal bourgeoisie in power, who, operating in direct concord with the Anglo-French imperialists, had wanted a minor court revolution. Under no circumstances were they willing to go beyond a constitutional monarchy with an electoral system conditioned by various qualifications. And when the revolution actually went further, completely abolishing the monarchy and establishing Soviets (of Workers', Soldiers' and Peasants' Deputies), the entire liberal bourgeoisie became counter-revolutionary.

Now, four months after the revolution, the counter-revolutionary character of the Cadets, the main party of the liberal bourgeoisie, is as clear as day. Everyone sees that. And everyone is compelled to admit it. But not nearly everyone is willing to face up to it and think about what it implies.

Russia today is a democratic republic governed by a free agreement between *political parties* which are freely advocating their views among the people. The four months since 27 February have fully consolidated and given final shape to *all* parties of any importance, showed them up during the elections (to the Soviets and to local bodies), and revealed their links with the various classes.

In Russia, the counter-revolutionary bourgeoisie are in power today, while the petty-bourgeois democrats, namely, the Socialist-Revolutionary and Menshevik parties, have become 'His Majesty's opposition'. The policy of these parties is essentially one of *compromise* with the counter-revolutionary bourgeoisie. The petty-bourgeois democrats are rising to power by filling local bodies to begin with (just as the liberals did under tsarism – by first winning places in the zemstvos).[1] These petty-bourgeois democrats want *to share power* with the bourgeoisie but not overthrow them, in exactly the same way as the Cadets wanted to share power with the monarchy but not overthrow it. The petty-bourgeois democrats (the Socialist-Revolutionaries and the Mensheviks) compromise with the Cadets because of the close class kinship between the petty and the big bourgeoisie, just as the class kinship between the capitalist and the landowner, living in the twentieth century, made them embrace each other at the feet of their 'adored' monarch.

---

1 Zemstvos – rural self-government bodies set up in the central *gubernias* ("governorates", administrative subdivisions) of tsarist Russia in 1864. They were dominated by the nobility, and their jurisdiction was limited to purely local economic and welfare matters: hospital and road building, statistics, insurance, etc.

It is the *form* of compromise that has changed. Under the monarchy it was crude, and the tsar allowed a Cadet no further than the Duma backyard. In a democratic republic, compromise has become as refined as in Europe, the petty bourgeoisie being permitted, in a harmless minority, to occupy harmless (for capital) posts in the Ministry.

The Cadets have taken the place of the monarchy. The Tseretelis and Chernovs have taken the place of the Cadets. Proletarian democracy has taken the place of a *truly* revolutionary democracy.

The imperialist war has hastened developments fantastically. Had it not been for this war, the Socialist-Revolutionaries and Mensheviks might have sighed for decades for ministerial posts. The same war, however, is hastening further developments. For it *poses* problems in a revolutionary rather than a reformist manner.

The Socialist-Revolutionary and Menshevik parties could have given Russia many a reform by agreement with the bourgeoisie. But the objective situation in world politics is revolutionary and it *cannot be dealt with* by reforms.

The imperialist war is crushing the peoples and threatens to crush them completely. The petty-bourgeois democrats can perhaps stave off disaster for a while. But it is only the revolutionary proletariat that can prevent a tragic end.

All Power to the Soviets!

Published 5 (18) July 1917

Editor's note:

On 3 (16) July spontaneous demonstrations occurred and threatened to grow into an armed uprising against the Provisional Government.

At that moment, the Bolshevik Party was against any armed action, for it believed that the revolutionary crisis had not yet matured, and that the army and the provinces were not yet ready to support the uprising in the capital. But the movement had already begun and it proved impossible to stop it.

In view of the mood of the masses, the CC decided to participate in the demonstration so as to lend it a peaceful and organised character. At the time, Lenin was away – he was ill due to overwork and had gone to the countryside for a few days' rest. He returned to Petrograd on the morning of 4 (17) July and took over direction of the events.

A mass demonstration had gathered outside the Smolny Institute, where tens of thousands of workers, soldiers and sailors stood ready and armed, demanding to carry out an insurrection. Lenin addressed the crowd, calling for "firmness, steadfastness and vigilance" (see 'An Answer', p. 243 of this volume).

More than 500,000 took part in the demonstration under Bolshevik slogans, including 'All Power to the Soviets!'

With the knowledge and consent of the Menshevik-SR Central Executive Committee, the Provisional Government decided to suppress the demonstration with armed force. Military cadet and counter-revolutionary Cossack regiments were thrown against the peaceable demonstration of workers and soldiers. They opened fire on the demonstrators. Reactionary military units were summoned from the front.

On the night of 4 (17) July, the Bolshevik leadership decided to stop the demonstration in an organised manner. This was a correct step taken by the Party, which succeeded in retreating at a right time and preserving the main forces of the revolution from being routed.

Lenin wrote this text the next morning, 5 (18) July, before the forces of the Provisional Government wrecked the offices of *Pravda*.

* * *

"Drive nature out of the door and she will rush back through the window." It seems that the Socialist-Revolutionary and Menshevik parties have to 'learn' this simple truth time and again by their own experience. They undertook to be 'revolutionary democrats' and found themselves in the shoes of revolutionary democrats – they are now forced to draw the conclusions which every revolutionary democrat must draw.

Democracy is the rule of the majority. As long as the will of the majority was not clear, as long as it was possible to make it out to be unclear, at least with a grain of plausibility, the people were offered a counter-revolutionary bourgeois government disguised as 'democratic'. But this delay could not last long. During the several months that have passed since 27 February the will of the majority of the workers and peasants, of the overwhelming majority of the country's population, has become clear in more than a general sense. Their will has found expression in mass organisations – the Soviets of Workers', Soldiers' and Peasants' Deputies.

How, then, can anyone oppose the transfer of all power in the state to the Soviets? Such opposition means nothing but renouncing democracy! It means no more no less than imposing on the people a government which *admittedly* can neither come into being nor hold its ground *democratically*, i.e. as a result of truly free, truly popular elections.

It is a farce, strange as it may seem at first sight, that the Socialist-Revolutionaries and Mensheviks have *forgotten* this perfectly simple, perfectly obvious and palpable truth. Their position is so false, and they are so badly confused and bewildered, that they are unable to 'recover' this truth they have lost. Following the elections in Petrograd and in Moscow, the convocation of the All-Russia Peasant Congress and the Congress of Soviets, the classes and parties throughout Russia have shown what they stand for so clearly and specifically that people who have not gone mad or deliberately got themselves into a mess simply cannot have any illusions on this score.

To tolerate the Cadet Ministers or the Cadet government or Cadet policies means challenging democrats and democracy. This is the source of the political crises since 27 February, and this also the source of the shakiness and vacillation of our government system. At every turn, daily and even hourly, appeals are being made to the people's revolutionary spirit and to their democracy on behalf of the most authoritative government institutions and congresses. Yet the government's policies in particular are all departures from revolutionary principles and breaches in democracy.

This sort of thing will not do.

It is inevitable that a situation like the present should show elements of instability now for one reason, now for another. And it is not exactly a clever policy of jib. Things are moving by fits and starts towards a point where power will be transferred to the Soviets, which is what our Party called for long ago.

Three Crises

Written on 7 (20) July 1917

Editor's note:
The offices of *Pravda,* having been wrecked on 5 (18) July by the Provisional Government, could not publish this article, which instead appeared two weeks later in *Rabotnitsa* (*Woman Worker*) on 19 July (1 August).

* * *

The more violent the slander and lies against the Bolsheviks these days, the more calmly must we, while refuting the lies and slander, reflect upon the historical interrelation of events and the political, i.e. *class*, significance of the revolution's present course.

To refute the lies and slander, we only have to refer again to *Listok 'Pravdy'* of 6 (19) July, and to call the reader's attention especially to the article printed below which gives documentary evidence that on 2 (15) July the Bolsheviks campaigned *against* the demonstration (as admitted by the Socialist-Revolutionaries' paper). The article indicates that on 3 (16) July the popular mood exploded into action and the demonstration started against our advice. It shows that on 4 (17) July, in a leaflet (reprinted by the Socialist-Revolutionary paper *Dyelo Naroda*), we called for a *peaceful* and *organised* demonstration, that on the night of 4 July we passed a decision to call off the demonstration. Slanderers, continue your slander! You can never refute these facts and their decisive significance in every connection!

Let us turn to the question of the historical interrelation of the events. When, as early as the beginning of April, we opposed support for the Provisional Government, we were attacked by both the SRs and the Mensheviks. But what has reality proved?

What have the three political crises proved – 20-21 April, 10 and 18 June, 3-4 July?

They have proved, in the first place, that the masses are becoming increasingly dissatisfied with the bourgeois policy of the Provisional Government's bourgeois majority.

It is rather interesting to note that the ruling Socialist-Revolutionaries' newspaper, *Dyelo Naroda*, despite its marked hostility to the Bolsheviks, is compelled to admit, in its 6 (19) July issue, the deep economic and political causes of the action of 3-4 July. The stupid, crude, infamous lie that this action was artificially created, that the Bolsheviks campaigned *in favour* of action, will daily be more and more exposed.

The common cause, the common origin, the deep common root of the three above-mentioned political crises is clear, especially if we look at them in their interrelation, as science demands that politics be looked at. It is absurd even to think that three such crises could be produced artificially.

In the second place, it is instructive to grasp what each one of them had in common with the others, and what was its specific features.

What is common to all three is a mass dissatisfaction overflowing all bounds, a mass resentment with the bourgeoisie and *their* government. Whoever forgets, ignores or underestimates *this essence of the matter*, renounces the ABC of socialism concerning the class struggle.

Let those who call themselves socialists, who know something about the character of the class struggle in European revolutions, think about the class struggle in the Russian revolution.

These crises are peculiar in the ways they manifested themselves. The first (20-21 April) was stormy and spontaneous, and completely unorganised. It led to Black Hundreds firing on the demonstrators and to unprecedentedly savage and lying accusations against the Bolsheviks. After the outburst came a political crisis.

In the second case, the demonstration was called by the Bolsheviks, and was cancelled after a stern ultimatum and direct ban by the Congress of Soviets; then, on 18 June, came a general demonstration in which the Bolshevik slogans clearly predominated. As the Socialist-Revolutionaries and Mensheviks themselves admitted on the evening of 18 June, a political crisis would certainly have broken out had it not been for the offensive at the front.

The third crisis broke out spontaneously on 3 July despite the Bolsheviks' efforts on 2 July to check it. Reaching its climax on 4 (17) July, it led to a furious outburst of counter-revolution on 5-6 July. The vacillation of the SRs and Mensheviks expressed itself in Spiridonova and a number of other SRs declaring for the transfer of power to the Soviets, and in the Menshevik internationalists, previously opposed to it, voicing the same idea.

The last, and perhaps the most instructive, conclusion to be drawn from considering the events in their interconnection is that *all* three crises manifested some form of demonstration that is new in the history of our revolution, a demonstration of a more complicated type in which the movement proceeds in waves, a sudden drop following a rapid rise, revolution and counter-revolution becoming more acute, and the middle elements being eliminated for a more or less extensive period.

In all three crises, the movement took the form of a *demonstration*. An anti-government demonstration – that would be the most exact, formal description of events. But the fact of the matter is that it was not an ordinary demonstration; it was something considerably more than a demonstration, but less than a revolution. It was an outburst of revolution and counter-revolution *together*, a sharp, sometimes almost sudden elimination of the middle elements, while the proletarian and bourgeois elements made a stormy appearance.

In this respect it is extremely typical that, for *each* of these movements, the middle elements blame *both* of the specific class forces – the proletariat as well as the bourgeoisie. Look at the SRs and Mensheviks. They lean over backwards to frantically shout that, by their extremes, the Bolsheviks are helping the counter-revolution. At the same time, however, they admit again and again that the Cadets (with whom they form a bloc in the government) are counter-revolutionary. "Our urgent task is to draw a line", wrote *Dyelo Naroda* yesterday, "to dig a deep moat between ourselves and all the Right elements, including *Yedinstvo*, which has gone militant" (with which, we may add, the SRs formed a bloc during the elections).

Compare that with today's (7 (20) July) issue of *Yedinstvo*, in which Plekhanov's editorial is compelled to state the indisputable fact that the Soviets (i.e. the SRs and Mensheviks) will "think over the matter for a fortnight" and that, if power were to pass to the Soviets, "it would be tantamount to victory for Lenin's supporters".

> If the Cadets don't stick to the rule – the worse, the better… [says Plekhanov] they themselves will have to admit that they have made a big mistake [by withdrawing from the Cabinet], making the work of Lenin's supporters easier.

Isn't that typical? The middle elements blame the Cadets for making the Bolsheviks' work easier, and the Bolsheviks for making the Cadets' work easier! Is it so hard to guess that if we substitute class names for political ones we have before us the dreams of the petty bourgeoisie about the disappearance of the class struggle between the proletariat and the bourgeoisie? Isn't the petty bourgeoisie complaining about the class struggle between the proletariat and the bourgeoisie? Is it really so hard to guess that no Bolsheviks in the world could have 'created' even a single 'popular movement', let alone three movements, if the deepest economic and political causes had not set the proletariat into action? Is it so difficult to guess that no Cadets and monarchists combined could have called forth any movement 'from the Right' if it had not been for the equally deep causes that make the bourgeoisie as a class counter-revolutionary?

Both we and the Cadets were blamed for the 20-21 April movement – for intransigence, extremes and for aggravating the situation. The

Bolsheviks were even accused (absurd as it may be) of the firing on Nevsky. When the movement was over, however, those same SRs and Mensheviks, in their joint, official organ, *Izvestia*, wrote that the 'popular movement' had 'swept away the imperialists, Milyukov, etc.', i.e. they *praised* the movement!! Isn't that typical? Doesn't it show very clearly that the petty bourgeoisie do not understand the workings, the meaning, of the class struggle between the proletariat and the bourgeoisie?

The objective situation is this. The vast majority of the country's population is petty-bourgeois by its living conditions and more so by its ideas. But big capital rules the country, primarily through banks and syndicates. There is an urban proletariat in this country, mature enough to go its own way, but not yet able to draw at once the majority of the semi-proletarians to its side. From this fundamental, class fact follows the inevitability of such crises as the three we are now examining, as well as their forms.

In future the forms of crises may, of course, change, but the substance of the issue will remain the same even if, for instance, the SR Constituent Assembly meets in October. The SRs have promised the peasants: (1) to abolish private landownership; (2) to transfer the land to the working people; (3) to confiscate the landed estates and transfer them to the peasants without compensation. These great reforms can never be realised without the most decisive revolutionary measures against the bourgeoisie, measures that can *only* be taken when the poor peasants join the proletariat, *only* when the banks and the syndicates are nationalised.

The credulous peasants, believing for a time that these beautiful things can be achieved by compromising with the bourgeoisie, will inevitably be disappointed and… 'dissatisfied' (mildly speaking) with the sharp class struggle of the proletariat against the bourgeoisie for the implementation of the promises of the SRs. So it was, and so it will be.

The Political Situation (Four Theses)

Written 10 (23) July 1917

Editor's note:

These theses were written by Lenin on 10 (23) July 1917, and defined the new tactical line of the Bolshevik Party in connection with the changed political situation following the demonstration on 4 (17) July.

* * *

1. The counter-revolution has become organised and consolidated, and has actually taken state power into its hands.

   The complete organisation and consolidation of the counter-revolution consists in a combination of its three main forces, a combination excellently conceived and already put into practice:

   i. The Constitutional-Democratic Party, i.e. the real leader of the organised bourgeoisie, has, by withdrawing from the Cabinet, confronted it with an ultimatum, thus clearing the way for the Cabinet's overthrow by the counter-revolution;

   ii. The General Staff and the military leaders, with the deliberate or semi-deliberate assistance of Kerensky, whom even the most prominent Socialist-Revolutionaries now call a

Cavaignac, have seized actual state power and have proceeded to shoot down revolutionary units at the front, disarm the revolutionary troops and workers in Petrograd and Moscow, suppress unrest in Nizhny Novgorod, arrest Bolsheviks and ban their papers, not only without trial, but even without a government order. At present, basic state power in Russia is virtually a military dictatorship. This fact is still obscured by a number of institutions that are revolutionary in words but powerless in deeds. Yet it is so obvious and fundamental a fact that, without understanding it, one cannot understand anything about the political situation.

iii. The Black-Hundred-monarchist and bourgeois press, which has switched from hounding Bolsheviks to hounding the Soviets, the 'incendiary' Chernov, etc. has indicated with the utmost clarity that the true meaning of the policy of military dictatorship, which now reigns supreme and is supported by the Cadets and monarchists, is preparation for disbanding the Soviets. Many of the leaders of the SRs and Mensheviks, i.e. the present majority in the Soviets, have admitted and expressed this during the past few days, but true to their petty-bourgeois nature, they shrug off this formidable reality with meaningless high-sounding phrases.

2. The leaders of the Soviets and of the Socialist-Revolutionary and Menshevik parties, headed by Tsereteli and Chernov, have completely betrayed the cause of the revolution by putting it in the hands of the counter-revolutionaries and by turning themselves, their parties and the Soviets into mere fig-leaves of the counter-revolution.

   Proof of this is that the Socialist-Revolutionaries and Mensheviks have betrayed the Bolsheviks and have tacitly agreed to close down their papers without daring to tell the people plainly and openly that they are doing so and why. By sanctioning the disarming of the workers and the revolutionary regiments, they have deprived themselves of all real power. They have turned into the most loud-mouthed ranters who help the reaction to 'divert' the people's attention until it is finally ready to disband the Soviets. It is impossible to understand anything at all about the present political situation without realising this complete and final bankruptcy of the SRs and Mensheviks and the present majority in the Soviets and without realising that their 'Directory' and other masquerades are an absolute sham.

3. All hopes for a peaceful development of the Russian revolution have vanished for good. This is the objective situation: either complete victory for the military dictatorship, or victory for the workers' armed uprising; the latter victory is only possible when it coincides with a deep mass upheaval, against the government and the bourgeoisie caused by economic disruption and the prolongation of the war.

   The slogan 'All Power to the Soviets!' was a slogan for peaceful development of the revolution which was possible in April, May, June and up to 5-9 (18-22) July, i.e. up to the time when actual power passed into the hands of the military dictatorship. This slogan is no longer correct, for it does not take into account that power has changed hands and that the revolution has in fact been completely betrayed by the SRs and Mensheviks. Reckless actions, revolts, partial resistance, or hopeless hit-and-run attempts to oppose reaction will not help. What will help is a clear understanding of the situation, endurance and determination of the workers' vanguard, preparation of forces for the armed uprising, for the victory of which conditions at present are extremely difficult, but still possible if the facts and trends mentioned in the thesis coincide. Let us have no constitutional or republican illusions of any kind, no more illusions about a peaceful path, no sporadic actions, no yielding *now* to provocation from the Black Hundreds and Cossacks. Let us muster our forces, reorganise them and resolutely prepare for the armed uprising, if the course of the crisis permits it on a really mass, country-wide scale. The transfer of land to the peasants is impossible at present without an armed uprising, since the counter-revolutionaries, having taken power, have completely united with the landowners as a class.

The aim of the insurrection can only be to transfer power to the proletariat, supported by the poor peasants, with a view to putting our Party programme into effect.

4. The party of the working class, without abandoning legal activity but never for a moment overrating it, must *combine* legal with illegal work, as it did in 1912-14.

   Don't let a single hour of legal work slip by. But don't cherish any constitutional or 'peaceful' illusions. Form illegal organisations or cells everywhere and at once for the publication of leaflets, etc. Reorganise immediately, consistently, resolutely, all along the line.

   Act as we did in 1912-14, when we could speak about overthrowing tsarism by a revolution and an armed uprising, without at the same time losing our legal base in the Duma, the insurance societies, the trade unions, etc.

Letter to the Editors of 'Proletarskoye Dyelo'

Published 15 (28) July 1917

Editor's note:

After the dispersal of the demonstration on 4 (17) July, the bourgeois Provisional Government intensified its reprisals. It attacked the Bolshevik Party with special ferocity.

On the night of 4 (17) July, the Minister for Justice PN Pereverzev gave the press papers that purported to show that Lenin was a German agent. The press waged a hysterical campaign against Lenin the next morning, and the offices of *Pravda, Soldatskaya Pravda* and others were wrecked by government forces. Workers were disarmed, and waves of raids, arrests, beatings and pogroms followed. The revolutionary units of the Petrograd garrison which had taken part in the demonstration were disbanded and sent to the front.

On 6 (19) July, the Provisional Government issued an order for the arrest of Lenin, Zinoviev and Kamenev. The leadership of the party convinced Lenin to go into hiding. He left Petrograd in the afternoon and hid with Zinoviev in safehouses around the city before making his way back to Finland on 10 (23) August, where he remained until October.

Proletarskoye Dyelo was the Kronstadt Bolshevik paper.

* * *

Comrades,

We have changed our minds about submitting to the Provisional Government's decree ordering our arrests, for the following reasons.

From the letter of Pereverzev, the former Minister of Justice, published on Sunday in *Novoye Vremya*, it became perfectly clear that the 'espionage' 'case' of Lenin and others was quite deliberately framed by the party of the counter-revolution.

Pereverzev has openly admitted that he took advantage of unconfirmed accusations to work up (his actual expression) the soldiers against our Party. This is admitted by the former Minister of Justice, a man who only yesterday called himself a socialist! Pereverzev is gone, but whether the new Minister of Justice will hesitate to adopt Pereverzev's and Alexinsky's methods, nobody can venture to say.

The counter-revolutionary bourgeoisie are trying to create a new Dreyfus case.[1] They believe in our 'espionage' as much as the leaders of Russian reaction, who framed the Beilis case,[2] believed that Jews drink children's blood. There are no guarantees of justice in Russia at present.

The Central Executive Committee, which considers it self the plenipotentiary organ of the Russian democrats, appointed a commission to investigate the espionage charges, but under pressure

1 The Dreyfus Affair began in 1894 when Captain Alfred Dreyfus, a Jewish officer, was convicted in a secret court martial of selling secrets to a foreign power, and sentenced to life on Devil's Island. This was a frame-up to protect another officer – a non-Jewish aristocrat – involving the General Staff. A scandal erupted that shook French society. Dreyfus was finally released from prison in 1899 and fully vindicated in 1906.

2 In 1913 the tsar's government staged a trial of Menahem Beilis, a Jewish man falsely accused of the ritual murder of a Christian boy. The murder was actually committed by the Black Hundreds. The government's aim was to stir up antisemitism and take advantage of anti-Jewish pogroms to divert the people's attention from the revolutionary movement growing throughout the country. The trial aroused public indignation. In a number of towns, workers held protest demonstrations. Beilis was eventually acquitted.

from the counter-revolutionary forces dismissed it. The Central Executive Committee refused to either directly confirm or to revoke the warrant for our arrest. It washed its hands of the case, virtually delivering us to the counter-revolution.

The charges of 'conspiracy' and 'moral incitement' to revolt proffered against us are of a very definite nature, but no precise indictment of our alleged crime is brought either by the Provisional Government or by the Soviet, both of which know full well that it is sheer nonsense to speak of 'conspiracy' in referring to a movement like that of 3-5 (16-18) July. The Menshevik and SR leaders *are* simply trying to appease the counter-revolution that is already bearing down on them too, by delivering a number of our Party members to the counter-revolutionaries in compliance with their demand.

At present there can be no legal basis in Russia, not even such constitutional guarantees as exist in the orderly bourgeois countries. To give ourselves up at present to the authorities would mean putting ourselves into the hands of the Milyukovs, Alexinskys, Pereverzevs, of rampant counter-revolutionaries who look upon all the charges against us as a simple civil war episode.

After what happened on 6-8 July, not a single Russian revolutionary can harbour constitutional illusions any longer. Revolution and counter-revolution are coming to grips in a decisive fashion. We shall continue to fight on the side of the former.

We shall continue to aid the proletariat's revolutionary struggle as far as we can. The Constituent Assembly alone, if it meets, and if its convocation is not the handiwork of the bourgeoisie, will have full authority to pass judgement upon the Provisional Government's decree ordering our arrest.

N Lenin

On Slogans

Written in mid-July 1917

Too often has it happened that, when history has taken a sharp turn, even progressive parties have for some time been unable to adapt themselves to the new situation and have repeated slogans which had formerly been correct but had now lost all meaning – lost it as 'suddenly' as the sharp turn in history was 'sudden'.

Something of the sort seems likely to recur in connection with the slogan calling for the transfer of all state power to the Soviets. That slogan was correct during a period of our revolution – say, from 27 February to 4 (17) July – that has now passed irrevocably. It has patently ceased to be correct now. Unless this is understood, it is impossible to understand anything of the urgent questions of the day. Every particular slogan must be deduced from the totality of specific features of a definite political situation. And the political situation in Russia now, after 4 July, differs radically from the situation between 27 February and 4 July.

During that period of the revolution now past, the so-called 'dual power' existed in the country, which both materially and formally expressed the indefinite and transitional condition of state power. Let us not forget that the issue of power is the fundamental issue of every revolution.

At that time state power was unstable. It was shared, by voluntary agreement, between the Provisional Government and the Soviets. The Soviets were delegations from the mass of free – i.e. not subject to external coercion – and armed workers and soldiers. What *really mattered* was that arms were in the hands of the people and that there was no coercion of the people from without. That is what opened up and ensured a peaceful path for the progress of the revolution. The slogan 'All Power Must be Transferred to the Soviets' was a slogan for the next step, the immediately feasible step, on that peaceful path of development. It was a slogan for the peaceful development of the revolution, which was possible and, of course, most desirable between 27 February and 4 July but which is now absolutely impossible.

Apparently, not all the supporters of the slogan 'All Power Must be Transferred to the Soviets' have given adequate thought to the fact that it was a slogan for peaceful progress of the revolution – peaceful not only in the sense that nobody, no class, no force of any importance, would then (between 27 February and 4 July) have been able to resist and prevent the transfer of power to the Soviets. That is not all. Peaceful development would then have been possible, even in the sense that the struggle of classes and parties *within* the Soviets could have assumed a most peaceful and painless form, provided full state power had passed to the Soviets in good time.

The latter aspect of the matter has similarly not yet received adequate attention. In their class composition, the Soviets were organs of the movement of the workers and peasants, a ready-made form of their dictatorship. Had they possessed full state power, the main shortcoming of the petty-bourgeois groups, their chief sin, that of trusting the capitalists, really would have been overcome, would have been criticised by the experience of their own measures. The change of classes and parties in power could have proceeded peacefully within the Soviets, provided the latter wielded exclusive and undivided power. The contact between all the Soviet parties and the people could have remained stable and unimpaired. One must not forget for a single moment that only such a close contact between the Soviet parties and the people, freely growing in extent and depth, could have helped peacefully to get rid of the illusion of petty-bourgeois compromise with the bourgeoisie. The transfer of power to the Soviets would not, and could not, in itself have changed the correlation of classes; it would in no way have changed the petty-bourgeois nature of the peasants. But it would have taken a big and timely step towards separating the peasants from the bourgeoisie, towards bringing them closer to, and then uniting them with, the workers.

This is what might have happened had power passed to the Soviets at the proper time. That would have been the easiest and the most advantageous course for the people. This course would have been the least painful, and it was therefore necessary to fight for it most energetically. Now, however, this struggle, the struggle for the timely transfer of power to the Soviets, has ended. A peaceful course of development has become impossible. A non-peaceful and most painful course has begun.

The turning-point of 4 July was precisely a drastic change in the objective situation. The unstable condition of state power has come to an end. At the decisive point, power has passed into the hands of the counter-revolution. The development of the parties on the basis of the collaboration of the petty-bourgeois Socialist-Revolutionary and Menshevik parties and the counter-revolutionary Cadets has brought about a situation in which both these petty-bourgeois parties have virtually become participants in and abettors of counter-revolutionary butchery. As the struggle between parties developed, the unreasoning trust which the petty bourgeoisie put in the capitalists led to their deliberate support of the counter-revolutionaries. The development of party relations has completed its cycle. On 27 February, all classes found themselves united against the monarchy. After 4 July, the counter-revolutionary bourgeoisie, working hand in glove with the monarchists and the Black Hundreds, secured the support of the petty-bourgeois Socialist-Revolutionaries and Mensheviks, partly by intimidating them, and handed over real state power to the Cavaignacs, the military gang, who are shooting insubordinate soldiers at the front and smashing the Bolsheviks in Petrograd.

The slogan calling for the transfer of state power to the Soviets would now sound quixotic or mocking. Objectively it would be deceiving the people; it would be fostering in them the delusion that even *now* it is enough for the Soviets to want to take power, or to pass such a decision, for power to be theirs, that there are still parties in the Soviets which have not been tainted by abetting the butchers, that it is possible to undo what has been done.

It would be a profound error to think that the revolutionary proletariat is capable of 'refusing' to support the Socialist-Revolutionaries and Mensheviks against the counter-revolution by way of 'revenge', so to speak, for the support they gave in smashing the Bolsheviks, in shooting down soldiers at the front and in disarming the workers. First, this would be applying philistine conceptions of morality to the proletariat (since, *for the good of the cause*, the proletariat will always support not only the vacillating petty bourgeoisie but even the big bourgeoisie); secondly – and that is the important thing – it would be a philistine attempt to obscure the political substance of the situation by 'moralising'.

And the political substance is that power can no longer be taken peacefully. It can be obtained only by winning a decisive struggle against those actually in power at the moment, namely, the military gang, the Cavaignacs, who are relying for support on the reactionary troops brought to Petrograd and on the Cadets and monarchists.

The substance of the situation is that these new holders of state power can be defeated only by the revolutionary masses, who, to be brought into motion, must not only be led by the proletariat, but must also turn their backs on the Socialist-Revolutionary and Menshevik parties, which have betrayed the cause of the revolution.

Those who introduce philistine morals into politics reason as follows: let us assume that the Socialist-Revolutionaries and Mensheviks did commit an 'error' in supporting the Cavaignacs, who are disarming the proletariat and the revolutionary regiments; still, they must be given a chance to 'rectify' their 'error'; the rectification of the 'error' 'should not be made difficult' for them;

the swing of the petty bourgeoisie towards the workers should be facilitated. Such reasoning would be childishly naive or simply stupid, if not a new deception of the workers. For the swing of the petty-bourgeois masses towards the workers would mean, and could only mean, that these masses had turned their backs upon the Socialist-Revolutionaries and Mensheviks. The Socialist-Revolutionary and Menshevik parties could now rectify their 'error' only by denouncing Tsereteli, Chernov, Dan and Rakitnikov as the butchers' aides. We are wholly and unconditionally in favour of their 'error' being 'rectified' in this way…

We said that the fundamental issue of revolution is the issue of power. We must add that it is revolutions that show us at every step how the question of *where* actual power lies is obscured, and reveal the divergence between formal and real power. That is one of the chief characteristics of every revolutionary period. It was not clear in March and April 1917 whether real power was in the hands of the government or the Soviet.

Now, however, it is particularly important for class-conscious workers to soberly face the fundamental issue of revolution, namely, who holds state power at the moment? Consider its material manifestations, do not mistake words for deeds, and you will have no difficulty in finding the answer.

Friedrich Engels once wrote the state is primarily contingents of armed men with material adjuncts, such as prisons.[1] Now it is the military cadets and the reactionary Cossacks, who have been specially brought to Petrograd, those who are keeping Kamenev and the others in prison, who closed down *Pravda*, who disarmed the workers and a certain section of the soldiers, who are shooting down an equally certain section of the soldiers, who are shooting down an equally certain section of troops in the army. These butchers are the real power. The Tseretelis and Chernovs are ministers without power, puppet Ministers, leaders of parties that support the butchery. That is a fact. And the fact is no less true because Tsereteli and Chernov

1 See Engels, Friedrich, *The Origin of the Family, Private Property and the State*, Wellred Books, 2020, p. 156.

themselves probably 'do not approve' of the butchery, or because their papers timidly dissociate themselves from it. Such changes of political garb change nothing in substance.

The newspaper of 150,000 Petrograd voters has been closed down. The military cadets on 6 (19) July killed the worker Voinov for carrying *Listok 'Pravdy'* out of the printers'. Isn't that butchery? Isn't that the handiwork of Cavaignacs? But neither the government nor the Soviets are to 'blame' for this, they may tell us.

So much the worse for the government and the Soviets, we reply; for that means that they are mere figureheads, puppets, and that real power is not in their hands.

Primarily, and above all, the people must know the *truth* – they must know who actually wields state power. The people must be told the whole truth, namely, that power is in the hands of a military clique of Cavaignacs (Kerensky, certain generals, officers, etc.), who are supported by the bourgeois class headed by the Cadet Party, and by all the monarchists, acting through the Black Hundred papers, *Novoye Vremya*, *Zhivoye Slovo*, etc., etc.

That power must be overthrown. Unless this is done, all talk of fighting the counter-revolution is so much phrase-mongering, 'self-deception and deception of the people'.

That power now has the support both of the Tseretelis and Chernovs in the Cabinet and of their parties. We must explain to the people the butcher's role they are playing and the fact that such a 'finale' for these parties was inevitable after their 'errors' of 21 April, 5 May, 9 June and 4 July and after their approval of the policy of an offensive, a policy which went nine-tenths of the way to predetermining the victory of the Cavaignacs in July.

All agitational work among the people must be reorganised to ensure that it takes account of the specific experience of the present revolution, and particularly of the July Days, i.e. that it clearly points to the real enemy of the people, the military clique, the Cadets and the Black Hundreds, and that it definitely unmasks the petty-bourgeois parties, the Socialist-Revolutionary and Menshevik parties, which played and are playing the part of butchers' aides.

All agitational work among the people must be reorganised so as to make clear that it is absolutely hopeless to expect the peasants to obtain land as long as the power of the military clique has not been overthrown, and as long as the Socialist-Revolutionary and Menshevik parties have not been exposed and deprived of the people's trust. That would be a very long and arduous process under the 'normal' conditions of capitalist development, but both the war and economic disruption will tremendously accelerate it. These are 'accelerators' that may make a month or even a week equal to a year.

Two objections may perhaps be advanced against what has been said above: first, that to speak now of a decisive struggle is to encourage sporadic action, which would only benefit the counter-revolutionaries; second, that their overthrow would still mean transferring power to the Soviets.

In answer to the first objection, we say: the workers of Russia are already class-conscious enough not to yield to provocation at a moment which is obviously unfavourable to them. It is indisputable that for them to take action and offer resistance at the moment would mean aiding the counter-revolutionaries. It is also indisputable that a decisive struggle will be possible only in the event of a new revolutionary upsurge in the very depths of the masses. But it is not enough to speak in general terms of a revolutionary upsurge, of the rising tide of revolution, of aid by the West-European workers, and so forth; we must draw a definite conclusion from our past, from the lessons we have been given. And that will lead us to the slogan of a decisive struggle against the counter-revolutionaries, who have seized power.

The second objection also amounts to a substitution of arguments of too general a character for concrete realities. No one, no force, can overthrow the bourgeois counter-revolutionaries except the revolutionary proletariat. Now, after the experience of July 1917, it is the revolutionary proletariat that must independently take over state power. Without that the victory of the revolution is *impossible*. The only solution is for power to be in the hands of the proletariat, and for the latter to be supported by the poor peasants or semi-proletarians. And we have already indicated the factors that can enormously accelerate this solution.

Soviets may appear in this new revolution, and indeed are bound to, but *not* the present Soviets, not organs collaborating with the bourgeoisie, but organs of revolutionary struggle against the bourgeoisie. It is true that even then we shall be in favour of building the whole state on the model of the Soviets. It is not a question of Soviets in general, but of combating the *present* counter-revolution and the treachery of the *present* Soviets.

The substitution of the abstract for the concrete is one of the greatest and most dangerous sins in a revolution. The present Soviets have failed, have suffered complete defeat, because they are dominated by the Socialist-Revolutionary and Menshevik parties. At the moment these Soviets are like sheep brought to the slaughterhouse and bleating pitifully under the knife. The Soviets *at present* are powerless and helpless against the triumphant and triumphing counter-revolution. The slogan calling for the transfer of power to the Soviets might be construed as a 'simple' appeal for the transfer of power to the present Soviets, and to say that, to appeal for it, would now mean deceiving the people. Nothing is more dangerous than deceit.

The cycle of development of the class and party struggle in Russia from 27 February to 4 July is complete. A new cycle is beginning, one that involves not the old classes, not the old parties, not the old Soviets, but classes, parties and Soviets rejuvenated in the fire of struggle, tempered, schooled and refashioned by the process of the struggle. We must look forward, not backward. We must operate not with the old, but with the new, post-July, class and party categories. We must, at the beginning of the new cycle, proceed from the triumphant bourgeois counter-revolution,which triumphed because the Socialist-Revolutionaries and Mensheviks compromised with it, and which can be defeated only by the revolutionary proletariat. Of course, in this new cycle there will be many and various stages, both before the complete victory of the counter-revolution and the complete defeat (without a struggle) of the Socialist-Revolutionaries and Mensheviks, and before a new upsurge of a new revolution. But it will only be possible to speak of this later, as each of these stages is reached.

Our Thanks to Prince GY Lvov

Published 19 July (1 August) 1917

In a farewell talk to members of the Committee of Journalists under the Provisional Government, Prince GY Lvov, former head of the Provisional Government, made some valuable admissions for which the workers will certainly be grateful.

> What strengthens my optimism above all else, [Lvov said] are the events of the past few days inside the country. I am convinced that our 'deep breach' in the Lenin front is incomparably more significant for Russia than the German breach in our South-Western Front.

How can the workers not be grateful to the prince for this sober appraisal of the class struggle? They will be more than grateful, they will take a lesson from Lvov.

What an endless flow of fine words and infinite hypocrisy all the bourgeois people and landowners, as well as the Socialist-Revolutionaries and Mensheviks trailing after them, pour out while orating against 'civil war'! But look at Prince Lvov's valuable admission and you will see that he very calmly appraises Russia's internal situation from the point of view of civil war. What the paltry truth of the prince's admissions amounts to is that the bourgeoisie, which head the counter-revolution, have made a deep breach in the revolutionary workers' front. Two enemies, two hostile camps, and one has made a breach in the front of the other – this is how Prince Lvov sums up Russia's internal situation. Let us, then, give Prince Lvov our heartfelt thanks for his frankness! After all, he is a thousand times more correct than those sentimental Socialist-Revolutionary and Menshevik philistines who imagine that the class struggle between the bourgeoisie and the proletariat, which inevitably becomes exceedingly aggravated during a revolution, is likely to disappear because of their curses and magic spells!

Two enemies, two hostile camps, and one has made a breach in the front of the other – this is Prince Lvov's correct philosophy of history. He is right in practically discounting the third camp, the petty bourgeoisie, the Socialist-Revolutionaries and Mensheviks. This third camp appears to be big, but, in fact, it cannot decide anything independently. That is clear to the sober-minded prince, just as it is clear to every Marxist who understands the economic position of the petty bourgeoisie, and as it is clear, lastly, to anyone who thinks about the lessons of the revolution's history, which have always revealed the impotence of the petty-bourgeois parties whenever the struggle between the bourgeoisie and the proletariat became acute.

Even in war-time, the internal class struggle is far more important than the struggle against the foreign enemy. What savage abuse the big and petty bourgeoisie have hurled at the Bolsheviks for recognising this truth! What efforts to deny it have been made by the numerous lovers of alluring words about 'unity', 'revolutionary democracy', and so on, and so forth!

But when a serious and decisive moment came, Prince Lvov at once fully admitted this truth, openly declaring that a 'victory' over the class enemy at home was more important than the position in the struggle against the foreign enemy. An incontestable truth. A useful truth. The workers will be very grateful to Prince Lvov for admitting it, for reminding them of it, for spreading it around. And to express their gratitude to the prince, the workers will use their Party to see that the greatest number of working and exploited people understand and assimilate this truth as well as possible. Nothing is more useful to the working class in the struggle for emancipation than this truth.

What is this 'breach' in the civil war front which Prince Lvov is so triumphant about? This question must be dealt with very carefully if the workers are to learn well from Lvov.

The 'breach in the front' of the internal war on this occasion came, firstly, from the fact that the bourgeoisie had poured oceans of filth and slander on their class enemies, the Bolsheviks, and had shown exceptional tenacity in this really infamous and vile business of slandering their political opponents. It was the 'ideological preparation', if we may call it that, for the 'breach in the front of the class struggle'.

Secondly, the material and really essential 'breach' came from the arrest and outlawing of people of hostile political trends, from the murder of some of them in the street without trial (Voinov was murdered on 6 (19) July for carrying publications out of the *Pravda* printers), from the closing down of their newspapers and the disarming of the workers and revolutionary soldiers.

This is what the 'breach in the front of the war against the class enemy' means. Let the workers think this over well so as to be able to apply it to the bourgeoisie when the time is ripe.

The proletariat will never resort to slander. They will close down the bourgeoisie's newspapers after openly declaring by law, by government decree, that the capitalists and their defenders are enemies of the people. The bourgeoisie, in the shape of our enemy, the government, and the petty bourgeoisie, in the shape of the Soviets, are afraid to say a single open and frank word about the ban on *Pravda*, about the reason for closing it down. The proletariat will tell the truth instead of resorting to slander. They will tell the peasants and everyone else the truth about the bourgeois newspapers and why they must be closed down.

Unlike the petty-bourgeois – Socialist-Revolutionary and Menshevik – windbags, the proletariat will know very well what is actually meant by a 'breach in the front' of the class struggle and by making the enemy, the exploiters, harmless. Prince Lvov has helped the workers realise this truth. Thank you, Prince Lvov.

An Answer

Written between 22-26 July (4-8 August) 1917

I

On 22 July the newspapers printed a report "from the Public Prosecutor of the Petrograd City Court" about the inquiry into the events of 3-5 (16-18) July, and about the prosecution of a group of Bolsheviks, including myself, who are charged with treason and the organisation of an armed uprising.

The government had to publish the report because this dirty business had already created too much of a scandal, having clearly been rigged, as every intelligent person realises, with the aid of the slanderer Alexinsky to meet a long-standing wish and demand of the counter-revolutionary Cadet Party.

But by publishing the report, the government of Tsereteli and co. will disgrace itself even more, for now the crudeness of the fabrication just hits one in the eye.

I left Petrograd on Thursday 29 June (12 July), on account of illness and did not return until Tuesday morning, 4 (17) July. But of course I assume full and unqualified responsibility for every single move or measure of our Party Central Committee, as well as of our Party as a whole. I call attention to my absence to account for my ignorance of certain details and for my allusion mainly to documents that have appeared in the press.

Obviously, it is documents of this nature, particularly if published in the anti-Bolshevik press, that the Public Prosecutor should have carefully collected, set in order and examined before anything else. But the 'republican' Prosecutor, who is carrying out the policies of the 'socialist' Minister Tsereteli, failed to perform his principal duty!

Shortly after 4 July, the ministerial newspaper *Dyelo Naroda* admitted that it was a fact that on 2 July the Bolsheviks had taken action in the Grenadier Regiment by campaigning *against* a demonstration.

Had the Prosecutor a right to keep quiet about this document? Had he any grounds for discounting the testimony of such a witness?

As it so happens, this testimony establishes the highly important fact that the movement developed spontaneously and that the Bolsheviks tried to put off rather than hasten the demonstration.

Furthermore, the same paper printed a still more important document, namely, the text of an appeal signed by our Party Central Committee and written on the night of 3-4 July. The appeal was written and sent to print *after* the movement, despite our efforts to check or rather control it, had 'spilled over', after the demonstration had become a fact.

The utter baseness and unscrupulousness of the Tseretelian Prosecutor, and his boundless treachery, show in his evasion of the question of exactly when, on what day and hour, whether before the Bolshevik appeal or after it, the demonstration began.

As a matter of fact, the appeal stressed the need to give the movement a *peaceable* and *organised* character!

Can you imagine a charge more laughable than that of 'organising an armed uprising', made against an organisation which on the night of 3-4 July, i.e. the night before the fateful day, issued an appeal for a 'peaceful and organised demonstration'? Or take another question: what difference is there between the Prosecutor of Dreyfus or Beilis and the 'republican' Prosecutor of the 'socialist' Minister Tsereteli, a Prosecutor who keeps completely quiet about the appeal?

Further, the Prosecutor does not say that on the night of 3-4 July our Party Central Committee wrote an appeal to stop the demonstration and printed it in *Pravda*, whose offices were wrecked by counter-revolutionary troops that very night.

Further, the Prosecutor does not say that on 4 July Trotsky and Zinoviev, in *several* speeches delivered before the workers and soldiers marching towards the Tauride Palace, called on them to *disperse* once they had made known their will.

Those speeches were heard by hundreds and thousands of people. Then, let every fair-minded citizen who does not want his country to be disgraced by another rigged 'Beilis case' see to it that irrespective of party affiliation, those who heard the speeches make written declarations to the Prosecutor (keeping copies for themselves), stating whether Trotsky's and Zinoviev's speeches contained an appeal to disperse. A decent Prosecutor would himself have made such an appeal to the population. But how on earth can there be decent Prosecutors in the Cabinet of Kerensky, Efremov, Tsereteli and co.? And isn't it high time Russian citizens themselves took care to make 'Beilis cases' impossible in their country?

By the way, owing to illness, I personally made only one speech on 4 July, from the balcony of Kshesinskaya's Palace. The Prosecutor mentions it, and tries to set out what I said, but far from naming any witnesses, he is again reticent about eyewitness reports given in the press. I have by no means been able to secure a complete set of the papers, but still I have seen two testimonies: (1) in the Bolshevik *Proletarskoye Dyelo* (Kronstadt) and (2) in the Menshevik ministerial *Rabochaya Gazeta*. Why not verify the contents of my speech by these documents and by a public appeal?

The speech contained the following points:

1. An apology for confining myself to just a few words on account of illness;
2. Greetings to the revolutionary people of Kronstadt on behalf of the Petrograd workers;

3. An expression of confidence that our slogan 'All Power to the Soviets' must and will win despite all the zigzags of history;
4. An appeal for "firmness, steadfastness and vigilance".

I bring out these particulars in order not to pass by the scant but truly factual evidence which the Prosecutor touched upon – barely touched upon – in such a cursory, indifferent and careless fashion.

However, the important thing is not the particulars, of course, but the overall picture, the overall significance of 4 July. The Prosecutor proved completely incapable of so much as even thinking about this.

On this question, we first of all have the highly valuable testimony given in the press by a rabid anti-Bolshevik, who turns upon us a veritable spate of invective and spiteful phrases. I refer to the ministerial *Rabochaya Gazeta* correspondent. He contributed his personal observations shortly after 4 July. The facts fully established by him show that his observations and experiences fall into two sharply differentiated parts. He contrasts the second with the first, saying that things had taken a "favourable turn" for him.

The first part of the author's experiences is the attempt he made to defend the ministers amid a raging crowd. He was insulted, pummelled, and eventually detained. He heard extremely violent outcries and slogans, of which he recalls in particular "Death to Kerensky" (because he ordered an offensive, "sent 40,000 men to death", etc.).

The second part of the author's experiences, the one that brought a "favourable" turn for him, as he puts it, began when the raging crowd led him "before the tribunal" at the Kshesinskaya Palace. There he was released at once.

Those are the facts which prompted the author to turn a torrent of abuse upon the Bolsheviks. Abuse coming from a political opponent is natural, particularly if the opponent is a Menshevik who senses that the people, crushed by capital and the imperialist war, are against instead of for him. Yet abuse cannot alter the facts, which even as stated by a most rabid anti-Bolshevik testify that the aroused crowd went as far as to shout "Death to Kerensky", that by and large the Bolshevik organisation gave the movement the slogan 'All Power to the Soviets', and that this organisation was the only one that carried any moral weight with the people and urged them to forgo violence.

Those are the facts. Let the willing and unwilling lackeys of the bourgeoisie shout and curse about the facts, accusing the Bolsheviks of 'conniving with the mob', etc., etc. We of the party of the revolutionary proletariat reply that our Party has always been and will always be with the oppressed whenever they voice their absolutely justified and legitimate indignation at the high cost of living, at the inaction and treachery of the 'socialist' Ministers, at the imperialist war and its prolongation. Our Party did its bounden duty by marching together with the justly indignant people on 4 July and by trying to make their movement, their demonstration, as peaceful and organised as possible. For on 4 July a peaceful transfer of power to the Soviets, a peaceful development of the Russian revolution, was *still* possible.

The crass stupidity of the Prosecutor's fairy-tale about the 'organisation of an armed uprising' can be seen from the following: no one will deny that the vast majority of the armed soldiers and sailors who crowded the Petrograd streets on 4 July were on our Party's side. Our Party had every opportunity to set about removing and arresting hundreds of high officials, taking over dozens of public and government buildings and institutions and so on. We did nothing of the kind. Only people so mixed up that they repeat all sorts of tall stories spread by the counter-revolutionary Cadets do not see the laughable absurdity of the assertion that on 3 or 4 July an 'armed uprising' was 'organised'.

The first question the investigation should have put, if it had at all been worthy of that name, was "who started the shooting?" The next question should have been: "How many killed and wounded were there on each side? In what circumstances did each killing and wounding take place?" Had the investigation been anything like a real investigation (and not like a trouble-making article in the papers of the Dans, the Alexinskys, etc.), it would have been the investigators' duty to hold an open, public cross-examination of the witnesses and then immediately publish the record of the interrogation.

That is what courts of inquiry always did in Britain when Britain was a free country. That, or roughly that, is what the Executive Committee of the Soviet felt it had to do at first, when fear of the Cadets had not yet completely numbed its conscience. We know the Executive Committee then promised in the press to issue two bulletins daily on the work of its investigating commission. We also know the Executive Committee (i.e. the Socialist-Revolutionaries and Mensheviks) deceived the people by *not* keeping its promise. But the text of that promise has gone down in history as an admission from our enemies, an admission of what any fair investigator should have done.

It is instructive, at any rate, to note that one of the first *bourgeois*, rabidly anti-Bolshevik papers to carry a report about the shooting on 4 July was the evening *Birzhevka*[1] of the same date. And it is this report that suggests that the shooting was *not* started by the demonstrators, and that the first shots were fired *against* them!! Of course, the 'republican' Prosecutor of the 'socialist' Cabinet preferred to say nothing about this testimony from *Birzhevka*!! And yet this testimony of the utterly anti-Bolshevik *Birzhevka* fully accords with the general picture of what happened as our Party sees it. Had it been an armed uprising, then, of course, the insurgents would not have fired on the counter-demonstrators but would have surrounded certain barracks and certain buildings; they would have wiped out certain army units, etc. On the other hand, if it was a demonstration against the government, with a counter-demonstration by government defenders, it was perfectly natural that the counter-revolutionaries should be the first to shoot, partly because they were enraged by the enormous number of demonstrators, and partly with provocative intent. And it was just as natural the demonstrators should counter shots with shots.

Lists of the dead, though probably incomplete, were published, nevertheless, in a few papers (I think in *Rech* and *Dyelo Naroda*).

1 *Birzhevyie Vedomosti* (*Stock-Exchange Recorder*) (*Birzhekva*) – bourgeois daily published in St. Petersburg from 1880.

The prime and immediate duty of the investigation was to verify, complete, and officially publish these lists. To evade this means *concealing* proof that the counter-revolutionaries started the shooting.

Indeed, even a cursory examination of the published lists shows that the two main and prominent groups, the Cossacks and the sailors, had each about the same number killed. Could this have been so if the ten thousand armed sailors who arrived in Petrograd on 4 July to join the workers and soldiers, particularly the machine-gunners who had many machine-guns, had been intent on an armed uprising?

Obviously, the number of dead among the Cossacks and other opponents of the insurrection would in that case have been ten times greater, for no one will deny that the predominance of the Bolsheviks among the armed people in the Petrograd streets on 4 July was enormous. There is a long list of relevant testimonies in the press from our Party opponents, and any fair investigating body would undoubtedly have collected and published all this evidence.

If the number of dead is approximately the same on both sides, this proves that the shooting was started by the counter-revolutionaries and that the demonstrators merely returned the fire. Otherwise there could not have been an equal number of dead.

Finally, the following piece of press information is exceedingly important: Cossacks are known to have been killed on 4 July during an open skirmish between the demonstrators and counter-demonstrators. Such skirmishes take place even in non-revolutionary times, if the population is at all aroused; for instance, they are not infrequent in the Latin countries, particularly in the South. Bolsheviks are also known to have been killed after 4 July, when there was no clash between excited demonstrators and counter-demonstrators, and hence when the murder of an unarmed by an armed person was really an act of butchery. Such was the murder of the Bolshevik Voinov in Shpalernaya Street on 6 July.

What kind of an investigating commission is it that does not fully collect even the evidence which has appeared in the press concerning the number of dead on both sides, and the time and circumstances of each killing? This is just a mockery of an investigation.

It is clearly futile to expect as much as an attempt at a historical evaluation of 4 July from such an 'investigating' commission. Yet this evaluation is indispensable to anyone wanting to maintain an intelligent attitude towards politics.

Whoever attempts a historical estimate of 3 and 4 July cannot shut his eyes to the exact identity of this movement and that of 20-21 April.

In both cases there was a spontaneous outburst of popular indignation.

In both cases armed people came on to the streets.

In both cases there was a skirmish between the demonstrators and counter-demonstrators, resulting in a certain (approximately equal) number of victims on both sides.

In both cases there was an extremely sharp outburst in the struggle between the revolutionary masses and the counter-revolutionaries, the bourgeoisie, while the neutral, intermediate elements which inclined towards compromise were temporarily inactive.

In both cases the special kind of anti-government demonstration (its special features have been listed above) was due to a deep and protracted crisis of power.

The difference between the two movements is that the latter was much more intense than the former and that the Socialist-Revolutionary and Menshevik parties, neutral on 20 and 21 April, have since got themselves into a tangle by their dependence on the counter-revolutionary Cadets (through the coalition Cabinet and the policy of taking offensive action), and so, on 3 and 4 July, found themselves on the side of the counter-revolution.

The counter-revolutionary Cadet Party brazenly lied even after the events of 20-21 April, shouting, "The shooting on Nevsky was done by Lenin's men", and, clown-like, they demanded an investigation. The Cadets and their friends then constituted the majority in the government and so the investigation was wholly in their hands. It was begun and abandoned, and nothing was published.

Why? Evidently because the facts in no way confirmed what the Cadets wanted. In other words, the investigation concerning 20-21 April was 'smothered' because the facts proved that the firing had been started by the counter-revolutionaries, the Cadets and their friends. This is clear.

The same thing apparently happened on 3 and 4 July and that explains the crude and glaring falsification used by the Prosecutor, who affronts all standards of reasonably conscientious investigation to please Tsereteli and co.

The movement on 3 and 4 July was the last attempt by means of a demonstration to induce the Soviets to take power. That was when the Soviets, i.e. the Socialist-Revolutionaries and Mensheviks controlling them, virtually handed over power to the counter-revolution by summoning counter-revolutionary troops to Petrograd, disarming and disbanding revolutionary regiments and the workers, approving and tolerating acts of tyranny and violence against the Bolsheviks, the introduction of the death penalty at the front, etc.

Military, and consequently political, power has now virtually passed into the hands of the counter-revolution represented by the Cadets and backed by the Socialist-Revolutionaries and Mensheviks. Now, a peaceful development of the Russian revolution is no longer possible and the historical alternative is either complete victory for the counter-revolution, or a new revolution.

II

The charge of espionage and relations with Germany is purely a Beilis case deserving only a brief comment. On this point, the 'investigation' merely repeats the slander of the notorious slanderer Alexinsky, distorting the facts in a particularly crude way.

It is not true that in 1914 Zinoviev and I were arrested in Austria. Only I was arrested.

It is not true that I was arrested as a Russian subject. I was arrested on suspicion of spying, the local gendarme having mistaken the graphs of agrarian statistics in my notebooks for 'plans'! Obviously, that Austrian gendarme was quite on a par with Alexinsky and the *Yedinstvo* group. But it appears that I have been persecuted for internationalism more than anyone else, for I have been persecuted by both belligerent coalitions as a spy – by the gendarme in Austria and by the Cadets, Alexinsky and co. in Russia.

It is not true that Hanecki played a part in my release from the Austrian prison. Victor Adler helped put the Austrian authorities to shame. Poles helped, being ashamed that such an infamous arrest of a Russian revolutionary could take place on Polish soil.

It is an infamous lie that I was in contact with Parvus, that I visited military camps, etc. Nothing of the kind happened, or could have happened. Upon the appearance of the very first issues of Parvus' journal *The Bell*, our newspaper, *Sotsial-Demokrat*, described Parvus as a renegade and a German Plekhanov.[2] Parvus is as much a social-chauvinist on the side of Germany as Plekhanov is on the side of Russia. Being revolutionary internationalists, we had and could have nothing in common with German, Russian, or Ukrainian (Union for the Liberation of the Ukraine) social-chauvinists.

Steinberg is a member of an exile committee in Stockholm, where I first met him. About 20 April or a little later, Steinberg came to Petrograd, where I remember him soliciting a subsidy for the exile society. The Prosecutor could have verified this quite easily if he had wanted to.

The Prosecutor's argument is that Parvus is connected with Hanecki, and that Hanecki is connected with Lenin! But this is just a big swindle, for everyone knows that Hanecki had financial dealings with Parvus, but none with me.

Hanecki, being a tradesman, worked for Parvus or did business with him. But then a great many Russian exiles associated with the press have worked in establishments and institutions belonging to Parvus.

The Prosecutor's argument is that business correspondence may have served as a screen for relations in the nature of espionage. One wonders how many members of the Cadet, Menshevik and Socialist-Revolutionary parties could be indicted for business correspondence according to this wonderful formula!

---

2 See Lenin, 'At the Uttermost Limit', 20 November 1915, *LCW*, Vol. 21, pp. 421-2.

But since the Prosecutor is in possession of several telegrams from Hanecki to Sumenson (which have already been published) and since the Prosecutor knows in which bank, when, and how much money Sumenson had (for the Prosecutor has published a few figures of this nature), why shouldn't he invite two or three office or business employees to take part in the investigation? It would surely take them no more than a couple of days to make a complete extract from all the business and bank records for him.

Hardly anything reveals the true nature of this 'Beilis case' as well as the fragmentary figures cited by the Prosecutor: within six months Sumenson drew 750,000 roubles; she has 180,000 roubles left on her account!! If you are going to publish figures, why not publish them all? When exactly, from whom exactly did Sumenson receive money "within six months", and to whom did she pay it out? When exactly, and exactly what consignments of goods were received?

What could be easier than to collect these complete data? This could and should have been done in a matter of two or three days! It would have disclosed the whole round of business dealings between Hanecki and Sumenson! It would have left no room for the obscure insinuations the Prosecutor is making!

How low the Socialist-Revolutionaries and Mensheviks have fallen is shown by Alexinsky's foulest and most infamous slander, paraphrased to read like a 'state' document by the officials of the Cabinet of Tsereteli and co.!

III

Of course, it would be extremely naive to regard the 'judicial cases' instituted by the Cabinet of Tsereteli, Kerensky and co. against the Bolsheviks as actual judicial cases. That would be an absolutely unpardonable constitutional illusion.

Having entered into a coalition with the counter-revolutionary Cadets on 6 May and having adopted the policy of an offensive, i.e. resumption and prolongation of the imperialist war, the Socialist-Revolutionaries and Mensheviks inevitably found themselves under the thumb of the Cadets.

Being captives, they are forced to participate in the filthiest Cadet deals, in the Cadets' lowest and most slanderous intrigues.

The 'case' of Chernov is rapidly beginning to enlighten even the backward, that is, to corroborate our view. After Chernov, *Rech* is now denouncing Tsereteli as well, calling him a "hypocrite" and a "Zimmerwaldist".

Now the blind will see and the stones will speak.

The counter-revolutionaries are closing their ranks. The Cadets form their basis. The General Staff, the military leaders and Kerensky are in their hands and the Black Hundred press is at their service. These are the allies of the bourgeois counter-revolution.

Foul slander against political opponents will help the workers to realise all the sooner where the counter-revolution is, and to sweep it away in the name of freedom, peace, bread for the hungry and land for the peasants.

The Beginning of Bonapartism

Published 29 July (11 August) 1917

Now that the Cabinet of Kerensky, Nekrasov, Avksentiev and co.[1] has been formed, the gravest and most disastrous error Marxists could make would be to mistake words for deeds, deceptive appearances for reality or generally for something serious.

Let's leave this pastime to the Mensheviks and Socialist-Revolutionaries who have already gone as far as to play the part of clowns around the Bonapartist Kerensky. Indeed, it certainly is buffoonery on the part of the Chernovs, Avksentievs and Tseretelis to start striking postures and uttering fancy words at a time when Kerensky, clearly at the Cadets' bidding, forms something of a secret Directory composed of himself, Nekrasov, Tereshchenko and Savinkov, keeps quiet about both the Constituent Assembly and the declaration of 8 (21) July,[2] proclaims the sacred union of classes in his

---

1 The coalition Provisional Government formed on 24 July (6 August) 1917. The cabinet was composed of Cadets, SRs, Mensheviks, Popular Socialists and non-party people who were close to the Cadets. It included Kerensky as Premier and War and Naval Minister (SR), Nekrasov as Deputy Premier and Minister of Finance (Cadet) and Avksentiev as Minister of the Interior (SR). Due to this composition, the cabinet was in the hands of the Cadets.

2 The declaration issued by the Provisional Government on 8 (21) July 1917, which contained a number of demagogic promises which the Provisional Government hoped would reassure the people after the July events. The

address to the people, concludes an agreement on terms unknown to anyone with Kornilov, who has presented a most brazen ultimatum, and continues the policy of scandalously outrageous arrests.

At a time like this, it certainly is buffoonery on the part of Chernov to challenge Milyukov to appear before a court of arbitration, of Avksentiev to shout about the futility of a narrow class point of view, or of Tsereteli and Dan to push through the Central Executive Committee of the Soviets the emptiest resolutions stuffed with utterly meaningless phrases, resolutions that call to mind the Cadet First Duma during its worst period of impotence in the face of tsarism.

Just as the Cadets in 1906 prostituted the first assembly of popular representatives in Russia by reducing it to a miserable talking shop in face of the growing tsarist counter-revolution, so the SRs and Mensheviks in 1917 have prostituted the Soviets by reducing them to a miserable talking-shop in face of the growing Bonapartist counter-revolution.

Kerensky's Cabinet is undoubtedly a cabinet taking the first steps towards Bonapartism.

We see the chief historical symptom of Bonapartism: the manoeuvring of state power, which leans on the military clique (on the worst elements of the army) for support, between two hostile classes and forces which more or less balance each other out.

The class struggle between the bourgeoisie and the proletariat has reached the limit and on 20 and 21 April, as well as on 3-5 July, the country was within a hair's breadth of civil war. This socio-economic condition certainly forms the classical basis for Bonapartism. And then, this condition is combined with others that are quite akin to it; the bourgeoisie are ranting and raving against the Soviets, but are as *yet* powerless to disperse them, while the Soviets, prostituted

---

government promised to hold elections to the Constituent Assembly on the appointed date of 17 (30) September, guarantee the early introduction of local – urban and *zemstvo* (rural) – self-government, abolish the social estates, take steps to remedy economic dislocation and draft legislation on an eight-hour day, labour safety and social insurance, as well as a land reform, to be considered by the Constituent Assembly. Not one of these promises was kept.

by Tsereteli, Chernov and co., are *now* powerless to put up serious resistance to the bourgeoisie.

The landowners and peasants, too, live as on the eve of civil war: the peasants demand land and freedom, they can be kept in check, if at all, only by a Bonapartist government capable of making the most unscrupulous promises to all classes without keeping any of them.

Add to this the situation created by a foolhardy offensive and military reverses, in which fancy phrases about saving the country are particularly fashionable (concealing the desire to save the imperialist programme of the bourgeoisie), and you have a perfect picture of the socio-political setting for Bonapartism.

Don't let us be deluded by phrases. Don't let us be misled by the idea that all we have is the first steps of Bonapartism. It is the first steps we must be able to discern unless we want to find ourselves in the ridiculous predicament of the stupid philistine who laments the second step although he himself helped to take the first.

It would now be nothing short of stupid philistinism to entertain constitutional illusions, such as, for instance, that the present Cabinet is probably more Left than all the preceding ones (see *Izvestia*), that well-meaning criticism by the Soviets could rectify the errors of the government, that the arbitrary arrests and suppression of newspapers were isolated incidents which, it is to be hoped, will never recur, or that Zarudny is an honest man and that in republican and democratic Russia a fair trial is possible and everyone should appear at it, and so on, and so forth.

The stupidity of these constitutional philistine illusions is too obvious to require special refutation.

The struggle against the bourgeois counter-revolution demands soberness and the ability to see and speak of things as they are.

Bonapartism in Russia is no accident but a natural product of the evolution of the class struggle in a petty-bourgeois country with a considerably developed capitalism and a revolutionary proletariat. Historical stages like 20-21 April, 6 May, 9-10 June, 18-19 June and 3-5 July are landmarks which show clearly how preparations for Bonapartism proceeded. It would be a very big mistake to think that a democratic situation rules out Bonapartism. On the contrary, it is exactly in a situation like this (the history of France has confirmed it twice) that Bonapartism emerges, given a certain relationship between classes and their struggle.

However, to recognise the inevitability of Bonapartism does not at all mean forgetting the inevitability of its downfall.

If we *only* said the counter-revolution had temporarily gained the upper hand here in Russia we should be dodging the issue.

If we analysed the origin of Bonapartism and, fearlessly facing the truth, told the working class and the whole people that the beginning of Bonapartism is a fact, we should thereby start a real and stubborn struggle to overthrow Bonapartism, a struggle waged on a large political scale and based on far-reaching class interests.

The Russian Bonapartism of 1917 differs from the beginnings of French Bonapartism in 1799 and 1849 in several respects, such as the fact that not a single important task of the revolution has been accomplished here. The struggle to settle the agrarian and the national questions is only just gathering momentum.

Kerensky and the counter-revolutionary Cadets who use him as a pawn can neither convoke the Constituent Assembly on the appointed date, nor postpone it, without in both cases promoting the revolution. And the catastrophe engendered by the prolongation of the imperialist war keeps on approaching with even greater force and speed than ever.

The advance contingents of the Russian proletariat succeeded in emerging from our June and July Days without losing too much blood. The proletarian party has every opportunity to choose the tactics and form, or forms, of organisation that will in any circumstances prevent unexpected (seemingly unexpected) Bonapartist persecutions from cutting short its existence and its regular messages to the people.

Let the Party loudly and clearly tell the people the whole truth that Bonapartism is beginning; that the 'new' government of Kerensky, Avksentiev and co. is merely a screen for the counter-revolutionary Cadets and the military clique which is in power at present; that the people can get no peace, the peasants no land, the workers no eight-hour day and the hungry no bread unless the counter-revolution is completely stamped out. Let the Party say so, and every step in the march of events will bear it out.

With remarkable speed Russia has gone through a whole epoch in which the majority of the people put their faith in the petty-bourgeois Socialist-Revolutionary and Menshevik parties. And now the majority of the working people are beginning to pay heavily for their credulity.

All indications are that the march of events is continuing at a very fast pace and that the country is approaching the next epoch, when the majority of the working people will have to entrust their fate to the revolutionary proletariat. The revolutionary proletariat will take power and begin a socialist revolution; despite all the difficulties and possible zigzags of development, it will draw the workers of all the advanced countries into the revolution and will defeat both war and capitalism.

Lessons of the Revolution

Written at the end of July; Afterword written 6 (19) September 1917

Every revolution means a sharp turn in the lives of a vast number of people. Unless the time is ripe for such a turn, no real revolution can take place. And just as any turn in the life of an individual teaches him a great deal and brings rich experience and great emotional stress, so a revolution teaches an entire people very rich and valuable lessons in a short space of time.

During a revolution, millions and tens of millions of people learn in a week more than they do in a year of ordinary, somnolent life. For at the time of a sharp turn in the life of an entire people it becomes particularly clear what aims the various classes of the people are pursuing, what strength they possess, and what methods they use.

Every class-conscious worker, soldier and peasant should ponder thoroughly over the lessons of the Russian revolution, especially now, at the end of July, when it is clear that the first phase of our revolution has failed.

I

Let us see, in fact, what the workers and peasants were striving for when they made the revolution. What did they expect of the revolution? As we know, they expected liberty, peace, bread and land.

But what do we see now?

Instead of liberty, the old tyranny is coming back. The death penalty is being introduced for the soldiers at the front.[1] Peasants are prosecuted for the unauthorised seizure of landed estates. Printing presses of workers' newspapers are wrecked. Workers' newspapers are closed down without trial. Bolsheviks are arrested, often without any charge or upon blatantly trumped-up charges.

It may be argued that the persecution of Bolsheviks does not constitute a violation of freedom, for only certain individuals are being prosecuted and on certain charges. Such an argument, however, would be a deliberate and obvious lie; for how can anyone wreck printing presses and close down newspapers for the crimes of individuals, even if these charges were proved and established by a court of law? It would be a different thing if the government had legally declared the whole party of the Bolsheviks, their very trend and views, to be criminal. But everybody knows that the government of free Russia could not, and did not, do anything of the kind.

What chiefly exposes the libellous character of the charges against the Bolsheviks is that the newspapers of the landowners and capitalists furiously abused the Bolsheviks for their struggle against the war and against the landowners and capitalists, and openly demanded the arrest and prosecution of the Bolsheviks even when not a single charge against a single Bolshevik had been trumped up.

The people want peace. Yet the revolutionary government of free Russia has resumed the war of conquest on the basis of those very same secret treaties which ex-Tsar Nicholas II concluded with the British and French capitalists so that the Russian capitalists might plunder other nations. Those secret treaties remain unpublished. The government of free Russia resorted to subterfuges, and to this day has not proposed a just peace to all nations.

---

1 On 12 (25) July the Provisional Government introduced capital punishment at the front. The divisional 'military revolutionary tribunals' that were set up passed sentences which became effective immediately and were carried out without delay.

There is no bread. Famine is again drawing near. Everybody sees that the capitalists and the rich are unscrupulously cheating the treasury on war deliveries (the war is now costing the nation 50 million roubles daily), that they are raking in fabulous profits through high prices, while nothing whatsoever has been done to establish effective control by the workers over the production and distribution of goods. The capitalists are becoming more brazen every day; they are throwing workers out into the street, and this at a time when the people are suffering from shortages.

A vast majority of the peasants, at congress after congress, have loudly and clearly declared that landed proprietorship is an injustice and robbery. Meanwhile, a government which calls itself revolutionary and democratic has been leading peasants by the nose for months and deceiving them by promises and delays. For months the capitalists did not allow Minister Chernov to issue a law prohibiting the purchase and sale of land. And when this law was finally passed, the capitalists started a foul slander campaign against Chernov, which they are still continuing. The government has become so brazen in its defence of the landowners that it is beginning to bring peasants to trial for 'unauthorised' seizures of land.

They are leading the peasants by the nose, telling them to wait for the Constituent Assembly. The convocation of the Assembly, however, is being steadily postponed by the capitalists. Now that owing to Bolshevik pressure it has been set for 30 September (13 October), the capitalists are openly clamouring about this being 'impossibly' short notice, and are demanding the Constituent Assembly's postponement. The most influential members of the capitalist and landowner party, the 'Cadet', or 'people's freedom', Party, such as Panina, are openly urging that the convocation of the Constituent Assembly be delayed until after the war.

As to land, wait until the Constituent Assembly. As to the Constituent Assembly, wait until the end of the war. As to the end of the war, wait until complete victory. That is what it comes to. The capitalists and landowners, having a majority in the government, are plainly mocking at the peasants.

II

But how could this happen in a free country, after the overthrow of the tsarist regime?

In a non-free country, the people are ruled by a tsar and a handful of landowners, capitalists and bureaucrats who are not elected by anybody.

In a free country, the people are ruled only by those who have been elected for that purpose by the people themselves. At the elections the people divide themselves into parties, and as a rule each class of the population forms its own party; for instance, the landowners, the capitalists, the peasants and the workers all form separate parties. In free countries, therefore, the people are ruled through an open struggle between parties and by free agreement between these parties.

For about four months after the overthrow of the tsarist regime on 27 February 1917, Russia was ruled as a free country, i.e. through an open struggle between freely formed parties and by free agreement between them. To understand the development of the Russian revolution, therefore, it is above all necessary to study the chief parties, the class interests they defended, and the relations among them all.

III

After the overthrow of the tsarist regime state power passed into the hands of the first Provisional Government, consisting of representatives of the bourgeoisie, i.e. the capitalists, who were joined by the landowners. The 'Cadet' Party, the chief capitalist party, held pride of place as the ruling and government party of the bourgeoisie.

It was no accident this party secured power, although it was not the capitalists, of course, but the workers and peasants, the soldiers and sailors, who fought the tsarist troops and shed their blood for liberty. Power was secured by the capitalist party because the capitalist class possessed the power of wealth, organisation and knowledge. Since 1905, and particularly during the war, the class of the capitalists, and the landowners associated with them, have made in Russia the greatest progress in organising.

The Cadet Party has always been monarchist, both in 1905 and from 1905 to 1917. After the people's victory over tsarist tyranny it proclaimed itself a republican party. The experience of history shows that whenever the people triumphed over a monarchy, capitalist parties were willing to become republican as long as they could uphold the privileges of the capitalists and their unlimited power over the people.

The Cadet Party pays lip-service to 'people's freedom'. But actually it stands for the capitalists, and it was immediately backed by all the landowners, monarchists and Black Hundreds. The press and the elections are proof of this. After the revolution, all the bourgeois papers and the whole Black Hundred press began to sing in unison with the Cadets. Not daring to come out openly, all the monarchist parties supported the Cadet Party at the elections, as, for example, in Petrograd.

Having obtained state power, the Cadets made every effort to continue the predatory war of conquest begun by Tsar Nicholas II, who had concluded secret predatory treaties with the British and French capitalists. Under these treaties, the Russian capitalists were promised, in the event of victory, the seizure of Constantinople, Galicia, Armenia, etc. As to the people, the government of the Cadets put them off with empty subterfuges and promises, deferring the decision of all matters of vital and essential importance to the workers and peasants until the Constituent Assembly met, without appointing the date of its convocation.

Making use of liberty, the people began to organise independently. The chief organisation of the workers and peasants, who form the overwhelming majority of the population of Russia, was the Soviets of Workers', Soldiers' and Peasants' Deputies. These Soviets already began to be formed during the February Revolution, and within a few weeks all class-conscious and advanced workers and peasants were united in Soviets in most of the larger cities of Russia and in many rural districts.

The Soviets were elected in an absolutely free way. They were genuine organisations of the people, of the workers and peasants. They were genuine organisations of the vast majority of the people. The workers and peasants in soldiers' uniforms were armed.

It goes without saying that the Soviets could and should have taken over state power in full. Pending the convocation of the Constituent Assembly there should have been no other power in the state but the Soviets. Only then would our revolution have become a truly popular and truly democratic revolution. Only then could the working people, who are really striving for peace, and who really have no interest in a war of conquest, have begun firmly and resolutely to carry out a policy which would have ended the war of conquest and led to peace. Only then could the workers and peasants have curbed the capitalists, who are making fabulous profits 'from the war' and who have reduced the country to a state of ruin and starvation. But in the Soviets only a minority of the deputies were on the side of the revolutionary workers' party, the Bolshevik Social-Democrats, who demanded that all state power should be transferred to the Soviets. The majority of the deputies to the Soviets were on the side of the parties of the Menshevik Social-Democrats and the Socialist-Revolutionaries, who were opposed to the transfer of power to the Soviets. Instead of removing the bourgeois government and replacing it by a government of the Soviets, these parties insisted on supporting the bourgeois government, compromising with it and forming a coalition government with it. This policy of compromise with the bourgeoisie pursued by the Socialist-Revolutionary and Menshevik parties, who enjoyed the confidence of the majority of the people, is the main content of the entire course of development of the revolution during the five months since it began.

IV

Let us first see how this compromising of the Socialist-Revolutionaries and Mensheviks with the bourgeoisie proceeded, and then let us try to explain why the majority of the people trusted them.

V

The Mensheviks and Socialist-Revolutionaries have compromised with the capitalists in one way or another at every stage of the Russian Revolution.

At the very close of February 1917, as soon as the people had triumphed and the tsarist regime had been overthrown, the capitalist Provisional Government admitted Kerensky as a 'socialist'. As a matter of fact, Kerensky has never been a socialist; he was only a Trudovik, and he enlisted himself with the 'Socialist-Revolutionaries' only in March 1917, when it was already safe and quite profitable to do so. Through Kerensky, as Deputy Chairman of the Petrograd Soviet, the capitalist Provisional Government immediately set about gaining control of and taming the Soviet. The Soviet, i.e. the Socialist-Revolutionaries and Mensheviks who predominated in it, allowed itself to be tamed, agreeing immediately after the formation of the capitalist Provisional Government to 'support it' – 'to the extent' that it carried out its promises.

The Soviet regarded itself as a body verifying and exercising control over the activities of the Provisional Government. The leaders of the Soviet established what was known as a Contact Commission to keep in touch with the government. Within that Contact Commission, the Socialist-Revolutionary and Menshevik leaders of the Soviet held continuous negotiations with the capitalist government, holding, properly speaking, the status of Ministers without portfolio or unofficial Ministers.

This state of affairs lasted throughout March and almost the whole of April. Seeking to gain time, the capitalists resorted to delays and subterfuges. Not a single step of any importance to further the revolution was taken by the capitalist government during this period. It did absolutely nothing even to further its direct and immediate task, the convocation of the Constituent Assembly; it did not submit the question to the localities or even set up a central commission to handle the preparations. The government was concerned with only one thing, namely, surreptitiously renewing the predatory international treaties concluded by the tsar with the capitalists of Britain and France, thwarting the revolution as cautiously and quietly as possible and promising everything without fulfilling any of its promises. The Socialist-Revolutionaries and Mensheviks in the Contact Commission acted like simpletons who were fed on fancy phrases, promises and more promises. Like the crow in the fable, the Socialist-Revolutionaries and Mensheviks succumbed to flattery and listened with pleasure to the assurances of the capitalists that they valued the Soviets highly and did not take a single step without them.

But time passed and the capitalist government did absolutely nothing for the revolution. On the contrary, during this period it managed, to the detriment of the revolution, to renew the secret predatory treaties, or, rather, to reaffirm them and 'vitalise' them by supplementary and no less secret negotiations with Anglo-French imperialist diplomats. During this period it managed, to the detriment of the revolution, to lay the foundations of a counter-revolutionary organisation of (or at least of a rapprochement among) the generals and officers in the army in the field. To the detriment of the revolution it managed to start the organisation of industrialists, of factory-owners, who, under the onslaught of the workers, were compelled to make concession after concession, but who at the same time began to sabotage (damage) production and prepare to bring it to a standstill when the opportunity came.

However, the organisation of the advanced workers and peasants in the Soviets made steady progress. The foremost representatives of the oppressed classes felt that, in spite of the agreement between the government and the Petrograd Soviet, in spite of Kerensky's pompous talk, in spite of the 'Contact Commission', the government remained an enemy of the people, an enemy of the revolution. The people felt that unless the resistance of the capitalists was broken, the cause of peace, liberty and the revolution, would inevitably be lost. The impatience and bitterness of the people kept on growing.

VI

It burst out on 20-21 April. The movement flared up spontaneously; nobody had cleared the ground for it. The movement was so markedly directed against the government that one regiment even appeared fully armed at the Mariinsky Palace to arrest the ministers. It became perfectly obvious to everybody that the government could not retain power. The Soviets could (and should) have taken over power without meeting the least resistance from any quarter. Instead, the Socialist-Revolutionaries and Mensheviks supported the collapsing capitalist government, entangled themselves even further in compromises with it and took steps that were even more fatal to the revolution, that tended to lead to its doom.

Revolution enlightens all classes with a rapidity and thoroughness unknown in normal, peaceful times. The capitalists, better organised and more experienced than anybody else in matters of class struggle and politics, learnt their lesson quicker than the others. Realising that the government's position was hopeless, they resorted to a method which for many decades, ever since 1848, has been practised by the capitalists of other countries in order to fool, divide and weaken the workers. This method is known as a 'coalition' government, i.e. a joint cabinet formed of members of the bourgeoisie and turncoats from socialism.

In countries where freedom and democracy have long existed side by side with a revolutionary labour movement, in Britain and France, the capitalists have repeatedly and very successfully resorted to this method. When the 'socialist' leaders entered a bourgeois cabinet, they invariably proved to be figureheads, puppets, screens for the capitalists, instruments for deceiving the workers. The 'democratic and republican' capitalists of Russia resorted to this very method. The Socialist-Revolutionaries and Mensheviks let themselves be fooled at once, and the 'coalition' cabinet, joined by Chernov, Tsereteli and co., became a fact on 6 May.

The simpletons of the Socialist-Revolutionary and Menshevik parties were jubilant and fatuously bathed in the rays of the ministerial glory of their leaders. The capitalists gleefully rubbed their hands at having found helpers against the people in the persons of the 'leaders of the Soviets' and at having secured their promise to support 'offensive operations at the front', i.e. a resumption of the imperialist predatory war, which had come to a standstill for a while. The capitalists were well aware of the puffed-up impotence of these leaders, they knew that the promises of the bourgeoisie – regarding control over production, and even the organisation of production, regarding a peace policy and so forth – would never be fulfilled.

And so it turned out. The second phase in the development of the revolution, 6 May to 9 June, or 18 June, fully corroborated the expectations of the capitalists as to the ease with which the Socialist-Revolutionaries and Mensheviks could be fooled.

While Peshekhonov and Skobelev were deceiving themselves and the people with florid speeches to the effect that 100 per cent of the profits of the capitalists would be taken away from them, that their 'resistance was broken' and so forth, the capitalists continued to consolidate their position. Nothing, absolutely nothing, was undertaken during this period to curb the capitalists. The ministerial turncoats from socialism proved to be mere talking machines for distracting the attention of the oppressed classes, while the entire apparatus of state administration actually remained in the hands of the bureaucracy (the officialdom) and the bourgeoisie. The notorious Palchinsky, Deputy Minister for Industry, was a typical representative of that apparatus, blocking every measure against the capitalists. While the ministers prated everything remained as of old.

The bourgeoisie used Minister Tsereteli in particular to fight the revolution. He was sent to 'pacify' Kronstadt when the local revolutionaries had the audacity to remove an appointed commissar. The bourgeoisie launched in their newspapers an incredibly vociferous, violent and vicious campaign of lies, slander and vituperation against Kronstadt, accusing it of the desire "to secede from Russia", and repeating this and similar absurdities in a thousand ways to intimidate the petty bourgeoisie and the philistines. A most typically stupid and frightened philistine,

Tsereteli, was the most 'conscientious' of all in swallowing the bait of bourgeois slander; he was the most zealous of all in *smashing up and subduing* Kronstadt, without realising that he was playing the role of a lackey of the counter-revolutionary bourgeoisie. He turned out to be the instrument of the 'compromise' arrived at with revolutionary Kronstadt, whereby the commissar for Kronstadt was not simply appointed by the government, but was elected locally and was *confirmed* by the government. It was on such miserable compromises that the ministers who had deserted socialism for the bourgeoisie wasted their time.

Wherever a bourgeois minister could not appear in defence of the government, before the revolutionary workers or in the Soviets, Skobelev, Tsereteli, Chernov or some other 'socialist' Minister appeared (or, to be precise, was sent by the bourgeoisie) and faithfully performed their assignment; he would do his level best to defend the Cabinet, whitewash the capitalists and fool the people by making promise after promise and by advising people to wait, wait and wait.

Minister Chernov particularly was engaged in bargaining with his bourgeois colleagues; down to July, to the new 'crisis of power' which began after the movement of 3-4 July, to the resignation of the Cadets from the Cabinet, Minister Chernov was continuously engaged in the useful and interesting work, so beneficial to the people, of 'persuading' his bourgeois colleagues, exhorting them to agree at least to prohibition of the purchase and sale of land. This prohibition had been most solemnly promised to the peasants at the All-Russia Congress of Peasant Deputies in Petrograd. But the promise remained only a promise. Chernov proved unable to fulfil it either in May or in June, until the revolutionary tide, the spontaneous outbreak of 3-4 July, which coincided with the resignation of the Cadets from the Cabinet, made it possible to enact this measure. Even then, however, it proved to be an isolated measure, incapable of promoting to any palpable extent the struggle of the peasants against the landowners for land.

Meanwhile, at the front, the counter-revolutionary, imperialist task of resuming the imperialist, predatory war, a task which

Guchkov, so hated by the people, had been unable to accomplish, was being accomplished successfully and brilliantly by the 'revolutionary democrat' Kerensky, that new-baked member of the Socialist-Revolutionary Party. He revelled in his own eloquence, incense was burned to him by the imperialists, who were using him as a pawn, he was flattered and worshipped – all because he served the capitalists faithfully, trying to talk the 'revolutionary troops' into agreeing to resume the war being waged in pursuance of the treaties concluded by Tsar Nicholas II with the capitalists of Britain and France, a war waged so that Russian capitalists might secure Constantinople and Lvov, Erzurum and Trebizond.

So passed the second phase of the Russian revolution – 6 May to 9 (22) June. Shielded and defended by the 'socialist' Ministers, the counter-revolutionary bourgeoisie grew in strength, consolidated their position and prepared an offensive both against the external enemy and against the internal enemy, i.e. the revolutionary workers.

VII

On 9 June, the revolutionary workers' party, the Bolsheviks, was preparing for a demonstration in Petrograd to give organised expression to the irresistibly growing popular discontent and indignation. The Socialist-Revolutionary and Menshevik leaders, entangled in compromises with the bourgeoisie and bound by the imperialist policy of an offensive, were horrified, feeling that they were losing their influence among the masses. A general howl went up against the demonstration, and the counter-revolutionary Cadets joined in this howl, this time together with the Socialist-Revolutionaries and Mensheviks. Under their direction, and as a result of their policy of compromise with the capitalists, the swing of the petty-bourgeois masses to an alliance with the counter-revolutionary bourgeoisie became quite definite and strikingly obvious. This is the historical significance and class meaning of the crisis of 9 June.

The Bolsheviks called off the demonstration, having no wish to lead the workers at that moment into a losing fight against the united Cadets, Socialist-Revolutionaries and Mensheviks. The latter, however, so as to retain at least a vestige of the people's confidence, were compelled to call a general demonstration for 18 June (1 July). The bourgeoisie were beside themselves with rage, rightly discerning in this a swing of the petty-bourgeois democrats towards the proletariat, and they decided to paralyse the action of the democrats by an offensive at the front.

In fact, 18 June was marked by an impressive victory for the slogans of the revolutionary proletariat, the slogans of Bolshevism, among the people of Petrograd. And on 19 June the bourgeoisie and the Bonapartist[2] Kerensky solemnly announced that the offensive at the front had begun on 18 June.

The offensive meant in effect the resumption of the predatory war in the interests of the capitalists and against the will of the vast majority of the working people. That is why the offensive was inevitably accompanied, on the one hand, by a gigantic growth of chauvinism and the transfer of military power (and consequently of state power) to the military gang of Bonapartists, and, on the other, by the use of violence against the masses, the persecution of the internationalists, the abolition of freedom of agitation and the arrest and shooting of those who were against the war.

Whereas 6 May bound the Socialist-Revolutionaries and Mensheviks to the triumphal chariot of the bourgeoisie with a rope, 19 June shackled them, as servants of the capitalists, with a chain.

VIII

Owing to the resumption of the predatory war, the bitterness of the people naturally grew even more rapidly and intensely. 3-4 July witnessed an outburst of their anger which the Bolsheviks attempted to restrain and which, of course, they had to endeavour to make as organised as possible.

---

2 Bonapartism (from Bonaparte, the name of the two French emperors) is a name applied to a government which endeavours to appear non-partisan by taking advantage of a highly acute struggle between the parties of the capitalists and the workers. Actually serving the capitalists, such a government dupes the workers most of all by promises and petty concessions. – *Lenin*

The Socialist-Revolutionaries and Mensheviks, being slaves of the bourgeoisie, shackled by their master, agreed to everything: dispatching reactionary troops to Petrograd, bringing back the death penalty, disarming the workers and revolutionary troops, arresting and hounding and closing down newspapers without trial. The power which the bourgeoisie in the government were unable to take entirely, and which the Soviets did not want to take, fell into the hands of the military clique, the Bonapartists, who, of course, were wholly backed by the Cadets and the Black Hundreds, by the landowners and capitalists.

Down the ladder, step by step. Having once set foot on the ladder of compromise with the bourgeoisie, the Socialist-Revolutionaries and Mensheviks slid irresistibly downwards, to rock bottom. On 28 February (13 March), in the Petrograd Soviet, they promised conditional support to the bourgeois government. On 6 May they saved it from collapse and allowed themselves to be made its servants and defenders by agreeing to an offensive. On 9 June they united with the counter-revolutionary bourgeoisie in a campaign of furious rage, lies and slander against the revolutionary proletariat. On 19 June they approved the resumption of the predatory war. On 3 July they consented to the summoning of reactionary troops, which was the beginning of their complete surrender of power to the Bonapartists. Down the ladder, step by step.

This shameful finale of the Socialist-Revolutionary and Menshevik parties was not fortuitous but a consequence of the economic status of the small owners, the petty bourgeoisie, as has been repeatedly borne out by experience in Europe.

IX

Everybody, of course, has seen the small owner bend every effort and strain every nerve to 'get on in the world', to become a real master, to rise to the position of a 'strong' employer, to the position of a bourgeois. As long as capitalism rules the roost, there is no alternative for the small owner other than becoming a capitalist (and that is possible at best in the case of one small owner out of a hundred), or becoming a ruined man, a semi-proletarian and ultimately a proletarian. The same is true in politics: the petty-bourgeois democrats, especially their leaders, tend to trail after the bourgeoisie. The leaders of the petty-bourgeois democrats console their people with promises and assurances about the possibility of reaching agreement with the big capitalists; at best, and for a very brief period, they obtain certain minor concessions from the capitalists for a small upper section of the working people; but on every decisive issue, on every important matter, the petty-bourgeois democrats have always tailed after the bourgeoisie as a feeble appendage to them, as an obedient tool in the hands of the financial magnates. The experience of Britain and France has proved this over and over again.

The experience of the Russian revolution from February to July 1917, when events developed with unusual rapidity, particularly under the influence of the imperialist war and the deep-going crisis brought about by it, has most strikingly and palpably confirmed the old Marxist truth that the position of the petty bourgeoisie is unstable.

The lesson of the Russian revolution is that there can be no escape for the working people from the iron grip of war, famine and enslavement by the landowners and capitalists unless they completely break with the Socialist-Revolutionary and Menshevik parties and clearly understand the latter's treacherous role, unless they renounce all compromises with the bourgeoisie and resolutely side with the revolutionary workers. Only the revolutionary workers, if supported by the peasant poor, are capable of smashing the resistance of the capitalists and leading the people in gaining land without compensation, complete liberty, victory over famine and the war and a just and lasting peace.

* * *

Afterword

This article was written at the end of July, as is apparent from the text.

The history of the revolution during August has fully corroborated what is said in this article. Then, at the end of August, the Kornilov revolt[3] caused a new turn in the revolution by clearly demonstrating to the whole people that the Cadets, in alliance with the counter-revolutionary generals, were striving to disband the Soviets and restore the monarchy. The near future will show how strong this new turn of the revolution is, and whether it will succeed in putting an end to the fatal policy of compromise with the bourgeoisie.

N Lenin
6 (19) September 1917

3 The Kornilov revolt against the revolution was organised by the bourgeoisie and landowners in August 1917. See 'To the CC of the RSDLP', p. 281 in this volume.

Kamenev's Speech in the CEC on the Stockholm Conference

Published 16 (29) August 1917

Editor's note:

The question of convening an international socialist conference in Stockholm arose in April 1917. The matter was discussed at a meeting of the Petrograd Soviet.

The Mensheviks and SRs accepted the invitation and decided to take the initiative in calling the conference. Lenin declared emphatically against participation in the Stockholm conference, a social-chauvinist affair.

On 6 (19) August 1917, at a meeting of the All-Russia Central Executive Committee of the Soviets of Workers' and Soldiers' Deputies (CEC) discussing preparations for the Stockholm conference, Kamenev insisted on participation in the conference. He said the Bolshevik resolution on the matter should be revised.

Simultaneously with the letter 'Kamenev's Speech in the CEC on the Stockholm Conference', which he sent to the Bolshevik paper *Proletary* for publication, Lenin on 17 (30) August wrote another letter, addressed to the Bureau of the Central Committee Abroad.

With reference to Kamenev's statement, Lenin wrote:

> I consider Kamenev's statement [...] the height of stupidity, if not of baseness, and have already written about this to the Central Committee and for the press. (Lenin, 'To the Bureau of the CC Abroad', 17 (30) August 1917, *LCW*, Vol. 35, p. 320.)

On 16 (29) August the Bolshevik Party's Central Committee, upon discussing the issue of the Stockholm conference, reaffirmed the decision not to attend.

The conference never met.

* * *

The speech made by Comrade Kamenev on 6 (19) August in the Central Executive Committee on the Stockholm Conference cannot but meet with reproof from all Bolsheviks who are faithful to their Party and principles.

In the very first sentence of his speech, Comrade Kamenev made a formal statement which gave his whole speech a monstrous ring. He made the reservation that he was speaking on his own behalf, and that "our group has not discussed this issue".

First of all, since when, in an organised party, do individual members speak about important issues "on their own behalf"? Since the group had not discussed the issue, Comrade Kamenev had no right to speak. This is the first conclusion to be drawn from his words.

Secondly, what right had Comrade Kamenev to ignore the decision of the Party Central Committee against participating in the Stockholm Conference? As long as this decision has not been rescinded by a congress or by a new decision of the Central Committee, it remains law for the Party. Had it been rescinded, Comrade Kamenev could not have kept quiet, could not have spoken in the present perfect: "We Bolsheviks have so far adopted a negative attitude to the Stockholm Conference."

Again the conclusion is that Kamenev had no right to speak and, moreover, directly violated a Party decision, directly spoke against the Party, and thwarted its will by not saying a word about the Central Committee decision, which is binding on him. Yet the decision was published in *Pravda*, even with the additional remark that the Party representative would withdraw from the Zimmerwald Conference should it favour participation in the Stockholm Conference.[1]

Kamenev gave an incorrect account of the reasons for the 'former' negative attitude of the Bolsheviks towards participation in the Stockholm Conference. He did not say that social-imperialists were going to attend the conference and that it would be a disgrace for a revolutionary Social-Democrat to have any truck with them.

Sad to admit, Starostin, who has often been very much in the wrong in the past, put the revolutionary Social-Democratic point of view a thousand times better, more correctly and more fittingly than Kamenev. To confer with social-imperialists, ministers, butchers' aides in Russia would be shameful treachery. There could then be no talk of internationalism.

Kamenev's arguments, which actually favour a 'change' in our view on the Stockholm Conference, are ludicrously feeble.

> It became clear to us, [Kamenev said] that from that [??] moment the Stockholm Conference ceased [??] to be a blind instrument of the imperialist countries.

That is not true. There is not a single fact to support it, and Kamenev could advance no serious argument in its favour. If the Anglo-French social-imperialists refuse to attend, while the German do attend, can that be regarded as a change in principle?? Is it a change at all from an internationalist point of view? Can Kamenev really have 'forgotten' the decision of our Party conference (29 April (12 May)) on the perfectly analogous case of the Danish social-imperialist?

According to newspaper reports, Kamenev further said:

> The broad revolutionary banner under which the forces of the world proletariat are mustering is beginning to wave over Stockholm.

This is a meaningless declamation in the spirit of Chernov and Tsereteli. It is a blatant untruth. In actual fact, it is not the revolutionary

1 See Lenin, 'On the Question of Convening an International, So-called Socialist Conference Jointly With the Social-chauvinists', 10 (23) May 1917, *LCW*, Vol. 24, p. 388.

banner that is beginning to wave over Stockholm, but the banner of deals, agreements, amnesty for the social-imperialists and negotiations among bankers for dividing up annexed territory.

We cannot tolerate a situation where the party of the internationalists, which is responsible to the whole world for revolutionary internationalism, compromises itself by winking at the dirty tricks of the Russian and German social-imperialists, of the ministers of the bourgeois imperialist government of the Chernovs, Skobelevs and co.

We have decided to build a Third International, and we must do so in face of all difficulties. Not a single step backward to deals with the social-imperialists and deserters from socialism!

N Lenin

To the CC of the RSDLP (On the Kornilov Revolt)

Written 30 August (12 September) 1917

Editor's note

The Kornilov revolt against the revolution was organised by the bourgeoisie and landowners in August 1917. It was led by the tsarist general Kornilov, then Supreme Commander-in-Chief of the Army. The conspirators aimed at capturing Petrograd, smashing the Bolshevik Party, disbanding the Soviets, establishing a military dictatorship, and paving the way for the restoration of the monarchy. Kerensky, head of the Provisional Government, first joined in the conspiracy, and then declared Kornilov to be a rebel against the Provisional Government. The revolt began on 25 August (7 September). Kornilov marched the Third Cavalry Corps against Petrograd.

In response to the call of the Bolshevik Party's CC, the workers of Petrograd and the revolutionary soldiers and sailors rose to fight the rebels. The Petrograd workers promptly formed Red Guard units. Revolutionary committees were set up in several localities. The Kornilov revolt was put down by the workers and peasants under the leadership of the Bolshevik Party. Under pressure from the people, the Provisional Government had to order the arrest and trial of Kornilov and his accomplices.

* * *

It is possible that these lines will come too late, for events are developing with a rapidity that sometimes makes one's head spin. I am writing this on Wednesday 30 August (12 September), and the recipients will read it no earlier than Friday 2 (15) September. Still, on chance, I consider it my duty to write the following.

The Kornilov revolt is a most unexpected (unexpected at such a moment and in such a form) and downright unbelievably sharp turn in events.

Like every sharp turn, it calls for a revision and change of tactics. And as with every revision, we must be extra-cautious not to become unprincipled.

It is my conviction that those who become unprincipled are people who (like Volodarsky) slide into defencism or (like other Bolsheviks) into a *bloc* with the SRs, into *supporting* the Provisional Government. Their attitude is absolutely wrong and unprincipled. We shall become defencists *only after* the transfer of power to the proletariat, *after* a peace offer, *after* the secret treaties and ties with the banks have been broken – *only afterwards*. Neither the capture of Riga *nor the capture of Petrograd* will make us defencists. (I should very much like Volodarsky to read this.) Until then we stand for a proletarian revolution, we are against the war, and we are *no* defencists.

Even now we must not support Kerensky's government. This is unprincipled. We may be asked: aren't we going to fight against Kornilov? Of course we must! But this is not the same thing; there is a 'dividing line' here, which is being stepped over by some Bolsheviks who fall into compromise and allow themselves to be *carried away* by the course of events.

We shall fight, we are fighting against Kornilov, *just as* Kerensky's *troops do*, but we do not support Kerensky. *On the contrary*, we expose his weakness. There is the difference. It is rather a subtle difference, but it is highly essential and must not be forgotten.

What, then, constitutes our change of tactics after the Kornilov revolt?

We are changing the *form* of our struggle against Kerensky. Without in the least relaxing our hostility towards him, without taking back a single word said against him, without renouncing the task of overthrowing him, we say that we must *take into account* the present situation. We shall not overthrow Kerensky right now. We shall approach the task of fighting against him *in a different way*, namely, we shall point out to the people (who are fighting against Kornilov) Kerensky's *weakness* and *vacillation*. That has been done in the past *as well*. Now, however, it has become the *all-important* thing and this constitutes the change.

The change, further, is that the *all-important* thing now has become the intensification of our campaign for some kind of 'partial demands' to be presented to Kerensky: arrest Milyukov, arm the Petrograd workers, summon the Kronstadt, Vyborg and Helsingfors troops to Petrograd, dissolve the Duma, arrest Rodzianko, legalise the transfer of the landed estates to the peasants, introduce workers' control over grain and factories, etc., etc. We must present these demands not only to Kerensky, and *not so much* to Kerensky, as to the workers, soldiers and peasants who have been *carried away* by the course of the struggle against Kornilov. We must keep up their *enthusiasm*, encourage them to deal with the generals and officers who have declared for Kornilov, urge *them* to demand the immediate transfer of land to the peasants, suggest to *them* that it is necessary to arrest Rodzianko and Milyukov, dissolve the Duma, close down *Rech* and other bourgeois papers and institute investigations against them. The 'Left' SRs must be especially urged on in this direction.

It would be wrong to think that we have moved farther away from the task of the proletariat winning power. No. We have come very close to it, *not directly*, but from the side. *At the moment* we must campaign not so much directly against Kerensky, as *indirectly* against him, namely, by demanding a more and more active, truly revolutionary war against Kornilov. The development of this war alone can lead *us* to power, but we must *speak* of this as little as possible in our propaganda (remembering very well that even tomorrow events may put power into our hands, and then we shall not relinquish it). It seems to me that this should be passed on in a letter (not in the papers) to the propagandists, to groups of agitators and propagandists, and to Party members in general.

We must relentlessly fight against phrases about the defence of the country, about a united front of revolutionary democrats, about supporting the Provisional Government, etc., etc., since they are just empty *phrases*. We must say: now is the time for *action*; you SR and Menshevik gentlemen have long since worn those phrases threadbare. Now is the time for *action*; the war against Kornilov must be conducted in a revolutionary way, by drawing the masses in, by arousing them, by inflaming them (Kerensky is *afraid* of the masses, *afraid* of the people). In the war against the Germans, *action* is required right now; *immediate and unconditional peace must be offered* on *precise* terms. If this is done, either a speedy peace *can* be attained or the war can be turned into a revolutionary war; if not, all the Mensheviks and Socialist-Revolutionaries remain lackeys of imperialism.

* * *

PS: Having read six issues of *Rabochy*, *after* this was written, I must say that our views fully coincide. I heartily welcome the splendid editorials, press review and articles by VM and V. As to Volodarsky's speech, I have read his letter to the editors, which likewise 'eliminates' my reproaches. Once more, best wishes and greetings!

On Compromises

Written 1-3 (14-16) September 1917

The term compromise in politics implies the surrender of certain demands, the renunciation of part of one's demands, by agreement with another party.

The usual idea the man in the street has about the Bolsheviks, an idea encouraged by a press which slanders them, is that the Bolsheviks will never agree to a compromise with anybody.

The idea is flattering to us as the party of the revolutionary proletariat, for it proves that even our enemies are compelled to admit our loyalty to the fundamental principles of socialism and revolution. Nevertheless, we must say that this idea is wrong. Engels was right when, in his criticism of the Manifesto of the Blanquist Communists,[1] he ridiculed their declaration: "No compromises!"[2] This, he said, was an empty phrase, for compromises are often unavoidably forced upon a fighting party by circumstances, and it is absurd to refuse once and for all to accept "payments on account".

1 Blanquists – supporters of a trend in the French socialist movement, headed by Louis-Auguste Blanqui (1805 – 1881), the French revolutionary and Utopian communist. Substituting the actions of a small group of conspirators for those of a revolutionary party, they ignored the actual situation necessary for a victorious insurrection and spurned contact with the masses.

2 See Engels, Friedrich, 'The Program of the Blanquist Commune Refugees', *MECW*, Vol. 24, p. 12.

The task of a truly revolutionary party is not to declare that it is impossible to renounce all compromises, but to be able, *through all compromises*, when they are unavoidable, to remain true to its principles, to its class, to its revolutionary purpose, to its task of paving the way for revolution and educating the mass of the people for victory in the revolution.

To agree, for instance, to participate in the Third and Fourth Dumas was a compromise, a temporary renunciation of revolutionary demands. But this was a compromise absolutely forced upon us, for the balance of forces made it impossible for us for the time being to conduct a mass revolutionary struggle, and in order to prepare this struggle over a long period we *had* to be able to work even from *inside* such a 'pigsty'. History has proved that this approach to the question by the Bolsheviks as a party was perfectly correct.

Now the question is not of a forced, but of a voluntary compromise.

Our Party, like any other political party, is striving after political domination *for itself*. Our aim is the dictatorship of the revolutionary proletariat. Six months of revolution have proved very clearly, forcefully and convincingly that this demand is correct and inevitable in the interests of *this particular* revolution, for otherwise the people will never obtain a democratic peace, land for the peasants, or complete freedom (a fully democratic republic). This has been shown and proved by the course of events during the six months of our revolution, by the struggle of the classes and parties and by the development of the crises of 20-21 April, 9-10 and 18-19 June, 3-5 July and 27-31 August.

The Russian revolution is experiencing so abrupt and original a turn that we, as a party, may offer a voluntary compromise – true, not to our direct and main class enemy, the bourgeoisie, but to our nearest adversaries, the 'ruling' petty-bourgeois-democratic parties, the Socialist-Revolutionaries and Mensheviks.

We may offer a compromise to these parties only by way of exception, and only by virtue of the particular situation, which will obviously last only a very short time. And I think we should do so.

The compromise on our part is our return to the pre-July demand of all power to the Soviets and a government of SRs and Mensheviks responsible to the Soviets.

Now, and only now, perhaps *during only a few days* or a week or two, such a government could be set up and consolidated in a perfectly peaceful way. In all probability it could secure the peaceful *advance* of the whole Russian revolution, and provide exceptionally good chances for great strides in the world movement towards peace and the victory of socialism.

In my opinion, the Bolsheviks, who are partisans of world revolution and revolutionary methods, may and should consent to this compromise only for the sake of the revolution's peaceful development – an opportunity that is *extremely* rare in history and *extremely* valuable, an opportunity that only occurs once in a while.

The compromise would amount to the following: the Bolsheviks, without making any claim to participate in the government (which is impossible for the internationalists unless a dictatorship of the proletariat and the poor peasants has been realised), would refrain from demanding the immediate transfer of power to the proletariat and the poor peasants and from employing revolutionary methods of fighting for this demand. A condition that is self-evident and not new to the SRs and Mensheviks would be complete freedom of propaganda and the convocation of the Constituent Assembly without further delays or even at an earlier date.

The Mensheviks and SRs, being the government bloc, would then agree (assuming that the compromise had been reached) to form a government wholly and exclusively responsible to the Soviets, the latter taking over all power locally as well. This would constitute the 'new' condition. I think the Bolsheviks would advance no other conditions, trusting that the revolution would proceed peacefully and party strife in the Soviets would be *peacefully overcome* thanks to really complete freedom of propaganda and to the immediate establishment of a new democracy in the composition of the Soviets (new elections) and in their functioning.

Perhaps this is *already* impossible? Perhaps. But if there is even one chance in a hundred, the attempt at realising this opportunity is still worthwhile.

What would both 'contracting' parties gain by this 'compromise', i.e. the Bolsheviks, on the one hand, and the SR and Menshevik bloc, on the other? If *neither* side gains anything, then the compromise must be recognised as impossible, and nothing more is to be said. No matter how difficult this compromise may be at present (after July and August, two months equivalent to two decades in 'peaceful', somnolent times), I think it stands a small chance of being realised. This chance has been created by the decision of the SRs and Mensheviks not to participate in a government together with the Cadets.

The Bolsheviks would gain the opportunity of quite freely advocating their views and of trying to win influence in the Soviets under a really complete democracy. In words, 'everybody' now concedes the Bolsheviks this freedom. In reality, this freedom is *impossible* under a bourgeois government or a government in which the bourgeoisie participate, or under any government, in fact, other than the Soviets. Under a Soviet government, such freedom would be *possible* (we do not say it would be a certainty, but still it would be possible). For the sake of such a possibility at such a difficult time, it would be worth compromising with the present majority in the Soviets. *We* have nothing to fear from real democracy, for reality is on our side, and even the course of development of trends within the SR and Menshevik parties, which are hostile to us, proves us right.

The Mensheviks and SRs would gain in that they would at once obtain every opportunity to carry out *their* bloc's programme with the support of the obviously overwhelming majority of the people and in that they would secure for themselves the 'peaceful' use of their majority in the Soviets.

Of course, there would probably be two voices heard from this bloc, which is heterogeneous both because it is a bloc, and because petty-bourgeois democracy is *always* less homogeneous than the bourgeoisie and the proletariat.

One voice would say: we cannot follow the same road as the Bolsheviks and the revolutionary proletariat. It will demand too much anyway and will entice the peasant poor by demagogy. It will demand peace and a break with the Allies. That is impossible. We are better off and safer with the bourgeoisie; after all, we have not parted ways with them but only had a temporary *quarrel*, and only over the Kornilov incident. We have quarrelled, but we shall make it up. Moreover, the Bolsheviks are not 'ceding' us anything, for their attempts at insurrection are as doomed to defeat as was the Commune of 1871.

The other voice would say: the allusion to the Commune is very superficial and even foolish. For, in the first place, the Bolsheviks have learnt something since 1871; they would not fail to seize the banks, and would not refuse to advance on Versailles. Under such conditions even the Commune might have been victorious. Furthermore, the Commune could not immediately offer the people what the Bolsheviks will be able to offer if they come to power, namely, land to the peasants, an immediate offer of peace, real control over production, an honest peace with the Ukrainians, Finns, etc. The Bolsheviks, to put it bluntly, hold ten times more 'trump' than the Commune did. In the second place, the Commune, after all, means a strenuous civil war, a set-back to peaceful cultural development for a long time to come, an opportunity for all sorts of MacMahons[3] and Kornilovs to operate and plot with greater ease – and such operations are a menace to our whole bourgeois society. Is it wise to risk a Commune?

Now a Commune is inevitable in Russia if we do not take power into our own hands, if things remain in as grave a state as they were between 6 May and 31 August. Every revolutionary worker and soldier will inevitably think about the Commune and believe in it; he will inevitably attempt to bring it about, for he will argue:

> 'The people are perishing; war, famine and ruin are spreading. Only the Commune can save us. So let us all perish, let us die, but let us set up the Commune.'

3 Marie Edme Patrice Maurice de MacMahon was the general of the Versailles army which suppressed the Paris Commune in May 1871.

Such thoughts are inevitable with the workers, and it will not be as easy to crush the Commune now as it was in 1871. The Russian Commune will have allies throughout the world, allies a hundred times stronger than those the Commune had in 1871... Is it wise for us to risk a Commune? I cannot agree, either, that the Bolsheviks virtually cede us nothing by their compromise. For, in all civilised countries, civilised ministers value highly every agreement with the proletariat in war-time, however small. They value it very, very highly. And these are men of action, real ministers. The Bolsheviks are rapidly becoming stronger, in spite of repression, and the weakness of their press... Is it wise for us to risk a Commune?

We have a safe majority; the peasant poor will not wake up for some time to come; we are safe for our lifetime. I do not believe that in a peasant country the majority will follow the extremists. And against an obvious majority, no insurrection is possible in a really democratic republic. This is what the second voice would say.

There may also be a third voice coming from among the supporters of Martov or Spiridonova, which would say: I am indignant, 'comrades', that both of you, speaking about the Commune and its likelihood, unhesitatingly side with its opponents. In one form or another, both of you side with those who suppressed the Commune. I will not undertake to campaign for the Commune and I cannot promise beforehand to fight in its ranks as every Bolshevik will do, but I must say that *if* the Commune does start *in spite* of my efforts, I shall rather help its defenders than its opponents.

The medley of voices in the 'bloc' is great and inevitable, for a host of shades is represented among the petty-bourgeois democrats – from the complete bourgeois, perfectly eligible for a post in the government, down to the semi-pauper who is not yet capable of taking up the proletarian position. Nobody knows what will be the result of this medley of voices at any given moment.

* * *

The above lines were written on Friday 1 (14) September, but due to unforeseen circumstances (under Kerensky, as history will tell, not all Bolsheviks were free to choose their domicile) they did not reach the editorial office that day. After reading Saturday's and today's (Sunday's) papers, I say to myself: perhaps it is already too late to offer a compromise. Perhaps the few days in which a peaceful development was *still* possible have passed *too*. Yes, to all appearances, they have already passed.[4] In one way or another, Kerensky will abandon both the SR Party and the SRs themselves, and will consolidate his position with the aid of the bourgeoisie *without* the SRs, and thanks to their inaction... Yes, to all appearances, the days when by chance the path of peaceful development became possible have *already* passed. All that remains is to send these notes to the editor with the request to have them entitled: 'Belated Thoughts'. Perhaps even belated thoughts are sometimes not without interest.

4 After the suppression of the Kornilov revolt the question of forming a new provisional cabinet came up for discussion. The new cabinet was expected to include Cadets in addition to Mensheviks and SRs. The Mensheviks and SRs, fearing that they might completely forfeit popular confidence, announced their refusal to join a cabinet which included Cadets.
On 1 (14) September 1917, the Provisional Government decided to form a Directory of five. Officially no Cadets were included in this cabinet, but its formation was a result of a behind-the-scenes compromise with them.

On Zimmerwald

Written not later than 3 (16) September 1917

It is now quite clear that we made a mistake by *not* withdrawing from it.

Everybody is being bamboozled by hopes from Stockholm. Meanwhile the Stockholm Conference is being 'postponed' from month to month.

And Zimmerwald is '*waiting*' for Stockholm! The Kautsky men plus the Italians; i.e. the Zimmerwald majority, are 'waiting' for Stockholm.

And we are joining in this comedy, bearing *responsibility* for it before the workers.

It is a disgrace.

We must withdraw from Zimmerwald *immediately*.

By staying there for information only, we lose nothing, but we are not going to be held *responsible* for the comedy of 'waiting' for Stockholm.

In leaving rotten Zimmerwald we must decide immediately, at the plenary meeting on 3 (16) September 1917, *to call a conference of the Left-wingers*, and entrust this to the Stockholm representatives.

What has happened is that, after we made a blunder by staying in Zimmerwald, our Party, the world's only internationalist party with seventeen newspapers etc., is *playing at compromise* with the German and Italian Martovs and Tseretelis, just as Martov is compromising with Tsereteli, just as Tsereteli is compromising with the Socialist-Revolutionaries and as the Socialist-Revolutionaries are compromising with the bourgeoisie.

And this is called 'standing for' the Third International!!!

The Bolsheviks Must Assume Power

A letter to the Central Committee and the Petrograd and Moscow Committees of the RSDLP(B)

Written 12-14 (25-27) September 1917

The Bolsheviks, having obtained a majority in the Soviets of Workers' and Soldiers' Deputies of both capitals, can and *must* take state power into their own hands.

They can because the active majority of revolutionary elements in the two chief cities is large enough to carry the people with it, to overcome the opponent's resistance, to smash him and to gain and retain power. For the Bolsheviks, by immediately proposing a democratic peace, by immediately giving the land to the peasants and by re-establishing the democratic institutions and liberties which have been mangled and shattered by Kerensky, will form a government which *nobody* will be able to overthrow.

The majority of the people are on *our side*. This was proved by the long and painful course of events from 6 May to 31 August and to 12 September. The majority gained in the Soviets of the metropolitan cities *resulted* from the people coming over to *our side*. The wavering of the Socialist-Revolutionaries and Mensheviks and the increase in the number of internationalists within their ranks prove the same thing.

The Democratic Conference[1] represents *not* a majority of the revolutionary people, but only *the compromising upper strata of the petty bourgeoisie*. We must not be deceived by the election figures: elections prove nothing. Compare the elections to the city councils of Petrograd and Moscow with the elections to the Soviets. Compare the elections in Moscow with the Moscow strike of 12 (25) August. Those are objective facts regarding that majority of revolutionary elements that are leading the people.

The Democratic Conference is deceiving the peasants; it is giving them neither peace nor land. A Bolshevik government *alone* will satisfy the demands of the peasants.

* * *

Why must the Bolsheviks assume power *at this very moment*?

Because the impending surrender of Petrograd will make our chances a hundred times less favourable.

And it is *not in our power* to prevent the surrender of Petrograd while the army is headed by Kerensky and co.

Nor can we 'wait' for the Constituent Assembly, for by surrendering Petrograd, Kerensky and co. *can* always frustrate its convocation. Our Party alone, on taking power, can secure the Constituent Assembly's

1 The All-Russia Democratic Conference was called by the Central Executive Committee of the Soviets, which was dominated by Mensheviks and SRs, to decide the question of state power, but its actual purpose was to draw the attention of the masses away from the mounting revolutionary movement. The Bolsheviks decided to attend.

The Democratic Conference adopted a resolution on the establishment of a Pre-parliament (Caretaker Council of the Republic), which was an attempt to create the impression that Russia now had a parliamentary system.

Lenin believed participation in the Democratic Conference was a mistake. When he heard that Trotsky was in favour of a boycott, he wrote "Bravo, Comrade Trotsky!", "Long live the boycott!" ('From a Publicist's Diary: The Mistakes of Our Party', in this volume, p. 339.)

convocation; it will then accuse the other parties of procrastination and will be able to substantiate its accusations.

A separate peace between the British and German imperialists must and can be prevented, but only by quick action.

The people are tired of the waverings of the Mensheviks and Socialist-Revolutionaries. It is only our victory in the metropolitan cities that will carry the peasants with us.

* * *

We are concerned now not with the 'day', or 'moment' of insurrection in the narrow sense of the word. That will be only decided by the common voice of those who are *in contact* with the workers and soldiers, with *the masses*.

The point is that now, at the Democratic Conference, our Party has virtually *its own congress*, and this congress (whether it wishes to or not) *must* decide the *fate of the revolution*.

The point is to make the *task* clear to the Party. The present task must be an *armed uprising* in Petrograd and Moscow (with its region), the seizing of power and the overthrow of the government. We must consider *how* to agitate for this without expressly saying as much in the press.

We must remember and weigh Marx's words about insurrection, "Insurrection is an art",[2] etc.

* * *

It would be naive to wait for a 'formal' majority for the Bolsheviks. No revolution ever waits for *that*. Kerensky and co. are not waiting either, and are preparing to surrender Petrograd. It is the wretched waverings of the Democratic Conference that are bound to exhaust the patience of the workers of Petrograd and Moscow! History will not forgive us if we do not assume power now.

There is no apparatus? There is an apparatus – the Soviets and the democratic organisations. The international situation *right* now, on *the eve* of the conclusion of a separate peace between the British and

2 Engels, Friedrich (in close collaboration with Marx and originally published under Marx's name), *Revolution and Counter-revolution in Germany*, *MECW*, Vol. 11, p. 85.

the Germans, is *in our favour*. To propose peace to the nations right now means *to win*.

By taking power both in Moscow and in Petrograd *at once* (it doesn't matter which comes first, Moscow may possibly begin), we shall win *absolutely and unquestionably*.

N Lenin

Marxism and Insurrection

A letter to the Central Committee of the RSDLP(B)

Written 13-14 (26-27) September 1917

One of the most vicious and probably most widespread distortions of Marxism resorted to by the dominant 'socialist' parties is the opportunist lie that preparation for insurrection, and generally the treatment of insurrection as an art, is 'Blanquism'.

Bernstein, the leader of opportunism, has already earned himself unfortunate fame by accusing Marxism of Blanquism, and when our present-day opportunists cry Blanquism they do not improve on or 'enrich' the meagre 'ideas' of Bernstein one little bit.

Marxists are accused of Blanquism for treating insurrection as an art! Can there be a more flagrant perversion of the truth, when not a single Marxist will deny that it was Marx who expressed himself on this score in the most definite, precise and categorical manner, referring to insurrection specifically as an *art*, saying that it must be treated as an art, that you must win the first success and then proceed from success to success, never ceasing the *offensive* against the enemy, taking advantage of his confusion, etc., etc.?

To be successful, insurrection must rely not upon conspiracy and not upon a party, but upon the advanced class. That is the first point. Insurrection must rely upon a *revolutionary upsurge of the people.* That is the second point. Insurrection must rely upon that *turning-point* in the history of the growing revolution when the activity of the advanced ranks of the people is at its height, and when the *vacillations* in the ranks of the enemy and *in the ranks of the weak, half-hearted and irresolute friends of the revolution* are strongest. That is the third point. And these three conditions for raising the question of insurrection distinguish *Marxism from Blanquism.*

Once these conditions exist, however, to refuse to treat insurrection as an *art* is a betrayal of Marxism and a betrayal of the revolution.

To show that it is precisely the present moment that the Party *must* recognise as the one in which the entire course of events has objectively placed *insurrection* on the order of the day and that insurrection must be treated as an art, it will perhaps be best to use the method of comparison, and to draw a parallel between 3-4 July and the September days.

On 3-4 July it could have been argued, without violating the truth, that the correct thing to do was to take power, for our enemies would in any case have accused us of insurrection and ruthlessly treated us as rebels. However, to have decided on this account in favour of taking power at that time would have been wrong, because the objective conditions for the victory of the insurrection did not exist.

1. We still lacked the support of the class which is the vanguard of the revolution.

   We still did not have a majority among the workers and soldiers of Petrograd and Moscow. Now we have a majority in both Soviets. It was created *solely* by the history of July and August, by the experience of the *ruthless treatment* meted out to the Bolsheviks, and by the experience of the Kornilov revolt.

2. There was no country-wide revolutionary upsurge at that time. There is now, after the Kornilov revolt; the situation in the provinces and assumption of power by the Soviets in many localities prove this.

3. At that time there was no *vacillation* on any serious political scale among our enemies and among the irresolute petty bourgeoisie. Now the vacillation is enormous. Our main enemy, Allied and world imperialism (for world imperialism is headed by the 'Allies'), *has begun to waver* between a war to a victorious finish and a separate peace directed against Russia. Our petty-bourgeois democrats, having clearly lost their majority among the people, have begun to vacillate enormously, and have rejected a bloc, i.e. a coalition, with the Cadets.

4. Therefore, an insurrection on 3-4 July would have been a mistake; we could not have retained power either physically or politically. We could not have retained it physically even though Petrograd was at times in our hands, because at that time our workers and soldiers would not have *fought and died* for Petrograd. There was not at the time that 'savageness', or fierce hatred *both of* the Kerenskys *and of* the Tseretelis and Chernovs. Our people had still not been tempered by the experience of the persecution of the Bolsheviks in which the Socialist-Revolutionaries and Mensheviks participated.

We could not have retained power politically on 3-4 July because, *before the Kornilov* revolt, the army and the provinces could and would have marched against Petrograd.

Now the picture is entirely different.

We have the following of the majority of a *class*, the vanguard of the revolution, the vanguard of the people, which is capable of carrying the masses with it.

We have the following of the *majority* of the people, because Chernov's resignation, while by no means the only symptom, is the most striking and obvious symptom that the peasants *will not receive land* from the Socialist-Revolutionaries' bloc (or from the Socialist-Revolutionaries themselves). And that is the chief reason for the popular character of the revolution.

We are in the advantageous position of a party that knows for certain which way to go at a time when *imperialism as a whole* and the Menshevik and Socialist-Revolutionary bloc as a whole are vacillating in an incredible fashion.

Our victory is assured, for the people are close to desperation, and we are showing the entire people a sure way out; we demonstrated to the entire people during the 'Kornilov days' the value of our leadership, and then *proposed* to the politicians of the bloc a compromise, *which they rejected*, although there is no let-up in their vacillations.

It would be a great mistake to think that our offer of a compromise had not *yet* been rejected, and that the Democratic Conference may *still* accept it. The compromise was proposed *by a party to parties*; it could not have been proposed in any other way. It was rejected by parties. The Democratic Conference is a *conference*, and nothing more. One thing must not be forgotten, namely, that the majority of the revolutionary people, the poor, embittered peasants, are not represented in it. It is a conference of a *minority of the people – this* obvious truth must not be forgotten. It would be a big mistake, sheer parliamentary cretinism on our part, if we were to regard the Democratic Conference as a parliament; for even *if it were* to proclaim itself a permanent and sovereign parliament of the revolution, it would nevertheless *decide nothing*. The power of decision lies *outside it* in the working-class quarters of Petrograd and Moscow.

All the objective conditions exist for a successful insurrection. We have the exceptional advantage of a situation in which only *our* victory in the insurrection can put an end to that most painful thing on earth, vacillation, which has worn the people out; in which only our victory in the insurrection will give the peasants land immediately; a situation in which only our victory in the insurrection can *foil* the game of a separate peace directed against the revolution – foil it by publicly proposing a fuller, juster and earlier peace, a peace that will *benefit* the revolution.

Finally, our Party alone *can*, by a victorious insurrection, save Petrograd; for if our proposal for peace is rejected, if we do not secure even an armistice, then *we* shall become 'defencists', we shall place ourselves at *the head of the war parties*, we shall be the *war party par excellence*, and we shall conduct the war in a truly revolutionary manner. We shall take away all the bread and boots from the capitalists. We shall leave them only crusts and dress them in bast shoes. We shall send all the bread and footwear to the front.

And then we shall save Petrograd.

The resources, both material and spiritual, for a truly revolutionary war in Russia are still immense; the chances are a hundred to one that the Germans will grant us at least an armistice. And to secure an armistice now would in itself mean to win the *whole world.*

* * *

Having recognised the absolute necessity for an insurrection of the workers of Petrograd and Moscow in order to save the revolution and to save Russia from a 'separate' partition by the imperialists of both groups, we must first adapt our political tactics at the Conference to the conditions of the growing insurrection; secondly, we must show that it is not only in words that we accept Marx's idea that insurrection must be treated as an art.

At the Conference we must immediately cement the Bolshevik group, without striving after numbers, and without fearing to leave the waverers in the waverers' camp. They are more useful to the cause of the revolution *there* than in the camp of the resolute and devoted fighters.

We must draw up a brief declaration from the Bolsheviks, emphasising in no uncertain manner the irrelevance of long speeches and of 'speeches' in general, the necessity for immediate action to save the revolution, the absolute necessity for a complete break with the bourgeoisie, for the removal of the present government, in its entirety, for a complete rupture with the Anglo-French imperialists, who are preparing a 'separate' partition of Russia, and for the immediate transfer of all power to *revolutionary democrats, headed by the revolutionary proletariat.*

Our declaration must give the briefest and most trenchant formulation of *this* conclusion in connection with the programme proposals of peace for the peoples, land for the peasants, confiscation of scandalous profits, and a check on the scandalous sabotage of production by the capitalists.

The briefer and more trenchant the declaration, the better. Only two other highly important points must be clearly indicated in it, namely, that the people are worn out by the vacillations, that they are fed up with the irresolution of the Socialist-Revolutionaries and Mensheviks; and that we are definitely breaking with these *parties* because they have betrayed the revolution.

And another thing. By immediately proposing a peace without annexations, by immediately breaking with the Allied imperialists and with all imperialists, either we shall at once obtain an armistice, or the entire revolutionary proletariat will rally to the defence of the country, and a really just, really revolutionary war will then be waged by revolutionary democrats under the leadership of the proletariat.

Having read this declaration, and having appealed for *decisions* and not talk, for *action* and not resolution-writing, we must *dispatch* our entire group to the *factories and the barracks.* Their place is there, the pulse of life is there, there is the source of salvation for our revolution, and there is the motive force of the Democratic Conference.

There, in ardent and impassioned speeches, we must explain our programme and put the alternative: either the Conference adopts it *in its entirety*, or else insurrection. There is no middle course. Delay is impossible. The revolution is lying.

By putting the question in this way, by concentrating our entire group in the factories and barracks, *we shall be able to determine the right moment to start the insurrection.*

In order to treat insurrection in a Marxist way, i.e. as an art, we must at the same time, without losing a single moment, organise a *headquarters* of the insurgent detachments, distribute our forces, move the reliable regiments to the most important points, surround the Alexandrinsky Theatre,[1] occupy the Peter and Paul Fortress, arrest the General Staff and the government, and move against the officer cadets and the Savage Division[2] those detachments which

1 Where the Democratic Conference was convened.

2 The Savage Division – formed during the First World War from volunteer mountaineers of the North Caucasus. General Kornilov tried to use it as a battering ram in his assault on revolutionary Petrograd.

would rather die than allow the enemy to approach the strategic points of the city. We must mobilise the armed workers and call them to fight the last desperate fight, occupy the telegraph and the telephone exchange at once, move *our* insurrection headquarters to the central telephone exchange and connect it by telephone with all the factories, all the regiments, all the points of armed fighting, etc.

Of course, this is all by way of example, only to illustrate the fact that at the present moment it is impossible to remain loyal to Marxism, to remain loyal to the revolution *unless insurrection is treated as an art.*

N Lenin

The Russian Revolution and Civil War

They Are Trying to Frighten Us With Civil War

Written 16 (29) September 1917

The bourgeoisie, frightened by the refusal of the Mensheviks and Socialist-Revolutionaries to join a bloc with the Cadets, and by the probability of the democrats being quite capable of forming a government without them and governing Russia against them, are doing their best to intimidate the democrats.

Scare them as much as you can! This is the slogan of the whole bourgeois press. Scare them with all your might! Lie, slander, but frighten them!

Birzhevka does its scaring by fabricating news about Bolshevik activities. Others by spreading rumours about Alexeyev's resignation, and about the imminent German offensive against Petrograd, as if the facts do not prove that it is the Kornilov generals (to whom Alexeyev undoubtedly belongs) who are capable of opening the front to the Germans in Galicia and near Riga and near Petrograd, and that it is the Kornilov generals who are arousing the greatest hatred in the army against the General Staff.

To make this method of intimidating the democrats more 'solid' and convincing, they refer to the danger of 'civil war'. Of all the methods of intimidation, that of scaring with civil war is perhaps the most widespread. Here is the way the Rostov-on-the-Don Committee of the People's Freedom Party [Cadets] formulated this widespread idea, heartily welcomed in philistine circles, in its resolution of 1 (14) September (*Rech*, No. 210):

> The Committee is convinced that civil war may sweep away all the gains of the revolution and drown in rivers of blood our young, still unstable freedom, and is of the opinion that it is necessary to make an energetic protest against developing the revolution as proposed by the unrealisable socialist utopias if we are to save the gains of the revolution.

Here, the fundamental idea which is to be met with innumerable times in *Rech* editorials, in the articles of Plekhanov and Potresov, in the editorials of Menshevik papers, etc., etc., is expressed in the clearest, most precise, well considered and substantial form. It will therefore be useful to take up this idea in greater detail.

Let us try to make a more concrete analysis of the civil war question, on the basis of the half year's experience of our revolution, among other things.

This experience, similarly to the experience of all European revolutions, from the end of the eighteenth century on shows that civil war is the sharpest form of the class struggle, it is that point in the class struggle when clashes and battles, economic and political, repeating themselves, growing, broadening, becoming acute, turn into an armed struggle of one class against another. More often than not – one may say almost always – in all more or less free and advanced countries the civil war is between those classes whose antagonistic position towards each other is created and deepened by the entire economic development of capitalism, by the entire history of modern society the world over – civil war is between the bourgeoisie and the proletariat.

During the past half year of our revolution, we have experienced very strong spontaneous outbursts (20-21 April, 3-4 July) in which the proletariat came very close to starting a civil war. On the other hand, the Kornilov revolt was a military conspiracy supported by the landowners and capitalists led by the Cadet Party, a conspiracy by which the bourgeoisie has actually begun a civil war.

Such are the facts. Such is the history of our own revolution. More than anything we must learn from this history, we must give a great deal of thought to the course it has taken and to its class significance.

Let us try to compare the germs of the proletarian civil war and the bourgeois civil war in Russia from the standpoint of (1) the spontaneous nature of the movement; (2) its aims; (3) the political consciousness of the masses participating in it; (4) the forces in the movement; (5) its tenacity.

We think that if all the parties which are now 'unnecessarily throwing about' the words 'civil war' were to approach the question in this way, and make a real attempt to study the germs of the civil war, the class-consciousness of the entire Russian revolution would gain a very great deal.

Let us begin with the spontaneous nature of the movement. For the 3-4 July movement we have the testimony of such witnesses as the Menshevik *Rabochaya Gazeta* and the Socialist-Revolutionary *Dyelo Naroda*, which have recognised the spontaneous origin of the movement. This testimony I quoted in an article published in *Proletarskoye Dyelo* and issued as a separate leaflet entitled 'An Answer'. For obvious reasons, however, the Mensheviks and the Socialist-Revolutionaries, who are defending themselves and the part they played in persecuting the Bolsheviks, officially continue to deny the spontaneous nature of the outburst of 3-4 July.

Let us put the controversial matter aside for the present. Let us take what is undisputed. No one denies the spontaneous nature of the 20-21 April movement. The Bolshevik Party joined this spontaneous movement under the slogan 'All Power to the Soviets'; independently of the Bolsheviks it was joined by the late Linde, who led 30,000 armed soldiers into the street ready to arrest the government.[1] (The action of

1 Linde, Fedor (1881 – 1917) – Revolutionary and sergeant in the Finland Regiment.

these troops, let us say in parenthesis, has not been investigated and studied. If it is examined closely, and 20 April is given its place in the historic sequence of events, i.e. if it is seen as a link in the chain which extends from 28 February to 29 August, it becomes clear that the fault and the error of the Bolsheviks was the insufficient revolutionism of their tactics, and by no means the excessive revolutionism the philistines accuse us of.)

The spontaneous nature of the movement leading to the proletariat beginning civil war is thus beyond doubt. On the other hand, there is not even a trace of anything resembling spontaneity in the Kornilov revolt; it was merely a conspiracy of generals who hoped by fraud and by the force of military command to carry part of the army with them.

It is beyond all doubt that the spontaneity of the movement is proof that it is deeply rooted in the masses, that its roots are firm and that it is inevitable. The proletarian revolution is firmly rooted, the bourgeois counter-revolution is without roots – this is what the facts prove if examined from the point of view of the spontaneous nature of the movement.

Let us now look at the aims of the movement. The movement of 20-21 April came very close to adopting the Bolshevik slogans, whereas that of 3-4 July was directly connected with them, was under their influence and guidance. The Bolshevik Party spoke quite openly, definitely, clearly, precisely, for all to hear, in its papers and in verbal propaganda of the chief *aims* of the proletarian civil war – the dictatorship of the proletariat and the poor peasantry, peace and an immediate offer of peace, confiscation of the landed estates.

We all know the aims of the Kornilov revolt, and no one among the democrats disputes that those aims were a dictatorship of the landowners and the bourgeoisie, dispersal of the Soviets, and preparations for the restoration of the monarchy. The Cadet Party, this main Kornilovite party (by the way, it ought to be called from now on the Kornilov party), possesses a larger press and greater forces for propaganda than the Bolsheviks, but it has never dared and still does not dare to tell the people openly either about the dictatorship of the bourgeoisie or about the dispersal of the Soviets, or about the Kornilovite aims in general!

As far as the aims of the movement are concerned, the facts tell us that the proletarian civil war can come out with an open exposition of its final aims before the people and win the sympathies of the working people, whereas the bourgeois civil war can attempt to lead part of the masses only by concealing its aims; this is the tremendous difference in them as far as the class-consciousness of the masses is concerned.

The only objective data on this question seem to be those on party affiliation and elections. There do not appear to be any other facts which allow a clear judgment of the class-consciousness of the masses. It is clear that the proletarian-revolutionary movement is represented by the Bolshevik Party, and the bourgeois counter-revolutionary movement by the Cadet Party, and this can hardly be disputed after six months experience of the revolution. Three comparisons of a factual nature can be made that concern the question under consideration. A comparison of the May elections to the local councils in Petrograd with the August elections to the city council shows a decrease in Cadet votes and a tremendous increase in Bolshevik votes. The Cadet press admits that, as a rule, Bolshevism is strong wherever masses of workers or soldiers are concentrated.

In the absence of any statistics concerning the fluctuation of the party membership, attendance at meetings, etc., the conscious support of the party by the *masses* may be judged only from published data concerning cash collections for the party. These data show a tremendous mass-scale heroism on the part of worker Bolsheviks in collecting money for *Pravda* for the papers that have been suppressed, etc. The reports of such collections have always been published. Among the Cadets we see nothing of the kind; their party work is obviously being 'nourished' by contributions from the rich. There is no trace of active aid on the part of the masses.

Lastly, a comparison of the movements of 20-21 April and 3-4 July on the one hand, and the Kornilov revolt on the other, shows that the Bolsheviks indicated point-blank to the masses who their enemy in the civil war is, namely, the bourgeoisie, the landowners and capitalists.

The Kornilov revolt has already demonstrated that the troops who followed Kornilov did so because they had been *completely deceived*, a fact made obvious the moment the Savage Division and Kornilov's contingents came up against the Petrograd masses.

Furthermore, what data indicate the *strength* of the proletariat and the bourgeoisie in the civil war? The Bolsheviks are strong only in the numbers and class-consciousness of the proletarians, in the sympathy with the Bolshevik slogans displayed by the Socialist-Revolutionary and Menshevik 'rank and file' (i.e. workers and poor peasants). It is a fact that these slogans actually won over the *majority* of the active revolutionary masses in Petrograd on 20-21 April, 18, 20 June and 3-4 July.

A comparison of the data on the 'parliamentary' elections and the data on the above-named mass movements fully corroborates, in respect of Russia, an observation often made in the West, namely, that the revolutionary proletariat is incomparably *stronger* in the *extra-parliamentary* than in the parliamentary struggle, as far as influencing the *masses* and drawing them into the struggle is concerned. This is a very important observation in respect of civil war.

It is quite clear why in all the circumstances and the entire situation of parliamentary struggle and elections the strength of the oppressed classes is less than the strength they can actually develop in civil war.

The strength of the Cadets and the Kornilov revolt is the strength of *wealth*. The press and a long series of political actions show that Anglo-French capital and imperialism are *in favour* of the Cadets and the Kornilov movement. It is common knowledge that the entire Right wing of the Moscow Conference of 12 (25) August gave frantic support to Kornilov and Kaledin.[2] It is common knowledge that the French and British bourgeois press 'aided' Kornilov. There are indications of his having been aided by the *banks*.

All the power of wealth stood behind Kornilov – and what a miserable and rapid failure! There are only two social forces among Kornilov's supporters apart from the wealthy – the Savage Division and the

2 Tsarist General.

Cossacks. In the case of the former it is *only* the power of ignorance and deception, and this power is the more formidable the longer the press remains in the hands of the bourgeoisie. After a victory in the civil war, the proletariat would undermine *this* source of 'power' once and for all.

As to the Cossacks, they are a section of the population consisting of rich, small or medium landed proprietors (the average holding is about fifty dessiatins) in one of those outlying regions of Russia that have retained many medieval traits in their way of life, their economy and their customs. We can regard this as the socio-economic basis for a Russian Vendée.[3] But what have the *facts* of the Kornilov-Kaledin movement proved? Not even Kaledin, the 'beloved leader' supported by the Guchkovs, Milyukovs, Ryabushinskys and co., has *succeeded* in creating a mass movement!! Kaledin marched towards civil war much more 'directly', much more forthrightly than did the Bolsheviks. Kaledin went specifically 'to rouse the Don', and still he has not aroused a mass movement in his 'home' region, in a Cossack region far removed from Russian democracy in general. On the part of the proletariat, on the contrary, we observe spontaneous outbursts of the movement in the very centre of the influence and power of anti-Bolshevik, all-Russia democracy.

Objective data on the attitude of various strata and economic groups of the Cossacks towards democracy and towards the Kornilov revolt are lacking. There are only indications to the effect that the majority of the poor and middle Cossacks are rather inclined towards democracy and that only the officers and the top layer of the well-to-do Cossacks are entirely in favour of Kornilov.

However that may be, the extreme weakness of a mass Cossack movement in favour of a bourgeois counter-revolution has been historically proved since the experience of 26-31 August.[4]

---

3 Vendée – a province in France, which was a hotbed of counter-revolution during the French bourgeois revolution at the end of the eighteenth century. The backward peasants of the Vendée, who were strongly influenced by the Catholic clergy, were a tool in the hands of the counter-revolutionaries in their fight against revolutionary France.

4 The Kornilov revolt of 8-13 September (New Style).

There remains the last question, that of the *tenacity* of the movement. As far as the Bolshevik, proletarian revolutionary movement is concerned, we have proof that the struggle against Bolshevism has been conducted during the six-month existence of a republic in Russia both ideologically, with a *gigantic* preponderance of press organs and propaganda forces on the side of the opponents of Bolshevism (even if we risk classing the campaign of slander as 'ideological' struggle), and *by means of repressions*, which include hundreds of people arrested, our main printing-plant demolished, and the chief newspaper and a number of other papers suppressed. The result can be seen in the facts – a tremendous growth of support for the Bolsheviks in the August Petrograd elections, and in both the Socialist-Revolutionary and Menshevik parties, a strengthening of the internationalist and Left trends that are drawing close to Bolshevism. This means that the tenacity of the proletarian revolutionary movement in republican Russia is very great. The facts tell us that the combined efforts of the Cadets, the Socialist-Revolutionaries and the Mensheviks *have not succeeded* in weakening that movement in the least. On the contrary, it was the alliance of the Kornilovites with 'democracy' that *strengthened* Bolshevism. The only possible means of struggle against the proletarian revolutionary trend are ideological influence *and* repressions.

Data on the tenacity of the Cadet-Kornilov movement are still lacking. The Cadets have suffered no persecution at all. Even Guchkov has been set free and Maklakov and Milyukov were not even arrested. *Rech* has not been suppressed. The Cadets are being spared. The Kornilovite Cadets are being courted by Kerensky's government. Suppose we put it this way: assuming that the Anglo-French and the Russian Ryabushinskys will give millions and millions more to the Cadets, to *Yedinstvo*, *Dyen*, etc., for the new election campaign in Petrograd, is it probable that the number of their votes will now increase, after the Kornilov revolt? Judging by meetings, etc., the answer to this question can hardly be anything but negative.

* * *

Summing up the results of the analysis in which we compared the data furnished by the history of the Russian revolution, we arrive at the conclusion that the beginning of the proletariat's civil war has revealed the strength, the class-consciousness, deep-rootedness, growth, and tenacity of the movement. The beginning of the bourgeoisie's civil war has revealed no strength, no class-consciousness among the masses, no depth whatsoever, no chance of victory.

The alliance of the Cadets with the Socialist-Revolutionaries and Mensheviks against the Bolsheviks, i.e. against the revolutionary proletariat, has been tried in practice for a number of months, and this alliance of the temporarily disguised Kornilovites with the 'democrats' has actually strengthened and not weakened the Bolsheviks, and led to the collapse of the 'alliance', and to the strengthening of the Left opposition among the Mensheviks.

An alliance of the Bolsheviks with the Socialist-Revolutionaries and Mensheviks against the Cadets, against the bourgeoisie, *has not yet been tried*; or, to be more precise, such an alliance *has been tried on one front only*, for *five days* only, from 26 August to 31 August, the period of the Kornilov revolt, and this alliance at that time scored a victory over the counter-revolution with an ease never yet achieved in any revolution; it was such a crushing suppression of the bourgeois, landowners', capitalist, Allied-imperialist and Cadet counter-revolution, that the civil war *from that side* ceased to exist, was a mere nothing from the very outset, collapsed before any 'battle' had taken place.

In the face of this historic fact the entire bourgeois press and all its chorus (the Plekhanovs, Potresovs, Breshko-Breshkovskayas, etc.) are shouting with all their might that an alliance of the Bolsheviks with the Mensheviks and Socialist-Revolutionaries 'threatens' the horrors of civil war!

This would be funny, if it were not so sad. It is sad indeed that such an open, self-evident, glaring absurdity, such a flouting of the facts of the whole history of our revolution, can still find listeners... This only proves that the selfish bourgeois lie is still widespread (and this cannot be avoided as long as the press is monopolised by the bourgeoisie), a lie that shouts down and drowns the most undoubted, palpably obvious lessons of the revolution.

If there is an absolutely undisputed lesson of the revolution, one fully proved by facts, it is that only an alliance of the Bolsheviks with the Socialist-Revolutionaries and Mensheviks, only an immediate transfer of all power to the Soviets would make civil war in Russia impossible, for a civil war begun by the bourgeoisie against such an alliance, against the Soviets of Workers', Soldiers' and Peasants' Deputies, is inconceivable; such a 'war' would not last even until the first battle; the bourgeoisie, for the second time since the Kornilov revolt, would not be able to move even the Savage Division, or the former number of Cossack units against the Soviet Government!

The peaceful development of any revolution is, generally speaking, extremely rare and difficult, because revolution is the maximum exacerbation of the sharpest class contradictions; but in a peasant country, at a time when a union of the proletariat with the peasantry *can* give *peace* to people worn out by a most unjust and criminal war, when that union can give the peasantry *all the land*, in that country, at that exceptional moment in history, a peaceful development of the revolution is *possible* and *probable* if all power is transferred to the Soviets. The struggle of parties for power within the Soviets may proceed peacefully, if the Soviets are made fully democratic, and 'petty thefts' and violations of democratic principles, such as giving the soldiers one representative to every five hundred, while the workers have one representative to every thousand voters, are eliminated. In a democratic republic such petty thefts will have to disappear.

When confronted with Soviets that have given all the land to the peasants without compensation and offer a just peace to all the peoples – when confronted with such Soviets the alliance of the British, French and Russian bourgeoisie, the Kornilovs, Buchanans, Ryabushinskys, Milyukovs, Plekhanovs and Potresovs is quite impotent and is not to be feared.

The bourgeoisie's resistance to the transfer of the land to the peasants without compensation, to similar reforms in other realms of life, to a just peace and a break with imperialism, is, of course, inevitable. But for such resistance to reach the stage of civil war, *masses* of some kind are necessary, masses capable of *fighting* and vanquishing the Soviets. The bourgeoisie does *not* have these masses, and has nowhere to get them. The sooner and the more resolutely the Soviets take all power, the sooner both Savage Divisions and Cossacks will split into an insignificant minority of politically-conscious Kornilov supporters and a huge majority of those in favour of a democratic and *socialist* (for it is with socialism that we shall then be dealing) alliance of workers and peasants.

When power passes to the Soviets, the resistance of the bourgeoisie will result in *scores and hundreds* of workers and peasants 'keeping track of', supervising, controlling and registering *every single* capitalist, for the interests of the workers and peasants will demand struggle against the capitalists' deception of the people. The forms and methods of this accountancy and control have been developed and simplified by capitalism itself, by such capitalist creations as banks, big factories, trusts, railways, the post office, consumers' societies and trade unions. If the Soviets punish those capitalists who evade the most detailed accounting or who deceive the people, punish them by confiscating all their property and arresting them for a short time, that will be sufficient to break all the resistance of the bourgeoisie by bloodless means. For it is through the banks, once they are nationalised, through the unions of employees, through the post office, the consumers' societies and the trade unions, that control and the accounting will become universal, all-powerful and irresistible.

And Russia's Soviets, the alliance of her workers and poor peasants, are not alone in the *steps* they take *towards* socialism. If we were alone, we should not be able to accomplish this task peacefully, for it is essentially an international task. But we have enormous reserves, the armies of the most advanced workers in other countries, where Russia's break with imperialism and the imperialist war will inevitably accelerate the workers' socialist revolution that is maturing.

* * *

Some speak about 'rivers of blood' in a civil war. This is mentioned in the resolution of the Kornilovite Cadets quoted above. This phrase is repeated in a thousand ways by all the bourgeois and opportunists. Since the Kornilov revolt all the class-conscious workers laugh, will continue to laugh and cannot help laughing at it.

However, the question of 'rivers of blood' in the present time of war can and must be studied by an approximate computation of forces, consequences and results; it must be taken seriously and not as an empty stock phrase, not as simply the hypocrisy of the Cadets, who have done *everything* in their power to *enable* Kornilov to drown Russia in 'rivers of blood', and to restore the dictatorship of the bourgeoisie, the power of the landowners and the monarchy.

'Rivers of blood', they say. Let us analyse *this* aspect of the question as well.

Let us assume that the vacillations of the Mensheviks and Socialist-Revolutionaries continue; that these parties do *not* hand over power to the Soviets; that they do not overthrow Kerensky; that they restore the old rotten compromise with the bourgeoisie in a somewhat different form (say, 'non-partisan' *Kornilovites* instead of Cadets); that they do not replace the apparatus of state power by the Soviet apparatus, do not offer peace, do not break with imperialism, and do not confiscate the landed estates. Let us assume that this is the outcome of the present wavering of the Socialist-Revolutionaries and Mensheviks, of this present '12 (25) September'.

The experience of our own revolution tells us most clearly that the consequence of this would be a still further weakening of the Socialist-Revolutionaries and Mensheviks, their further separation from the masses, an incredible growth of indignation and bitterness among the masses, a tremendous growth of sympathy with the revolutionary proletariat, with the Bolsheviks.

Under such conditions, the proletariat of the capital will be still closer to a Commune, to a workers' uprising, to the conquest of power, to a civil war in its highest and most decisive form, than it is at present; after the experience of 20-21 April and 3-4 July such a result must be recognised as historically inevitable.

'Rivers of blood', shout the Cadets. But such rivers of blood would give victory to the proletariat and the poor peasantry, and it is a hundred to one that this victory would bring *peace* in place of the imperialist war, i.e. that it would save the lives of *hundreds of thousands* of men who are now shedding their blood for the sake of a division of spoils and seizures (annexations) by the capitalists. If 20-21 April had ended by the transfer of all power to the Soviets, and the Bolsheviks in alliance with the poor peasantry had won in the Soviets, it would have saved the lives of the *half million* Russian soldiers, who certainly perished in the battles of 18 June, even if it had cost 'rivers of blood'.

This is how every class-conscious Russian worker and soldier figures, this is how he must figure, if he weighs and analyses the question of civil war now being raised everywhere; and, of course, such a worker or soldier, who has experienced many things and given thought to them, will not be frightened by the cries of 'rivers of blood' raised by individuals, parties and groups willing to sacrifice more millions of Russian soldiers for the sake of Constantinople, Lvov, Warsaw and 'victory over Germany'.

No 'rivers of blood' in an internal civil war can even approximately equal those *seas* of blood which the Russian imperialists have shed since 19 June (2 July) (in spite of the very great chances they had of avoiding this by handing over power to the Soviets).

All you Milyukovs, Potresovs and Plekhanovs be careful about your arguments *against* 'rivers of blood' in civil war while this present war continues, for the soldiers have seen *seas* of blood and know what they mean.

The international situation of the Russian revolution now, in 1917, the fourth year of a terrifically burdensome and criminal war, that has worn out the peoples, is such that an offer of a just peace on the part of a Russian proletariat victorious in the civil war would have a hundred to one chance of achieving an armistice and peace *without the shedding of further seas of blood.*

For a combination of warring Anglo-French and German imperialism *against* the proletarian socialist Russian Republic is *impossible* in practice, while a combination of British, Japanese and American imperialism against us is extremely difficult to realise and is not at all dangerous to us, if only because of Russia's geographical position. On the other hand, the existence of revolutionary and socialist proletarian masses in *all* the European states is a fact; the maturing and the inevitability of the worldwide socialist revolution is beyond doubt, and such a revolution can be seriously aided only by the progress of the Russian revolution and not by delegations and not by playing at Stockholm conferences with the foreign Plekhanovs or Tseretelis.

The bourgeoisie wails about the inevitable defeat of a Commune in Russia, i.e. defeat of the proletariat if it were to conquer power.

These are false, selfish class wailings.

If the proletariat gains power it will have *every* chance of retaining it and of leading Russia until there is a victorious revolution in the West.

In the first place, we have learned much since the Commune, and we would not repeat its fatal errors, we would not leave the banks in the hands of the bourgeoisie, we would not confine ourselves to defence against the Versaillais (or the Kornilovites) but would take the offensive against them and crush them.

Secondly, the victorious proletariat would give Russia peace, and no power on earth would be able to overthrow a government of *peace*, a government of an honest, sincere, just peace, after all the horrors of more than three years butchery of the peoples.

Thirdly, the victorious proletariat would give the peasantry the land immediately and without compensation. And a tremendous majority of the peasantry – worn out and embittered by the 'playing around with the landowners' practised by our government, particularly the coalition government, particularly the Kerensky government – would support the victorious proletariat absolutely, unreservedly, with every means in its power.

You Mensheviks and Socialist-Revolutionaries are all talking about the 'heroic efforts' of the people. Only recently I came across this phrase for the nth time in the leading article of your *Izvestia* of the Central Executive Committee. With you it is a mere phrase. But the workers and peasants read it and *think* about it, and such deliberation – reinforced by the experience of the Kornilov revolt, by the 'experience' of Peshekhonov's ministry, by the 'experience' of Chernov's ministry *and so forth* – every such deliberation inevitably leads to the conclusion that this 'heroic effort' is nothing but confidence of the poor peasantry in the city workers as their most faithful allies and leaders. The heroic effort is nothing but the victory of the Russian proletariat over the bourgeoisie in civil war, for such a victory alone will save the country from painful vacillations, it alone will show the way out, it alone will give land and peace.

If an alliance between the city workers and the poor peasantry can be effected through an immediate transfer of power to the Soviets, so much the better. The Bolsheviks will do *everything* to secure this *peaceful* development of the revolution. Without this, even the Constituent Assembly, by itself, will not save the situation, for even there the Socialist-Revolutionaries may continue their 'playing' at agreements with the Cadets, with Breshko-Breshkovskaya and Kerensky (in what way are they better than Cadets?) and so on, and so forth.

If even the experience of the Kornilov revolt has taught the 'democrats' nothing, and they continue the destructive policy of vacillation and compromise, we say that nothing is more ruinous to the proletarian revolution than these vacillations. That being the case, do not frighten us, gentlemen, with civil war. Civil war is inevitable, if you do not wish to break with Kornilovism and the 'coalition' right now, once and for all. This war will bring victory over the exploiters, it will give the land to the peasants, it will give peace to the peoples, it will open the right road to the victorious revolution of the world socialist proletariat.

Heroes of Fraud and the Mistakes of the Bolsheviks

Written 22 September (5 October) 1917

The so-called Democratic Conference is over. Thank God, one more farce is behind us and still we are advancing, provided fate has no more than a certain number of farces in store for our revolution.

In order correctly to judge the political results of the Conference, we must attempt to ascertain its precise class significance as indicated by objective facts.

Further break-up of the government parties, the Socialist-Revolutionaries and Mensheviks; their obvious loss of the majority among the revolutionary democrats; one more step towards linking up Mr. Kerensky and Messrs. Tsereteli, Chernov and co. and exposing the Bonapartism they share – such is the class significance of the Conference.

In the Soviets, the Socialist-Revolutionaries and Mensheviks have lost their majority. They therefore have had to resort to a fraud – they have violated their pledge to call a new congress of the Soviets in three months. They have evaded reporting back to those who elected the Central Executive Committee of the Soviets; and they have rigged the 'Democratic' Conference. The Bolsheviks spoke of this fraud prior to the Conference, and the results fully confirmed their correctness. The Liberdans[1] and the Tseretelis, Chernovs and co. saw that their majority in the Soviets was dwindling, therefore they resorted to a fraud.

Arguments like that which say that co-operatives and also 'properly' elected city and zemstvo representatives 'are already of great significance among the democratic organisations', are so flimsy that it is nothing but crass hypocrisy to advance them seriously. First of all, the Central Executive Committee was elected by the Soviets, and its refusal to deliver a report and relinquish office to *the Soviets*, is a Bonapartist fraud. Secondly, the Soviets represent revolutionary democracy insofar as they are joined by those who wish to fight in a revolutionary way. Their doors are not closed to members of the co-operatives and city dwellers. Those same Socialist-Revolutionaries and Mensheviks ran the Soviets.

Those who remained *only* in the co-operatives, who confined themselves *only* to municipal (city and zemstvo) work, voluntarily separated themselves from the ranks of revolutionary democracy, thereby attaching themselves to a democracy that was either reactionary or neutral. Everybody knows that cooperative and municipal work is done *not only* by revolutionaries, but *also* by reactionaries; everybody knows that people are elected to co-operatives and municipalities primarily for work that is *not* of general political scope and importance.

The aim of the Liberdans, Tsereteli, Chernov and co. when they rigged the Conference was to bring up reserves secretly from among the adherents of *Yedinstvo* and 'non-partisan' reactionaries. That was the fraud they perpetrated. That was their Bonapartism, which allies them with the Bonapartist Kerensky. They robbed democracy while hypocritically keeping up democratic appearances – this is the essence of the matter.

Nicholas II stole, figuratively, large sums from democracy. He convened representative institutions but gave the landowners a hundredfold greater representation than the peasants. The Liberdans,

1 Liberdan was an ironical nickname for the Mensheviks Mikhail Liber and Fyodor Dan.

Tseretelis and Chernovs steal petty sums from democracy; they convoke a Democratic Conference where *both* workers and peasants point with full justice to the curtailment of their representation, to lack of proportionality, to *discrimination* in favour of members of the co-operatives and municipal councils closest to the bourgeoisie (and reactionary democracy).

The Liberdans, Tseretelis and Chernovs have parted ways with the masses of poor workers and peasants. They saved themselves by the fraud that keeps their Kerensky going.

The demarcation of classes is progressing. A protest is growing in the Socialist-Revolutionary and Menshevik parties, a direct split is maturing because the 'leaders' have betrayed the interests of the majority of the population. The leaders are relying on the support of a *minority*, in defiance of the principles of democracy. Fraud is *inevitable* as far as they are concerned.

Kerensky is revealing himself more and more as a Bonapartist. He was considered a Socialist-Revolutionary. Now we know that he is not merely a 'March' Socialist-Revolutionary who ran over to them from the Trudoviks 'for advertising purposes'. He is an adherent of Breshko-Breshkovskaya, the Socialist-Revolutionary Mr. Plekhanov, or Mr. Potresov in their *Dyen*. The so-called Right wing of the so-called socialist parties, the Plekhanovs, Breshkovskayas, Potresovs, is where Kerensky *belongs*; this wing, however, does not differ substantially from the Cadets *in anything*.

The Cadets have good reason to praise Kerensky. He pursues *their* policies and confers with them and with Rodzianko *behind the back of the people*; he has been exposed by Chernov and others as conniving with Savinkov, a friend of Kornilov's. Kerensky is a *Kornilovite*; by sheer *accident* he has had a quarrel with Kornilov himself, but he remains in the most intimate alliance with other Kornilovites. This is a *fact*, proved by the revelations about Savinkov, by *Dyelo Naroda* and by the continuation of the political game, Kerensky's 'ministerial leapfrog' with the Kornilovites disguised under the name of the 'commercial and industrial class'.

Secret pacts with the Kornilov gang, secret hobnobbing (through Tereshchenko and co.) with the imperialist 'Allies'; secret obstruction and sabotage of the Constituent Assembly; secret deception of the peasants by way of service to Rodzianko, i.e. the landowners (by doubling the price of bread) – this is what Kerensky is *really* doing. This is his *class* policy. This is his Bonapartism.

To conceal this from the Conference, the Liberdans, Tseretelis and Chernovs had to resort to a fraud.

The Bolshevik participation in this hideous fraud, in this farce, had the same justification as their participation in the Third Duma;[2] even in a 'pigsty' we must uphold our line, even from a 'pigsty' we must send out material exposing the enemy for the instruction of the people.

The difference, however, is this, that the Third Duma was convened when the revolution was obviously ebbing, while at present there is an obvious upsurge of a *new revolution*; of the scope and the pace of this upsurge, however, we unfortunately know very little.

* * *

The most characteristic episode of the Conference was, in my opinion, Zarudny's speech. He tells us that as soon as Kerensky 'as much as hinted' at reorganising the government, all the ministers began to hand in their resignations. "The following day", continues the naive, childishly naive (a good thing if he is *only* naive), Zarudny, "the following day, notwithstanding our resignation, we were called, we were consulted, and finally we were prevailed upon to stay."

"General laughter in the hall", remarks at this point the official *Izvestia*.

Gay folk, those participants in the Bonapartist deception of the people by the republicans. We are all revolutionary democrats – no joking!

---

2 On 3 (16) June 1907, the tsar issued a manifesto dissolving the Second State Duma and amending the electoral law. The landowners, industrialists and merchants were given many more seats in the Duma, and the workers and peasants many less. The Third Duma, which was elected under the new law and met on 1 (14) November 1907, was out-and-out reactionary.

> From the very beginning, [says Zarudny], we heard two things; we were to strive to make the army capable of fighting, and to hasten peace on a democratic basis. Well, as far as peace is concerned, I do not know whether, during the six weeks I have been a member of the Provisional Government, the Provisional Government has done anything about it. I did not notice it. (*Applause and a voice from the audience:* "It did nothing" [*Izvestia* remarks].) When I, as a member of the Provisional Government, inquired about it, I received no reply…

Thus speaks Zarudny, according to the report of the official *Izvestia*. And the Conference listen in silence, tolerate such things, do not stop the orator, do not interrupt the session, do not jump to their feet and chase out Kerensky and the government! How could they? These 'revolutionary democrats' are for Kerensky to a man!

Very well, gentlemen, but then, wherein does the term 'revolutionary democrat' differ from the terms 'lackey' and 'scoundrel'?

It is natural that these lackeys are capable of roaring with laughter when 'their' Minister, noted for his rare naivety or rare stupidity, tells them how Kerensky keeps removing and replacing ministers (in order to come to terms with the Kornilov gang behind the back of the people and 'in full privacy'). It is not surprising that the lackeys keep silent when 'their' Minister, who seems to have taken general phrases about peace seriously without seeing their hypocrisy, admits that he did not even receive a reply to his question about real steps towards peace. Such is the fate of lackeys, to allow themselves to be fooled by the government. But what has this to do with revolution, what has it to do with democracy?

Would it be surprising if revolutionary soldiers and workers were to get the idea that it would be good if the ceiling of the Alexandrinsky Theatre were to fall and crush all that gang of pitiful scoundrels who can sit there in silence when it is being demonstrated to them that Kerensky and co. are fooling them with their talk about peace, who can roar with laughter when they are told as clearly as can be by their own ministers that ministerial leapfrog is a farce (concealing Kerensky's dealings with the Kornilovites). God save us from our friends, we can cope with our enemies ourselves! God save us from these claimants to revolutionary democratic leadership, we can cope with the Kerenskys, Cadets and Kornilovites ourselves!

* * *

And now I come to the errors of the Bolsheviks. To have confined themselves to ironic applause and exclamations at such a moment was an error.

The people are weary of vacillations and delays. Dissatisfaction is obviously growing. A new revolution is approaching. The reactionary democrats, the Liberdans, Tseretelis and others, wish only to *distract* the attention of the people with their farce of a 'conference', *keep them busy* with it, *cut* the Bolsheviks *off* from the masses and *provide* the Bolshevik delegates with the unworthy occupation of sitting and listening to the Zarudnys! And the Zarudnys are not the least sincere of them!

The Bolsheviks should have walked out of the meeting in protest and not allowed themselves to be caught by the conference trap set to divert the people's attention from serious questions. The Bolsheviks should have left two or three of their 136 delegates for 'liaison work', that is, to report by telephone the moment the idiotic babbling came to an end and the voting began. They *should not have allowed themselves to be kept busy* with obvious nonsense for the obvious purpose of deceiving the people with the obvious aim of *extinguishing* the growing revolution by wasting time on trivial matters.

Ninety-nine per cent of the Bolshevik delegation ought to have gone to the factories and barracks; that was the proper place for delegates who had come from all ends of Russia and who, after Zarudny's speech, could see the full depth of the Socialist-Revolutionary and Menshevik rottenness. There, closer to the masses, at hundreds and thousands of meetings and talks, they ought to have discussed the lessons of this farcical conference whose obvious purpose was only to give a respite to the Kornilovite Kerensky and make it easier for him to try new variations of the 'ministerial leapfrog' game.

The Bolsheviks, it turned out, had a wrong attitude to parliamentarianism in moments of revolutionary (and not constitutional) crises, an incorrect attitude to the Socialist-Revolutionaries and Mensheviks.

How it happened can be understood – history made a *very* sharp turn at the time of the Kornilov revolt. The Party failed to keep pace with the incredibly fast tempo of history at this turning-point. The Party allowed itself to be diverted, for the time being, into the trap of a despicable talking-shop.

They should have left one hundredth of their forces for that talking-shop and devoted ninety-nine hundredths to the *masses.*

If the turn taken by history called for a compromise with the Socialist-Revolutionaries and Mensheviks (personally I believe it did) the Bolsheviks should have proposed it clearly, openly and speedily, so that they could *immediately turn to account* the possible and probable refusal of the Bonapartist Kerensky's friends to agree to a compromise with them.

The refusal was already indicated by articles in *Dyelo Naroda* and *Rabochaya Gazeta on the eve* of the Conference. The masses should have been told as officially, openly and clearly as possible, they should have been told without the *loss of a minute,* that the Socialist-Revolutionaries and Mensheviks had rejected our offer of a compromise – Down with the Socialist-Revolutionaries and Mensheviks! The Conference could have afforded 'to laugh' at the naivety of Zarudny to the accompaniment of *this* slogan in the factories and barracks!

The atmosphere of a certain enthusiasm for the Conference and the situation surrounding it seems to have been built up from various sides. Comrade Zinoviev made a mistake in writing about the Commune so ambiguously (ambiguously, to say the least) that it appeared that the Commune, although victorious in Petrograd, might be defeated *as in France in 1871.* This is absolutely untrue. If the Commune were victorious in Petrograd *it would be victorious* throughout Russia. It was a mistake on his part to write that the Bolsheviks did right in proposing a proportional composition for the Presidium of the Petrograd Soviet. The revolutionary proletariat would never do anything worthwhile *in the Soviet* as long as the Tseretelis were allowed proportional participation; to let them in meant *depriving ourselves* of the opportunity to work, it meant *the ruin* of Soviet work. Comrade Kamenev was wrong in delivering the first speech at the Conference in a purely 'constitutional' spirit when he raised the foolish question of confidence or non-confidence in the government. If, at such a meeting, it was *not possible* to tell *the truth* about the Kornilovite Kerensky that had *already* been told both in *Rabochy Put* and the Moscow *Sotsial-Demokrat*, why not refer to those papers and *make it well known to the masses* that the Conference did not want to listen to the truth about the Kornilovite Kerensky?

It was a mistake on the part of the Petrograd workers' delegations to send speakers to *such* a conference after Zarudny had spoken and the situation had been made clear. Why cast pearls before Kerensky's friends? Why divert the attention of proletarian forces to a farcical conference? Why did those delegations not go quite peacefully and legally to the barracks and the more backward factories? That would have been a million times more useful, essential, serious and to the point than the journey to the Alexandrinsky Theatre and chats with cooperators who sympathise with *Yedinstvo* and Kerensky.

Ten soldiers or ten workers from a backward factory who have become politically enlightened *are worth a thousand times more* than a *hundred* delegates hand-picked from various delegations by the Liberdans. Parliamentarianism should be used, especially in revolutionary times, not to waste valuable time over representatives of what is rotten, but *to use the example of what is rotten to teach the masses.*

Why should those same proletarian delegations not 'use' the Conference to publish, say, two posters explaining that the Conference is a farce and *to display* them in barracks and factories? One of the posters could depict Zarudny in a fool's cap, dancing on the stage and singing the song "Kerensky *sacked* us, Kerensky *took* us *back*". Around him stand Tsereteli, Chernov, Skobelev and a cooperator arm-in-arm with Liber and Dan, all rolling with laughter. Caption: *They are happy.*

Poster number two. Zarudny again in front of the same audience saying: "I asked about peace for six weeks. *I got no answer.*" The audience is silent, their faces express 'statesmanlike importance'. Tsereteli looks particularly important as he writes in his notebook:

> 'What a fool that Zarudny is! The imbecile should be carting dung instead of being a minister. He is an advocate of the coalition and undermines it worse than a hundred Bolsheviks! He was a minister but he never learned to speak like one, he should have said: "I continuously followed the campaign for peace for six weeks and I am fully convinced of its final success precisely under the coalition government in accordance with the great idea of Stockholm, etc., etc." Then even *Russkaya Volya* would have praised Zarudny as the knight of the Russian revolution.'

Caption: 'Revolutionary-democratic' conference of male prostitutes.

* * *

Written before the end of the Conference; change the first phrase to something like "In all essentials the so-called Democratic…"

From a Publicist's Diary: The Mistakes of Our Party

Written 22-24 September (5-7 October) 1917

Friday 22 September 1917

The more one reflects on the meaning of the so-called Democratic Conference, and the more attentively one observes from outside – and it is said that the bystander sees most – the more firmly convinced one becomes that our Party committed a mistake by participating in it. We should have boycotted it. One may ask if there is any use in analysing such a question since the past cannot be remedied. Such an objection to criticising the tactics of yesterday, however, would be clearly unfounded. We have always condemned, and as Marxists we must condemn, the tactics of those who live 'from hand to mouth'. Momentary success is not enough for us. In general, plans calculated for a minute or a day are not enough for us. We must constantly test ourselves by a *study* of the chain of political events in their entirety, in their causal connection, in their results. By analysing the errors of yesterday, we learn to avoid errors today and tomorrow.

A new revolution is obviously maturing in the country, a revolution of *other* classes (other than those that carried out the revolution against tsarism). At that time it was a revolution of the proletariat, the peasantry and the bourgeoisie in alliance with Anglo-French finance capital against tsarism.

The revolution now maturing is one of the proletariat and the majority of the peasants, more specifically, of the poor peasants, against the bourgeoisie, against its ally, Anglo-French finance capital and against its government apparatus headed by the Bonapartist Kerensky.

At the moment we shall not dwell on the facts testifying to the rise of a new revolution, since, judging by the articles in *Rabochy Put*, our Central Organ, the Party has already made clear its views on this point. The new revolutionary upsurge seems to be a phenomenon commonly recognised by the Party. Data on this process of maturing, of course, still have to be summarised, but they must form the subject of other articles.

At the present moment it is more important to call the closest attention to the class differences between the old revolution and the new, to weigh up the political situation and our tasks from the point of view of this basic fact, class relations. At the time of the first revolution the vanguard was formed by the workers and soldiers, i.e. by the proletariat and the advanced sections of the peasantry.

This vanguard *carried along* not only many of the worst vacillating elements of the petty bourgeoisie (remember the indecision of the Mensheviks and Trudoviks on the question of a republic), but also the monarchist party of the Cadets, the liberal bourgeoisie, thereby making it a republican party. Why was such a change possible?

Because economic domination is everything to the bourgeoisie, and the form of political domination is of very little importance; the bourgeoisie can rule just as well under a republic, its domination is even more certain under a republic, in the sense that under a republican political order, no changes in the composition of the government or in the composition and the grouping of the ruling parties affect the bourgeoisie.

Of course, the bourgeoisie stood for and will stand for a monarchy, because the cruder armed protection of capital by monarchist institutions is more obvious and 'closer' to all the capitalists and landowners. However, under a strong pressure 'from below', the bourgeoisie has always and everywhere 'reconciled' itself to a republic, as long as it could maintain its economic domination.

The relation of the proletariat and the poor peasantry, i.e. the *majority* of the people, in respect of the bourgeoisie and Allied (and world) imperialism is such that it is impossible for them to '*carry*' the bourgeoisie *with them*. Moreover, the upper strata of the *petty* bourgeoisie and the more well-to-do strata of the *democratic* petty bourgeoisie are patently against a new revolution. This fact is so obvious that there is no need to dwell on it here. The Liberdans, Tseretelis and Chernovs illustrate this most clearly.

The class relations have changed. This is the crux of the matter.

Different classes now stand 'on the one and the other side of the barricade'.

That is the main thing.

That, and that *alone*, is the *scientific* reason for speaking of a *new* revolution which – arguing purely theoretically, taking the question in the abstract – could be accomplished legally if, for instance, the Constituent Assembly, convoked by the bourgeoisie, produced a majority opposed to the bourgeoisie, if the majority belonged to the parties of the workers and poor peasants.

The objective relations of the classes, their role (economic and political) outside and inside representative institutions of the given type; the rise or decline of the revolution; the relation of extra-parliamentary to parliamentary means of struggle – these are the chief, the basic objective facts which must be considered if the tactics of boycott or participation are to be deduced in a Marxist way and not arbitrarily, according to our 'sympathies'.

The experience of our revolution clearly demonstrates how to approach the boycott question in a Marxist way.

Why did the boycott of the Bulygin Duma[1] prove correct tactics?

---

1 The Bulygin Duma of 1905, named after Alexander Bulygin, Minister of the Interior, had no legislative functions, and was permitted merely to discuss certain questions as a consultative body under the tsar. The Bolsheviks boycotted the Duma. It was swept away by the general political strike in October 1905.

Because it was in accordance with the objective alignment of social forces in their development. It provided the maturing revolution with a slogan for the overthrow of an old order which, to distract the people from the revolution, was convoking a clumsily fabricated compromise institution (the Bulygin Duma) which did not show promise of any earnest 'anchoring' in parliamentarianism. The extra-parliamentary means of struggle of the proletariat and the peasantry were stronger. These are the elements that went into shaping the correct tactics of boycotting the Bulygin Duma, tactics which took account of the objective situation.

Why did the tactics of boycotting the Third Duma prove incorrect?

Because they were based only on the 'catchiness' of the boycott slogan and on the revulsion felt towards the brutal reaction of the 3 (16) June 'pigsty'. The objective situation, however, was such that on the one hand the revolution was in a state of collapse and declining fast. For the upsurge of the revolution a parliamentary base (even inside a 'pigsty') was of tremendous political importance, since extra-parliamentary means of propaganda, agitation and organisation were almost non-existent or extremely weak. On the other hand, the most openly reactionary nature of the Third Duma did not prevent it from being an organ reflecting real class relations, namely, the Stolypin combination of the monarchy and the bourgeoisie. This new relation of classes was something the country had to get rid of.

These very elements shaped the tactics of participation in the Third Duma that took proper account of the objective situation.

It is sufficient to give thought to these lessons gained from experience and the conditions required by a Marxist approach to the question of boycott or participation, to realise that participation in the Democratic Conference, the Democratic Council or the Pre-parliament would be wrong tactics.

On the one hand, a new revolution is maturing. The war is on the upgrade. The extra-parliamentary means of propaganda, agitation and organisation are tremendous. The 'parliamentary' tribune in the given Pre-parliament is insignificant. On the other hand, this

Pre-parliament neither reflects nor serves a new relation of classes; for instance, the peasantry is here *more poorly* represented than in the already existing organs (Soviets of Peasants' Deputies). The Pre-parliament is in substance a Bonapartist *fraud*, not only because the filthy gang of the Liberdans, Tseretelis and Chernovs, together with Kerensky and co. *have given* this Tsereteli-Bulygin Duma a *fake*, hand-picked composition, but also more profoundly because the only aim of the Pre-parliament is to trick the masses, to deceive the workers and peasants, to distract them from the new upsurge of the revolution, to dazzle the eyes of the oppressed classes by a new dress for the *old*, long tried-out, bedraggled, threadbare 'coalition' with the bourgeoisie (i.e. the bourgeoisie's transformation of Tsereteli and co. into jesters helping to subordinate the people to imperialism and the imperialist war).

"We are weak now," said the tsar in August 1905 to his feudal landowners. "Our power is wavering. The tide of the workers' and peasants' revolution is rising. We must trick the 'plain man', we must dangle something before his eyes..."

"We are weak now", says the present 'tsar', the Bonapartist Kerensky, to the Cadets, the non-party Tit Tityches,[2] Plekhanovs, Breshkovskayas and co. "Our power is tottering. A wave of workers' and peasants' revolution against the bourgeoisie is rising. We must hoodwink the democrats by dying in new colours that jester's costume which the Socialist-Revolutionary and Menshevik 'leaders of revolutionary democracy', our dear friends the Tseretelis and Chernovs, have been wearing to fool the people since 6 (19) May 1917.[3] We can easily dangle a 'Pre-parliament' before their eyes."

"We are strong now," said the tsar to his feudal landowners in June 1907. "The wave of workers' and peasants' revolution is receding, but we cannot maintain ourselves as of old; deception alone will not suffice. We must have a new policy in the village, we must have a new economic and political bloc with the Guchkovs and Milyukovs, with the bourgeoisie."

2 A merchant from Alexander Ostrovsky's comedy *Shouldering Another's Troubles*, personifying the petty tyranny of the rich.

3 The date the first coalition Provisional Government was announced.

It is in this way that the three situations, August 1905, September 1917 and June 1907, may be presented to illustrate most vividly the objective basis for the boycott tactics and its connection with class relations. The oppressed classes are always being deceived by the oppressors, but the meaning of this deception differs at different moments in history. Tactics cannot be based on the bare fact that the oppressors deceive the people; tactics must be shaped after analysing class relations *in their entirety* and the development of both extra-parliamentary and parliamentary struggle.

Participation in the Pre-parliament is *incorrect* tactics that does not correspond to the objective relations of classes, to the objective conditions of the moment.

We should have boycotted the Democratic Conference; we all erred by not doing so, but mistakes are no crime. We shall correct the mistake only if we have a sincere desire to support the revolutionary struggle of the masses, only if we give earnest thought to the objective foundations of our tactics.

We must boycott the Pre-parliament. We must leave it and go to the Soviets of Workers', Soldiers' and Peasants' Deputies, to the trade unions, to the masses in general. We must call on *them* to struggle. We must give *them* a correct and clear slogan: disperse the Bonapartist gang of Kerensky and *his* fake Pre-parliament, with this Tsereteli-Bulygin Duma. The Mensheviks and Socialist-Revolutionaries, even after the Kornilov revolt, refused to accept our compromise of peacefully transferring the power to the Soviets (in which we *then* had *no* majority); they have again sunk into the morass of filthy and mean bargaining with the Cadets. Down with the Mensheviks and Socialist-Revolutionaries! Struggle against them ruthlessly. Expel them ruthlessly from all revolutionary organisations. No negotiations, no communication with those *friends of the Kishkins*,[4] the friends of the Kornilovite landowners and capitalists.

* * *

4 A leading Cadet and minister in the third Provisional Government.

Saturday 23 September

Trotsky was for the boycott. Bravo, Comrade Trotsky!

Boycottism was defeated in the Bolshevik group at the Democratic Conference.

Long live the boycott!

We cannot and must not under any circumstances reconcile ourselves to participation. A group at one of the conferences is not the highest organ of the party and even the decisions of the highest organs are subject to revision on the basis of experience.

We must at all costs strive to have the boycott question solved both at a plenary meeting of the Executive Committee and at an extraordinary Party congress. The boycott question must now be made the platform for elections to the Congress and for *all* elections inside the Party.

We must draw the *masses* into the discussion of this question. Class-conscious workers must take the matter into their own hands, organise the discussion and exert pressure on *those at the top*.

There is not the slightest doubt that at the 'top' of our Party there are noticeable vacillations that may become *ruinous*, because the struggle is developing; under certain conditions, at a certain moment, vacillations may *ruin* the cause.

We must put all our forces into the struggle, we must uphold the correct line of the party of the revolutionary proletariat before it is too late.

Not all is well with the 'parliamentary' leaders of our Party; greater attention must be paid to them, there must be greater workers' supervision over them; the competency of parliamentary groups must be more clearly defined.

Our Party's mistake is obvious. The fighting party of the advanced class need not fear mistakes. What it should fear is persistence in a mistake, refusal to admit and correct a mistake out of a false sense of shame.

* * *

Sunday 24 September

The Congress of Soviets has been postponed until 20 October (2 November). The tempo of Russian life is such that this almost means postponing it to the Greek calends.[5] The farce staged by the Socialist-Revolutionaries and Mensheviks after 20-21 April is being repeated for the second time.

5 The calends was a feature of the Roman calendar, but it was not included in the Greek calendar. Consequently, to postpone something *ad Kalendas Graecas* – until the Greek calends – was a colloquial expression for postponing something forever.

The Tasks of the Revolution

Published 26 September (10 October) 1917

Russia is a country of the petty bourgeoisie, by far the greater part of the population belonging to this class. Its vacillations between the bourgeoisie and the proletariat are inevitable, and only when it joins the proletariat is the victory of the revolution, of the cause of peace, freedom, and land for the working people assured easily, peacefully, quickly and smoothly.

The course of our revolution shows us these vacillations in practice. Let us then not harbour any illusions about the Socialist-Revolutionary and Menshevik parties; let us stick firmly to the path of our proletarian class. The poverty of the poor peasants, the horrors of the war, the horrors of hunger – all these are showing the masses more and more clearly the correctness of the proletarian path, the need to support the proletarian revolution.

The 'peaceful' hopes of the petty bourgeoisie that there might be a 'coalition' with the bourgeoisie and agreements with them, that it will be possible to wait 'calmly' for the 'speedy' convocation of the Constituent Assembly, etc., have been mercilessly, cruelly, implacably destroyed by the course of the revolution. The Kornilov revolt was the last cruel lesson, a lesson on a grand scale, supplementing thousands upon thousands of small lessons in which workers and peasants were deceived by local capitalists and landowners, in which soldiers were deceived by the officers etc., etc.

Discontent, indignation and wrath are growing in the army, among the peasantry and among the workers. The 'coalition' of the Socialist-Revolutionaries and Mensheviks with the bourgeoisie, promising everything and fulfilling nothing, is irritating the masses, is opening their eyes, is pushing them towards insurrection.

There is a growing Left opposition among the Socialist-Revolutionaries (Spiridonova and others) and among the Mensheviks (Martov and others), and has already reached 40 per cent of the Council and Congress of those parties. And down *below*, among the proletariat and the peasantry, particularly the poorest sections, the *majority* of the Socialist-Revolutionaries and Mensheviks belong to the *Lefts*.

The Kornilov revolt is instructive and has proved a good lesson.

It is impossible to know whether the Soviets will be able to go farther than the leaders of the Socialist-Revolutionaries and Mensheviks, and thus ensure a peaceful development of the revolution, or whether they will continue to mark time, thus making a proletarian uprising inevitable.

We cannot know this.

Our business is to help get everything possible done to make sure the 'last' chance for a peaceful development of the revolution, to help by the presentation of our programme, by making clear its national character, its absolute accord with the interests and demands of a vast majority of the population.

The following lines are an essay in the presentation of such a programme.

Let us take it more to those down below, to the masses, to the office employees, to the workers, to the peasants, not only to our supporters, but particularly to those who follow the Socialist-Revolutionaries, to the non-party elements, to the ignorant. Let us lift them up so that they can pass an independent judgment, make their own decisions, send *their own* delegations to the Conference, to the Soviets, to the government and our work will not have been in vain, *no matter what* the outcome of the Conference. This will then prove useful for the Conference, for the elections to the Constituent Assembly, and for all other political activity in general.

Experience teaches us that the Bolshevik programme and tactics are correct. So little time passed, so much happened from 20 April to the Kornilov revolt.

The experience of the *masses,* the experience of *oppressed* classes taught them very, very much in that time; the leaders of the Socialist-Revolutionaries and Mensheviks have completely cut adrift from the masses. This will most certainly be revealed in the discussion of our concrete programme insofar as we are able to bring it to the notice of the masses.

Agreements with the capitalists are disastrous

1. To leave in power the representatives of the bourgeoisie, even a small number of them, to leave in power such notorious Kornilovites as Generals Alexeyev, Klembovsky, Bagration, Gagarin and others, or such as have proved their complete powerlessness in face of the bourgeoisie, and their ability of acting Bonaparte-fashion like Kerensky, is, on the one hand, merely opening the door wide to famine and the inevitable economic catastrophe which the capitalists are purposely accelerating and intensifying; on the other hand, it will lead to a military catastrophe, since the army hates the General Staff and cannot enthusiastically participate in the imperialist war. Besides, there is no doubt that Kornilovite generals and officers remaining in power will *deliberately open the front to the Germans,* as they have done in Galicia and Riga. This can be prevented only by the formation of a new government on a new basis, as expounded below. To continue any kind of agreements with the bourgeoisie after all that we have gone through since 20 April would be, on the part of the Socialist-Revolutionaries and Mensheviks, not only an error but a direct betrayal of the people and of the revolution.

Power to the soviets

2. All power in the country must pass exclusively to the representatives of the Soviets of Workers', Soldiers' and Peasants' Deputies on the basis of a definite programme and under the condition of the government being fully responsible to the Soviets. New elections to the Soviets must be held immediately, both to record the experience of the people during the recent weeks of the revolution, which have been particularly eventful, and to eliminate crying injustices (lack of proportional representation, unequal elections, etc.) which in some cases still remain.

   All power locally, wherever there are not yet any democratically elected institutions, and also in the army, must be taken over exclusively by the local Soviets and by commissars and other institutions elected by them, but only those that have been properly elected.

   Workers and revolutionary troops, i.e. those who have in practice shown their ability to suppress the Kornilovites, must everywhere be armed, and this must be done with the full support of the state.

Peace to the peoples

3. The Soviet Government must *straight away* offer to *all* the belligerent peoples (i.e. simultaneously both to their governments and to the worker and peasant masses) to conclude an immediate general peace on democratic terms, and also to conclude an immediate armistice (even if only for three months).

   The main condition for a democratic peace is the renunciation of annexations (seizures) – not in the incorrect sense that all powers get back what they have lost, but in the only correct sense that *every* nationality without any exception, both in Europe and in the colonies, shall obtain its freedom and the possibility to decide for itself whether it is to form a *separate* state or whether it is to enter into the composition of some other state.

In offering the peace terms, the Soviet Government must itself immediately take steps towards their fulfilment, i.e. it must publish and repudiate the secret treaties by which we have been bound up to the present time, those which were concluded by the tsar and which give Russian capitalists the promise of the pillaging of Turkey, Austria, etc. Then we must immediately satisfy the demands of the Ukrainians and the Finns, ensure them, as well as all other non-Russian nationalities in Russia, full freedom, including freedom of secession, applying the same *to all* Armenia, undertaking to evacuate that country as well as the Turkish lands occupied by us, etc.

Such peace terms will not meet with the approval of the capitalists, but they will meet with such tremendous sympathy on the part of all the peoples and will cause such a great world-wide outburst of enthusiasm and of general indignation against the continuation of the predatory war that it is extremely probable that we shall at once obtain a truce and a consent to open peace negotiations. For the workers' revolution against the war is irresistibly growing everywhere, and it can be spurred on, not by phrases about peace (with which the workers and peasants have been deceived by *all* the imperialist governments including our own Kerensky government), but by a break with the capitalists and by the offer of peace.

If the least probable thing happens, i.e. if not a single belligerent state accepts even a truce, then as far as we are concerned the war becomes truly forced upon us, it becomes a truly just war of defence. If this is understood by the proletariat and the poor peasantry Russia will become many times stronger even in the military sense, especially after a complete break with the capitalists who are robbing the people; furthermore, under such conditions it would, as far as we are concerned, be a war in league with the oppressed classes of all countries, a war in league with the oppressed peoples of the whole world, not in word, but in deed.

The people must be particularly cautioned against the capitalists' assertion which sometimes influences the petty bourgeoisie and others who are frightened, namely, that the British and other capitalists are capable of doing serious damage to the Russian revolution if we break the present predatory alliance with them. Such an assertion is false through and through, for 'Allied financial aid' enriches the bankers and 'supports' the Russian workers and peasants in exactly the same way as a rope supports a man who has been hanged. There is plenty of bread, coal, oil and iron in Russia; for these products to be properly distributed it is only necessary for us to rid ourselves of the landowners and capitalists who are robbing the people. As to the possibility of the Russian people being threatened with war by their present Allies, it is obviously absurd to assume that the French and Italians could unite their armies with those of the Germans and move them against Russia who offers a just peace. As to Britain, America and Japan, even if they were to declare war against Russia (which for them is extremely difficult, both because of the extreme unpopularity of such a war among the masses and because of the divergence of material interests of the capitalists of those countries over the partitioning of Asia, especially over the plunder of China), they could not cause Russia one-hundredth part of the damage and misery which the war with Germany, Austria and Turkey is causing her.

Land to those who till it

4. The Soviet Government must immediately declare the abolition of private landed estates without compensation and place all these estates under the management of the peasant committees pending the solution of the problem by the Constituent Assembly. These peasant committees are also to take over all the landowners' stock and implements, with the proviso that they be placed primarily at the disposal of the poor peasants for their use free of charge.

Such measures, which have long been demanded by an immense majority of the peasantry, both in the resolutions of congresses and in hundreds of mandates from local peasants (as may be seen, for instance, from a summary of 242 mandates published by *Izvestia Soveta Krestyanskikh Deputatov*), are absolutely and urgently necessary. There must be no further procrastination like that from which the peasantry suffered so much at the time of the 'coalition' government.

Any government that hesitates to introduce these measures should be regarded as a government *hostile to the people* that should be overthrown and crushed by an uprising of the workers and peasants. On the other hand, only a government that realises these measures will be a government of all the people.

Struggle against famine and economic ruin

5. The Soviet Government must immediately introduce workers' control of production and distribution on a nation-wide scale. Experience since 6 (19) May has shown that in the absence of such control all the promises of reforms and attempts to introduce them are powerless, and famine, accompanied by unprecedented catastrophe is becoming a greater menace to the whole country week by week.

   It is necessary to nationalise the banks and the insurance business immediately, and also the most important branches of industry (oil, coal, metallurgy, sugar, etc.), and at the same time, to abolish commercial secrets and to establish unrelaxing supervision by the workers and peasants over the negligible minority of capitalists who wax rich on government contracts and evade accounting and just taxation of their profits and property.

   Such measures, which do not deprive either the middle peasants, the Cossacks or the small handicraftsmen of a single kopek, are urgently needed for the struggle against famine and are absolutely just because they distribute the burdens of the war equitably. Only after capitalist plunder has been curbed and the deliberate sabotage of production has been stopped will it be possible to work for an improvement in labour productivity, introduce universal labour conscription and the proper exchange of grain for manufactured goods, and return to the Treasury thousands of millions in paper money now being hoarded by the rich.

Without such measures, the abolition of the landed estates without compensation is also impossible, for the major part of the estates is mortgaged to the banks, so that the interests of the landowners and capitalists are inseparably linked up.

The latest resolution of the Economic Department of the All-Russia Central Executive Committee of Soviets of Workers' and Soldiers' Deputies (*Rabochaya Gazeta*, No. 152) recognises not only the '*harm*' caused by the government's measures (like the raising of grain prices for the enrichment of the landowners and kulaks), not only "the fact of the *complete inactivity* on the part of the central organs set up by the government for the regulation of economic life", but even the "contravention of the laws" by this government. This admission on the part of the ruling parties, the Socialist-Revolutionaries and Mensheviks, proves once more the criminal nature of the policy of conciliation with the bourgeoisie.

Struggle against the counter-revolution of the landowners and capitalists

6. The Kornilov and Kaledin revolt was supported by the entire class of the landowners and capitalists, with the party of the Cadets ('people's freedom' party) at their head. This has already been fully proved by the facts published in *Izvestia* of the Central Executive Committee.

However, nothing has been done either to suppress this counter-revolution completely or even to investigate it, and nothing serious can be done without the transfer of power to the Soviets. No commission can conduct a full investigation, or arrest the guilty, etc., unless it holds state power. Only a Soviet government can do this, and must do it. Only a Soviet government can make Russia secure against the otherwise inevitable repetition of 'Kornilov' attempts by arresting the Kornilovite generals and the ringleaders of the bourgeois counter-revolution (Guchkov, Milyukov, Ryabushinsky, Maklakov and co.), by disbanding the counter-revolutionary associations (the State Duma, the officers' unions, etc.), by placing their members under the surveillance of the local Soviets and by disbanding counter-revolutionary armed units.

This government alone can set up a commission to make a full and public investigation of the Kornilov case and all the other cases, even those started by the bourgeoisie; and the party of the Bolsheviks, in its turn, would appeal to the workers to give full cooperation and to submit only to such a commission.

Only a Soviet government could successfully combat such a flagrant injustice as the capitalists' seizure of the largest printing presses and most of the papers with the aid of millions squeezed out of the people. It is necessary to suppress the bourgeois counter-revolutionary papers (*Rech*, *Russkoye Slovo*), presses, to declare private advertisements in the papers a state monopoly, to transfer them to the paper published by the Soviets, the paper that tells the peasants the truth. Only in this way can and must the bourgeoisie be deprived of its powerful weapon of lying and slandering, deceiving the people with impunity, misleading the peasantry and preparing a counter-revolution.

Peaceful development of the revolution

7. A possibility very seldom to be met with in the history of revolutions now faces the democracy of Russia, the Soviets and the Socialist-Revolutionary and Menshevik parties – the possibility of convening the Constituent Assembly at the appointed date without further delays, of making the country secure against a military and economic catastrophe, and of ensuring the peaceful development of the revolution.

If the Soviets now take full state power exclusively into their own hands for the purpose of carrying out the programme set forth above, they will not only obtain the support of nine-tenths of the population of Russia, the working class and an overwhelming majority of the peasantry; they will also be assured of the greatest revolutionary enthusiasm on the part of the army and the majority of the people, an enthusiasm without which victory over famine and war is impossible.

There could be no question of any resistance to the Soviets if the Soviets themselves did not waver. No class will dare start an uprising against the Soviets, and the landowners and capitalists, taught a lesson by the experience of the Kornilov revolt, will give up their power peacefully and yield to the ultimatum of the Soviets. To overcome the capitalists' resistance to the programme of the Soviets, supervision over the exploiters by workers and peasants and such measures of punishing the recalcitrants as confiscation of their entire property coupled with a short term of arrest will be sufficient.

By seizing full power, the Soviets could still today – and this is probably their last chance – ensure the peaceful development of the revolution, peaceful elections of deputies by the people, and a peaceful struggle of parties inside the Soviets; they could test the programmes of the various parties in practice and power could pass peacefully from one party to another.

The entire course of development of the revolution, from the movement of 20 April to the Kornilov revolt, shows that there is bound to be the bitterest civil war between the bourgeoisie and the proletariat if this opportunity is missed. Inevitable catastrophe will bring this war nearer. It must end, as all data and considerations accessible to human reason go to prove, in the full victory of the working class, in that class, supported by the poor peasantry, carrying out the above programme; it may, however, prove very difficult and bloody, and may cost the lives of tens of thousands of landowners, capitalists and officers who sympathise with them. The proletariat will not hesitate to make every sacrifice to save the revolution, which is possible only by implementing the programme set forth above. On the other hand, the proletariat would support the Soviets in every way if they were to make use of their last chance to secure a peaceful development of the revolution.

The Crisis Has Matured

Written 29 September (13 October) 1917

Editor's note:

This article consisted of six chapters, the last not being intended for publication but for circulation among members of the CC, the Petrograd and Moscow Committees and the Soviets. The article was first published in four chapters in *Rabochy Put*, No. 30 of 7 (20) October 1917; a comparison of the newspaper text and the manuscript shows that one of the chapters was omitted and Chapter V was headed as Chapter IV.

* * *

I

The end of September undoubtedly marked a great turning-point in the history of the Russian revolution and, to all appearances, of the world revolution as well.

The world working-class revolution began with the action of individuals, whose boundless courage represented everything honest that remained of that decayed official 'socialism' which is in reality social-chauvinism. Liebknecht in Germany, Adler in Austria, Maclean in Britain – these are the best-known names of the isolated heroes who have taken upon themselves the arduous role of forerunners of the world revolution.

The second stage in the historical preparation for this revolution was a widespread mass discontent, expressing itself in the split of the official parties, in illegal publications and in street demonstrations. The protest against the war became stronger, and the number of victims of government persecution increased. The prisons of countries famed for their observance of law and even for their freedom – Germany, France, Italy and Britain – became filled with tens and hundreds of internationalists, opponents of the war and advocates of a working-class revolution.

The third stage has now begun. This stage may be called the eve of revolution. Mass arrests of party leaders in free Italy, and particularly the beginning of mutinies in the German Army, are indisputable symptoms that a great turning-point is at hand, that we are *on the eve of a world wide revolution.*[1]

Even before this there were, no doubt, individual cases of mutiny among the troops in Germany, but they were so small, so weak and isolated that it was possible to hush them up – and that was the chief way of checking the *mass contagion* of seditious action. Finally, there developed such a movement in the navy that it was *impossible* to hush it up, despite all the severity of the German regime of military servitude, severity elaborated with amazing minuteness of detail and observed with incredible pedantry.

Doubt is out of the question. We are on the threshold of a world proletarian revolution. And since of all the proletarian internationalists in all countries only we Russian Bolsheviks enjoy a measure of freedom – we have a legal party and a score or so of papers, we have the Soviets of Workers' and Soldiers' Deputies of both capitals on our side, and

---

1 Revolts broke out in the German Navy in early August. Sailors of the warship *Prinzregent Luitpold*, which was at Wilhelmshaven, took absence without leave to fight for the release of their comrades who had earlier been arrested for staging a strike. On 16 August, the firemen of the *Westphalia* refused to work; at the same time the crew of the cruiser *Nürnberg*, which was out at sea, staged an uprising. The sailors' movement spread to the ships of several squadrons at Wilhelmshaven.

These revolts were brutally crushed. Its leaders were shot and other active participants were sentenced to long terms of hard labour.

we have the support of a *majority* of the people in a time of revolution – to us the saying: "to whom much has been given, of him much shall be required" in all justice can and must be applied.

II

The crucial point of the revolution in Russia has undoubtedly arrived.

In a peasant country, and under a revolutionary, republican government which enjoys the support of the Socialist-Revolutionary and Menshevik parties that only yesterday dominated petty-bourgeois democracy, a *peasant revolt* is developing.

Incredible as this is, it is a fact.

We Bolsheviks are not surprised by this fact. We have always said that the government of the notorious 'coalition' with the bourgeoisie is a government that *betrays* democracy and the revolution, that it is a government of *imperialist* slaughter, a government that *protects* the capitalists and landowners *from* the people.

Owing to the deception practised by the Socialist-Revolutionaries and the Mensheviks, there still exists in Russia, under a republic and in a time of revolution, a government of capitalists and landowners side by side with the Soviets. This is the bitter and sinister reality. Is it then surprising, in view of the incredible hardship inflicted on the people by prolonging the imperialist war and by its consequences, that a peasant revolt has begun and is spreading in Russia?

Is it then surprising that the enemies of the Bolsheviks, the leaders of the *official* Socialist-Revolutionary Party, the very party that supported the 'coalition' all along, the party that until the last few days or weeks had the majority of the people on its side, the party that continues to harry and abuse the 'new' Socialist-Revolutionaries, who have realised that the policy of coalition is a betrayal of the interests of the peasants – is it surprising that these leaders of the official Socialist-Revolutionary Party wrote the following in an editorial in their official organ, *Dyelo Naroda* of 29 September (12 October):

> So far practically nothing has been done to put an end to the relations of bondage that still prevail in the villages of central Russia… The bill for

> the regulation of land relations in the countryside, which was introduced in the Provisional Government long ago, and which has even passed through such a purgatory as the Judicial Conference, has got hopelessly stuck in some office... Are we not right in asserting that our republican government is still a long way from having rid itself of the old habits of the tsarist administration, and that the dead hand of Stolypin is still making itself strongly felt in the methods of the revolutionary ministers?

This is written by the official Socialist-Revolutionaries! Just think: the supporters of the coalition are *forced* to admit that in a peasant country, after seven months of revolution, "practically nothing has been done to put an end to the bondage" of the peasants, to their enslavement by the landowners! These Socialist-Revolutionaries are *forced* to give the name of *Stolypins* to their colleague, Kerensky, and his gang of ministers.

Could we get more eloquent testimony than this from the camp of our opponents, not only to the effect that the coalition has collapsed and that the official Socialist-Revolutionaries who tolerate Kerensky have become an *anti-popular*, *anti-peasant* and *counter-revolutionary* party, but also that the whole Russian revolution has reached a turning-point?

A peasant revolt in a peasant country against the government of the Socialist-Revolutionary Kerensky, the Mensheviks Nikitin and Gvozdev, and other ministers who represent capital and the interests of the landowners! The crushing of this revolt by *military measures* by a republican government!

In the face of such facts, can one remain a conscientious champion of the proletariat and yet deny that a crisis has matured, that the revolution is passing through an extremely critical moment, that the government's victory over the peasant revolt would now sound the death knell of the revolution, would be the final triumph of the Kornilov revolt?

III

It is obvious that if in a peasant country, after seven months of a democratic republic, matters could come to a peasant revolt, it irrefutably proves that the revolution is suffering nation-wide collapse, that it is experiencing a crisis of unprecedented severity, and that the forces of counter-revolution have gone the *limit*.

That is obvious. In the face of such a fact as a peasant revolt all other political symptoms, even were they to contradict the fact that a nation-wide crisis is maturing, would have no significance whatsoever.

But on the contrary, all the symptoms do indicate that a nation-wide crisis has matured.

Next to the agrarian question, the most important question in Russia's state affairs is the national question, particularly for the petty-bourgeois masses of the population. And at the 'Democratic' Conference, which was fixed by Mr. Tsereteli and co., we find that the 'national' curia takes second place for radicalism, yielding only to the trade unions, and *exceeding* the curia of the Soviets of Workers' and Soldiers' Deputies in the percentage of votes cast *against* the coalition (forty out of fifty-five). The Kerensky government – a government suppressing the peasant revolt – is withdrawing the revolutionary troops from Finland in order to strengthen the reactionary Finnish bourgeoisie. In the Ukraine, the conflicts of the Ukrainians in general, and of the Ukrainian troops in particular, with the government are becoming more and more frequent.

Furthermore, let us take the army, which in war-time plays an exceptionally big role in all state affairs. We find that the army in Finland and the fleet in the Baltic have completely *parted ways* with the government. We have the testimony of the officer Dubasov, a non-Bolshevik, who speaks in the name of the whole front and declares in a manner more revolutionary than that of any Bolsheviks that the soldiers will not fight any longer. We have governmental reports stating that the soldiers are in a state of "agitation" and that it is impossible to guarantee the maintenance of "order" (i.e. participation of these troops in the suppression of the peasant revolt). We have, finally, the voting in Moscow, where 14,000 out of 17,000 soldiers voted for the Bolsheviks.

This vote in the elections to the district councils in Moscow is in general one of the most striking symptoms of the profound change which has taken place in the mood of the whole nation. It is generally known that Moscow is more petty-bourgeois than Petrograd. It is a fact frequently corroborated and indisputable that the Moscow proletariat has an incomparably greater number of connections with the countryside, that it has greater sympathy for the peasant and is closer to the sentiments of the peasant.

In Moscow the vote cast for the Socialist-Revolutionaries and the Mensheviks nevertheless dropped from 70 per cent in June to 18 per cent. There can be no doubt that the petty bourgeoisie and the people have turned away from the coalition. The Cadets have increased their strength from 17 to 30 per cent, but they remain a minority, a hopeless minority, despite the fact that they have obviously been joined by the 'Right' Socialist-Revolutionaries and the 'Right' Mensheviks. *Russkiye Vedomosti* states that the *absolute* number of votes cast for the Cadets fell from 67,000 to 62,000. Only the votes cast for the Bolsheviks increased – from 34,000 to 82,000. They received 47 per cent of the total vote. There can be no shadow of doubt that we, together with the Left Socialist-Revolutionaries, now have a majority in the Soviets, in the army and *in the country.*

Among the symptoms that have not only a symptomatic, but also a very real significance is the fact that the armies of railway and postal employees, who are of immense importance from the general economic, political and military point of view, continue to be in sharp conflict with the government,[2] even the Menshevik defencists are dissatisfied with 'their' Minister, Nikitin, and the official Socialist-Revolutionaries call Kerensky and co. 'Stolypins'. Is it not clear that if such 'support' of the government by the Mensheviks and Socialist-Revolutionaries has any value at all it can be only a negative value?

IV

* * *

2 From 23-26 September (6-9 October) 1917 there was a nationwide strike of railwaymen over wages.

V

Yes, the leaders of the Central Executive Committee are pursuing the correct tactics of defending the bourgeoisie and the landowners. And there is not the slightest doubt that if the Bolsheviks allowed themselves to be caught in the trap of constitutional illusions, 'faith' in the Congress of Soviets and in the convocation of the Constituent Assembly, 'waiting' for the Congress of Soviets and so forth – these Bolsheviks would most certainly be *miserable traitors* to the proletarian cause.

They would be traitors to the cause, for by their conduct they would be betraying the German revolutionary workers who have started a revolt in the navy. To 'wait' for the Congress of Soviets and so forth under such circumstances would be a *betrayal of internationalism*, a betrayal of the cause of the world socialist revolution.

For internationalism consists of *deeds* and not phrases, not expressions of solidarity, not resolutions.

The Bolsheviks would be traitors to the *peasants*, for to tolerate the suppression of the peasant revolt by a government which *even Dyelo Naroda* compares with the Stolypin government would be *to ruin* the whole revolution, to ruin it for good. An outcry is raised about anarchy and about the increasing indifference of the people, but what else can the people be but indifferent to the elections, when the peasants have been *driven to revolt* while the so-called 'revolutionary democrats' are patiently tolerating its suppression by military force!

The Bolsheviks would be traitors to democracy and to freedom, for to tolerate the suppression of the peasant revolt at such a moment would *mean* allowing the elections to the Constituent Assembly to be fixed *in exactly the same* way as the Democratic Conference and the 'pre-parliament' were fixed, only even worse and more crudely.

The crisis has matured. The whole future of the Russian revolution is at stake. The honour of the Bolshevik Party is in question. The whole future of the international workers' revolution for socialism is at stake.

The crisis has matured...

29 September (12 October) 1917

* * *

Everything to this point may be published, but what follows is *to be distributed* among the members of the *Central Committee, the Petrograd Committee, the Moscow Committee and the Soviets.*

VI

What, then, is to be done? We must *aussprechen was ist*, 'state the facts', admit the truth that there is a tendency, or an opinion, in our Central Committee and among the leaders of our Party which favours *waiting* for the Congress of Soviets, and is *opposed* to taking power immediately, is *opposed* to an immediate insurrection. That tendency, or opinion, must be *overcome.*

Otherwise, the Bolsheviks will cover themselves with eternal *shame* and *destroy themselves* as a party.

For to miss such a moment and to 'wait' for the Congress of Soviets would be *utter idiocy*, or *sheer treachery.*

It would be sheer treachery to the German workers. Surely we should not wait until their revolution begins. In that case even the Liberdans would be in favour of 'supporting' it. But it *cannot* begin as long as Kerensky, Kishkin and co. are in power.

It would be sheer treachery to the peasants. To allow the peasant revolt to be suppressed when we control the Soviets of both *capitals* would be to *lose*, and *justly lose*, every ounce of the peasants' confidence. In the eyes of the peasants we would be putting ourselves on a level with the Liberdans and other scoundrels.

To 'wait' for the Congress of Soviets would be utter idiocy, for it would mean losing *weeks* at a time when weeks and even days decide *everything*. It would mean faint-heartedly *renouncing* power, for on 1-2 November it will have become impossible to take power (both politically and technically, since the Cossacks would be mobilised for the day of the insurrection so foolishly 'appointed').[3]

---

3 To 'convene' the Congress of Soviets for 20 October (2 November) in order to decide upon 'taking power' – how does that differ from foolishly 'appointing' an insurrection? It is possible to take power now, whereas on 20-29 October (2-11 November) you will not be given a chance to. – *Lenin*

To 'wait' for the Congress of Soviets is idiocy, for the Congress will *give nothing, and can give nothing*!

'Moral' importance? Strange indeed, to talk of the 'importance' of resolutions and conversations with the Liberdans when we know that the Soviets *support* the peasants and that the peasant revolt is *being suppressed!* We would be reducing the *Soviets* to the status of wretched debating parlours. First defeat Kerensky, then call the Congress.

The Bolsheviks are now *guaranteed* the success of the insurrection:

1. We can (if we do not 'wait' for the Soviet Congress) launch a *surprise* attack from three points – from Petrograd, from Moscow and from the Baltic fleet;[4]
2. We have slogans that guarantee us support – 'down with the government that is suppressing the revolt of the peasants against the landowners!'
3. We have a majority *in the country*;
4. The disorganisation among the Mensheviks and the Socialist-Revolutionaries is complete;
5. We are technically in a position to take power in Moscow (where the start might even be made, so as to catch the enemy unawares);
6. We have *thousands* of armed workers and soldiers in Petrograd who could *at once* seize the Winter Palace, the General Staff building, the telephone exchange and the large printing presses. Nothing will be able to drive us out, while agitational work in the *army* will be such as to make it *impossible* to combat this government of peace, of land for the peasants, and so forth.

If we were to attack at once, suddenly, from three points, Petrograd, Moscow and the Baltic fleet, the chances are a hundred to one that we would succeed with smaller sacrifices than on 3-5 (16-18) July, because *the troops will not advance* against a government of peace.

4 What has the Party done to *study* the disposition of the troops, etc? What has it done to conduct the insurrection as an art? Mere talk in the Central Executive Committee, and so on! – *Lenin*

Even though Kerensky *already* has 'loyal' cavalry etc., in Petrograd, if we were to attack from two sides, he would be compelled to *surrender* since *we* enjoy the sympathy of the army. If with such chances as we have at present we do not take power, then all talk of transferring the power to the Soviets becomes *a lie.*

To refrain from taking power now, to 'wait', to indulge in talk in the Central Executive Committee, to confine ourselves to 'fighting for the organ' (of the Soviet), 'fighting for the Congress', is *to doom the revolution to failure.*

In view of the fact that the Central Committee has *even left unanswered* the persistent demands I have been making for such a policy ever since the beginning of the Democratic Conference, in view of the fact that the Central Organ is *deleting* from my articles all references to such glaring errors on the part of the Bolsheviks as the shameful decision to participate in the Pre-parliament, the admission of Mensheviks to the Presidium of the Soviet, etc., etc. – I am compelled to regard this as a 'subtle' hint at the unwillingness of the Central Committee even to consider this question, a subtle hint that I should keep my mouth shut, and as a proposal for me to retire.

I am compelled to *tender my resignation from the Central Committee,* which I hereby do, reserving for myself freedom to campaign among the *rank and file* of the Party and at the Party Congress.

For it is my profound conviction that if we 'wait' for the Congress of Soviets and let the present moment pass, we shall *ruin* the revolution.

N Lenin,
29 September (12 October) 1917

* * *

PS: There are a number of facts which serve to prove that even the Cossack troops will not go against a government of peace! And how many are there? Where are they? And will not the entire army dispatch units *for our support?*

Can the Bolsheviks Retain State Power? (Extract)

Written 1 (14) October 1917

Editor's note:

Due to its length, only the afterword of this text has been reproduced below. The full text is available online on the *Marxists Internet Archive* and in *LCW*, Vol. 26, pp. 87-136.

* * *

Afterword

The foregoing lines were already written when the leading article in *Novaya Zhizn* of 1 (14) October produced another gem of stupidity which is all the more dangerous because it professes sympathy with the Bolsheviks and offers most sagacious philistine admonitions 'not to allow yourselves to be provoked' (not to allow ourselves to be caught in the trap of screams about provocation, the object of which is to frighten the Bolsheviks and cause them to *refrain* from taking power).

Here is this gem:

> The lessons of movements, like that of 3-5 (16-18) July, on the one hand, and of the Kornilov days, on the other, have shown quite clearly

> that the democracy, having at its command organs that exercise immense influence among the population, is invincible when it takes a defensive position in civil war, and that it suffers defeat, loses all the middle vacillating groups when it takes the initiative and launches an offensive.

If the Bolsheviks were to yield in any form and in the slightest degree to the philistine stupidity of this argument they would ruin their Party and the revolution.

For the author of this argument, taking it upon himself to talk about civil war (just the subject for a lady with many good points), has distorted *the lessons of history* on this question in an incredibly comical manner.

This is how *these* lessons, the lessons of history on *this* question, were treated by the representative and founder of proletarian revolutionary tactics, Karl Marx:

> Now, insurrection is an art quite as much as war or any other art, and is subject to certain procedural rules which, when neglected, will bring about the downfall of the party neglecting them. These rules, logical deductions from the nature of the parties and the circumstances you have to deal with in such a case, are so plain and simple that the brief experience of 1848 made the Germans fairly well acquainted with them. Firstly, never play with insurrection unless you are fully prepared to go the whole way [literally: face the consequences of your game].
>
> Insurrection is an equation with very indefinite magnitudes, the value of which may change every day; the forces opposed to you have all the advantage of organisation, discipline and habitual authority [Marx has in mind the most 'difficult' case of insurrection: against the 'firmly established' old authority, against the army not yet disintegrated by the influence of the revolution and the vacillation of the government]; unless you bring strong odds against them you are defeated and ruined.
>
> Secondly, once you have entered upon the insurrectionary career, act with the greatest determination, and on the offensive. The defensive is the death of every armed rising; it is lost before it measures itself with its enemies. Surprise your antagonists while their forces are scattered,

> prepare the way for new successes, however small, but prepare daily; keep up the moral superiority which the first successful rising has given to you; rally in this way those vacillating elements to your side which always follow the strongest impulse and which always look out for the safer side; force your enemies to retreat before they can collect their strength against you; in the words of Danton, the greatest master of revolutionary tactics yet known: *de l'audace, de l'audace, encore de l'audace!*[1]

We have changed all that, the 'would-be Marxists' of *Novaya Zhizn* may say about themselves; instead of triple audacity they have two virtues: "We have two, sir: moderation and accuracy." For 'us', the experience of world history, the experience of the Great French Revolution, is nothing. The important thing for 'us' is the experience of the two movements in 1917, distorted by Molchalin spectacles.[2]

Let us examine this experience without these charming spectacles.

You compare 3-5 July with 'civil war', because you believed Alexinsky, Pereverzev and co. It is typical of the gentlemen of *Novaya Zhizn* that they believe *such* people (and do absolutely nothing themselves to *collect information* about 3-5 July, although they have the huge apparatus of a big daily newspaper at their disposal).

Let us assume for a moment, however, that 3-5 July was not the rudiment of civil war that was kept within the rudimentary stage by the Bolsheviks, but actual civil war. Let us assume this.

In that case, then, what does this lesson prove?

First, the Bolsheviks did *not* take the offensive, for it is indisputable that on the night of 3-4 July, and even on 4 July, they would have gained a great deal if they had taken the offensive. Their defensive position was their weakness, if we are to speak of civil war (as *Novaya Zhizn* does, and not of converting a spontaneous outburst into a demonstration of the type of 20-21 April, as the *facts* show).

---

1 "Audacity, audacity, more audacity!"
Engels, Friedrich (in close collaboration with Marx and originally published under Marx's name), *Revolution and Counter-revolution in Germany*, *MECW*, Vol. 11, pp. 85-6.

2 Reference to the words of Molchalin, a character from Alexander Griboyedov's comedy *Wit Works Woe*, who became a symbol of sycophancy and toadyism.

The 'lesson' therefore proves that the wise men of *Novaya Zhizn* are *wrong*.

Secondly, if the Bolsheviks did not even set out to start an insurrection on 3 or 4 July, if *not a single* Bolshevik *body* even raised such a question, the reason for it lies *beyond* the scope of our controversy with *Novaya Zhizn*. For we are arguing about the *lessons* of 'civil war', i.e. of insurrection, and not about the point that obvious lack of a majority to support it restrains the revolutionary party from thinking of insurrection.

Since everybody knows that the Bolsheviks received a majority in the metropolitan Soviets and in the country (over 49 per cent of the Moscow votes) *much later* than July 1917, it again follows that the 'lessons' are far, far from what *Novaya Zhizn*, that lady with many good points, would like them to be.

No, no, you had better not meddle with politics, citizens of *Novaya Zhizn*!

If the revolutionary party has no majority in the advanced contingents of the revolutionary classes and in the country, insurrection is out of the question. Moreover, insurrection requires:

1. Growth of the revolution on a country-wide scale;
2. The complete moral and political bankruptcy of the old government, for example, the 'coalition' government;
3. Extreme vacillation in the camp of all middle groups, i.e. those who do *not* fully support the government, although they did fully support it yesterday.

Why did *Novaya Zhizn*, when speaking of the 'lessons' of 3-5 July, fail even to note this very important lesson? Because a political question was not dealt with by politicians but by a circle of intellectuals who had been terrified by the bourgeoisie.

To proceed. Thirdly, the facts show that it was *after* 3-4 July that the *rot* set in among the Socialist-Revolutionaries and Mensheviks, precisely because the Tseretelis had *exposed* themselves by their *July* policy, precisely because the mass of the *people* realised that the

Bolsheviks were *their own* front-rank fighters and that the 'social-bloc' advocates were traitors. *Even before* the Kornilov revolt this rot was fully revealed by the Petrograd elections on 20 August, which resulted in a victory for the Bolsheviks and the rout of the 'social-bloc' advocates. (*Dyelo Naroda* recently tried to refute this *by concealing* the returns for *all* parties, but this was both self-deception and deception of its readers; according to the figures published in *Dyen* of 24 August, covering only the city, the Cadets' share of the total vote increased from 22 to 23 per cent, but the absolute number of votes cast for the Cadets dropped 40 per cent; the Bolsheviks' share of the total vote increased from 20 to 33 per cent, while the absolute number of votes cast for the Bolsheviks dropped only 10 per cent; the share of all 'middle groups' dropped from 58 to 44 per cent, but the absolute number of votes cast for them dropped 60 per cent!)

That a rot had set in among the Socialist-Revolutionaries and Mensheviks after the July Days and before the Kornilov days is also proved by the growth of the Left wings in both parties, reaching almost 40 per cent: this is 'retribution' for the persecution of the Bolsheviks by the Kerenskys.

In spite of the 'loss' of a few hundred members, the proletarian party *gained* enormously from 3-4 July, for it was precisely during those stern days that the *people* realised and saw its devotion and the *treachery* of the Socialist-Revolutionaries and Mensheviks. So, the 'lesson' is far, very far from being of the *Novaya Zhizn* sort, it is one entirely different, namely: don't desert the seething masses for the 'Molchalins of democracy'; and if you launch an insurrection, go over to the offensive while the enemy forces are scattered, catch the enemy unawares.

Is that not so, gentlemen 'would-be Marxists' of *Novaya Zhizn*?

Or does 'Marxism' mean *not* basing tactics on an exact appraisal of the *objective* situation but senselessly and uncritically lumping together "civil war" and "a Congress of Soviets and the convocation of the Constituent Assembly"?

But this is simply ridiculous, gentlemen, this is a sheer mockery of Marxism and of logic in general!

If there is *nothing* in the *objective* situation that warrants the intensification of the class struggle to the point of "civil war", why did you speak of "civil war" *in connection* with "a Congress of Soviets and the Constituent Assembly"? (For this is the title of the leading article in *Novaya Zhizn* here under discussion.) In that case you should clearly have told the reader and proved to him that there is *no* ground in the objective situation for civil war and that, therefore, peaceful, constitutionally-legal, juridically and parliamentarily 'simple' things like a Congress of Soviets and a Constituent Assembly can and should be the cornerstone of tactics. In that case it is *possible* to hold the opinion that such a congress and such an assembly are really capable *of making decisions.*

If, however, the present objective conditions harbour the inevitability or even only the probability of civil war, if you did not 'idly' speak about it, but did so clearly seeing, feeling, sensing the existence of a situation of civil war, how could you make a Congress of Soviets or a Constituent Assembly the cornerstone? This is a sheer mockery of the starving and tormented people! Do you think the starving will consent to 'wait' two months? Or that the ruin, about the increase of which you yourselves write every day, will consent to 'wait' for the Congress of Soviets or for the Constituent Assembly? Or that the German offensive, in the absence of serious steps on our part towards peace (i.e. in the absence of a formal offer of a just peace to all belligerents), will consent to 'wait' for the Congress of Soviets or for the Constituent Assembly? Or are you in possession of facts which permit you to conclude that the history of the Russian revolution, which from 28 February to 30 September had proceeded with extraordinary turbulence and unprecedented rapidity, will, from 1 October to 29 November, proceed at a super-tranquil, peaceful, legally balanced pace that will preclude upheavals, spurts, military defeats and economic crises? Or will the army at the front, concerning which the *non*-Bolshevik officer Dubasov said officially, in the name of the front, "it will not fight", quietly starve and freeze until the 'appointed' date? Or will the peasant revolt cease to be a factor of civil war because you call it 'anarchy' and 'pogrom', or because Kerensky will send 'military' forces *against the peasants*? Or is it possible, *conceivable*, that the government can work calmly, honestly, and *without* deception to convene the Constituent Assembly in a *peasant* country when that same government is *suppressing* the peasant revolt?

Don't laugh at the "confusion in the Smolny Institute", gentlemen![3] There is no less confusion in your own ranks. You answer the formidable questions of civil war with confused phrases and pitiful constitutional illusions. That is why I say that if the Bolsheviks were to give in to these moods they would ruin both their Party and their revolution.

N Lenin
1 (14) October 1917

3 A quotation from Nikolai Sukhanov's article 'Another Thunderbolt' in *Novaya Zhizn* (*New Life*). From August 1917, the Smolny Institute was the headquarters of the Bolshevik groups of the All-Russia Central Executive Committee, and the Petrograd Soviet of Workers' and Soldiers' Deputies. The Revolutionary Military Committee also had its premises there from October.

To Workers, Peasants and Soldiers!

Written 1-2 (14-15) October 1917

Comrades! The Party of Socialist-Revolutionaries, to which Kerensky belongs, appeals to you in its paper *Dyelo Naroda* (of 30 September (12 October)) "*to be patient*".

The paper asks us "to be patient" and urges that power be left in the hands of Kerensky's government, that power should not pass to the Soviets of Workers' and Soldiers' Deputies. Let Kerensky rely on the landowners, capitalists and kulaks, let the Soviets that have carried through the revolution and vanquished the Kornilovite generals "be patient", we are told. Let them have patience until the Constituent Assembly, which will soon be convened.

Comrades! Look around you, see what is happening in the countryside, see what is happening in the army, and you will realise that the peasants and the soldiers cannot tolerate it any longer. *An uprising of the peasants* from whom the land has hitherto been withheld by fraud is sweeping like a broad river over the whole of Russia. The peasants cannot tolerate it any longer. Kerensky sends *troops* to suppress the peasants and to defend the landowners. Kerensky has again come to an agreement with the Kornilovite generals and officers who stand for the landowners.

Neither the workers in the cities nor the soldiers at the front can tolerate this military suppression of the just struggle of the peasants for the land.

As to what is going on in the army at the front, Dubasov, a non-Party officer, has declared before all of Russia: "The soldiers will not fight any longer." The soldiers are tired out, the soldiers are barefooted, the soldiers are starving, the soldiers do not want to fight for the interests of the capitalists, they do not want to "*be patient*" when they are treated only to beautiful words about peace, while for months there has been a delay (as Kerensky is delaying it) in the *peace proposal*, the proposal for a just peace without annexations, to be offered to all the belligerent peoples.

Comrades! Know that Kerensky is again negotiating with the Kornilovite generals and officers to *lead troops against the Soviets* of Workers' and Soldiers' Deputies, to *prevent* the Soviets *from obtaining power!* Kerensky "*will under no circumstances submit*" to the Soviets, *Dyelo Naroda* openly admits.

Go, then, to the barracks, go to the Cossack units, go to the working people and explain the *truth* to them.

If power is in the hands of the Soviets, then not later than 25 October (7 November) (if the Congress of Soviets opens on 20 October (2 November)) *a just peace will be offered* to all the belligerent peoples. There will be *a workers' and peasants' government* in Russia; it will *immediately*, without losing a single day, *offer a just peace to all the belligerent peoples*. Then the people will learn who wants the unjust war. Then in the Constituent Assembly the people will decide.

If power is in the hands of the Soviets, the *landowners* estates will *immediately* be declared the *inalienable property of the whole people.*

This is what Kerensky and his government fight against, relying on the village exploiters, capitalists and landowners!

This is for whom and for whose interests you are asked to "be patient".

Are you willing to "be patient" in order that Kerensky may use armed force to suppress the peasants who have risen for land?

Are you willing to "be patient" in order that the *war may be dragged out longer, in order that the offer of peace* and the annulling of the former tsar's secret treaties with the Russian and Anglo-French capitalists may be postponed?

Comrades, remember that Kerensky deceived the people once when he promised to convene the Constituent Assembly! On 8 July he solemnly promised to convene it not later than 17 September, and he has *deceived the people*. Comrades! Whoever believes in the Kerensky government is a traitor to his brothers, the peasants and soldiers!

No, *not for one more day* are the people willing to suffer postponement. *Not for a single day longer* can we suffer the peasants to be suppressed by armed force, thousands upon thousands to perish in the war, when a *just peace* can and must be *offered* at once.

Down with the government of Kerensky, who is conniving with the Kornilovite landowning generals to suppress the peasants, to fire on the peasants, to drag out the war!

All power to the Soviets of Workers' and Soldiers' Deputies!

Letter to the CC, the Moscow and Petrograd Committees and the Bolshevik Members of the Petrograd and Moscow Soviets

Written 1 (14) October 1917

Dear Comrades,

Events are prescribing our task so clearly for us that procrastination is becoming positively *criminal.*

The peasant movement is developing. The government is intensifying its severe repressive measures. Sympathy for us is growing in the army (99 per cent of the soldiers' votes were cast for us in Moscow, the army in Finland and the fleet are against the government, and there is Dubasov's evidence about the front in general).

In Germany the beginning of a revolution is obvious, especially since the sailors were shot. The elections in Moscow – 47 per cent Bolsheviks – are a tremendous victory. Together with the Left Socialist-Revolutionaries we have an *obvious* majority *in the country.*

The railway and postal employees are in conflict with the government. Instead of calling the Congress for 20 October (2

November), the Liberdans are already talking of calling it at the end of October, etc., etc.

Under such circumstances to 'wait' would be a crime.

The Bolsheviks have no right to wait for the Congress of Soviets, they must *take power at once*. By so doing they will save the world revolution (for otherwise there is danger of a deal between the imperialists of all countries, who, after the shootings in Germany, will be more accommodating to each other and *will unite against us*), the Russian revolution (otherwise a wave of real anarchy may become stronger *than we are*) and the lives of hundreds of thousands of people at the front.

Delay is criminal. To wait for the Congress of Soviets would be a childish game of formalities, a disgraceful game of formalities and a betrayal of the revolution.

If power cannot be achieved without insurrection, we must *resort to insurrection at once*. It may very well be that right now power can be achieved without insurrection, for example, if the Moscow Soviet were to take power at once, immediately, and proclaim itself (together with the Petrograd Soviet) the government. Victory in Moscow is guaranteed, and there is no need to fight. Petrograd can wait. The government cannot do anything to save itself; it will surrender.

For, by seizing power and taking over the banks, the factories and *Russkoye Slovo*, the Moscow Soviet would secure a tremendous basis and tremendous strength, it would be able to campaign throughout Russia and raise the issue thus: we shall propose *peace tomorrow* if the Bonapartist Kerensky surrenders (and if he does not, we shall overthrow him). We shall hand over the *land* to the peasants *at once*, we shall make concessions to the railway and postal employees *at once*, and so on.

It is not necessary to 'begin' with Petrograd. If Moscow 'begins' without any blood being shed, it will certainly be supported by (1) the army at the front by its sympathy, (2) the peasants everywhere and (3) the fleet and the troops in Finland, which will *proceed to Petrograd*.

Even if Kerensky has a corps or two of mounted troops near Petrograd, he will be obliged to surrender. The Petrograd Soviet can wait and campaign for the Moscow Soviet Government. The slogan is: Power to the Soviets, Land to the Peasants, Peace to the Nations, Bread to the Starving!

Victory is certain, and the chances are ten to one that it will be a bloodless victory.

To wait would be a crime to the revolution.

Greetings,
N Lenin

Letter to the Petrograd City Conference

Written 7 (20) October 1917

To be read in closed session

Comrades,

Permit me to call the attention of the Conference to the extreme seriousness of the political situation. I base my opinion on the news in the Saturday morning papers alone. That news, however, compels me to raise the question in this way.

The absolute inaction of the British fleet in general, and also of British submarines during the occupation of Esel by the Germans, coupled with the government's plan to move from Petrograd to Moscow – does not all this prove that the Russian and British imperialists, Kerensky and the Anglo-French capitalists, *have conspired* to surrender Petrograd to the Germans and *thus* stifle the Russian revolution?

I think it does.

Perhaps there was no direct conspiracy, but an agreement reached through some Kornilovites (Maklakov or other Cadets, 'non-party' Russian millionaires, etc.), but this does not in any way change the nature of it.

The conclusion is clear.

We must admit that unless the Kerensky government is overthrown by the proletariat and the soldiers in the near future the revolution is ruined. The question of an uprising is on the order of the day.

We must mobilise all forces to convince the workers and soldiers that it is absolutely imperative to wage a last, desperate and decisive fight for the overthrow of the Kerensky government.

We must appeal to the Moscow comrades, persuade them to seize power in Moscow, declare the Kerensky government deposed and declare the Soviet of Workers' Deputies in Moscow the provisional government of Russia in order to offer immediate peace and save Russia from the conspiracy. Let the Moscow comrades raise the question of the uprising in Moscow immediately.

We must use the opportunity offered by the Congress of the Soviets of Soldiers' Deputies of the Northern Region, called for 8 (21) October in Helsingfors, and mobilise all our forces to win the delegates over for the uprising (as they go back through Petrograd).

We must put the request and proposal to the Central Committee of our Party that it hasten the withdrawal of the Bolsheviks from the Pre-parliament and devote all efforts to exposing to the masses Kerensky's conspiracy with the imperialists of other countries and to preparing the uprising so that the right *moment* for it is chosen.

* * *

PS: The resolution of the *soldiers'* section of the Petrograd Soviet against moving the government from Petrograd shows that the soldiers are also becoming *more* convinced of Kerensky's conspiracy. We must gather all forces to support this *correct* conviction and to carry on propaganda among the soldiers.

* * *

I move that the following resolution be adopted:

> The Conference, having discussed the present situation, which is generally admitted to be highly critical, establishes the following facts:

1. The aggressive operations of the German fleet, accompanied by the very strange inactivity of the British fleet and coupled with the Provisional Government's plan to move from Petrograd to Moscow, arouse a very strong suspicion that the government of Kerensky (or, what is the same thing, the Russian imperialists behind him) have entered into a conspiracy with the Anglo-French imperialists to surrender Petrograd to the Germans and *in this way* to suppress the revolution.
2. These suspicions are greatly strengthened, and are being confirmed, as far as is possible in such cases, by the following:
   - First, the conviction has long been growing and strengthening in the army that it was betrayed by the tsarist generals and is also being betrayed by the generals of Kornilov and Kerensky (particularly in the surrender of Riga);
   - Second, the Anglo-French bourgeois press does not conceal its fierce, even frenzied hatred for the Soviets and its readiness to drown them in any quantity of blood;
   - Third, Kerensky, the Cadets, Breshkovskaya, Plekhanov and similar politicians are conscious or unconscious tools in the hands of Anglo-French imperialism, as six months' history of the Russian revolution has proved in full;
   - Fourth, the vague but persistent rumours of a separate peace between Britain and Germany at the expense of Russia could not have arisen without cause;
   - Fifth, all the circumstances of the Kornilov conspiracy, as admitted even by *Dyelo Naroda* and *Izvestia*, papers that on the whole sympathise with Kerensky, have proved that Kerensky was to a very large extent mixed up in the Kornilov affair, that Kerensky was and is the most dangerous Kornilovite; Kerensky, in fact, has shielded such leaders of the Kornilov revolt as Rodzianko, Klembovsky, Maklakov and others.

The Conference, therefore, recognises that all the shouting by Kerensky and the bourgeois papers that support him about the defence of Petrograd is sheer deception and hypocrisy, and the soldiers' section of the Petrograd Soviet was perfectly right when it sharply condemned the plan to move from Petrograd; furthermore, that Petrograd cannot be defended and the revolution saved unless the tired army is absolutely and urgently convinced of the sincerity of the government and is given bread, clothing and footwear at the cost of revolutionary measures against the capitalists, who hitherto have sabotaged the struggle against economic ruin (as admitted even by the Economic Department of the Menshevik-Socialist-Revolutionary Central Executive Committee).

The Conference therefore declares that only the overthrow of the Kerensky government with its packed Council of the Republic, and the substitution for it of a workers' and peasants' revolutionary government, can ensure:

1. The transfer of the land to the peasants instead of suppressing the peasant uprising;
2. The offer of an immediate and just peace so that our entire army will believe that truth exists;
3. Adoption of the most decisive revolutionary measures against the capitalists in order to provide the army with bread, clothing and footwear and in order to fight against economic ruin.

The Conference urgently requests the Central Committee to take all measures to lead the inevitable uprising of the workers, soldiers and peasants for the overthrow of the anti-popular, feudal Kerensky government.

The Conference decides on the immediate dispatch of delegations to Helsingfors, Vyborg, Kronstadt and Revel, to the military units south of Petrograd, and also to Moscow, to carry on propaganda in favour of adopting this resolution and in favour of a swift, general uprising and the overthrow of Kerensky as the steps necessary to open the road to peace, to save Petrograd and the revolution, and to give the land to the peasants and power to the Soviets.

Advice of an Onlooker

Written 8 (21) October 1917

I am writing these lines on 8 (21) October and have little hope that they will reach Petrograd comrades by the 9th. It is possible that they will arrive too late, since the Congress of the Northern Soviets has been fixed for 10 October. Nevertheless, I shall try to give my 'Advice of an Onlooker' in the event that the probable action of the workers and soldiers of Petrograd and of the whole 'region' will take place soon but has not yet taken place.

It is clear that all power must pass to the Soviets. It should be equally indisputable for every Bolshevik that proletarian revolutionary power (or Bolshevik power – which is now one and the same thing) is assured of the utmost sympathy and unreserved support of all the working and exploited people all over the world in general, in the belligerent countries in particular, and among the Russian peasants especially. There is no need to dwell on these all too well known and long established truths.

What must be dealt with is something that is probably not quite clear to all comrades, namely, that in practice the transfer of power to the Soviets now means armed uprising. This would seem obvious, but not everyone has or is giving thought to the point. To repudiate armed uprising now would mean to repudiate the key slogan of

Bolshevism ('All Power to the Soviets') and proletarian revolutionary internationalism in general.

But armed uprising is a *special* form of political struggle, one subject to special laws to which attentive thought must be given. Karl Marx expressed this truth with remarkable clarity when he wrote that "*insurrection is an art quite as much as war*".[1]

Of the principal rules of this art, Marx noted the following:

1. *Never play* with insurrection, but when beginning it realise firmly that you must *go all the way*.
2. Concentrate a *great superiority of forces* at the decisive point and at the decisive moment, otherwise the enemy, who has the advantage of better preparation and organisation, will destroy the insurgents.
3. Once the insurrection has begun, you must act with the greatest *determination*, and by all means, without fail, take the *offensive*. "The defensive is the death of every armed rising."
4. You must try to take the enemy by surprise and seize the moment when his forces are scattered.
5. You must strive for *daily* successes, however small (one might say hourly, if it is the case of one town), and at all costs retain "*moral superiority*".

Marx summed up the lessons of all revolutions in respect to armed uprising in the words of "Danton, the greatest master of revolutionary policy yet known: *de l'audace, de l'audace, encore de l'audace.*"[2]

Applied to Russia and to October 1917, this means: a simultaneous offensive on Petrograd, as sudden and as rapid as possible, which must without fail be carried out from within and from without, from the working-class quarters and from Finland, from Revel and

1 Engels, Friedrich (in close collaboration with Marx and originally published under Marx's name), *Revolution and Counter-revolution in Germany*, *MECW*, Vol. 11, p. 85.

2 Ibid., p. 86.

from Kronstadt, an offensive of the *entire* navy, the concentration of a *gigantic superiority* of forces over the 15,000 or 20,000 (perhaps more) of our 'bourgeois guard' (the officers' schools), our 'Vendée troops' (part of the Cossacks), etc.

Our *three* main forces – the fleet, the workers and the army units – must be so combined as to occupy without fail and to hold *at any cost*: (a) the telephone exchange; (b) the telegraph office; (c) the railway stations; (d) and above all, the bridges.

The *most determined* elements (our 'shock forces' and *young workers*, as well as the best of the sailors) must be formed into small detachments to occupy all the more important points and to *take part* everywhere in all important operations, for example:

1. To encircle and cut off Petrograd; to seize it by a combined attack of the sailors, the workers and the troops – a task which requires *art and triple audacity*;
2. To form detachments from the best workers, armed with rifles and bombs, for the purpose of attacking and surrounding the enemy's 'centres' (the officers' schools, the telegraph office, the telephone exchange, etc.). Their watch word must be: "*Better die to a man than let the enemy pass!*"

Let us hope that if action is decided on, the leaders will successfully apply the great precepts of Danton and Marx.

The success of both the Russian and the world revolution depends on two or three days' fighting.

Letter to the Bolshevik Comrades Attending the Congress of Soviets of the Northern Region

Written 8 (21) October 1917

Comrades,

Our revolution is passing through a highly critical period. This crisis coincides with the great crisis – the growth of the world socialist revolution and the struggle waged against it by world imperialism. A gigantic task is being presented to the responsible leaders of our Party, and failure to perform it will involve the danger of a complete collapse of the internationalist proletarian movement. The situation is such that, in truth, delay would be fatal.

Take a glance at the international situation. The growth of a world revolution is beyond dispute. The outburst of indignation on the part of the Czech workers has been suppressed with incredible ferocity, testifying to the government's extreme fright. Italy too has witnessed a mass outbreak in Turin. Most important, however, is the revolt in the German Navy. One can imagine the enormous difficulties of a revolution in a country like Germany, especially under present conditions. It cannot be doubted that the revolt in the German navy is indicative of the great crisis – the growth of the world revolution. While our chauvinists, who are advocating Germany's defeat, demand a revolt of the German workers immediately, we Russian revolutionary internationalists know from the experience of 1905-17 that a more impressive sign of the growth of revolution than a revolt among the troops cannot be imagined.

Just think what our position is now in the eyes of the German revolutionaries. They can say to us: We have only Liebknecht who openly called for a revolution. His voice has been stifled in a convict prison. We have not a single newspaper which openly explains the necessity for a revolution; we have not got freedom of assembly. We have not a single Soviet of Workers' or Soldiers' Deputies. Our voice barely reaches the real, broad mass of people. Yet we made an attempt at revolt, although our chance was only one in a hundred. But you Russian revolutionary internationalists have behind you a half-year of free agitation, you have a score of newspapers, you have a number of Soviets of Workers' and Soldiers' Deputies, you have gained the upper hand in the Soviets of Petrograd and Moscow, you have on your side the entire Baltic fleet and all the Russian troops in Finland. And still you do not respond to our call for an uprising, you do not overthrow your imperialist, Kerensky, although the chances are a hundred to one that your uprising will be successful.

Yes, we shall be real traitors to the International if, at such a moment and under such favourable conditions, we respond to this call from the German revolutionaries with… *mere* resolutions.

Add to this, as we all perfectly well know, that the plotting and conspiracy of the international imperialists against the Russian revolution are rapidly growing. International imperialism is coming closer to the idea of stifling the revolution at all costs, stifling it both by military measures and by a peace made at the expense of Russia. It is this that is making the crisis in the world socialist revolution so acute, and is rendering our delay of the uprising particularly dangerous – I would almost say criminal.

Take, further, Russia's internal situation. The petty-bourgeois compromising parties which expressed the naive confidence of the masses in Kerensky and in the imperialists in general, are absolutely bankrupt. Their collapse is complete. The vote cast against coalition by the Soviet curia at the Democratic Conference, the vote cast against coalition by a *majority* of the local Soviets of Peasants' Deputies (in spite of their central Soviet, where Avksentiev and other friends of Kerensky's are installed), the elections in Moscow, where the working-class population has the closest ties with the peasants, and where *over 49 per cent* voted for the Bolsheviks (and among the soldiers 14,000 out of 17,000) – does this not signify that the confidence of the people in Kerensky and in those who are compromising with Kerensky and co. has completely collapsed? Can one imagine any way in which the people could say more clearly to the Bolsheviks than they did by this vote, "Lead us, we shall follow you"?

And we, who have thus won the majority of the people over to our side, and who have gained the Soviets in both the capital cities – are we to wait? What for? For Kerensky and his Kornilovite generals to surrender Petrograd to the Germans, and thus enter directly or indirectly, openly or secretly, into a conspiracy with *both* Buchanan *and* Wilhelm for the purpose of completely stifling the Russian revolution.

By the Moscow vote and by the re-elections to the Soviets, the people have expressed their confidence in us, but that is not all. There are signs of growing apathy and indifference. That is understandable. It implies not the ebb of the revolution, as the Cadets and their henchmen vociferate, but the ebb of confidence in resolutions and elections. In a revolution, the masses demand action, not words from the leading parties, they demand victories in the struggle, not talk. The moment is approaching when the people may conceive the idea that the Bolsheviks are no better than the others, since they were unable *to act* when the people placed confidence in them…

The peasant revolt is spreading over the whole country. It is perfectly clear that the Cadets and their hangers-on are minimising it in every way and are claiming it to be nothing but 'riots' and 'anarchy'. That lie is being refuted because in the revolt centres the land is beginning to be handed over to the peasants. 'Riots' and 'anarchy' have never led to such splendid political results! The tremendous strength of the peasant revolt is shown by the fact that the compromisers and the Socialist-Revolutionaries of *Dyelo Naroda*, and *even* Breshko-Breshkovskaya, have begun to talk of transferring the land to the peasants in order to check the movement before it has finally engulfed them.

Are we to wait until the Cossack units of the Kornilovite Kerensky (who was recently exposed as a Kornilovite by the Socialist-Revolutionaries themselves) succeed in suppressing this peasant revolt *piecemeal*?

Apparently, many leaders of our Party have failed to note the *specific* meaning of the slogan which we all adopted and which we have repeated endlessly. The slogan is 'All Power to the Soviets'. There were periods, there were moments during the six months of the revolution, when this slogan did not mean insurrection. Perhaps those periods and those moments blinded some of our comrades and led them to forget that now, at least since the middle of September, this slogan for us too has become *equivalent to a call for insurrection.*

There can be no shadow of doubt on this score. *Dyelo Naroda* recently explained this 'in a popular way', when it said "Kerensky will under no circumstances submit!" As if he could!

The slogan 'All Power to the Soviets' is nothing but a call for insurrection. And the blame will be wholly and undoubtedly ours, if we, who for months have been calling upon the people to revolt and repudiate compromise, fail to lead them to revolt on the eve of the revolution's collapse, after the people have expressed their confidence in us.

The Cadets and compromisers are trying to scare us by citing the example of 3-5 July, by pointing to the intensified agitation of the Black Hundreds, and so forth. But if any mistake was made on 3-5 July, it was that we did not take power. I do not think we made a mistake then, for at that time we were not *yet* in a majority. But now it would be a fatal mistake, worse than a mistake. The spread of Black Hundred agitation is understandable. It is an aggravation of extremes in an atmosphere of a developing proletarian and peasant revolution. But to use this as an argument *against* an uprising is ridiculous, for the impotence of the Black Hundreds, hirelings of the capitalists, *the impotence of the Black Hundreds in the struggle*, does not even require proof. In the struggle they are not worth considering. In the struggle Kornilov and Kerensky can only rely on the Savage Division and the Cossacks. And now demoralisation has set in even among the Cossacks; furthermore, the peasants are threatening them with civil war within their Cossack regions.

I am writing these lines on Sunday 8 (21) October. You will read them not earlier than 10 October. I have heard from a comrade who passed through here that people travelling on the Warsaw railway say: "Kerensky is bringing Cossacks to Petrograd!" This is quite probable, and it will be entirely our fault if we do not verify it *most carefully* and do not *make a study* of the strength and distribution of *the Kornilovite troops of the second draft.*

Kerensky has again brought Kornilovite troops into the vicinity of Petrograd in order to prevent state power from passing into the hands of the Soviets, in order to prevent this power from proposing an immediate peace, in order to prevent all the land from being immediately handed over to the peasants, in order to surrender Petrograd to the Germans, and himself escape to Moscow! That is the slogan of the insurrection which we must circulate as widely as possible and which will have a tremendous success.

We must not wait for the All-Russia Congress of Soviets, which the Central Executive Committee may delay even until November. We must not delay and permit Kerensky to bring up more Kornilovite troops. Finland, the fleet and Revel are represented at the Congress of Soviets. These can together start an immediate movement on Petrograd against the Kornilovite regiments, a movement of the fleet, artillery, machine-guns and two or three army corps, such as have shown, for instance in Vyborg, the intensity of their hatred for the Kornilovite generals, with whom Kerensky is again in collusion.

It would be a great mistake to refuse to seize the opportunity of immediately smashing the Kornilovite regiments of the second draft on the ground that the Baltic fleet, by moving into Petrograd, would allegedly expose the front to the Germans. The Kornilovite slanderers will say this, as they will tell any lie, but it is unworthy of revolutionaries to allow themselves to be intimidated by lies and slanders. Kerensky will surrender Petrograd to the Germans, that is now as clear as daylight. No assertions to the contrary can destroy our full conviction that this is so, for it follows from the entire course of events and Kerensky's entire policy.

Kerensky and the Kornilovites will surrender Petrograd to the Germans. And it is in order to save Petrograd that Kerensky must be overthrown and power taken by the *Soviets of both capital cities.* These Soviets will immediately propose a peace to all the nations and will thereby fulfil their duty to the German revolutionaries. They will thereby also be taking a decisive step towards frustrating the criminal conspiracies against the Russian revolution, the conspiracies of international imperialism.

Only the immediate movement of troops from Finland, and of the Baltic fleet, Revel and Kronstadt against the Kornilovite forces quartered near Petrograd can save the Russian and the world revolution. Such a movement has a hundred to one chance of leading *within a few days* to the surrender of a part of the Cossack troops, to the utter defeat of the other part, and to the overthrow of Kerensky, for the workers and the soldiers of both capital cities will support such a movement.

In truth, delay would be fatal.

The slogan 'All Power to the Soviets' is a slogan of insurrection. Whoever uses this slogan without having grasped this and given thought to it will have only himself to blame. And insurrection must be treated as an *art.* I insisted on this during the Democratic Conference and I insist on it now, because *that* is what Marxism teaches us, and it is what is being taught us by the present situation in Russia and in the world generally.

It is not a question of voting, of attracting the Left Socialist-Revolutionaries, of additional provincial Soviets, or of a congress of these Soviets. It is a question of insurrection, which *can* and must be decided by Petrograd, Moscow, Helsingfors, Kronstadt, Vyborg and Revel. It is *in the vicinity of Petrograd* and in Petrograd itself that the insurrection can, and must be decided on and effected, as earnestly as possible, with as much preparation as possible, as quickly as possible and as energetically as possible.

The fleet, Kronstadt, Vyborg and Revel can and must advance on Petrograd; they can and must smash the Kornilovite regiments, rouse both the capital cities, start a mass agitation for a government which will immediately give land to the peasants and immediately make proposals for peace, overthrow Kerensky's government and establish such a government.

Delay would be fatal.

N Lenin

8 (21) October 1917

Meeting of the CC of the RSDLP(B)

10 (23) October 1917

Editor's note:

At this CC meeting, Lenin gave a report on the current situation, and the CC adopted the resolution motioned by Lenin proposing the immediate preparations for an armed uprising. Only Zinoviev and Kamenev voted against the proposal.

* * *

Report Minutes

Comrade Lenin maintains that a sort of indifference to the question of insurrection has been noticeable since the beginning of September. But this is impermissible if we are issuing the slogan of the seizure of power by the Soviets in all seriousness. It is therefore high time to pay attention to the technical aspect of the question. Apparently a lot of time has already been lost.

Nevertheless the question is an urgent one, and the decisive moment is near.

The international situation is such that we must take the initiative.

What is being done to surrender territory as far as Narva, and to surrender Petrograd makes it still more imperative for us to take decisive action.

The political situation is also working impressively in this direction. Decisive action on our part on 3, 4 and 5 July would have failed because we did not have the majority behind us. Since then we have made tremendous progress.

Absenteeism and indifference on the part of the masses is due to their being tired of words and resolutions.

We now have the majority behind us. Politically, the situation is fully ripe for taking power.

The agrarian movement is also developing in that direction, for it is obvious that extreme effort would be needed to stem that movement. The slogan of the transfer of all land has become the general slogan of the peasants. The political situation, therefore, is mature. We must speak of the technical aspect. That is the crux of the matter. Nevertheless we, like the defencists, are inclined to regard the systematic preparation of an uprising as something in the nature of a political sin.

It is senseless to wait for the Constituent Assembly that will obviously not be on our side, for this will only make our task more involved.

The regional congress and the proposal from Minsk must be used for the beginning of decisive action.[1]

* * *

Resolution

The Central Committee recognises that the international position of the Russian revolution (the revolt in the German navy which is an extreme manifestation of the growth throughout Europe of the world

1 The reference is to Yakov Sverdlov's report to the Central Committee on 10 (23) October 1917, on the third item of the agenda: 'Minsk and the Northern Front'. He said that there was a technical possibility of staging an armed uprising in Minsk, and that Minsk had offered to send a revolutionary corps to help Petrograd.

socialist revolution; the threat of peace by the imperialists with the object of strangling the revolution in Russia) as well as the military situation (the indubitable decision of the Russian bourgeoisie and Kerensky and co. to surrender Petrograd to the Germans), and the fact that the proletarian party has gained a majority in the Soviets – all this, taken in conjunction with the peasant revolt and the swing of popular confidence towards our Party (the elections in Moscow), and, finally, the obvious preparations being made for a second Kornilov revolt (the withdrawal of troops from Petrograd, the dispatch of Cossacks to Petrograd, the encircling of Minsk by Cossacks, etc.) – all this places the armed uprising on the order of the day.

Considering therefore that an armed uprising is inevitable, and that the time for it is fully ripe, the Central Committee instructs all Party organisations to be guided accordingly, and to discuss and decide all practical questions (the Congress of Soviets of the Northern Region, the withdrawal of troops from Petrograd, the action of our people in Moscow and Minsk, etc.) from this point of view.

Meeting of the CC of the RSDLP(B)

16 (29) October 1917

Report Minutes

Comrade Lenin read the resolution adopted by the Central Committee at the previous meeting. He stated that the resolution had been adopted with two dissenting votes. If the dissident comrades wished to make a statement, a discussion could be held; meanwhile he continued with the motives of the resolution.

If the Menshevik and Socialist-Revolutionary parties were to break with their policy of conciliation, a compromise with them could be proposed. The proposal had been made, but those parties had obviously rejected the compromise. On the other hand, by that time it had become definitely clear that the masses were following the Bolsheviks. That had been before the Kornilov revolt. Lenin cited election returns from Petrograd and Moscow as evidence. The Kornilov revolt had pushed the masses still more decisively to the side of the Bolsheviks. The alignment of forces at the Democratic Conference. The position was clear – either Kornilov's dictatorship or the dictatorship of the proletariat and the poorer strata of the peasantry. The Party could not be guided by the temper of the masses because it was changeable and incalculable; the Party must be guided by an objective analysis and an appraisal of the revolution. The masses had put their trust in the Bolsheviks and demanded deeds from them and not words, a decisive policy both in the struggle against the war and in the struggle against economic ruin. If the political analysis of the revolution were taken as the basis, it would be perfectly clear that even anarchic outbursts confirmed that.

Lenin went on to analyse the situation in Europe and showed that revolution would be even more difficult in Europe than in Russia; if matters had gone as far as a revolt in the navy in such a country as Germany, there too they must already have gone very far. Certain objective data on the international situation showed that by acting at that moment the Bolsheviks would have all proletarian Europe on their side; he showed that the bourgeoisie wanted to surrender Petrograd. That could only be prevented by the Bolsheviks taking over Petrograd. The obvious conclusion from all this was – the armed uprising was on the order of the day as was stated in the resolution of the Central Committee.

It would be better to draw practical conclusions from the resolution after hearing the reports of representatives from the centres.

From a political analysis of the class struggle in Russia and in Europe there emerged the necessity to pursue the most determined and most active policy, which could be only the armed uprising.

Speeches in Discussion (Minutes)

1. Comrade Lenin argued against Milyutin and Shotman and showed that it was not a matter of armed forces, that it was not a question of fighting against the troops but of one part of the army fighting against another. He could see no pessimism in what had been said there. He demonstrated that the forces on the side of the bourgeoisie were small. The facts showed that ours were superior to the enemy. Why could the Central

Committee not begin? There was no reason that derived from the facts. To reject the resolution of the Central Committee it would have to be proved that there was no economic ruin and that the international situation would not lead to complications. If trade union leaders were in favour of full power they knew very well what they wanted. Objective conditions showed that the peasantry must be led; they would follow the proletariat.

Some were afraid that Bolsheviks would not be able to maintain power, but at that moment there was a better chance than ever that they would be able to.

Lenin expressed the wish that the debate be confined to the substance of the resolution.

2. If all resolutions were defeated in that manner nothing better could be wished for. Zinoviev was saying: do away with the 'Power to the Soviets' slogan and bring pressure to bear on the government. When it was said that the time was ripe for insurrection there could be no question of conspiracy. Since an insurrection was inevitable politically, it must be regarded as an art. Politically, an insurrection was due.

   Because there was only enough bread for a day the Party could not wait for the Constituent Assembly. Comrade Lenin proposed that the resolution be approved, that energetic preparations be begun and that it be left to the Central Committee and the Soviet to decide when.

3. Comrade Lenin opposed Zinoviev, saying that the revolution could not be contrasted to the February Revolution. He proposed a resolution straight to the point.

Resolution

The meeting fully welcomes and fully supports the resolution of the Central Committee and calls upon all organisations and on workers and soldiers to make all-round, energetic preparations for an armed uprising and to support the centre set up for that purpose by the

Central Committee; the meeting expresses its complete confidence that the Central Committee and the Soviet will indicate in good time the favourable moment and the most appropriate methods of attack.

Letter to Comrades

Written 17 (30) October 1917

Comrades,

We are living in a time that is so critical, events are moving at such incredible speed that a publicist, placed by the will of fate somewhat aside from the mainstream of history, constantly runs the risk either of being late or proving uninformed, especially if some time elapses before his writings appear in print. Although I fully realise this, I must nevertheless address this letter to the Bolsheviks, even at the risk of its not being published at all, for the vacillations against which I deem it my duty to warn in the most decisive manner are of an unprecedented nature and may have a disastrous effect on the Party, the movement of the international proletariat and the revolution. As for the danger of being too late, I will prevent it by indicating the nature and date of the information I possess.

It was not until Monday morning, 16 (29) October, that I saw a comrade who had on the previous day participated in a very important Bolshevik gathering in Petrograd, and who informed me in detail of the discussion.[1] The subject of discussion was that same

1 A reference to the enlarged Central Committee meeting on 16 (29) October 1917. Lenin was in fact at the meeting, but for security reasons he has here claimed otherwise and has given an incorrect date of the meeting.

question of the uprising discussed by the Sunday papers of all political trends. The gathering represented all that is most influential in all branches of Bolshevik work in the capital. Only a most insignificant minority of the gathering, namely, all in all two comrades, took a negative stand. The arguments which those comrades advanced are so weak, they are a manifestation of such an astounding confusion, timidity and collapse of all the fundamental ideas of Bolshevism and proletarian revolutionary internationalism that it is not easy to discover an explanation for such shameful vacillations. The fact, however, remains, and since the revolutionary party has no right to tolerate vacillations on such a serious question, and since this pair of comrades, who have scattered their principles to the winds, might cause some confusion, it is necessary to analyse their arguments, to expose their vacillations and to show how shameful they are. The following lines are an attempt to do this.

* * *

> We have no majority among the people, and without this condition the uprising is hopeless…

People who can say this are either distorters of the truth or pedants who want an advance guarantee that throughout the whole country the Bolshevik Party has received exactly one-half of the votes plus one, this they want at all events, without taking the least account of the real circumstances of the revolution. History has never given such a guarantee, and is quite unable to give it in any revolution. To make such a demand is jeering at the audience, and is nothing but a cover to hide one's own *flight* from reality.

For reality shows us clearly that it was after the July Days that the majority of the people began quickly to go over to the side of the Bolsheviks. This was demonstrated first by the 20 August (2 September) elections in Petrograd, even before the Kornilov revolt, when the Bolshevik vote rose from 20 to 33 per cent in the city not including the suburbs, and then by the district council elections in Moscow in September, when the Bolshevik vote rose from 11 to 49.3 per cent (one

Moscow comrade, whom I saw recently, told me that the correct figure is 51 per cent). This was proved by the new elections to the Soviets. It was proved by the fact that a majority of the peasant Soviets, their 'Avksentiev' central Soviet notwithstanding, has expressed itself *against* the coalition. To be against the coalition means *in practice* to follow the Bolsheviks. Furthermore, reports from the front prove more frequently and more definitely that the soldiers are passing *en masse* over to the side of the Bolsheviks with ever greater determination, in spite of the malicious slanders and attacks by the Socialist-Revolutionary and Menshevik leaders, officers, deputies, etc., etc.

Last, but not least, the most outstanding fact of present day Russian life is *the revolt of the peasantry*. This shows objectively, not by words but by deeds, that the people are going over to the side of the Bolsheviks. But the fact remains, notwithstanding the lies of the bourgeois press and its miserable yes-men of the 'vacillating' *Novaya Zhizn* crowd, who shout about riots and anarchy. The peasant movement in Tambov Gubernia[2] was an uprising both in the physical and political sense, an uprising that has yielded such splendid political results as, in the first place, agreement to transfer the land to the peasants. It is not for nothing that the Socialist-Revolutionary rabble, including *Dyelo Naroda*, who are frightened by the uprising, now *scream* about the need to transfer the land to the peasants. Here is a *practical* demonstration of the correctness of Bolshevism and of its success. It proved to be impossible to 'teach' the Bonapartists and their lackeys in the Pre-parliament otherwise than by an uprising.

This is a fact and facts are stubborn things. And such a factual 'argument' *in favour* of an uprising is stronger than thousands of 'pessimistic' evasions on the part of confused and frightened politicians.

2 The peasant movement in Tambov Gubernia in September 1917 assumed great proportions: the peasants seized tracts of landed estates, destroyed and burned landowners' mansions and confiscated grain stocks. The commanding officer of the Moscow Military District sent military units to Tambov Gubernia to crush the peasant uprising, and imposed martial law, but the peasants' revolutionary struggle for land continued to grow in scope.

If the peasant uprising were not an event of nation-wide political import, the Socialist-Revolutionary lackeys from the Pre-parliament would not be shouting about the need to hand over the land to the peasants.

Another splendid political and revolutionary consequence of the peasant uprising, as already noted in *Rabochy Put*, is the delivery of grain to the railway stations in Tambov Gubernia. Here is another 'argument' for you, confused gentlemen, an argument in favour of the uprising as the only means to save the country from the famine that is knocking at our door and from a crisis of unheard-of dimensions. While the Socialist-Revolutionary and Menshevik betrayers of the people are grumbling, threatening, writing resolutions, promising to feed the hungry by convening the Constituent Assembly, the people are beginning to solve the bread problem *Bolshevik-fashion, by rebelling* against the landowners, capitalists and speculators.

Even the *bourgeois* press, even *Russkaya Volya*, was compelled to admit the wonderful results of *such* a solution (the only real solution) of the bread problem, by publishing information to the effect that the railway stations in Tambov Gubernia were swamped with grain… *And this after the peasants had revolted!*

To doubt now that the majority of the people are following and will follow the Bolsheviks is shameful vacillation and in practice is the abandoning of *all* the principles of proletarian revolutionism, the complete renunciation of Bolshevism.

* * *

> We are not strong enough to seize power, and the bourgeoisie is not strong enough to hinder the convening of the Constituent Assembly.

The first part of this argument is a simple paraphrase of the preceding one. It does not gain in strength or power of conviction, when the confusion of its authors and their fear of the bourgeoisie are expressed in terms of pessimism in respect of the workers and optimism in respect of the bourgeoisie. If the officer cadets and the Cossacks say that they will fight against the Bolsheviks to the last drop of blood, this deserves full credence; if, however, the workers and soldiers at hundreds of meetings express full confidence in the Bolsheviks and affirm their readiness to defend the transfer of power to the Soviets, then it is 'timely' to recall that voting is one thing and fighting another!

If you argue like that, of course, you 'refute' the possibility of an uprising. But, we may ask, in what way does this peculiarly orientated 'pessimism' with its peculiar urge differ from a political shift to the side of the bourgeoisie?

Look at the facts. Remember the Bolshevik declarations, repeated thousands of times and now 'forgotten' by our pessimists. We have said thousands of times that the Soviets of Workers' and Soldiers' Deputies are a force, that they are the vanguard of the revolution, that they *can* take power. Thousands of times have we upbraided the Mensheviks and Socialist-Revolutionaries for phrase-mongering about the 'plenipotentiary organs of democracy' accompanied by *fear* to transfer power to the Soviets.

And what has the Kornilov revolt proved? It has proved that the Soviets are a real force.

And, now, after this has been proved by experience, by facts, we are expected to repudiate Bolshevism, deny ourselves, and say that we are not strong enough (although the Soviets of Petrograd and Moscow and a majority of the provincial Soviets are on the side of the Bolsheviks)! Are these not shameful vacillations? As a matter of fact, our 'pessimists' are abandoning the slogan of 'All Power to the Soviets', though they *are afraid* to admit it.

How can it be proved that the bourgeoisie are not strong enough to hinder the calling of the Constituent Assembly?

If the Soviets *have not the strength* to overthrow the bourgeoisie, this *means* the latter are strong enough to prevent the convocation of the Constituent Assembly, for there is nobody else to stop them. To trust the promises of Kerensky and co., to trust the resolutions of the servile Pre-parliament – is this worthy of a member of a proletarian party and a revolutionary?

Not only has the bourgeoisie *strength enough* to hinder the convocation of the Constituent Assembly if the present government is not overthrown, but it can also achieve this result *indirectly* by surrendering Petrograd to the Germans, laying open the front, increasing lockouts and sabotaging deliveries of foodstuffs. It has been proved by *facts* that the bourgeoisie have already been partly doing this, which means that they are capable of doing it *to the full extent*, if the workers and soldiers do not overthrow them.

* * *

> The Soviets must be a revolver pointed at the head of the government with the demand to convene the Constituent Assembly and stop all Kornilovite plots.

This is how far one of the two sad pessimists has gone.

He had to go that far, for to reject the uprising is *the same as* rejecting the slogan 'All Power to the Soviets'.

Of course, a slogan is 'not sacred'; we all agree to that. But then why has *no one* raised the question of changing this slogan (in the same way as I raised the question after the July Days)? Why be *afraid* to say it openly, when the Party, since September, has been discussing the question of the uprising, which is now *the only way* to realise the slogan 'All Power to the Soviets'.

There is no way for our sad pessimists to turn. A renunciation of the uprising is a renunciation of the transfer of power to the Soviets and implies a 'transfer' of all hopes and expectations to the kind bourgeoisie, which has 'promised' to convoke the Constituent Assembly.

Is it so difficult to understand that once *power* is in the hands of the Soviets, the Constituent Assembly and its success are *guaranteed*? The Bolsheviks have said so thousands of times and *no one* has ever attempted to refute it. Everybody has recognised this 'combined type', but to smuggle in a *renunciation* of the transfer of power to the Soviets under cover of the words 'combined type', to smuggle it in *secretly* while *fearing* to renounce our slogan openly is a matter for wonder. Is there any parliamentary term to describe it?

Someone has very pointedly retorted to our pessimist: "Is it a revolver with no cartridges?" If so, it means going over directly to the Liberdans, who have declared the Soviets a 'revolver' thousands of times and have deceived the people thousands of times. For *while they were in control* the Soviets proved to be worthless.

If, however, it is to be a revolver 'with cartridges', this cannot mean anything but *technical* preparation for an uprising; the cartridges have to be procured, the revolver has to be loaded – and cartridges alone will not be enough.

Either go over to the side of the Liberdans and *openly* renounce the slogan 'All Power to the Soviets', or start the uprising.

There is no middle course.

* * *

> The bourgeoisie cannot surrender Petrograd to the Germans, although Rodzianko wants to, for the fighting is done not by the bourgeoisie, but by our heroic sailors.

This argument again reduces itself to the same 'optimism' *in respect of the bourgeoisie* which is fatally manifested at every step by those who are pessimistic about the revolutionary forces and capabilities of the proletariat.

The fighting is done by the heroic sailors, *but* this did not prevent *two* admirals from *disappearing* before the capture of Esel!

That is a fact and facts are stubborn things. The facts prove that admirals *are capable* of treachery no less than Kornilov. It is an undisputed fact that Field Headquarters has not been reformed, and that the commanding staff is Kornilovite in composition.

If the Kornilovites (with Kerensky at their head, for he is also a Kornilovite) *want* to surrender Petrograd, they can do it in two or even in three ways.

First, they can, through an act of treachery on the part of the Kornilovite officers, open the northern land front.

Second, they can 'agree' on freedom of action for the entire German navy, which is *stronger* than we are; they can agree both with the German and the British imperialists. Moreover, the admirals who have disappeared may have delivered the *plans* to the Germans *as well.*

Third, they can, by means of lockouts, and by sabotaging the delivery of food, bring our troops to complete *desperation* and impotence.

Not a single one of these three ways can be denied. The facts have proved that the bourgeois-Cossack party of Russia has already knocked at all three doors and has tried to force open each of them.

What follows? It follows that we have no right to *wait* until the bourgeoisie strangle the revolution.

Experience has proved that Rodzianko's wishes are no trifle. Rodzianko is a man of affairs. Rodzianko is backed by *capital.* This is beyond dispute. Capital is tremendous strength as long as the proletariat do not have power. *For decades,* Rodzianko has faithfully and truly carried out the policies of capital.

What follows? It follows that to vacillate on the question of an uprising as the only means to save the revolution means to sink into that cowardly credulity in the bourgeoisie which is half-Liberdan, Socialist-Revolutionary-Menshevik and half 'peasant-like' unquestioning credulity, against which the Bolsheviks have been battling most of all.

Either fold your idle arms on your empty chest, wait and swear 'faith' in the Constituent Assembly until Rodzianko and co. have surrendered Petrograd and strangled the revolution or start an uprising. There is no middle course.

Even the convocation of the Constituent Assembly does not, in itself, change anything, for no 'constituting', no voting by any arch-sovereign assembly will have any effect on the famine, or on Wilhelm. Both the convocation and the *success* of the Constituent Assembly depend upon the transfer of power to the Soviets. This old Bolshevik truth is being proved by reality ever more strikingly and ever more *cruelly.*

* * *

> We are becoming stronger every day. We can enter the Constituent Assembly as a strong opposition; why should we stake everything?

This is the argument of a philistine who has 'read' that the Constituent Assembly is being called, and who trustingly acquiesces in the most legal, most loyal, most constitutional course.

It is a pity, however, that *waiting* for the Constituent Assembly does not solve either the question of famine or the question of surrendering Petrograd. This 'trifle' is forgotten by the naive or the confused or those who have allowed themselves to be frightened.

The famine will not wait. The peasant uprising did not wait. The war will not wait. The admirals who have disappeared did not wait.

Will the famine agree to wait, because we Bolsheviks *proclaim* faith in the convocation of the Constituent Assembly? Will the admirals who have disappeared agree to wait? Will the Maklakovs and Rodziankos agree to stop the lockouts and the sabotaging of grain deliveries, or to denounce the secret treaties with the British and the German imperialists?

This is what the arguments of the heroes of 'constitutional illusions' and parliamentary cretinism amount to. The living reality disappears, and what remains is only a *paper* dealing with the convocation of the Constituent Assembly; there is nothing left – but to hold elections.

And blind people are still wondering why hungry people and soldiers betrayed by generals and admirals are indifferent to the elections! Oh, wiseacres!

* * *

> Were the Kornilovites to start again, we would show them! But why should we take risks and start?

This is extraordinarily convincing and revolutionary. History does not repeat itself, but if we turn our *backs* on it, contemplate the first Kornilov revolt and repeat: "If only the Kornilovites would start" – if we do that, what excellent revolutionary strategy it would be. How much like a waiting game it is! Maybe the Kornilovites will start again at an inopportune time. Isn't this a 'weighty' argument? What kind of an earnest foundation for a proletarian policy is this?

And what if the Kornilovites of the second draft will have learned a thing or two? What if they *wait* for the hunger riots to begin, for the front to be broken through, for Petrograd to be surrendered, *before they begin*? What then?

It is proposed that we build the tactics of the proletarian party on the possibility of the Kornilovites' repeating one of their old errors!

Let us forget all that was being and *has been demonstrated* by the Bolsheviks a hundred times, all that the six months' history of our revolution has proved, namely, that there is *no* way out, that there is no objective way out and can be none *except* a dictatorship of the Kornilovites or a dictatorship of the proletariat. Let us forget this, let us renounce all this and wait! Wait for what? Wait for a miracle, for the tempestuous and catastrophic course of events from 20 April to 29 August to be succeeded (due to the prolongation of the war and the spread of famine) by a peaceful, quiet, smooth, legal convocation of the Constituent Assembly and by a fulfilment of its most lawful decisions. Here you have the 'Marxist' tactics! Wait, ye hungry! Kerensky has promised to convene the Constituent Assembly.

* * *

> There is really nothing in the international situation that makes it obligatory for us to act immediately, we would be more likely to damage the cause of a socialist revolution in the West, if we were to allow ourselves to be shot...

This argument is truly magnificent: Scheidemann 'himself', Renaudel 'himself' would not be able to 'manipulate' more cleverly the workers' sympathies for the international socialist revolution!

Just think of it: under devilishly difficult conditions, having but *one* Liebknecht (and he in prison) with no newspapers, with no freedom of assembly, with no Soviets, with *all* classes of the population, including every well-to-do peasant, incredibly hostile to the idea of internationalism, with the imperialist big, middle and petty bourgeoisie splendidly organised – the Germans, i.e., the German revolutionary internationalists, the German workers dressed in sailors' jackets, started a mutiny in the navy with one chance in a hundred of winning.

But we, with dozens of papers at our disposal, freedom of assembly, a *majority* in the Soviets, we, the best situated proletarian internationalists in the world, should refuse to support the German revolutionaries by our uprising. We ought to reason like the Scheidemanns and Renaudels, that it is most prudent not to revolt, for if we are shot, then the world will lose such excellent, reasonable, ideal internationalists!

Let us prove how reasonable we are. Let us pass a resolution of sympathy with the *German insurrectionists*, and let us renounce the *insurrection* in Russia. This would be genuine, reasonable internationalism. Imagine how fast world internationalism would blossom forth, if the same wise policy were to triumph *everywhere!*

The war has fatigued and tormented the workers of all countries to the utmost. Outbursts are becoming frequent in Italy, Germany and Austria. We *alone* have Soviets of Workers' and Soldiers' Deputies. Let us then *keep on waiting*. Let us betray the German internationalists as we are betraying the Russian peasants, who, not by words but by deeds, by their uprising against the landowners, appeal to us to rise against Kerensky's government…

Let the clouds of the imperialist conspiracy of the capitalists of all countries who are ready to strangle the Russian revolution gather – we shall wait patiently until we are strangled *by the rouble!* Instead of attacking the conspirators and breaking their ranks by a victory of the Soviets of Workers' and Soldiers' Deputies, let us wait for the Constituent Assembly, where all international plots will be vanquished by *voting*, provided Kerensky and Rodzianko conscientiously convene the Constituent Assembly. Have we any right to doubt the honesty of Kerensky and Rodzianko?

* * *

> But 'everyone' is against us! We are isolated; the Central Executive Committee, the Menshevik internationalists, the *Novaya Zhizn* people, and the Left Socialist-Revolutionaries have been issuing and will continue to issue appeals against us!

A crushing argument. Up to now we have been mercilessly scourging the vacillators for their vacillations. *By so doing*, we have won the sympathies of the people. *By so doing*, we have won over the Soviets, without which the uprising could not be safe, quick and sure. Now let us use the Soviets which we have won over in order *to move into the camp of the vacillators*. What a splendid career for Bolshevism!

The whole essence of the policy of the Liberdans and Chernovs, and also of the Left Socialist-Revolutionaries and Mensheviks, consists in *vacillations*. The Left Socialist-Revolutionaries and Menshevik internationalists have *tremendous* political importance as an *indication* of the fact that the *masses are moving to the left*. Two such facts as the passing of some 40 per cent of both Mensheviks and Socialist-Revolutionaries into the camp of the Left, on the one hand, and the peasant uprising, on the other, are clearly and obviously interconnected.

But it is the very character of this connection that reveals the abysmal spinelessness of those who have now undertaken to whimper over the fact that the Central Executive Committee, which has rotted away, or the vacillating Left Socialist-Revolutionaries and co., have come out against us. For *these* vacillations of the petty-bourgeois leaders – the Martovs, Kamkovs, Sukhanovs and co. – have to be compared to the *uprising* of the peasants. Here is a *realistic* political comparison. With whom shall we go? Should it be with the vacillating handfuls of Petrograd leaders, who have expressed *indirectly* the *leftward swing* of the masses, but who, at *every* political turn, have shamefully whimpered, vacillated, run to ask forgiveness of the Liberdans, Avksentievs and co., *or with those masses that have moved to the left?*

Thus, and only thus, can the question be presented.

Because the peasant uprising has been betrayed by the Martovs, Kamkovs and Sukhanovs, we, the workers' party of revolutionary internationalists, are asked to betray it, too. This is what the policy of blaming the Left Socialist-Revolutionaries and Menshevik internationalists reduces itself to.

But we have said that to help the vacillating, we must stop vacillating ourselves. Have those 'nice' Left petty-bourgeois democrats not 'vacillated' in favour of the coalition? In the long run we succeeded in making them follow us because we ourselves did not vacillate. Events have shown we are right.

These gentlemen by their vacillations have always held back the revolution. We alone have saved it. Shall we now give up, when the famine is knocking at the gates of Petrograd and Rodzianko and co. are preparing to surrender the city?!

* * *

> But we have not even firm connections with the railwaymen and the postal employees. Their official representatives are the Plansons.[3] And can we win without the post office and without railways?

Yes, yes, the Plansons here, the Liberdans there. What confidence have the *masses* shown them? Have we not always shown that those leaders betrayed the *masses*? Did the masses not turn away from those leaders *towards us*, both at the elections in Moscow and at the elections to the Soviets? Or perhaps the mass of railway and postal employees are not starving! Or do not strike against Kerensky and co.?

"Did we have connections with these unions before 28 February?" one comrade asked a pessimist. The latter replied by pointing out that the two revolutions could not be compared. But this reply only *strengthens* the position of the one who asked the question. For it is the Bolsheviks who have spoken thousands of times about prolonged preparation for the *proletarian* revolution *against the bourgeoisie* (and they have not spoken about it in order to forget their words when the decisive moment is at hand). The political and economic life of the unions of postal and telegraph employees and railwaymen is characterised by the very *separation* of the proletarian elements of the masses from the petty-bourgeois and bourgeois upper layer. It is not absolutely necessary to secure 'connections' with one or the

3 Anton Planson was a Popular Socialist, and member of the Central Executive Committee (First Convocation). A leader of Vikzhel – the All-Russia Executive Committee of the Railwaymen's Trade Union, an organisation run by the compromisers.

other union beforehand; what matters is that only a victory of a proletarian and peasant uprising *can* satisfy the *masses* both of the army of railwaymen and of postal and telegraph employees.

* * *

> There is only enough bread in Petrograd for two or three days. Can we give bread to the insurrectionists?

This is one of a thousand sceptical remarks (the sceptics can *always* 'doubt' and cannot be refuted by anything but experience), one of those remarks that put the blame on the wrong shoulders.

It is Rodzianko and co., it is the bourgeoisie that are preparing the famine and speculating on strangling the revolution by famine. There is no escaping the famine and *there can be none* except by an uprising of the peasants against the landowners in the countryside and by a victory of the workers over the capitalists in the cities and Petrograd and Moscow. There is *no other way* to get grain from the rich, or to transport it despite their sabotage, or to break the resistance of the corrupt employees and the capitalist profiteers, or to establish strict accounting. The history of the supply organisations and of the food difficulties of the 'democracy' with its millions of *complaints* against the sabotage of the capitalists, with its *whimpering* and *supplication,* is proof of this.

There is no power on earth apart from the power of a victorious proletarian revolution that would advance from complaints and begging and tears to *revolutionary action*. And the longer the proletarian revolution is delayed, the longer it is put off by events or by the vacillations of the wavering and confused, the more victims it will claim and the more difficult it will be to *organise* the transportation and distribution of food.

"In insurrection delay is fatal" this is our answer to those having the sad 'courage' to look at the growing economic ruin, at the approaching famine, and still *dissuade* the workers from the uprising (*that is, persuade them to wait and place confidence in the bourgeoisie for some further time*).

* * *

> There is not yet any danger at the front either. Even if the soldiers conclude an armistice themselves, it is still not a calamity.

But the soldiers will not conclude an armistice. For this state power is necessary and that cannot be obtained without an uprising. The soldiers will simply *desert*. Reports from the front tell that. We must not wait because of the risk of aiding collusion between Rodzianko and Wilhelm and the risk of *complete* economic ruin, with the soldiers deserting in masses, once they (*being already close to desperation*) sink into absolute despair and leave everything to the mercy of fate.

* * *

> But if we take power, and obtain neither an armistice nor a democratic peace, the soldiers may not be willing to fight a revolutionary war. What then?

An argument which brings to mind the saying: one fool can ask ten times more questions than ten wise men can answer.

We have never denied the difficulties of *those in power* during an imperialist war. Nevertheless, we have always *preached* the dictatorship of the proletariat and the poor peasantry. Shall we renounce this, when the moment to act has arrived?

We have always said that the dictatorship of the proletariat in one country creates gigantic changes in the international situation, in the economic life of the country, in the condition of the army and in its mood – shall we now 'forget' all this, and allow ourselves to be frightened by the 'difficulties' of the revolution?

* * *

> As everybody reports, the masses are not in a mood that would drive them into the streets. Among the signs justifying pessimism may be mentioned the greatly increasing circulation of the pogromist and Black-Hundred press.

When people allow themselves to be frightened by the bourgeoisie, all objects and phenomena naturally appear yellow to them. First, they substitute an impressionist, intellectualist criterion for the Marxist criterion of the movement; they *substitute* subjective impressions of moods *for* a political analysis of the development of the class struggle and of the course of events in the entire country against the entire international background. They 'conveniently' forget, of course, that a firm party line, its unyielding resolve, is *also* a mood-creating *factor*, particularly at the sharpest revolutionary moments. It is sometimes very 'convenient' for people to forget that the responsible leaders, by their vacillations and by their readiness to burn their yesterday's idols, cause the most unbecoming vacillations in the mood of certain strata of the masses.

Secondly – and this is at present the main thing – in speaking about the mood of the masses, the spineless people forget to add:

- That 'everybody' reports it as a tense and expectant mood;
- That 'everybody' agrees that, called upon by the Soviets for the defence of the Soviets, the workers will rise to a man;
- That 'everybody' agrees that the workers are greatly dissatisfied with the indecision of the centres concerning the 'last decisive struggle', the inevitability of which they clearly recognise;
- That 'everybody' unanimously characterises the mood of the broadest masses as close to desperation and points to the anarchy developing therefrom;
- That 'everybody' also recognises that there is among the class-conscious workers a definite unwillingness to go out into the streets *only* for demonstrations, *only* for partial struggles, since a general and not a partial struggle is in the air, while the hopelessness of individual strikes, demonstrations and acts to influence the authorities has been seen and is fully realised.

And so forth.

If we approach this characterisation of the mass mood from the point of view of the entire development of the class and political struggle and of the entire course of events during the six months of our revolution, it will become clear to us how people frightened by the bourgeoisie are distorting the question. Things are not as they were before 20-21 April, 9 June, 3 July, for then it was a matter of *spontaneous excitement* which we, as a party, either failed to comprehend (20 April) or held back and shaped into a peaceful demonstration (9 June and 3 July), for we knew very well at that time that the Soviets were *not yet* ours, that the peasants *still* trusted the Liberdan-Chernov and not the Bolshevik course (uprising), that consequently we could not have the majority of the people behind us, and that consequently the uprising would be premature.

At that time the majority of the class-conscious workers did *not* raise the question of the last decisive struggle at all; not one of all our Party units would have raised it at that time. As for the unenlightened and very broad masses, there was neither a concerted effort nor the resolve born out of despair; there was only a spontaneous *excitement* with the naive hope of 'influencing' Kerensky and the bourgeoisie by 'action', by a demonstration pure and simple.

What is needed for an uprising is not this, but, on the one hand, a conscious, firm and unswerving resolve on the part of the class-conscious elements to fight to the end; and on the other, a mood of despair among the broad masses who *feel* that nothing can now be saved by half-measures; that you cannot 'influence' anybody; that the hungry will 'smash everything, destroy everything, even anarchically', *if* the Bolsheviks are not able to lead them in a decisive battle.

The development of the revolution has in practice brought *both* the workers *and* the peasantry to precisely this combination of a tense mood resulting from experience among the class-conscious and a mood of hatred towards those using the lockout weapon and the capitalists that is close to despair among the broadest masses.

We can also understand the 'success' on this very soil of the scoundrels of the reactionary press who imitate Bolshevism. The malicious glee of the reactionaries at the approach of a decisive battle between the bourgeoisie and the proletariat has been observed in all revolutions without exception; it has always been so, and it is absolutely unavoidable. And if you allow yourselves to be frightened by *this* circumstance, then you have to renounce not only the uprising but the proletarian revolution in general. For in a capitalist society this revolution *cannot* mature *without* being accompanied by malicious glee on the part of the reactionaries and by hopes that they would be able to feather their nest in this way.

The class-conscious workers know perfectly well that the Black Hundreds work hand in hand with the bourgeoisie, and that a decisive victory of the workers (in which the petty bourgeoisie do not believe, which the capitalists are afraid of, which the Black Hundreds sometimes wish for out of sheer malice, convinced as they are that the Bolsheviks cannot retain power) – that this victory will completely *crush* the Black Hundreds, that the Bolsheviks *will be able* to retain power firmly and to the greatest advantage of all humanity tortured and tormented by the war.

Indeed, is there anybody in his senses who can doubt that the *Rodziankos* and Suvorins are acting in concert, that the roles have been distributed among them?[4]

Has it not been proved by facts that Kerensky acts on Rodzianko's orders, while the State Printing Press of the Russian Republic (don't laugh!) prints the Black-Hundred speeches of reactionaries in the 'Duma' at the expense of the state. Has not this fact been exposed *even* by the lackeys from *Dyelo Naroda*, who serve 'their own mannikin'? Has not the experience of *all* elections proved that the Cadet lists were fully supported by *Novoye Vremya*, which is a venal paper controlled by the 'interests' of the tsarist landowners?

Did we not read yesterday that commercial and industrial capitalists (non-partisan capitalists, of course; oh, non-partisan capitalists, to be sure, for the Vikhlayevs and Rakitnikovs, the Gvozdevs and Nikitins are not in coalition with the Cadets – God forbid – but with *non-partisan* commercial and industrial circles!) have donated the goodly sum of 300,000 roubles to the Cadets?

4 Mikhail Rodzianko was a landowner and a leading Octobrist, who supported Kornilov's revolt. A Suvorin Jr. published the reactionary Black Hundred newspaper *Malenkaya Gazeta*, which, speculating on the people's sympathy for socialism, from May 1917 carried the subheading: "The paper of the non-party socialists."

The whole Black-Hundred press, if we look at things from a class and not a sentimental point of view, is a *branch* of the firm 'Ryabushinsky, Milyukov and co.'. Capitalists buy, on the one hand, the Milyukovs, Zaslavskys, Potresovs and so on; on the other, the Black Hundreds.

The *victory of the proletariat* is the only means of putting an end to this most hideous poisoning of the people by the cheap Black-Hundred venom.

Is it any wonder that the crowd, tired out and made wretched by hunger and the prolongation of the war, clutches at the Black-Hundred poison? Can one imagine a capitalist society on the eve of collapse in which the oppressed masses are *not* desperate? Is there any doubt that the desperation of the masses, a large part of whom are still ignorant, *will* express itself in the increased consumption of all sorts of poison?

Those who, in arguing about the mood of the masses, blame the masses for their own personal spinelessness, are in a hopeless position. The masses are divided into those who are consciously biding their time and those who unconsciously are ready to sink into despair; but the masses of the oppressed and the hungry are *not* spineless.

* * *

> On the other hand, the Marxist party cannot reduce the question of an uprising to that of a military conspiracy…

Marxism is an extremely profound and many-sided doctrine. It is, therefore, no wonder that *scraps* of quotations from Marx – especially when the quotations are made *inappropriately* – can always be found among the 'arguments' of those who break with Marxism. Military conspiracy is Blanquism, *if* it is organised not by a party of a definite class, *if* its organisers have not analysed the political moment in general and the international situation in particular, *if* the party has not on its side the sympathy of the majority of the people, as proved by objective facts, *if* the development of revolutionary events has not brought about a practical refutation of the conciliatory illusions of the petty bourgeoisie, *if* the majority of the Soviet-type organs of revolutionary struggle that have been recognised as authoritative or have shown themselves to be such in practice have not been won over, *if* there has not matured a sentiment in the army (if in war-time) against the government that protracts the unjust war against the will of the whole people, *if* the slogans of the uprising (like 'All power to the Soviets' 'Land to the peasants', or 'Immediate offer of a democratic peace to all the belligerent nations, with an immediate abrogation of all secret treaties and secret diplomacy', etc.) have not become widely known and popular, *if* the advanced workers are not sure of the desperate situation of the masses and of the support of the countryside, a support proved by a serious peasant movement or by an uprising against the landowners and the government that defends the landowners, *if* the country's economic situation inspires earnest hopes for a favourable solution of the crisis by peaceable and parliamentary means.

This is probably enough.

In my pamphlet entitled: *Can the Bolsheviks Retain State Power?* (I hope it will appear in a day or two), there is a quotation from Marx which really bears upon the question of insurrection and which enumerates the features of insurrection as an 'art'.

I am ready to wager that if we were to propose to all those chatterers in Russia who are now shouting against a military conspiracy, to open their mouths and explain the difference between the 'art' of an insurrection and a military conspiracy that deserves condemnation, they would either repeat what was quoted above or would cover themselves, with shame and would call forth the general ridicule of the workers. Why not try, my dear would-be Marxists! Sing us a song *against* 'military conspiracy'!

Postscript

The above lines had been written when I received, at eight o'clock Tuesday evening, the morning Petrograd papers; there was an article by Mr. V Bazarov in *Novaya Zhizn*. Mr. V Bazarov asserts that "a handwritten manifesto was distributed in the city, in which arguments were presented in the name of two eminent Bolsheviks, against immediate action."

If this is true, I beg the comrades, whom this letter cannot reach earlier than Wednesday noon, to *publish it* as quickly as possible.

I did not write it for the press; I wanted to talk to the members of our Party by letter. But we cannot remain silent when the heroes of *Novaya Zhizn*, who do not belong to the Party and who have been ridiculed by it a thousand times for their contemptible spinelessness (they voted for the Bolsheviks the day before yesterday, for the Mensheviks yesterday, and who *almost* united them at the world-famous unity congress) – when such individuals receive a *manifesto* from members of our Party in which they carry on propaganda against an uprising.

We must agitate also *in favour* of an uprising. Let the anonymous individuals come right out into the light of day, and let them bear the punishment they deserve for their shameful vacillations, even if it be only the ridicule of all class-conscious workers. I have at my disposal only one hour before I send the present letter to Petrograd, and I therefore can say only a word or two about one of the 'methods' of the sad heroes of the brainless *Novaya Zhizn* trend. Mr. V Bazarov attempts to polemise against Comrade Ryazanov, who has said, and who is a thousand times correct in saying, that "all those who create in the masses a mood of despair and indifference are preparing an uprising".

The sad hero of a sad cause 'rejoins' as follows: "Have despair and indifference ever conquered?"

O contemptible fools from *Novaya Zhizn*! Do they know such examples of uprising in history, in which the masses of the oppressed classes were victorious in a desperate battle without having been reduced to despair by long sufferings and by an extreme sharpening of all sorts of crises, in which those masses had not been seized by indifference towards various lackey-like pre-parliaments, towards idle playing at revolution, towards the Liberdans' reduction of the Soviets from organs of power and uprising to empty talking shops?

Or have the contemptible little fools from *Novaya Zhizn* perhaps discovered among the masses an *indifference* – to the question of bread, to the prolongation of the war, to and for the peasants?

Letter to Bolshevik Party Members

Written 18 (31) October 1917

Comrades,

I have not yet been able to obtain the Petrograd papers for Wednesday 18 (31) October. When the full text of Kamenev's and Zinoviev's statement in the non-Party paper *Novaya Zhizn* was transmitted to me by telephone, I refused to believe it. But, as it has turned out, there can be no doubt about it and I have to avail myself of this opportunity to get a letter to Party members by Thursday evening or Friday morning; for to remain silent in the face of such unheard-of *strikebreaking* would be a crime.

The more serious the practical problem, and the more responsible and 'prominent' the persons guilty of strikebreaking, the more dangerous it is, the more resolutely must the strikebreakers be kicked out, and the more unpardonable would it be to stop even to consider the past 'services' of the strikebreakers.

Just think of it! It has been known in Party circles that the Party has been discussing the question of an insurrection since September. Nobody has ever heard of a single letter or manifesto by either of the persons named! Now, on the eve, one might say, of the Congress of

Soviets, two prominent Bolsheviks come out *against* the majority, and, obviously, *against the Central Committee.* It is not said plainly, but the harm done to the cause is all the greater, for to speak in hints is even more dangerous.

It is perfectly clear from the text of Kamenev's and Zinoviev's statement that they have gone against the Central Committee, for otherwise their statement would be meaningless. But they do not say *what* specific decision of the Central Committee they are disputing.

Why?

The reason is obvious: because it has not been published by the Central Committee.

What does this boil down to?

On a burning question of supreme importance, on the eve of the critical day of 20 October (2 November), two 'prominent Bolsheviks' attack an *un*published decision of the Party centre and attack it in the *non*-Party press and, furthermore, in a paper which on this very question is *hand in glove with the bourgeoisie against the workers' party!*

This is a thousand times more despicable and a *million times more harmful* than all the statements Plekhanov, for example, made in the non-Party press in 1906-07, and which the Party so sharply condemned! At that time it was only a question of elections, whereas now it is a question of an insurrection for the conquest of power!

On such a question, *after* a decision has been taken by the centre, to dispute this *unpublished* decision in front of the Rodziankos and Kerenskys in a non-Party paper – can you imagine an act more treacherous, or blacklegging any worse?

I should consider it disgraceful on my part if I were to hesitate to condemn these former comrades because of my earlier close relations with them. I declare outright that I no longer consider either of them comrades and that I will fight with all my might, both in the Central Committee and at the Congress, to secure the expulsion of both of them from the Party.

A workers' party, which the course of events is confronting more and more frequently with the need for an insurrection, is unable to accomplish that difficult task if, after their adoption, unpublished decisions of the centre are disputed in the non-Party press, and vacillation and confusion are brought into the ranks of the fighters.

Let Mr. Zinoviev and Mr. Kamenev found their own party with the dozens of perplexed people or with candidates for election to the Constituent Assembly. The workers will not join such a party, for its first slogan will be:

> Members of the Central Committee who are defeated at a meeting of the Central Committee on the question of a decisive fight are permitted to resort to the non-Party press for the purpose of attacking the unpublished decisions of the Party.

Let them build themselves *such* a party; our workers' Bolshevik Party will only gain from it.

When all the documents are published, the strikebreaking act of Zinoviev and Kamenev will stand out even more glaringly. Meanwhile, let the workers consider the following question:

> 'Let us assume that the Executive Committee of an all-Russia trade union had decided, after a month of deliberation and by a majority of over 80 per cent, that preparations must be made for a strike, but that for the time being neither the date nor any other details should be divulged. Let us assume that, *after* the decision had been taken, two members, under the false pretext of a 'dissenting opinion', not only began to write to local groups urging a reconsideration of the decision, but also permitted their letters to be communicated to *non*-Party newspapers. Let us assume, finally, that they themselves attacked the decision in non-Party papers, although it had not yet been published, and began to vilify the strike in front of the capitalists.
>
> 'We ask, would the workers hesitate to expel such blacklegs from their midst?'

* * *

As to the situation with regard to an insurrection now, when 20 October is so close at hand, I cannot judge from afar to what exact extent the cause has been damaged by the strikebreaking statement in the non-Party press. There is no doubt that very great *practical* damage has been done. In order to remedy the situation, it is necessary first of all to restore unity in the Bolshevik front by expelling the blacklegs.

The weakness of the ideological arguments against an insurrection will become clearer, the more we drag them into the light of day. I recently sent an article on this subject to *Rabochy Put*, and if the editors do not find it possible to print it, Party members will probably acquaint themselves with it in the manuscript.

There are basically two so-called 'ideological' arguments. First, that it is necessary to 'wait' for the Constituent Assembly. Let us wait, perhaps we can hold on until then – that is the whole argument. Perhaps, despite famine, despite economic chaos, despite the fact that the patience of the soldiers is exhausted, despite Rodzianko's steps to surrender Petrograd to the Germans, despite the lockouts, perhaps we can hold on.

Perhaps and maybe – that is the whole point of the argument.

The second is noisy pessimism. Everything is fine with the bourgeoisie and Kerensky; everything is wrong with us. The capitalists have prepared everything wonderfully; everything is wrong with the workers. The 'pessimists' are shouting at the top of their voices about the military side of the matter, but the 'optimists' are silent, for to disclose certain things to Rodzianko and Kerensky is hardly pleasant to anybody but blacklegs.

* * *

Difficult times. A hard task. A grave betrayal.

Nevertheless, the task will be accomplished; the workers will consolidate their ranks, the peasant revolt and the extreme impatience of the soldiers at the front will do their work! Let us close our ranks – the proletariat must win!

N Lenin

Letter to the CC of the RSDLP(B)

Written 19 October (1 November) 1917

Dear Comrades,

No self-respecting party can tolerate strikebreaking and blacklegs in its midst. That is obvious. The more we reflect upon Zinoviev's and Kamenev's statement in the non-Party press, the more self-evident it becomes that their action is strikebreaking in the full sense of the term.

Kamenev's evasion at the meeting of the Petrograd Soviet is something really despicable. He is, don't you see, in full agreement with Trotsky. But is it so difficult to understand that in the face of the enemy, Trotsky *could not* have said, he had no right to say, and should not have said more than he did? Is it so difficult to understand that it is a *duty* to the Party which has concealed *its* decision from the enemy (on the necessity for an armed uprising, on the fact that the time for it is fully ripe, on the thorough preparations to be made for it, etc.), and it is this decision that makes it *obligatory* in public statements to fasten not only the 'blame', but also the initiative upon the adversary? Only a child could fail to understand that.

Kamenev's evasion is a sheer fraud. The same must be said of Zinoviev's evasion, at least of his letter of 'justification' (written, I think, to the Central Organ), which is the only document I have seen (for, as to a dissenting opinion, 'an alleged dissenting opinion', which has been trumpeted in the *bourgeois* press, I, a member of the Central Committee, have *to this very day* seen nothing of it). Among Zinoviev's 'arguments' there is this: Lenin, he says, sent out his letters "*before* any decisions were adopted", and you did not protest. That is literally what Zinoviev wrote, himself underlining the word *before* four times. Is it really so difficult to understand that *before* a decision has been taken on a strike by the centre, it is permissible to agitate for and against it; but that *after* a decision in favour of a strike (with the additional decision to conceal this from the enemy), to carry on agitation against the strike is strikebreaking?

Any worker will understand that. The question of insurrection has been discussed in the centre since September. That is when Zinoviev and Kamenev could and *should* have come out in writing, so that *everybody*, upon seeing their arguments, would have realised that they had completely lost their heads. To conceal one's views from the Party for a whole month *before* a decision is taken, and to send out a dissenting opinion *after* a decision is taken – that is strikebreaking.

Zinoviev pretends not to understand this difference, he pretends not to understand that after a decision to strike has been taken by the centre, only blacklegs can carry on agitation among the lower bodies against that decision. Any worker will understand that.

And Zinoviev did agitate and attempted to defeat the centre's decision, both at Sunday's meeting, where he and Kamenev secured not a single vote, and in his present letter. For Zinoviev has the effrontery to assert that "the opinion of the Party has not been canvassed" and that such questions "cannot be decided by ten men". Just think! Every member of the Central Committee knows that more than ten CC members were present at the decisive meeting, that a *majority of the plenary meeting* were present, that Kamenev himself declared at the meeting that "this meeting is decisive", that it was known with absolute certainty that the *majority* of the absent members of the Central Committee *were not in agreement* with Zinoviev and Kamenev. And now, *after* the Central Committee has adopted a decision at a meeting which Kamenev himself admitted to be *decisive*, a member of the Central Committee has the audacity to write that "the opinion of the Party has not been canvassed", and that such questions "cannot be decided by ten men". That is strikebreaking in the full sense of the term. Between Party congresses, the Central Committee decides. The Central Committee has decided. Kamenev and Zinoviev, who did not come out in writing *before* the decision was taken, began to *dispute* the Central Committee's decision *after* it had been taken.

That is strikebreaking in the full sense of the term. After a decision has been taken, any dispute is *impermissible* when it concerns immediate and *secret* preparations for a strike. Now Zinoviev has the insolence to blame *us* for "warning the enemy". Is there any limit to his brazenness? Who is it that has damaged the cause, frustrated the strike by "warning the enemy", if not those who came out in the *non-Party* press?

How can one come out *against* a "decisive" resolution of the Party in a paper which on *this* question is hand in glove with the entire bourgeoisie?

If that is tolerated, the Party will become impossible, the Party will be destroyed.

It is ridiculing the Party to give the name of 'dissenting opinion' to that which Bazarov learns about and publishes in a non-Party paper.

Kamenev's and Zinoviev's statement in the non-Party press was especially despicable for the additional reason that the Party is not in a position to refute their *slanderous lie* openly. I know of no decisions regarding the date, Kamenev writes and publishes his writings in his own name and in the name of Zinoviev. (After such a statement, Zinoviev bears full responsibility for Kamenev's conduct and statements.)

How can the Central Committee refute this?

We cannot tell the capitalists the truth, namely, that we have *decided* on a strike and have decided *to conceal the moment chosen* for it.

We cannot refute the slanderous lie of Zinoviev and Kamenev *without doing even greater damage to the cause*. And the utter baseness, the real treachery of these two individuals is precisely in their having revealed the strikers' plan to the capitalists, for, since we remain silent in the press, everybody will guess *how* things stand.

Kamenev and Zinoviev have *betrayed* to Rodzianko and Kerensky the decision of the Central Committee of their Party on insurrection and the decision to conceal from the enemy preparations for insurrection and the date appointed for it. That is a fact and no evasions can refute it. Two members of the Central Committee have by a slanderous lie *betrayed* the decision of the workers to the capitalists. There can and must be only one answer to that: an immediate decision of the Central Committee:

> 'The Central Committee, regarding Zinoviev's and Kamenev's statement in the non-Party press as strikebreaking in the full sense of the term, expels both of them from the Party.'

It is not easy for me to write in this way about former close comrades. But I should regard any hesitation in this respect as a crime, for otherwise a party of revolutionaries which does not punish prominent blacklegs would *perish*.

The question of insurrection, even if the blacklegs have now delayed it for a long time by betraying it to Rodzianko and Kerensky, has not been *removed from the agenda*, it has not been removed by the Party. But how can we prepare ourselves for insurrection and lay plans for it, if we *tolerate* 'prominent' strikebreakers in our midst? The more prominent, the *more dangerous* they are, and the less deserving of 'forgiveness'. *On n'est trahi que par les siens*, the French say. Only your *own people* can betray you.

The more '*prominent*' the strikebreakers are, the more imperative it is to punish them by immediate expulsion.

That is the only way for the workers' party to recuperate, rid itself of a dozen or so spineless intellectuals, rally the ranks of the revolutionaries, and advance to meet great and momentous difficulties hand in hand *with the revolutionary workers*.

We cannot publish the truth, namely, that *after* the decisive meeting of the Central Committee, Zinoviev and Kamenev at Sunday's meeting had the audacity to demand a *revision*, that

Kamenev had the effrontery to shout: "The Central Committee has collapsed, for it has done nothing for a whole week" (I could *not* refute that because to say *what really had been done* was impossible), while Zinoviev with an air of innocence proposed this resolution, which was rejected by the meeting: "No action shall be taken before consulting with the Bolsheviks who are to arrive on 20 October (2 November) for the Congress of Soviets."

Just imagine! After the *centre* has taken a decision to call a strike, it is proposed at a meeting of the rank and file that it be postponed (until 20 October, when the Congress was to convene. The Congress was subsequently postponed – the Zinovievs trust the Liberdans) and be referred to a body *such* as the Party Rules do not provide for, that has *no* authority over the Central Committee, and that does *not* know Petrograd.

And *after this* Zinoviev still has the insolence to write: "This is hardly the way to strengthen the unity of the Party."

What else can you call it but a threat to effect a split?

My answer to this threat is that I shall go the limit, I shall win freedom of speech for myself before the workers, and I shall, *at whatever cost*, brand the blackleg Zinoviev as a blackleg. My answer to the threat of a split is to declare war to a finish, war for the expulsion of both blacklegs from the Party.

The Executive Committee of a trade union, after a *month* of deliberation, decides that a strike is inevitable, that the time is ripe, but that the date is to be concealed from the employers. After that, two members of the Executive Committee appeal *to the rank and file*, disputing the decision, and are defeated. Thereupon these two come out in the press and with a slanderous lie betray the decision of the Executive Committee to the capitalists, thus more than half wrecking the strike, or delaying it to a less favourable time by warning the enemy.

Here we have strikebreaking in the full sense of the term. And that is why I demand the expulsion of both the blacklegs, reserving for myself the right (in view of their threat of a split) to publish *everything* when publication becomes possible.

Letter to CC Members

Written 24 October (6 November) 1917

Comrades,

I am writing these lines on the evening of the 24th. The situation is critical in the extreme. In fact it is now absolutely clear that to delay the uprising would be fatal.

With all my might I urge comrades to realise that everything now hangs by a thread; that we are confronted by problems which are not to be solved by conferences or congresses (even congresses of Soviets), but exclusively by peoples, by the masses, by the struggle of the armed people.

The bourgeois onslaught of the Kornilovites and the removal of Verkhovsky show that we must not wait.[1] We must at all costs, this very evening, this very night, arrest the government, having first disarmed the officer cadets (defeating them, if they resist) and so on.

We must not wait! We may lose everything!

The value of the immediate seizure of power will be the defence of the *people* (not of the congress, but of the people, the army and the

1 Aleksandr Verkhovsky was at this time the Minister of War and Major General of the General Staff. He was temporarily dismissed on 21 October (3 November) for advocating concluding peace with Germany.

peasants in the first place) from the Kornilovite government, which has driven out Verkhovsky and has hatched a second Kornilov plot.

Who must take power?

That is not important at present. Let the Revolutionary Military Committee[2] do it, or 'some other institution' which will declare that it will relinquish power only to the true representatives of the interests of the people, the interests of the army (the immediate proposal of peace), the interests of the peasants (the land to be taken immediately and private property abolished), the interests of the starving.

All districts, all regiments, all forces must be mobilised at once and must immediately send their delegations to the Revolutionary Military Committee and to the Central Committee of the Bolsheviks with the insistent demand that under no circumstances should power be left in the hands of Kerensky and co. until the 25th – not under any circumstances; the matter must be decided without fail this very evening, or this very night.

History will not forgive revolutionaries for procrastinating when they could be victorious today (and they certainly will be victorious today), while they risk losing much tomorrow, in fact, they risk losing everything.

If we seize power today, we seize it not in opposition to the Soviets but on their behalf.

The seizure of power is the business of the uprising; its political purpose will become clear after the seizure.

It would be a disaster, or a sheer formality, to await the wavering vote of 25 October (7 November). The people have the right and are in duty bound to decide such questions not by a vote, but by force; in critical moments of revolution, the people have the right and are in duty bound to give directions to their representatives, even their best representatives, and not to wait for them.

---

2 The Revolutionary Military Committee was established by the Petrograd Soviet in October 1917 on the instigation of Trotsky, who was its President. It was renamed from the 'Committee of Revolutionary Defence' and formed the General Staff of the October Insurrection.

This is proved by the history of all revolutions; and it would be an infinite crime on the part of the revolutionaries were they to let the chance slip, knowing that the *salvation of the revolution*, the offer of peace, the salvation of Petrograd, salvation from famine, the transfer of the land to the peasants depend upon them.

The government is tottering. It must be *given the death-blow* at all costs.

To delay action is fatal.

To the Citizens of Russia!

Written 25 October (7 November) 1917

Editor's note:

On the night of the 24th, the insurrection Lenin had been calling for since the July Days began. Leon Trotsky, as leader of the Revolutionary Military Committee, spent the entire night co-ordinating the movement of battalions of workers from the Smolny Institute. One by one, the telephone interchange, the railway terminals, and finally, during the next day, the Winter Palace itself – all the important points in the city were handed over to the workers and soldiers with little resistance.

That morning, a few hours before the Winter Palace was seized, Lenin penned this statement on behalf of the Revolutionary Military Committee.

* * *

The Provisional Government has been deposed. State power has passed into the hands of the organ of the Petrograd Soviet of Workers' and Soldiers' Deputies – the Revolutionary Military Committee, which heads the Petrograd proletariat and the garrison.

The cause for which the people have fought, namely, the immediate offer of a democratic peace, the abolition of landed proprietorship, workers' control over production and the establishment of Soviet power – this cause has been secured.

Long live the revolution of workers, soldiers and peasants!

Revolutionary Military Committee of the
Petrograd Soviet of Workers' and
Soldiers' Deputies,

10 am, 25 October (7 November) 1917

Meeting of the Petrograd Soviet of Workers' and Soldiers' Deputies

25 October (7 November) 1917

Editor's note:
The meeting opened at 2:35 pm on 25 October (7 November) and heard a report of the Revolutionary Military Committee on the overthrow of the Provisional Government and the triumph of the revolution. Lenin gave a report on the tasks facing Soviet power. The resolution motioned by Lenin was adopted by an overwhelming majority.

* * *

Report on the Tasks of the Soviet Power

Newspaper Report

Comrades, the workers' and peasants' revolution, about the necessity of which the Bolsheviks have always spoken, has been accomplished.

What is the significance of this workers' and peasants' revolution? Its significance is, first of all, that we shall have a Soviet government, our own organ of power, in which the bourgeoisie will have no share whatsoever. The oppressed masses will themselves create a power. The old state apparatus will be shattered to its foundations and a new administrative apparatus set up in the form of the Soviet organisations.

From now on, a new phase in the history of Russia begins, and this, the third Russian revolution, should in the end lead to the victory of socialism.

One of our urgent tasks is to put an immediate end to the war. It is clear to everybody that in order to end this war, which is closely bound up with the present capitalist system, capital itself must be fought.

We shall be helped in this by the world working-class movement, which is already beginning to develop in Italy, Britain and Germany.

The proposal we make to international democracy for a just and immediate peace will everywhere awaken an ardent response among the international proletarian masses. All the secret treaties must be immediately published in order to strengthen the confidence of the proletariat.[1]

Within Russia a huge section of the peasantry have said that they have played long enough with the capitalists, and will now march with the workers. A single decree putting an end to landed proprietorship will win us the confidence of the peasants. The peasants will understand that the salvation of the peasantry lies only in an alliance with the workers. We shall institute genuine workers' control over production.

We have now learned to make a concerted effort. The revolution that has just been accomplished is evidence of this. We possess the

1 The reference is to secret diplomatic documents, such as the secret treaties concluded by the tsarist and later by the bourgeois Provisional Government of Russia with the governments of Britain, France, Germany, Japan and other imperialist powers. From 10 (23) November 1917, these documents were published in *Pravda* and *Izvestia*, and in December were put out in a series entitled *Collection of Secret Documents from the Archives of the Former Ministry of Foreign Affairs*. Seven volumes were published from December 1917 to February 1918. By publishing the secret treaties, the Soviet Government's revolutionary propaganda struck a great blow for a general democratic peace, without annexations and indemnities, and exposed the imperialist nature of the First World War.

strength of mass organisation, which will overcome everything and lead the proletariat to the world revolution.

We must now set about building a proletarian socialist state in Russia.

Long live the world socialist revolution! (*Stormy applause.*)

* * *

Resolution

The Petrograd Soviet of Workers' and Soldiers' Deputies hails the victorious revolution of the proletariat and the garrison of Petrograd. The Soviet particularly emphasises the solidarity, organisation, discipline and complete unanimity displayed by the masses in this unusually bloodless and unusually successful uprising.

It is the unshakable conviction of the Soviet that the workers' and peasants' government which will be created by the revolution, as a Soviet government, and which will ensure the urban proletariat the support of the whole mass of the poor peasantry, will firmly advance towards socialism, the only means of saving the country from the untold miseries and horrors of war.

The new workers' and peasants' government will immediately propose a just and democratic peace to all belligerent nations.

It will immediately abolish landed proprietorship and hand over the land to the peasants. It will institute workers' control over the production and distribution of goods and establish national control over the banks, at the same time transforming them into a single state enterprise.

The Petrograd Soviet of Workers' and Soldiers' Deputies calls on all workers and all peasants to support the workers' and peasants' revolution devotedly and with all their energy. The Soviet expresses the conviction that the urban workers, in alliance with the poor peasants, will display strict, comradely discipline and establish the strictest revolutionary order, which is essential for the victory of socialism.

The Soviet is convinced that the proletariat of the West European countries will help us to achieve a complete and lasting victory for the cause of socialism.

Timeline

1917

9 (22) January	Lenin delivers a lecture on the 1905 Revolution at a youth meeting in Zurich
23 February (8 March)	February Revolution begins with protests erupting on International Working Women's Day; wide layers of the working class take part in protests, which last eight days; Soviets of Workers' and Soldiers' deputies formed
2 (15) March	Nicholas II abdicates; Provisional Government formed
7 (20) March	Lenin writes the first of his *Letters from Afar*
3 (16) April	Lenin arrives at the Finland Station in Russia
7 (20) April	Lenin's article 'The Tasks of the Proletariat in the Present Revolution' containing the *April Theses* is published in *Pravda*
20 April (3 May)	April Crisis begins, following the public revelation of Foreign Minister Milyukov's Note to the Allied governments, in which the Provisional Government reaffirmed its intention to honour all the treaties of the tsarist government and to carry on the war to a victorious end

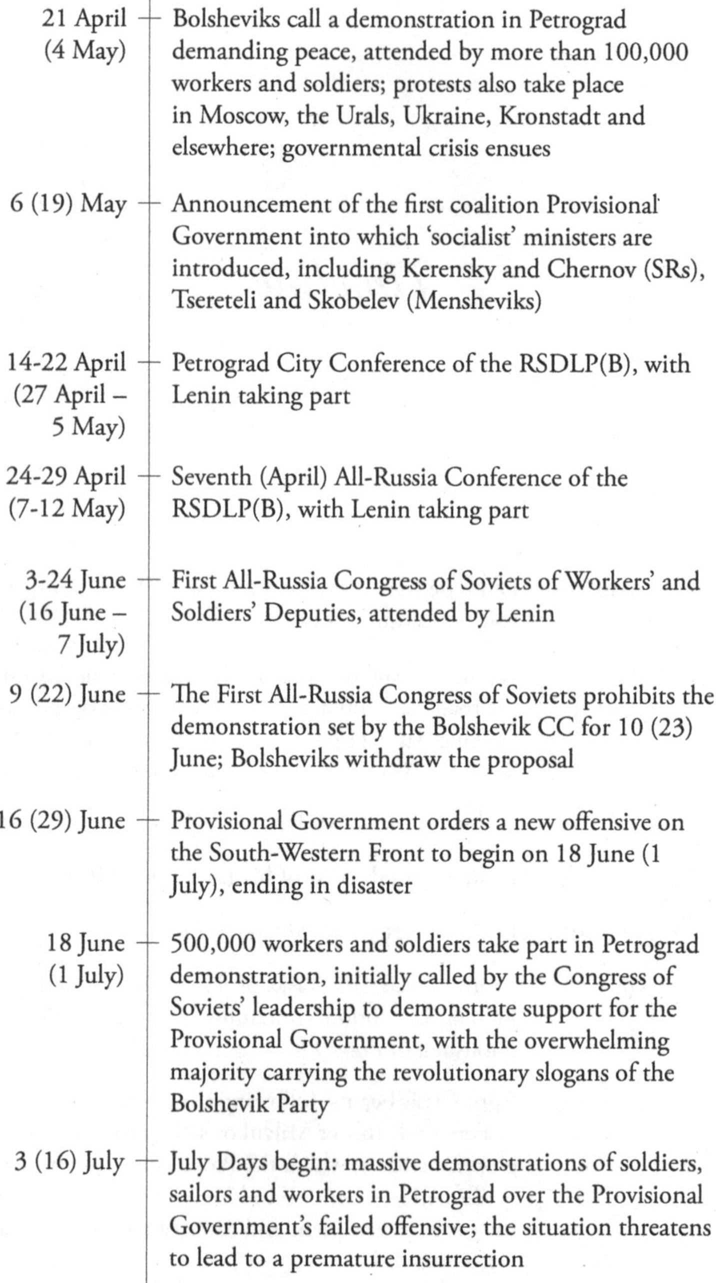

21 April (4 May)	Bolsheviks call a demonstration in Petrograd demanding peace, attended by more than 100,000 workers and soldiers; protests also take place in Moscow, the Urals, Ukraine, Kronstadt and elsewhere; governmental crisis ensues
6 (19) May	Announcement of the first coalition Provisional Government into which 'socialist' ministers are introduced, including Kerensky and Chernov (SRs), Tsereteli and Skobelev (Mensheviks)
14-22 April (27 April – 5 May)	Petrograd City Conference of the RSDLP(B), with Lenin taking part
24-29 April (7-12 May)	Seventh (April) All-Russia Conference of the RSDLP(B), with Lenin taking part
3-24 June (16 June – 7 July)	First All-Russia Congress of Soviets of Workers' and Soldiers' Deputies, attended by Lenin
9 (22) June	The First All-Russia Congress of Soviets prohibits the demonstration set by the Bolshevik CC for 10 (23) June; Bolsheviks withdraw the proposal
16 (29) June	Provisional Government orders a new offensive on the South-Western Front to begin on 18 June (1 July), ending in disaster
18 June (1 July)	500,000 workers and soldiers take part in Petrograd demonstration, initially called by the Congress of Soviets' leadership to demonstrate support for the Provisional Government, with the overwhelming majority carrying the revolutionary slogans of the Bolshevik Party
3 (16) July	July Days begin: massive demonstrations of soldiers, sailors and workers in Petrograd over the Provisional Government's failed offensive; the situation threatens to lead to a premature insurrection

4 (17) July	Lenin addresses the Kronstadt sailors from the balcony of Kshesinskaya's Palace, calling on the sailors to exercise restraint and be staunch and vigilant; later that day over 500,000 people demonstrate carrying the Bolshevik slogan 'All Power to the Soviets'; with the knowledge and consent of the Menshevik and SR-led CEC, the Provisional Government sends military cadets, Cossacks and counter-revolutionary units from the front line against the peaceful demonstration; the troops open fire
5-7 (16-20) July	*Pravda* and other Bolshevik papers closed down by the Provisional Government; campaign of slander against Lenin and the Bolsheviks begins; order for Lenin's arrest is issued; Lenin forced into hiding and escapes to Finland; workers disarmed; wave of house searches and arrests; the revolutionary-minded units in the Petrograd garrison sent off to the front line; Soviets become a mere appendage to the Provisional Government, all with complicity of the Mensheviks and SRs
8 (21) July	Kerensky becomes Prime Minister of the Provisional Government
24 July (6 August)	Second coalition Provisional Government is formed, headed by Kerensky
26 July – 3 August (8-16 August)	Sixth Congress of RSDLP takes place, where the Mezhraiontsy (Inter-District) organisation affiliates; Trotsky formally joins the Bolshevik Party and is immediately elected to the CC
28-31 August (10-13 September)	Kornilov attempts a coup against the Provisional Government; Bolsheviks spearhead the struggle against his putsch
31 August (13 September)	The Petrograd Soviet of Workers' and Soldiers' Deputies passes a Bolshevik resolution calling for the establishment of a Soviet Government

August – September	Lenin writes *The State and Revolution*
14-22 September (27 September – 5 October)	The Democratic Conference (originally set to open on 12 (25) September) takes place; it founds the Provisional Council, also known as the 'Pre-parliament', which meets for the first time on 23 September (6 October)
23 September (6 October)	The Fourth Duma is dissolved
25 September (8 October)	The Directorate, the second cabinet formed by Kerensky, is abolished and a new, third coalition is formed
10 (23) October	At the CC, Lenin tables a motion for an armed uprising; Zinoviev and Kamenev vote against
16 (29) October	At the enlarged Central Committee Lenin again proposes an armed insurrection; again Zinoviev and Kamenev vote against
18 (31) October	Zinoviev and Kamenev publicly reveal the plans for an insurrection; Lenin proposes their expulsion
Night of 24 October (6 November)	The insurrection begins, led by Trotsky and the Revolutionary Military Committee
25 October (7 November)	At 10 am, on behalf of the Revolutionary Military Committee, Lenin announces the overthrow of the Provisional Government; Lenin drafts decrees on peace, land, and the formation of a Soviet government

Glossary

People

Adler, Victor (1852-1918) – A founder and leader of the Austrian social democracy. He took a social-chauvinist position in the war.

Alexinsky, Grigory (1879-1967) – Early member of the Bolsheviks in Moscow. Became a social-chauvinist in the war. In 1917, Alexinsky joined Plekhanov's *Yedinstvo* group. After July, he became a counter-revolutionary and an author of forgeries claiming Lenin was a German agent.

Avilov, Boris (1874-1938) – Left the Bolsheviks in 1917 and joined Vladimir Bazarov, Gavriil Lindov and others to form the United Social-Democrat Internationalists, who aimed to bring together the Menshevik-Internationalists with the more moderate Bolsheviks into a new group. The group's organ was *Novaya Zhizn*.

Avksentiev, Nikolai (1878-1943) – A leading SR.

Axelrod, Pavel (1850-1928) – A leading Menshevik.

Bazarov, Vladimir (1874-1939) – Attended first meetings of St. Petersburg Bolshevik committee after February 1917 before breaking with the Bolsheviks. Held a position close to the Menshevik-Internationalists.

Bernstein, Eduard (1850-1932) – German Social-Democrat who tried to revise Marx's revolutionary theory on the lines of bourgeois liberalism. Bernsteinism, the opportunist trend in German and International Social-Democracy, hostile to Marxism, derives its name from his ideas.

Blanc, Louis (1811-1882) – French petty-bourgeois socialist and historian. He opposed the proletarian revolution, and wanted a compromise with the bourgeoisie. Lenin frequently used his name as an epithet to denote the opportunist and conciliatory tactics of the Mensheviks and other traitors to the cause of the revolution and the interests of the working class.

Blanqui, Louis-Auguste (1805-1881) – French socialist who put forward that the revolution must be carried out, not by the masses, but as a *coup de main* of a small revolutionary minority. The term 'Blanquism', as properly used for example by Marx, Engels and Lenin, denotes this conspiratorial conception of the revolution. However, the term was often falsely used by reformists and conciliators to denote the idea of insurrection. See Lenin's 'Letters on Tactics' (p. 59) and 'Marxism and Insurrection' (p. 299).

Breshko-Breshkovskaya, Catherine (1844-1934) – Narodnik and a founding SR member. She returned to Russia from exile in 1917. Supported the Provisional Government, and was elected to the Pre-parliament in October.

Buchanan, Sir George William (1854-1924) – British diplomat and ambassador to Russia (1910-1918). Supported Kornilov's revolt.

Cavaignac, Louis-Eugène (1802-1857) – Notorious French general who, as Minister of War, led the suppression of the Paris workers' uprising in June 1848. Appointed Chief of the Executive Power in France from June-December 1848.

Chernov, Victor (1873-1952) – A founder and the main theoretician of the SRs. Minister of Agriculture in the first and second Provisional Government.

Chkheidze, Nikolai (1864-1926) – Georgian Menshevik. President of the EC of the Soviet of Petrograd until September 1917.

Chkhenkeli, Akaki (1874-1959) – Georgian Menshevik.

Dan, Fyodor (1871-1947) – A founding member of the Mensheviks who took a defencist position. Member of the EC of the Petrograd Soviet after February 1917. Dan and Mikhail Liber were together ironically nicknamed 'Liberdan'.

David, Eduard (1863-1930) – Reichstag member for the German SPD after 1903, leading the social-chauvinist majority.

Grimm, Robert (1881-1958) – A leader of the Swiss Social-Democratic Party, belonging to the centrist trend.

Guchkov, Alexander (1862-1936) – Moscow landowner and industrialist. He was the founder and leader of the Octobrists. Minister of War and Navy in the Provisional Government from March-May 1917. He was forced to resign in the wake of public unrest when Milyukov's Note was revealed.

Gvozdev, Kuzma (1859-1932) – Menshevik, on the Petrograd Soviet EC from February. Minister of Labour in the third Provisional Government.

Kaledin, Alexey (1861-1918) – Tsarist General.

Kamenev, Lev (1883-1936) – Joined the Bolshevik faction in 1903, elected to the CC in 1907. After the February Revolution, Kamenev sided with Zinoviev and Stalin and pursued a policy of conciliation with the Provisional Government. In October, Kamenev and Zinoviev went to the public press and disclosed the plans for an insurrection, for which Lenin called for their immediate expulsion.

Kamkov, Boris (1885-1938) – A leading SR. Elected to the Petrograd Soviet in April 1917. Joined the Left SRs.

Kautsky, Karl (1854-1938) – One of the leading theoreticians of the Social Democratic Party of Germany and the Second International. By the outbreak of the First World War, he had abandoned revolutionary Marxism and took up an indecisive position between revolutionary opposition to the war and patriotic support for the German bourgeoisie. As such, he became the theoretician of this 'centrism' in the socialist movement, and a bitter opponent of the Russian Revolution.

Kerensky, Alexander (1881-1970) – Lawyer and nominal member of the SRs. After the February Revolution, he became the outstanding representative of petty-bourgeois conciliationism, first as Minister of Justice, then as War Minister. Kerensky then headed the Provisional Government from July-October 1917, at which point he fled the country.

Kishkin, Nikolai (1864-1930) – A leading Cadet. Minister of Healthcare and Minister of Public Charities in the third Provisional Government.

Klembovsky, Vladislav (1860-1921) – Supreme Commander-in-chief of the Russian Army in August 1917, replacing Kornilov.

Konovalov, Aleksandr (1875-1949) – Cadet and one of Russia's biggest textile manufacturers. Minister of Trade and Industry in the first Provisional Government, maintaining the post when he became Vice-President in the third.

Kornilov, Lavr (1870-1918) – Siberian Cossack and Commander on the South Western Front in 1917. Appointed Commander-in-Chief by the Provisional Government in July 1917. Kornilov was arrested after his attempted counter-revolutionary uprising against the Provisional Government on 28-31 August (10-13 September) which was repelled by the workers, headed by the Bolsheviks. He later escaped and led the White Volunteer Army.

Kutler, Nikolai (1859-1924) – Cadet and prominent politician in Russia from 1904.

Legien, Carl (1861-1920) – Reichstag member of the German SPD. Leader of the right wing of the SPD and a virulent social-chauvinist.

Liber, Mikhail (1880-1937) – A leading Menshevik, with a defencist position. Supported Kerensky's Provisional Government. Liber and Fyodor Dan were together ironically nicknamed 'Liberdan'.

Liberdan – An ironical nickname which stuck to the Mensheviks Mikhail Liber and Fyodor Dan and their followers.

Liebknecht, Karl (1871-1919) – German socialist and internationalist. In 1914, together with Luxemburg, Mehring and Zetkin, he publicly opposed the German SPD's support for the war. He co-organised the Spartacus League from 1915 and was expelled from the SPD parliamentary group the following year. Liebknecht was imprisoned for anti-war agitation. On the day of his trial, 50,000 munitions workers downed tools, as demonstrations and strikes spread across the country. He was murdered during the Spartacist Uprising in January 1919.

Lloyd George, David (1863-1945) – Welsh MP for the Liberal Party from 1890-1945. British Prime Minister from 1916-22.

Luxemburg, Rosa (1871-1919) – Joined the social-democratic movement in Poland in 1887 and joined the SPD in Germany 1898. She was on the bureau of the Second International from 1903. She was a leader of the left wing against the revisionist right in Germany and, after 1910, against the Kautskyist group. A leading revolutionary opponent of war and a founding member of the Spartacus group.

Lvov, Prince Georgy (1861-1925) – Aristocrat and Cadet. First Prime Minister of the first Provisional Government and Minister of the Interior until his resignation in July.

Maclean, John (1879-1923) – Scottish schoolteacher and revolutionary socialist, arrested for his opposition to the war.

Maklakov, Vasily (1869-1957) – Moscow landowner, lawyer and Cadet. A member of the Provisional Committee of the State Duma formed by the Provisional Government in February 1917. Supported Kornilov's revolt.

Martov, Yuri (Julius) (1873-1913) – A leading Menshevik, on its left wing. He advocated against Mensheviks joining the Provisional Government. He strongly criticised Mensheviks such as Irakli Tsereteli and Fyodor Dan who, as members of the Russian government, supported the war effort.

Milyukov, Pavel (1859-1943) – A founder and leader of the Cadets, ideologue of the imperialist bourgeoisie. Foreign Minister in the first Provisional Government. He advocated continuing the war effort at all costs. On 20 April (3 May), his Note to the Allied governments was made public, in which the Provisional Government reaffirmed its intention to honour all the treaties of the tsarist government and to carry on the war to a victorious end. This provoked mass demonstrations and a governmental crisis. He resigned shortly after, remaining the leader of the Cadets. Supported Kornilov's revolt.

Nekrasov, Nikolai (1879-1940) – A founder and leader of the Cadets. Transportation Minister in the first and Vice-president and Minister of Finance in the second Provisional Government. Supported Kornilov's revolt.

Nicholas II, (Nikolai Romanov) (1868-1918) – Last tsar of Russia, reigning from 1894 until his abdication on 2 (15) March 1917.

Nikitin, Alexey (1876-1939) – Menshevik. Post and Telegraph Minister in the second and third Provisional Government, as well as Minister for Internal Affairs in the third.

Pereverzev, Pavel (1871-1944) – SR. Justice Minister in the first Provisional Government. During the July Days, he published documents allegedly showing the connections between Lenin and the German General Staff.

Peshekhonov, Alexey (1867-1933) – Member of the Popular Socialist Party. Minister of Food in the first and second Provisional Government.

Plekhanov, Georgi (1856-1918) – The founder of Russian Marxism and a leading member of the RSDLP. After joining the Menshevik faction in 1903, he became extremely hostile to Lenin and the Bolsheviks. He took a defencist, social-chauvinist position in the war. He initially opposed the February Revolution on the grounds that it disorganised the war effort, before supporting the Provisional Government. Founded and edited *Yedinstvo* in 1917, which had a small group of supporters. Denounced Lenin as a German agent in the July Days.

Potresov, Alexander (1869-1934) – A leading Menshevik, on the extreme right. He held a defencist position to the war, advocating its continuation at all costs in 1917.

Rakitnikov, Nikolai (b. 1864) – A leading SR.

Rasputin, Grigori (1869-1916) – Russian Orthodox mystic in the tsarist court, close with the family of Nicholas II and exercising colossal power through his ties with the tsarina. He was a divisive figure both outside and within the court, and was assassinated by a group of noblemen.

Renaudel, Pierre (1871-1935) – A founder and leader of the Socialist Party of France, on its right wing.

Ribot, Alexandre (1842-1923) – Four-time French Prime Minister including during 1914 and March-September 1917.

Ryabushinsky, Pavel (1871-1924) – Industrialist and founder of the liberal Progressive Party along with Aleksandr Konovalov. Supported Kornilov's revolt.

Savinkov, Boris (1879-1925) – SR and Assistant Minister of War in the Provisional Government from July-August. Supported Kornilov's revolt.

Scheidemann, Philipp (1865-1939) – Leader of the extreme right-wing section of the German SPD. Chairman of the SPD parliamentary group together with Hugo Haase. Voted for war credits at the outbreak of the war.

Shingarev, Andrei (1869-1918) – A leading Cadet. Minister of Agriculture in the first and Minister of Finance in the second Provisional Government.

Skobelev, Matvey (1885-1938) – Menshevik and a leader of the Petrograd Soviet after the February Revolution. Elected deputy chairman of the All-Russia Soviet EC at the first Soviet Congress in June 1917. Minister of Labour in the first and second Provisional Governments.

Sonnino, Sidney (1847-1922) – Prime Minister of Italy in 1909-10 and Minister of Foreign Affairs in 1914-1919.

Spiridonova, Maria (1884-1941) – Prominent SR, joining the Left SRs in October 1917, siding with the Bolsheviks. Broke with the Bolsheviks in 1918.

Stalin, Joseph (1878-1953) – Joined the Bolshevik faction of the RSDLP in 1904 and was co-opted onto the CC in 1912. After the February Revolution, Stalin, Kamenev and Zinoviev pursued a policy of conciliation with the Provisional Government.

Stolypin, Pyotr (1862-1911) – Landowner who was appointed Prime Minister and Minister of the Interior from 1906 until his assassination in 1911. He oversaw the counter-revolutionary terror after the 1905 Revolution, for which he was nicknamed 'Stolypin the Hangman'.

Sukhanov, Nikolai (1882-1940) – Initially an SR. In February was elected to the Petrograd Soviet EC as an independent. He helped to negotiate the formation of Provisional Government, and became a member of the Contact Commission. Became a left Menshevik, on the editorial board of their paper *Novaya Zhizn*.

Tereshchenko, Mikhail (1886-1956) – Major Ukrainian landowner and factory owner. Finance Minister in the first Provisional Government, and then Foreign Minister from the second until the October Revolution.

Trotsky, Leon (Lev Davidovich Bronstein) (1879-1940) – Ukrainian-born revolutionary who joined the socialist movement in 1897. Growing close to Lenin in his youth, he ended up supporting the Mensheviks at the RSDLP Congress in 1903, upset at Lenin's sharp approach. He vacillated amongst the various groups during the period of reaction after 1905, but consistently took an internationalist position. He was in exile in New York at the time of the February Revolution, and independently formulated the same perspectives as Lenin. He now recognised the impossibility of unity with the left-wing of the Mensheviks. With Lenin's complete agreement, Trotsky did not immediately join the Bolshevik Party, but instead joined the 4,000-strong Petrograd Inter-District Committee – the Mezhraiontsy – in order to win them over to Bolshevism. He formally joined the Bolsheviks at the Sixth Congress in late-July to early-August (Old Style) along with the Mezhraiontsy, and was elected to the CC. Together with Lenin, he was one of the main leaders of the Russian Revolution. As leader of the Revolutionary Military Committee, he was responsible for co-ordinating the insurrection on the night of 24-25 October (6-7 November).

Tsereteli, Irakli (1881-1959) – Menshevik who had a leading position in the Petrograd Soviet from February 1917. Minister of Post and Telegraph (and part of Prince Lvov's 'inner cabinet') in the first and Minister of the Interior in the second Provisional Government.

Volodarsky, V (1891-1918) – Joined the Bund in 1905, before joining the Mensheviks. Exiled in 1911, Volodarsky returned to Russia in May 1917 and joined the Mezhraiontsy (Inter-District Group). This group joined the Bolsheviks in July and he quickly became one of the best agitators in the party, focusing his work around the Putilov Ironworks.

Wilhelm II (1859-1941) – German Emperor and King of Prussia from 1888 until his abdication in 1918.

Zarudny, Alexander (1863-1934) – Petrograd lawyer and member of the Popular Socialists. Minister of Justice in the second Provisional Government. He issued orders for the arrest of Lenin, Trotsky, Kamenev and Zinoviev.

Zinoviev, Grigory (1883-1936) – Joined the Bolshevik faction in 1903, elected to the CC in 1907. After the February Revolution, Zinoviev sided with Kamenev and Stalin and pursued a policy of conciliation with the Provisional Government. Zinoviev and Kamenev went to the public press and disclosed the plans for an insurrection in October, for which Lenin called for their immediate expulsion.

Groups, periodicals and other terms

Birzhevka (abb.), *Birzhevyie Vedomosti* (*Stock-Exchange Recorder*) – A bourgeois daily published in St. Petersburg from 1880. Its abbreviated name, '*Birzhevka*' became a generic term for the unscrupulous and venal bourgeois press.

Black Hundreds (Union of the Russian People) – Ultra-reactionary terrorist bands, loyal to the tsar, responsible for state-sanctioned pogroms against Jews and social-democrats.

Blanquism – Theory named after the French nineteenth century socialist Louis-Auguste Blanqui, who put forward that the revolution must be carried out, not by the masses, but as a *coup de main* of a small revolutionary minority. The term Blanquism, as properly used for example by Marx, Engels and Lenin, denotes this conspiratorial conception of the revolution. However, the term was often falsely used by reformists and conciliators to denote the idea of insurrection. See Lenin's 'Letters on Tactics' (p. 59), and 'Marxism and Insurrection' (p. 299).

Bolsheviks – The revolutionary faction in the RSDLP. The word Bolshevik means 'majority' in Russian, a reference to the fact that the Bolsheviks made up a majority at the 1903 Congress. They defended the class independence of the working class in relation to bourgeois parties, implacable firmness in questions of theory, as well as tactical and organisational flexibility. Until 1918, the party went under the name Russian Social-Democratic Labour Party (Bolsheviks), abbreviated as RSDLP(B).

Cadets (Constitutional-Democratic Party) – The chief party of the Russian liberal-monarchist bourgeoisie. Founded in October 1905, it was composed chiefly of capitalists, *zemstvo* leaders, landlords and bourgeois intellectuals. Actively supported the tsarist government's predatory policies and the ambitions of the imperialist bourgeoisie in the war. Attempted to save the monarchy during the February Revolution. They were the dominant force in the Provisional Government, following a policy advantageous to US, British and French imperialism.

Duma – During the reign of Nicholas II the State Duma was the name given to the national parliament, which only had an advisory role. There were also local dumas, the equivalent of local councils.

Dyelo Naroda (*People's Cause*) – Daily organ of the Centrist group of the SRs from March 1917, becoming the organ of the CC in June. The paper took a defencist and conciliatory stand and supported the Provisional Government.

Internationale, Die – See 'Spartacus League'.

Izvestia – Daily paper of the Petrograd Soviet of Workers' and Soldiers' Deputies, which in July 1917 became the organ of its

Central Executive Committee led by the SRs and Mensheviks. After the October Revolution, the paper became the official organ of the Soviet government.

Listok 'Pravdy' (*A Leaf of Truth*) – A renaming of *Pravda* due to the Provisional Governments persecution of the paper.

Menshevik-Internationalists – Menshevik adherents of Martov and non-aligned intellectuals of a semi-Menshevik trend.

Mensheviks – Originated as the opposition faction in the RSDLP. They pursued a policy of class collaboration with the bourgeoisie. Their leading body was the Organising Committee (OC).

Mezhraiontsy (Inter-District Group) – A non-Party organisation in Petrograd. With Lenin's complete agreement, Trotsky did not immediately join the Bolshevik Party on his return to Russia in 1917, but instead joined the Mezhraiontsy in order to win them over to Bolshevism. They formally joined the Bolsheviks at the Sixth Congress in late-July to early-August (Old Style).

Narodniks – A revolutionary movement active in the 1860s and 1870s, led by students and the intelligentsia. Believing the peasantry was the revolutionary class that would overthrow the monarchy, they regarded the village commune as the embryo of socialism. This tactic eventually proved to be a dead end, which provoked the movement to enter into crisis. In 1917, Lenin often used the term 'Narodnik' to denote the three petty-bourgeois parties of the Narodnik trend, namely, the Trudoviks, the SRs and the Popular Socialists.

Novaya Zhizn (*New Life*) – Daily newspaper of a Menshevik trend, organ of a group of Social-Democrats known as Menshevik-Internationalists, adherents of Martov and non-aligned intellectuals.

Novoye Vremya (*New Times*) – Daily newspaper, published in St. Petersburg from 1868. In 1905 it became an organ of the Black Hundreds. Lenin called it a model of a corrupted newspaper.

After the February Revolution, *Novoye Vremya* fully supported the policy of the Provisional Government and the Black Hundreds.

Octobrists (The League of October Seventeenth) – Party of the big merchants, industrialists and big landowners who ran their estates on capitalist lines. Their name derives from their support for the tsar's 'October Manifesto' in 1905.

Organising Committee (OC) – See Mensheviks.

Peaceful Renovation Party – Constitutional-monarchist organisation of the big bourgeoisie and landlords.

Popular Socialist Party – Formed in 1906 from right-wing elements of the SRs who stood for a bloc with the Cadets. After the February Revolution they merged with the Trudoviks and actively supported the Provisional Government, in which it was represented.

Pravda – Main organ of the Bolsheviks.

Proletarskoye Dyelo – Organ of the Bolsheviks in Kronstadt.

Rabochaya Gazeta (*Workers' Newspaper*) – Central organ of the Mensheviks, published as a daily in Petrograd from March-November 1917. It supported the Provisional Government and fought against the Bolshevik Party.

Rabochy Put (*The Workers' Path*) – The central organ of the Bolshevik Party, from 3 (16) September to 26 October (8 November) 1917 in place of *Pravda*, which was closed down by the Provisional Government.

Rech (*Speech*) – Central organ of the Cadets.

Russian Social-Democratic Labour Party (RSDLP) – The Russian Marxist party formed in 1898 in Minsk. It united the various isolated revolutionary groups in Russia into a single, unified party based on the principles of Marxism. At its Second Congress, the party was divided into the Bolshevik and Menshevik factions, before forming separate parties in 1912. Until 1918, the Bolsheviks went under the name Russian Social-Democratic Labour Party (Bolsheviks), abbreviated as RSDLP(B).

Russkaya Volya (*Russian Freedom*) – Daily newspaper founded and run by the big banks in Moscow from December 1916. Lenin called it one of the most disreputable bourgeois newspapers.

Russkoye Slovo (*Russian World*) – Daily newspaper published in Moscow from 1895. Ostensibly independent, it aligned with the Russian bourgeoisie. In 1917 the paper sided with the Provisional Government.

Socialist-Revolutionary Party (SRs) – Petty-bourgeois party of agrarian socialists, who based themselves on the peasantry. They were the ideological heirs of the Narodniks. In the summer of 1917 they split into the Left SRs and Right SRs.

Sotsial-Demokrat – Central organ of the RSDLP, published as an underground newspaper from February 1908 to January 1917. It featured more than eighty articles and other items by Lenin, who became its editor in December 1911.

Spartacus League (Spartacists, *Internationale* group) – The *Internationale* group, who produced the organ *Die Internationale*, was formed by the German Left Social-Democrats Karl Liebknecht, Rosa Luxemburg, Franz Mehring, Clara Zetkin and others at the beginning of the First World War. Soon after, the group denounced the SPD, and formed the Spartacus League. They carried out propaganda among the masses against the imperialist war, exposing the aggressive policy of German imperialism and the treachery of the leaders of Social-Democracy. In 1917 they became affiliated to the centrist Independent Social-Democratic Party of Germany, preserving their organisational independence.

Social Democratic Party of Germany (SPD) – Considered the leading party in the Second International, with over 1 million members in 1914. The near-unanimous vote for war credits amongst its members in the Reichstag at the opening of the First World War signified the death of the International.

Trudoviks – Party formed in a split from the SRs in 1906, with an agrarian peasant programme. Alexander Kerensky, later Prime Minister of the Provisional Government in 1917, was elected to the Fourth Duma as a Trudovik in 1912. In 1917 they supported the Provisional Government.

Yedinstvo (*Unity*) – Organ of the extreme-right Mensheviks, led by Plekhanov.

Zimmerwald Conference – The first conference of internationalists held in Zimmerwald from 5-8 September 1915. During the conference a struggle developed between the revolutionary internationalists led by Lenin and the Kautskyite majority. Lenin formed and led the Zimmerwald Left group.

Zimmerwald Left – Formed by Lenin at the first socialist conference of internationalists at Zimmerwald, Switzerland, in early September 1915. It was, Lenin said, the first step in the development of the internationalist movement against the war. The group also included a number of inconsistent internationalists.

Further Reading

The best account of the revolutions of 1917 is *History of the Russian Revolution* by Leon Trotsky, over three volumes.

In Defence of Lenin by Rob Sewell and Alan Woods, over two volumes, follows the events and Lenin's political ideas and activity over his entire life.

For more on Lenin's approach to the question of war in 1917, see *Lenin Selected Writings: On Imperialist War* by Wellred Books.

For more on Lenin's approach to the state, see *The State and Revolution*, written by Lenin in August – September 1917.

The History of the Russian Revolution to Brest-Litovsk by Leon Trotsky is a brief yet insightful analysis of the 1917-18 period.

Lenin's writings and speeches during 1917 in English are contained in *Collected Works*, Vols. 23-25, 41-44, by Progress Publishers.

Bolshevism: The Road to Revolution by Alan Woods provides a comprehensive history of the Bolshevik Party up to the October Revolution of 1917.

Titles by Wellred Books

Wellred Books is a publishing house specialising in works of Marxist theory. Among the titles we publish are:

Anti-Dühring, Friedrich Engels
Bolshevism: The Road to Revolution, Alan Woods
Chartist Revolution, Rob Sewell
China: From Permanent Revolution to Counter-Revolution, John Peter Roberts
The Civil War in France, Karl Marx
Class Struggle in the Roman Republic, Alan Woods
The Class Struggles in France, 1848-1850, Karl Marx
The Classics of Marxism: Volumes One & Two, Various authors
Dialectics of Nature, Friedrich Engels
The Eighteenth Brumaire of Louis Bonaparte, Karl Marx
The First Five Years of the Communist International, Leon Trotsky
The First World War: A Marxist Analysis of the Great Slaughter, Alan Woods
Germany: From Revolution to Counter-Revolution, Rob Sewell
Germany 1918-1933: Socialism or Barbarism, Rob Sewell
History of British Trotskyism, Ted Grant

The History of Philosophy: A Marxist Perspective, Alan Woods
The History of the Russian Revolution: All Volumes, Leon Trotsky
The History of the Russian Revolution to Brest-Litovsk, Leon Trotsky
The Ideas of Karl Marx, Alan Woods
Imperialism: The Highest Stage of Capitalism, VI Lenin
In Defence of Lenin, Rob Sewell & Alan Woods
In Defence of Marxism, Leon Trotsky
In the Cause of Labour, Rob Sewell
Ireland: Republicanism and Revolution, Alan Woods
'Left-Wing' Communism: An Infantile Disorder, VI Lenin
Lenin and Trotsky: What They Really Stood For,
Alan Woods & Ted Grant
Lenin Selected Writings, VI Lenin
On Imperialist War
On the National Question
The Revolutions of 1917
Lenin, Trotsky & the Theory of the Permanent Revolution, John Roberts
Marxism and Anarchism, Various authors
Marxism and the USA, Alan Woods
Materialism and Empirio-criticism, VI Lenin
My Life, Leon Trotsky
Not Guilty, Dewey Commission Report
The Origin of the Family, Private Property & the State, Friedrich Engels
The Permanent Revolution and Results & Prospects, Leon Trotsky
Permanent Revolution in Latin America, John Roberts & Jorge Martin
Reason in Revolt, Alan Woods & Ted Grant
Reformism or Revolution, Alan Woods
Revolution and Counter-Revolution in Spain, Felix Morrow
The Revolution Betrayed, Leon Trotsky
The Revolutionary Legacy of Rosa Luxemburg, Marie Frederiksen
The Revolutionary Philosophy of Marxism, John Peterson (Ed.)
Russia: From Revolution to Counter-Revolution, Ted Grant
Spain's Revolution Against Franco, Alan Woods

Stalin, Leon Trotsky

The State and Revolution, VI Lenin

Ted Grant: The Permanent Revolutionary, Alan Woods

Ted Grant Writings: Volumes One and Two, Ted Grant

Thawra hatta'l nasr! - Revolution until Victory!, Alan Woods & others

What Is Marxism?, Rob Sewell & Alan Woods

What Is to Be Done?, VI Lenin

Women, Family and the Russian Revolution, John Roberts & Fred Weston

Writings on Britain, Leon Trotsky

To make an order or for more information, visit wellred-books.com, email books@wellred-books.com or write to Wellred Books, 152-160 Kemp House, City Road, London, EC1V 2NX, United Kingdom.

www.ingramcontent.com/pod-product-compliance
Ingram Content Group UK Ltd.
Pitfield, Milton Keynes, MK11 3LW, UK
UKHW012253290726
14090UKWH00016B/627

9 781916 936126